# NUREMBERG DIARY

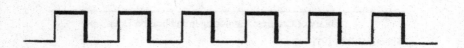

# Nuremberg Diary

### BY G. M. GILBERT, Ph.D.

*Formerly Prison Psychologist at the Nuremberg Trial
of the Nazi War Criminals*

## DA CAPO PRESS
A Member of the Perseus Books Group

Library of Congress Cataloging in Publication Data

Gilbert, G. M., 1911–
    Nuremberg diary / by G.M. Gilbert.—1st Da Capo Press ed.
        p.      cm.
    Originally published: New York: Farrar, Straus, 1947. With the addition of
24 photos from the 1961 ed.
    Includes index.
    ISBN 0-306-80661-4
    1. Gilbert, G. M., 1911– —Diaries. 2. Nuremberg War Crime Trials, Nurem-
berg, Germany, 1946–1949. 3. War criminals—Germany—Psychology. 4. Prison
psychologists—United States—Diaries. I. Title.
D804.G42G5    1995
341.6′9026843—dc20                                                    95-20429
                                                                           CIP

First Da Capo Press edition 1995

This Da Capo Press paperback edition of *Nuremberg Diary* is an unabridged
republication of the edition first published in 1947, with the addition of
24 photos from the 1961 edition. It is reprinted by arrangement with
Farrar, Straus & Giroux, Inc.

Published by Da Capo Press, Inc.
A member of the Perseus Books Group

TO MY WIFE

# Acknowledgments

I am indebted to Colonel B. C. Andrus, prison commandant, and Dr. Douglas M. Kelley, prison psychiatrist for the first two months, for facilitating my assignment to the Nuremberg jail with free access to all the prisoners from the very beginning of my stay there. I also wish to express gratitude for the encouragement and stimulating discussions afforded by my association with Dr. Leon N. Goldensohn, prison psychiatrist during most of the trial.

In preparing the Diary for publication, I had the expert assistance of John Farrar, whose practised editorial hand and keen interest proved invaluable in the final editing. The historical details were checked and the Chronology was prepared by Mr. Robert Katz, formerly of OWI, who also rendered valuable editorial assistance. The legal details were checked by Mr. William Jackson, formerly assistant to the United States Chief of Counsel.

Finally, I wish to express my thanks to Justice Robert H. Jackson, former United States Chief of Counsel at the Nuremberg Trial for permission to publish my Diary because he felt it would benefit history and science.

THE AUTHOR.

# Contents

# Introduction—The Indicted

I ARRIVED IN NUREMBERG with a load of prisoners on October 20, 1945, the day that the International Military Tribunal received the indictment against the 23 Nazi war criminals then in custody. As a German-speaking military intelligence officer, I had seen the collapse of the Nazi war machine and the evidence of Nazi barbarism in places like Dachau concentration camp before V-E Day. Being a psychologist by profession, I had naturally been interested in finding out what made human beings join the Nazi movement and do the things they did.

My interrogation of prisoners of war and German civilians had proved inconclusive. The "little men" had only protested their lack of responsibility and their obedience to leaders who had betrayed them. These leaders were now in the Nuremberg jail, and that was the one place I wanted to be. Fortunately, I was able to replace the prison commandant's interpreter, and was thereupon also designated as prison psychologist for the duration of the trial.

My principal duty was to maintain close daily contact with the prisoners in order to keep the prison commandant, Colonel B. C. Andrus, aware of the state of their morale, and to help in any way possible to assure their standing trial with orderly discipline. I also collaborated with the psychiatric commissions and the prison psychiatrist* in any mental examinations that were required.

I was allowed free access to the prisoners at all times, from the time of the indictment up to the time of the execution. This made possible a study of their reactions under controlled conditions for a whole year. The method was simply that of casual conversation in my role as psychologist and liaison man, supplementing the trial itself as a vehicle for examining the Nazi system and the men who made it. I never took notes in their presence, but kept a careful record of my conversations and observations, setting down my notes in private immediately each time after

*The position of prison psychiatrist was first held by Major Douglas M. Kelley, who left after the first month of the trial and was succeeded by Major Leon N. Goldensohn for most of the trial. The position was also held by Captain Richard Worthington and Lt. Colonel W. H. Dunn for briefer periods of time.

3

leaving their cells, the courtroom, or the lunchroom, then making my daily Diary entries from these notes. This Diary constitutes the "raw data" of this study, and is presented for its historical as well as psychological value.

As one might expect, a good deal of the Nazis' conversation was consumed in rationalization, self-justification and recrimination; but even in thus protesting too much, and by being more frank in their opinions about each other than about themselves, they inevitably revealed their personalities and motives. Indeed, for the most part, they were more than eager to express themselves to a psychologist and the only American officer on the prison staff (except for the chaplains) who could speak German. I refrained from embroidering the data with too much psychological speculation, leaving that to later collaborative studies which would be more comprehensive and objective than my own immediate reactions could possibly be.

During the month that intervened between the indictment and the beginning of the trial, the Nazi leaders were in solitary confinement. I used this period to establish my personal contact with the prisoners, getting their reactions to the indictment and administering psychological tests. For them it served as a relief from their isolation. For me it served as an introduction to the Nazi leaders as individuals. The study of this period will therefore be presented informally in this introductory chapter, rather than in chronological sequence.

## ———— REACTIONS TO THE INDICTMENT ————

The reactions to the indictment were soon crystallized. I asked each of the defendants to autograph my copy of the indictment with a brief statement giving his opinion of it. Their first spontaneous reactions, as quoted below, will introduce the main characters:

HERMANN GOERING, Reichsmarschall and Luftwaffe-Chief, President of the Reichstag, Plenipotentiary of the Four Year Plan, etc., etc., wrote his favorite cynical formula, *"The victor will always be the judge, and the vanquished the accused."*

JOACHIM VON RIBBENTROP, Foreign Minister, made the evasive statement, "The indictment is directed against the wrong people." He wanted to add, "We were all under Hitler's shadow," but cautiously refrained from putting it in writing.

RUDOLF HESS, having been in a state of total amnesia since his arrival from England, could only write (in English), "I can't remember."

ERNST KALTENBRUNNER, Chief of Himmler's Security Headquarters (including the Gestapo and SD) protested his formal innocence, "I do not feel guilty of any war crimes, I have only done my duty as an intelligence organ, and I refuse to serve as an ersatz for Himmler."

ALFRED ROSENBERG, Chief Nazi philosopher and Reichsminister for the Eastern Occupied Territories, also declared his innocent intentions. "I must reject an indictment for 'conspiracy.' The anti-Semitic movement was only protective."

HANS FRANK, Hitler's lawyer and later Governor-General of occupied Poland, reflected his recent religious conversion, "I regard this trial as a God-willed world court, destined to examine and put to an end the terrible era of suffering under Adolf Hitler."

WILHELM FRICK, Minister of the Interior, gave his legalistic reaction, "The whole indictment rests on the assumption of a fictitious conspiracy."

FRITZ SAUCKEL, Chief of slave labor recruitment, found it hard to reconcile the indictment with his love of the workers. "The abyss between the ideal of a social community which I imagined and advocated as a former seaman and worker, and the terrible happenings in the concentration camps, has shaken me deeply."

ALBERT SPEER, Reichsminister of Armaments and Munitions frankly admitted the guilt of the Nazi regime. "The trial is necessary. There is a common responsibility for such horrible crimes even in an authoritarian system."

HJALMAR SCHACHT, Reichsbank President and Minister of Economics before the war, declared, "*I do not understand at all why I have been accused!*"

WALTER FUNK, Schacht's successor as Minister of Economics was somewhat more verbose and emotional in his protestations of his innocence. "*I have never in my life consciously done anything which could contribute to such an indictment. If I have been made guilty of the acts which stand in the indictment, through error or ignorance, then my guilt is a human tragedy and not a crime.*"

FRANZ VON PAPEN, Reich Chancellor before Hitler, and Ambassador to Austria and Turkey during the Hitler regime, was even more verbose in disassociating himself from the Nazi guilt. "*The indictment has horrified me because of (1) the irresponsibility with which Germany was thrown into this war and the world-wide catastrophe and (2) the accumulation of crimes which some of my people have committed. The latter is psychologically inexplicable. I believe that paganism and the years of totalitarianism bear the main guilt. Through both of these Hitler became a pathological liar in the course of the years.*"

BARON VON NEURATH, Foreign Minister in the early years of the Nazi regime and later Protector of Bohemia and Moravia, singled out one aspect of Nazi lawlessness. "*I was always against punishment without the possibility of a defense.*"

BALDUR VON SCHIRACH, Hitler Youth Leader and Gauleiter of Vienna, had a belated but apparently sincere awakening. "*The whole misfortune came from racial politics.*"

ARTUR SEYSS-INQUART, Austrian Chancellor and later Reichs-Commissioner for the Netherlands, did not bother protesting his innocence, but wrote with cool fatalism, "*Last act of the tragedy of the second World War, I hope!*"

JULIUS STREICHER, Nazi Germany's No. 1 Jew-baiter, as editor of Der Stürmer and Gauleiter of Franconia, expressed his obsession even with respect to the trial. "*This trial is a triumph of World Jewry!*"

FIELD MARSHAL KEITEL, Chief of Staff of the High Command of the Wehrmacht, gave the Prussian officer's expected reaction: "For a soldier, orders are orders!"

GENERAL JODL, Chief of Operations for the High Command, regarded the indictment with mixed feelings. "I regret the mixture of justified accusations and political propaganda."

ADMIRAL DOENITZ, Grand Admiral of the German Navy and Hitler's successor after the latter's suicide, tried to laugh the whole thing off as something that didn't concern him. "None of these indictment counts concerns me in the least.—Typical American humor."

HANS FRITZSCHE, Radio Propaganda Chief in Goebbels' Propaganda Ministry, felt impelled to speak for the German people. "It is the most terrible indictment of all times. Only one thing is more terrible: the indictment the German people will make for the abuse of their idealism."

The autographed reactions of Admiral Raeder and Robert Ley were missing. Admiral Raeder had just been brought to the jail from Russian captivity and refused to commit himself either in writing or in discussion. The eccentric, emotionally unstable labor leader, Robert Ley, had given a prompt and decisive reaction to his indictment as a war criminal by committing suicide.

——————— ROBERT LEY'S SUICIDE ———————

I visited Robert Ley with the prison psychiatrist the day before Ley killed himself. He was in an agitated state, pacing up and down his cell in his felt boots and GI field jacket, which some of the prisoners were wearing at that time. Asked how he was getting along in preparing his defense after reading the indictment, he launched into a tirade:

OCTOBER 23. (Ley's Cell)
"How can I prepare a defense? Am I supposed to defend myself against all these crimes which I knew nothing about? If after all

the bloodshed of this war some more s-sacrifices are needed to satisfy the v-vengeance of the victors, all well and good—" (Here he placed himself against the wall, crucifix-like, and declaimed with a dramatic gesture) "Stand us against a wall and shoot us!— All well and good—you are the victors. But why should I be brought before a Tribunal like a c——, c——, like a c——, c——?" He stammered and blocked completely at the word "criminal" until I supplied it, then added: "Yes, I can't even get the word out." He repeated this trend of thought several times, pacing up and down the cell, gesticulating and stuttering in great agitation.

The next night he was found strangled in his cell. He had made a noose from the stripped edges of an army towel tied together and fastened to the toilet pipe. In his suicide note he said that he could not stand the shame any longer.

Ley's suicide created considerable consternation in the prison detachment. The guard was quadrupled so that there was one sentry on each cell 24 hours a day. For fear of suggesting to the other defendants how to commit suicide, Colonel Andrus, prison commandant, did not reveal immediately what had happened, but circulated an ambiguous note a few days later, announcing Ley's death.

I was sitting in Goering's cell when this note was brought around on October 29. He read the announcement without any show of emotion. After the officer left the cell, he turned to me:

OCTOBER 29. (Goering's Cell)
"It's just as well that he's dead, because I had my doubts about how he would behave at the trial. He's always been so scatter-brained—always making such fantastic and bombastic speeches. I'm sure he would have made a spectacle of himself at the trial. Well, I'm not surprised that he's dead, because he's been drinking himself to death anyway . . . "

Similar attitudes were expressed by the other defendants. The only one who seemed to mourn Robert Ley's passing at all was the vulgar fanatic, Julius Streicher. The eccentric labor leader, who had forced German workers to subscribe to Streicher's journal, Der Stürmer, had been the only one who had seen fit to associate with Streicher during their previous internment in Mondorf prison camp. However, Streicher thought it was cowardly of Ley to commit suicide and leave behind a "Political Testament" calling the Nazi anti-Semitic policy "a big mistake."

## STREICHER

Streicher had achieved an all-time low in social prestige, being considered unfit for other war criminals to associate with. His lewd, perverted mentality had rated the lowest IQ on the psychological tests, but even his own defense counsel wondered whether his anti-Semitic obsession did not spring from a diseased mind. Streicher was accordingly examined by a psychiatric commission consisting of Dr. Krasnushkin of Moscow, Colonel Schroeder of Chicago, and Dr. Delay of Paris. Streicher turned the examination into another harangue on anti-Semitism, lecturing the psychiatrists on the subject, explaining how he had devoted 25 years to the study of the Jewish problem, and how he knew more about it than anybody else. When the doctors asked him to undress for a physical examination, the female Russian interpreter stepped to the door and turned her back to the examining group. Streicher leered and said, "What's the matter? Are you afraid of seeing something nice?" The girl shivered in revulsion as she turned her back to him.

As a result of the examination, the psychiatrists decided that while he suffered from a neurotic obsession, he was not insane.

This obsession was often illustrated in casual talks in his cell before the trial began. Streicher would continually lecture anybody who came to visit him on his scholarship in the subject of anti-Semitism, while revealing that it was essentially his lewd and sacrilegious perversity that made him delight in the subject. A Diary note illustrates this trend of thought:

NOVEMBER 14. (*Streicher's Cell*)
"I am the only one in the world who clearly saw the Jewish menace as an historical problem. I didn't become anti-Semitic because of any personal mistreatment or grudge—not at all—I was called to it! My realization of the Jewish menace came from the Talmud itself—the so-called Holy Book which the Jews have cam-

ouflaged with Christianity, and so they call it the Holy Book. You know all this about the Christians and Jews believing in the same God is tommyrot. The Talmud itself shows that the Jews are governed by racial law. And this is the main thing—now pay attention. Isn't it diabolical how the Talmud says that God told the Jews: 'Thou shalt be circumcised, and thou shalt beget only Jewish children from Jewish women.'? And that is how they maintained their racial purity and survived for centuries. Now if they want to maintain their racial purity, let them, that's all I say. But let them keep away from the German race, which is a Nordic race. We have to preserve our racial purity too. Ah yes," he added, squinting his eyes wisely and wagging a pedantic finger, "one can learn much from the Talmud. The Jews knew about such things. But we must be the masters, not they."

"Well, Goering and the others are at least willing to admit that it was a terrible mistake, aside from anything else."

"Ach, der Goering!—He never really even consummated his marriage.—Yes, I know it was Goering who was responsible for having me kicked out of my position as Gauleiter in 1940, on account of that story about his child being a test-tube baby. But I can't help that. I must speak what I believe to be the truth."

"I understand that many people tried to stop you from publishing the Stürmer, but Hitler always supported you. What was the secret of your favoritism with the Führer?"

"Oh, well, you know that I marched in the front rank with him in the Munich putsch, and he never forgot that. He even said in prison that he would never forget it, and he kept his word. And I remained faithful too. Even after I was kicked out, he sent Goebbels and Ley to visit me, a couple of years ago, to ask if I desired anything. So I told them [with a dramatic gesture] 'Tell my Führer that I desire nothing except to die beside my Führer in case a catastrophe should befall the Fatherland!'" Streicher held the pose for a moment, then added, "—And that impressed him no end."

------------ HESS ------------

The chief candidate for a mental examination was Rudolf Hess, Hitler's deputy as Nazi Party leader, whose mysterious flight to England in 1941 had created a sensation. He had recently come to the Nuremberg jail from England in a state of total amnesia. Among his belongings were small packages of food samples which he had wrapped and sealed and labeled in England during a period of paranoid delusions concerning food poisoning. He sat in his cell all day in a state of apathetic absent-mindedness, unable to give the slightest inkling of familiarity with any subject mentioned out of the past, including his flight to England. Occasionally he would seem to be deliberately suppressing a recollection that flickered through his clouded mind, but there was little doubt in our minds that he was essentially in a state of complete amnesia.

When confronted by Goering and von Papen, he failed to recognize either of them. When shown a Nazi film including his own picture, he likewise showed no reaction.

He had to be kept handcuffed on his walks in the exercise yard, because of his suicide attempt in England.

The psychological tests I gave him in his cell showed a severely limited mentality, although he was slightly above average in intelligence. The reactions were typical of the hysterical personality.

A few days before the beginning of the trial, he was examined in his cell by an American psychiatric commission consisting of Dr. Nolan D. C. Lewis of Columbia University, Dr. Donald E. Cameron of McGill University, and Colonel Paul Schroeder of Chicago. I acted as interpreter during this examination. Continuous questioning gave no suggestion whatever that his amnesia was anything but genuine, though the psychiatrists concluded that he was not legally insane.

----------- GOERING -----------

Aside from the suicide of Robert Ley and the psychiatric examinations of Julius Streicher and Rudolf Hess, no question was raised as to the sanity of any of the defendants in the jail.

Goering had already been weaned away from his drug addiction by Doctors Miller and Kelley, using gradually diminishing doses of paracodeine pills. Colonel Andrus, prison commandant, was fond of saying, "When Goering came to me at Mondorf, he was a simpering slob with two suitcases full of paracodeine. I thought he was a drug salesman. But we took him off his dope and made a man of him."

In our conversations in his cell, Goering tried to give the impression of a jovial realist who had played for big stakes and lost, and was taking it all like a good sport. Any question of guilt was adequately covered by his cynical attitude toward the "justice of the victors." He had abundant rationalizations for the conduct of the war, his alleged ignorance of the atrocities, the "guilt" of the Allies, and a ready humor which was always calculated to give the impression that such an amiable character could have meant no harm. Nevertheless, he could not conceal a pathological egotism and inability to stand anything but flattery and admiration for his leadership, while freely expressing scorn for other Nazi leaders.

OCTOBER 29. (*Goering's Cell*)

(After commenting on Robert Ley's suicide) " . . . I hope Ribbentrop doesn't break down. I'm not afraid of the soldiers; they'll behave themselves. But Hess—he's insane. He's been insane for a long time. We knew it when he flew to England. Do you think Hitler would have sent the third man in the Reich on such a lone mission to England without the slightest preparation? Hitler really blew up when he found out. Do you think it was a pleasure for us to have to state publicly that one of our leading figures was crazy? If he had really wanted to deal with the British, there were reliable para-diplomatic channels through neutral countries. My own connections with England were such that I could have arranged it within 48 hours. No, Hess took off without a word, without papers, without anything. Just left a crazy note behind."

In discussing Hitler, I remarked: "The people now say that it's too bad that the assassination attempt on July 20th last year didn't succeed. They seem pretty disillusioned about the Nazi leadership."

This reference to the German people really irritated him. "Never mind what the people say *now!* That is the one thing that doesn't interest me a damn bit! I know what they said *before!* I know how they cheered and praised us when things were going well. I know too much about people!"

NOVEMBER 11. (*Goering's Cell*)

"As far as the trial is concerned," Goering said, "it's just a cut-and-dried political affair, and I'm prepared for the consequences.

I have no doubt that the press will play a bigger part in the decision than the judges.—And I'm sure that the Russian and French judges, at least, already have their instructions. I can answer for anything I've done, and can't answer for anything I haven't done. But the victors are the judges . . . I know what's in store for me. I'm even writing my farewell letter to my wife today . . .

"I'm sorry to see Ribbentrop breaking down. If I had been Foreign Minister, I would simply say, 'This was my foreign policy and I stick to it. As Foreign Minister of the sovereign German State that was strictly my business and my right. If you want to put me on trial for it, go ahead. You've got the power; you're the victors.' But I would stick to my guns. I hate to see him wavering like this, excusing himself with endless memoranda and verbose explanations.

"I have nothing against him personally, but I never did think much of him as Foreign Minister. Von Neurath was a man of standing and insight. He would contradict Hitler on occasion and reason with him . . . But Ribbentrop was a boundless egotist— a wine salesman who was successful in business, but had neither the background nor the tact for diplomacy. I tried to advise Hitler to remove him, for two reasons. First of all, he was *persona non grata* with the British, and even Hitler wanted to keep on good terms with the British. They disliked Ribbentrop because of that stupid tactlessness. He had hardly gotten off the train when he went on his mission to London, before he started giving them expert advice on controlling the balance of power against Russia, completely insensitive to the fact that the British considered themselves the experts on power politics and were trying to give us advice on protecting ourselves in the East. Then, when he was presented to the King, he greeted him with the *Heil Hitler* salute, which the British, of course, regarded as an insult to the crown. I was even able to make Hitler see that point. 'Suppose Russia sent a good-will ambassador to you,' I said, 'and he came and greeted you with "Long live the Communist revolution!" ' Hahahaha!" Here Goering raised his fist in the Communist salute and laughed heartily.

"The second reason was that Ribbentrop didn't have the background for international diplomacy. Hitler was in no position to judge this, because he had never travelled abroad himself. Just because the wine merchants Ribbentrop associated with happened to include some English counts, Hitler thought he had a man with 'connections.' I told Hitler that if he wanted to have any dealings with England he could do much better through my connections—with Lord Halifax, for example. But in spite of his ignorance, Ribbentrop was as arrogant as a peacock about his position. Just imagine—at the time of the signing of the Axis pact with Japan and Italy, with the newsreels, and all that, he wanted me—the second man in the Reich—to stand *behind him* in approval. Can you imagine the gall? I told him that if I did pose with him, I would sit down and he could stand *behind me.*—But I didn't want to be in it altogether, because I hadn't read the pact yet, and might take exception to it later, only to find that I had identified myself with it.

"He was certainly cocky in those days. He's not that way now. At Mondorf he wrote an 85-page document and asked everybody to read it. Some of them told him that if he was too stuck-up to consult them before, he could take his document and stick it up now." Goering had another good laugh at that one. "I've got nothing against him personally," he repeated.

NOVEMBER 12. (Goering's Cell)

Goering considers Hitler's suicide certain. He understands that Eva Braun said to Speer as early as April 22 that she and Hitler would end their lives then. That was the day Goering was supposed to succeed Hitler, but the latter changed his mind and ordered him arrested and shot instead. He does not think it was cowardly of Hitler to commit suicide.

"After all, he was the Chief of the German State. It would be absolutely unthinkable for me to have Hitler sitting in a cell like this awaiting trial as a war criminal before a foreign tribunal.— Even if he hated me at the end.—He was, after all, the symbol of Germany.—It would have been the same as if they had brought the Kaiser to trial after the last war. Why, even the Japanese insisted on not bringing their Emperor to trial.—No matter how much harder it is for me now, I would still rather suffer any consequences than to have Hitler alive as a prisoner before a foreign court—no, it is absolutely unthinkable.

"But with Himmler it is a different story. He should at least have stood up to answer for himself and his subordinates. He could have cleared many of these defendants of any knowledge of his orders for mass murder.—I'll never understand how he could have done all those things and gotten away with it."

"Didn't you hear about the atrocities that the whole world knew about?" I asked.

"Oh, one heard lots of rumors, but naturally one didn't believe those things. But some of those SS generals who had to carry out those orders must have known all about it. How could they reconcile that with their own consciences? I can't understand it."

NOVEMBER 15. (Goering's Cell)

I administered the Intelligence test in his cell. He was in a slightly depressed mood when I came in, but livened up after a few minutes' conversation. He reacted with keen interest to the challenge of an intelligence test, and by the end of the first sub-test (memory-span), he was acting like a bright and egotistical schoolboy, anxious to show off before the teacher. He chuckled with glee as I showed surprise at his accomplishment at the increasingly difficult digit series. He slapped his thighs and pounded his bed impatiently when he failed on 9 forward and 7 backward, and pleaded for a third and a fourth try at it. "Oh, come on, give me another crack at it; I can do it!" When he finally succeeded, to my expressed amazement, he could hardly contain himself for joy, and swelled with pride. This pattern of rapport was maintained throughout the entire test; the examiner encouraging him with remarks of how few people are able to do the next problem, and Goering responding like a show-off schoolboy. Goering was given to understand that he had the highest rating so far. He decided the American psychologists really had something there. "The method is good—much better than the stuff our psychologists were fooling around with."

"Maybe you should have become an Akademiker instead of a politician," I suggested.

"Perhaps. I'm convinced that I would have done better than the average man no matter what I went into. But you can't fathom your fate. It depends on such little things. For instance, the little thing that prevented me from becoming a Freemason. I had a date to meet some friends to join the Freemasons in 1919. While waiting for them, I saw a pretty blonde pass by, and I picked her up. Well, I just never did get around to joining the Freemasons. If I hadn't picked up that blonde that day, it would have been impossible for me to get into the Party, and I wouldn't be here today."

—————— VON RIBBENTROP ——————

As may be inferred from Goering's remarks, the von Ribbentrop of cell no. 7 did not bear much resemblance to the arrogant Nazi Ambassador at the Court of St. James, nor to the Foreign Minister who had cracked Hitler's whip over the foreign offices of Europe and forged the Rome-Berlin-Tokyo Axis. The collapse of the system that had backed up his diplomacy with armed force had taken all the false backbone out of his weak character. What was left was a confused and demoralized opportunist in defeat, without even a consistent argument to maintain a presentable front.

Slovenly in his physical as well as mental habits, he gave the impression of a German businessman in moral and material bankruptcy, with nothing in the world—not even a mind—he could call his own. If there ever had been any respectable purpose behind his activities, von Ribbentrop seemed to have forgotten what it was and was hoping that someone would tell him. In the preliminary interrogations by the prosecution staff, von Ribbentrop frequently complained of defective memory and would ask the interrogators what they thought about it all. In his cell he spent his time writing endless memoranda and asking all within reach for advice on his defense—the doctors, the cell guards, mess attendants, barber, etc. As the German prison doctor remarked, if there had been a prison janitor, von Ribbentrop would have consulted him too for advice on his defense of Nazi foreign policy.

Under these conditions, any attempts to get expressions of basic attitudes in our early conversations were doomed to failure, because von Ribbentrop did not seem to have any basic attitudes. Even in trying out the excuse that he had only obeyed Hitler, he betrayed the passive ambivalence and lack of moral integrity in his character. He claimed on the one hand that he had only done

his duty in supporting Hitler and on the other hand that he had
always warned the British and French against Hitler. Besides, Hitler had once screamed at him in 1940 and he could never contradict him after that.

The trial filled him with apprehension. He kept complaining
that he was not being given enough time to prepare his defense, and
hoped that the trial would be postponed indefinitely. He seemed
to dread the day when his record would be laid bare in open
court and he would have to stand up and make some kind of a
defense of his activities in the Nazi regime. He sensed that many
of his co-defendants—especially the elder statesmen, von Papen
and von Neurath, whom he had eclipsed—would be all too eager
to condemn him and Hitler for the reckless foreign policy that
had brought war and defeat to Germany, and he kept repeating:
"Really, this trial is a big mistake.—It will not be a very dignified
spectacle to let Germans denounce Germans." He even considered forestalling an open examination of the record by making
some superficial confession and throwing himself on the mercy
of the American authorities. But nothing came of this, and von
Ribbentrop continued to bury his anxiety in a sea of memoranda
and sleeping pills.

———————— SCHACHT ————————

Schacht shared Goering's contempt of von Ribbentrop as well
as their contempt of each other and admiration of themselves.
There was clearly no love lost among the egotistical rivals for
power in the Third Reich. Goering's insatiable lust for supremacy
in all fields had naturally crossed Schacht's in the economic
field. But it manifested itself even the minor matter of the IQ
tests I gave in the jail while they were awaiting trial.

Goering did not actually rank highest on the Intelligence tests
after they were completed, much to his annoyance. (See table on
page 31.) The top man turned out to be his old rival and enemy,
"financial wizard" Hjalmar Schacht. If this was a surprise to
Goering, it wasn't a surprise to Schacht, who made no secret of
the fact that he was the most innocent man in the entire prison,
and the most brilliant. His indignation at being imprisoned as a
supporter of Hitler was not entirely without foundation, since he

had just completed 10 months in a concentration camp under suspicion of plotting against Hitler, before he was thrown into jail by the Americans after the Armistice. He let it be known to all who came to visit him that as far as he was concerned it was all a mistake, and he hoped that the trial would take a short time, so that they could hang those other criminals and let him go home.

OCTOBER 23. (*Schacht's Cell*)
"I have full confidence in the judges, and I am not afraid of the outcome. A few of the defendants are not guilty, most of them are sheer criminals. Even Ribbentrop should be hung for his stupidity; there is no worse crime than stupidity."

NOVEMBER 1. (*Schacht's Cell*)
Still resentful at being incarcerated as a criminal like the others, he hopes the trial won't take too long. I told him that depended to some degree on how long the defendants talked.

"As for me, all I need is a half hour, since my opposition to Hitler's aggressive policies is an open book. After all, he threw me into concentration camp for it, and I was imprisoned for 10 months—only to be dragged here as a war criminal.—That's why I resent it so much."

"Well, you must admit that the government leadership has much to answer for," I replied. "Of course, anyone who is innocent will not be punished."

"I have no doubt about that. That's why I can put up with this without a troubled conscience, which is more than some of those other gentlemen can say. Everybody knows that I was against war. It is even mentioned in Ambassador Davies' book, *Mission to Moscow*. All I wanted was to build up Germany industrially. The so-called financial wizardry was nothing but an efficient unification and exploitation of Germany's finances and resources. The only thing they can accuse me of is breaking the Versailles Treaty. But if that's a crime, then the judges should be tried too. England not only tacitly approved our rearmament but actually made a pact to limit our navy to ⅓ the size of her navy, in 1935. When we re-established universal conscription, not one of the world powers let out a peep. Their military attachés witnessed our parades as guests. They even condoned aggression. After trying sanctions on Italy, they recognized her conquest of Ethopia. No one did anything about the Russian aggression against Finland. No, they can ill afford to make an issue of the Versailles Treaty. Even America's bankers loaned us money which I didn't want, just to get their commissions and maintain a fiction that couldn't last.

"I'll admit that I was fool enough to believe in Hitler's peaceful intentions in the beginning. I did support rearmament only to the point of insuring Germany's security. But I became more and more suspicious as he tried to absorb all of the country's financial resources in armament. The turning point came when he dismissed the Chief of Staff, General von Fritsch, who never wanted an aggressive war, and put in his lackey, Keitel. I then withheld funds for further armament and got kicked out as a result. The more aggressive he became, the more defeatist I became. Finally he threw me into concentration camp, in 1944.

"As for anti-Semitism, I did exact an understanding from him as early as 1934, that there was to be no discrimination in the industrial field, and as long as I was in my post there wasn't any discrimination in that field. The real reason wasn't racial anyway —that's a lot of nonsense. It was just a question of curtailing Jewish overrepresentation in the professions. I first found out about the atrocities while I was interned in Flossenburg. I could hear the people being forced to undress and march out to their death—and the shooting in the woods. It was beastly. I was terrified at the thought that this was a camp from which no one came out alive. The only reason I can imagine why they kept me alive was as a possible hostage or negotiator."

## FRANK

Not all of the defendants shared Goering's cynicism or Schacht's hurt innocence. Two or three of them appeared to show some signs of remorse. One of these was Hans Frank, former Governor-General of Poland, who had recently been converted to the Catholic faith. He would sit in his cell reading the Bible or German literature, turning the pages with the little finger of his left hand, because he had slashed his wrists in his suicide attempt when he was captured. (He did not have free movement of his fingers and sometimes kept his left hand covered with a glove.) A healed gash was also visible at his throat as a result of the same suicide attempt. Interrogators described him as surly and evasive upon questioning, and he had once left the interrogation room, cursing, "Swine!" It was, therefore, all the more surprising to me that in our conversations in his cell he was all sweetness and light, full of abject remorse, and could curse Hitler with an amazing vehemence and literary facility.

NOVEMBER 7. (*Frank's Cell*)

"Yes, many things have become clear to me in the loneliness of this cell. The trial is neither here nor there, but what a spectacle of the irony of fate and heavenly justice! You know, there is a divine punishment which is far more devastating in its irony than any punishment man has yet devised! Hitler represented the spirit of evil on earth and recognized no power greater than his own. God watched this band of heathens puffed up with their puny power and then simply brushed them aside in scorn and amusement." Frank brushed them aside with his gloved hand. "I tell you, the scornful laughter of God is more terrible than any vengeful lust of man! When I see Goering, stripped of his uniform and decorations, meekly taking his 10-minute walk under the curious, amused eyes of the American guards, I think of how he revelled in his glory as President of the Reichstag. It is grotesque! Here are the would-be rulers of Germany—each in a cell like this, with four walls and a toilet, awaiting trial as ordinary criminals. Is that not a proof of God's amusement with men's sacrilegious quest for power?" His smile gradually froze and his eyes narrowed to slits. "But are these people thankful for these last few weeks in which to atone for their sins of egotism and indifference, and to recognize that they have been in league with the *devil incarnate?* Do they get on their knees and pray to God for forgiveness?—No, they worry about their own little necks and cast about for all kinds of little excuses to absolve themselves of blame! Can't they see that this is a horrible tragedy in the history of mankind, and that we are the symbols of an evil that God is brushing aside?" His voice had been raised in anger and he apologized as the guard peeked into the cell curiously.

He continued in cold, quiet anger: "If only one of us had had the courage to shoot him dead! That's the one thing for which I reproach myself. What misery, death, and destruction would have been spared! I began to come to my senses in 1942, and realized what evil was embodied in him. When I protested against terror measures in public at that time, he deprived me of military rank and political power—but he let me sit as the figurehead Governor-General of Poland, to go down in history as the symbol of the crimes in that miserable country.—That was the satanical evil in him. And so here I sit—but it serves me right—I was in league with the devil in the beginning. In later years I realized what a cold-blooded, hard, insensitive psychopath he really was. That so-called fascinating look of his was nothing but the stare of an insensitive psychopath! He was moved by sheer primitive, wilful egotism, unrestrained by form and convention.—That's why he hated all legal, diplomatic, and religious institutions—all the social values that represented restrictions to his impulsive ego-expression. He played art-and-music-lover, but he had no conception of art. He liked Wagner, naturally, because he could see himself playing god with dramatic splendor. And his adoration of the nude.—One can appreciate the nude in art as the epitome of human beauty, form, and feeling—but Hitler was incapable of appreciating these things. To him the nude represented merely a protest against convention which he was able to understand.

"No, the psychopathic hatred of form and convention was the real keynote of Hitler's personality. That's why he took only such diabolical 'men of action' as Himmler and Bormann into his confidence. Bormann was his *Sekretär Wurm*\*—a contemptible flatterer and brutal intriguer, a clear reflection on Hitler's character, by the way. I am convinced that all these atrocities were secretly planned by these three who shared a common contempt for all standards of humanity and honor . . . "

We discussed the attitude of the German people toward Hitler. He raised a warning forefinger. "Beware of the legend-builders, *Herr Doktor!* Himmler would not have dared to carry out this program of mass murder if Hitler had not directly approved it or ordered it!"

NOVEMBER 15. (*Frank's Cell*)
Frank said that he now felt liberated spiritually as never before

---

\**The intriguing secretary in Schiller's play, Kabale und Liebe.*

in his life. His dreams especially take him far beyond the confines
of his cell—they show him vast vistas of endless sea and high
mountains, and sky, and he awakes with an extraordinary feeling
of spiritual and physical relief. (Recently he dreamed of Hitler
and that made him doubly resolved to take an upright stand and
admit common guilt.) It is all so realistic. Sometimes he has noc-
turnal emissions. In one recent dream he was standing at the sea-
shore and watching the waves, and then a girl appeared—he thinks
his daughter—then the mountains and the yodelling and the vast
spaces.—He awoke with an incredible feeling of emotional relief.
(Implies this was one of the sex dreams.) Went on talking about
how independent one could be of the restrictions of the environment if one had inner fortitude.

## ———— VON SCHIRACH ————

Less hysterical in his remorse but equally resigned to death was
handsome Baldur von Schirach, former Hitler Youth Leader. He
was grave and tremulous when interviewed in his cell, but showed
his aesthetic inclinations by writing a poem "To Death." Conscious of his heritage in German nobility and culture, he told his
defense counsel at their first meeting, "As long as I can keep my
head, I'll keep it high." Our first long interview, a week after he
received the indictment, gave a good insight into his background
and guilt feelings.

OCTOBER 27. (Von Schirach's Cell)
After finishing the ink-blot test,* we discussed the indictment
and the question of his guilt. Since the stirring up of anti-Semitism
was mentioned in the specifications against him, he offered to explain how he became anti-Semitic:
"In my youth I moved in aristocratic circles and never even
came in contact with Jews. I had no reason to be anti-Semitic,
but I did notice a sort of underhanded quiet prejudice against the
Jews 'in the best circles.' This did not impress me, however, until
someone made me read the American book, The International

*The Rorschach ink-blot test in which the subject reveals certain personal-
ity traits by using his imagination for "seeing things" in a series of large ink-
blot figures.

Jew, at the impressionable age of 17. You have no idea what a great influence this book had on the thinking of German Youth, who did not have the maturity to think for themselves. At about the same time I came under the influence of Julius Streicher, who had a knack for clothing anti-Semitism in pseudo-scientific garb. Since many of the older people in social gatherings took a similar tack, it was natural for a youngster to accept their opinions as authoritative. Then at the age of 18 I met Adolf Hitler. I must admit I was inspired by him, went to Munich to study because he was there, and became one of his staunchest supporters. From then on I was a convinced anti-Semite until the recent bitter tragedy showed me the utter falsity of such a belief. But why did our elders betray us? Why didn't anybody tell us that Ford had repudiated *The International Jew* and that the *Protocols of Zion* was a forgery? Why all the historical and scientific lies to breed hatred in impressionable young minds? I will not deny my guilt. I made the mistake of approving the Vienna evacuation, and I am prepared to die for it. But German Youth must not be forever punished for their betrayal. German Youth can and must be re-educated. I don't think there will ever be anti-Semitism in the world again, after this horrible example. But people must fight this quiet underhanded social stigmatization which was the breeding ground for the disease."

Elaborating further on his relationship to the Führer, he said that he had noticed a distinct change coming over Hitler in the course of the years. "Before 1934 he was *menschlich* [human]; from 1934 to 1938 he was *übermenschlich* [superhuman]; from 1938 on he was *unmenschlich* [inhuman] and a tyrant. I believe that power went to his head in 1934 when Hindenburg died and he became Reichsführer. Then it drove him mad when legal and judiciary processes were abolished and he became a dictator with plans of world domination before the war. My first disappointment in him was when he broke the Munich Pact, because I realized that Germany's reputation in the world had been damaged. But still he managed to convince me that it would turn out all right. About 1942 I think I first began to notice that he was becoming slightly insane. His stare would suddenly go blank in the midst of a conversation and he would wander off, or you would look behind you to see if he was looking at someone else; or else he would seem to close his ears against something he didn't want

to hear. In 1943 we had a serious quarrel. My wife had seen how
Jews were being dragged out of their homes, and being an outspoken idealist, she asked the Führer whether he knew about such
disgraceful action. He was silent. I also chimed in with some question about how the deported Jews were being treated. He flew
at me with such a rage that I thought that I would surely be arrested. I fell from grace after that."

The twilight filtering through the cell window had faded out
and we could hardly see each other in the dim prison light that
peered through the portal opening. But in the semidarkness I
could hear his voice beginning to break with emotion.

"When all the atrocities came to light at the end of the war,
my worst fears were realized, and I knew that I must die for it.
But I would not commit suicide like a coward. I did not evade
arrest. I even proposed to the American authorities that all Youth
leaders be called together in Buchenwald for a reeducation program, and then I would deliver myself as a hostage to take the
consequences of our earlier blind mistakes.—I hoped in that way
to make good somehow for what I had done . . . " His voice
choked and there was silence in the cell.

——————— SPEER ———————

The tall shaggy-browed Armaments Minister of the Hitler war
machine attracted little attention at first, but appeared to have
a more sincere and less demonstrative conception of the Nazi
guilt than anybody else.

OCTOBER 23. (Speer's Cell)
Speer seems to be the most realistic of all. He said he had no
illusions about his fate before, so the indictment was no particular shock to him. He realizes that history demands such a trial in
view of the enormity of the crimes committed, and considers it a
good thing in general. He doesn't think there's any point in bawling about individual fate, although his own guilt is as much in
doubt in his mind as anybody else's. He claimed that he had no
idea of all the crimes listed in the indictment, having been made
War Production Chief in 1942 without any previous experience.
He knew no more about concentration camps than any other

minister knew about V-2. He told Hitler in March that all was lost and that they ought to save Germany from utter destruction regardless of personal consequences. Hitler answered that if Germany couldn't win the war, it didn't deserve to survive.

The realization that Hitler was a destructive maniac and not a patriot bent on building up Germany at the expense of others had apparently completely shattered the illusions of the architect Speer. Re-examining the whole Nazi leadership and system of values in his cell for the first time since the dawn of the Third Reich, he came to the belated realization that it had been rotten to the core. In acknowledging the validity of the indictment in charging a common responsibility of the Nazi leadership "for such horrible crimes" and the inadmissability of obeying orders as an excuse, he indicated at the outset the cleavage between his basic attitudes and those of the military caste.

Though he had little to say before the trial started, he did occasionally give vent to his feelings about Germany's military leaders. On one occasion he remarked with quiet bitterness, "Yes, I know—they made great heroic speeches about fighting and dying for the Fatherland, without risking their own necks. And now when their own lives are at stake, they shiver and look for all kinds of excuses.—So that's the kind of heroes we had leading Germany to destruction!"

---

## KEITEL

Speer's remarks were directed mostly against bombastic Goering, but they also included the weak-kneed chief representative of Prussian militarism in the jail, Field Marshal Wilhelm Keitel.

Though bred to the Prussian military tradition, Keitel's behavior was almost obsequious when interviewed in his cell. The Chief of Staff of the High Command of the German Wehrmacht that had overrun most of Europe and had required a world coalition to beat, bowed and scraped before any lieutenant who came to see him, and exclaimed what an unimportant little man he really was. Shorn of his military insignia, he still looked very much like a Prussian officer of the old school, but without his rank and power he had no more backbone than a jellyfish. The idea that a field marshal could be held criminally responsible for orders he gave or executed was apparently something that had never dawned on him. These attitudes were reflected in some of our early interviews.

OCTOBER 26. (Keitel's Cell)
I asked Keitel about his reaction to the indictment, now that he has had an opportunity to study it. He had underlined the statement in the indictment that holds all the members of the conspiracy responsible for the acts of each, and rules out "following orders" as an excuse.

"How in heaven's name can they accuse me of conspiring to wage aggressive war when I was nothing but the mouthpiece to carry out the Führer's wishes? As Chief of Staff I had no authority whatever—no command function—nothing. All I could do was to transmit his orders to the staff and see that they were carried out. I had no idea of his general plan, and he made it clear that I was to stick strictly to military business. I can see now that he probably made all his ministers and chiefs of staff mind their own business so that no one had any clear idea of what his plans were.

"I can understand lots of things now that I was too stupid to understand then. The question of a new commander in chief of the armed forces in 1940, for instance. When General von Blomberg disgraced himself with that affair (please spare me a repetition of the details), Hitler asked me to recommend a successor. I suggested Goering, but he said Goering wasn't suited for the command. Then he decided to take it over himself. I couldn't understand why at the time, because I thought he had enough to do with affairs of state. But now I realize that he had plans of his own and didn't want to confide in anyone else.

"The charges in the indictment are terrible, and, believe me, I had many a miserable moment as I saw how things were developing. But what could I do? There were only 3 possibilities: (a) refusal to follow orders, which naturally meant death; (b) resign my post, or (c) commit suicide. I was on the point of resigning my post 3 times, but Hitler made it clear that he considered resignation in time of war the same as desertion. What could I do?

"As for the persecution of the Jews, all I could do was to defend the army against anti-Semitic measures. When the Nuremberg Laws began to dispossess and disenfranchise Jews, I prevailed upon the Führer not to discharge and disqualify decorated World War veterans, for the sale of army morale. He agreed. But outside of the army, it was clearly none of my business. To be sure, I heard later that even decorated World War veterans were being abused, but what could I do?"

NOVEMBER 17. (*Keitel's Cell*)

Keitel said he was "fit as a fiddle this morning." Before taking the IQ test, he cleared the table, neatly rearranged his cell, and made some remarks about the interrogation he had just had. "That was a silly hypothesis they put to me: 'Would you have objected at that meeting of the General Staff, if you had known that it meant war?' Of course there was no such thing as objecting. How can an officer object? Naturally I had to say 'No' to that question. An officer can't stand right up before the Führer, his Commander in Chief, and object! We can only receive orders and obey. Well, I know that this doesn't interest you because you're not assigned to the interrogation, but I thought it would interest you psychologically. It's hard for Americans to understand the Prussian code of discipline."

After he signified that he was ready, we proceeded with the test. He was co-operative and very responsive to assurances that he was doing well. On performance tests he went about the task in a businesslike manner. On the block designs test, for example, he kept the used cards in a neat pile to one side, removed the blocks from the working space after each item, and cleaned the decks for the next one. He became increasingly impressed with the objectivity of the test, and remarked how much better it was than the "silly nonsense" the German psychologists resorted to in the Wehrmacht testing stations. "Why, they even flunked my son on an officers' candidate examination, because of some stupid business in a dark room, and an exercise to make a speech, where his voice wasn't loud enough for the audience that wasn't there. I just kicked that stuff out."

After the test he returned to the subject of officers and politics. "In my opinion, the naval officers are much smarter politically than the army officers, because they travel a lot. They've been in England, Valparaiso, etc., and they get to know foreign temperaments, while we don't. It was a big mistake on our part that our army officers were restricted to the narrow army life on home territory."

JODL

Even more Prussian in his bearing than Keitel was the Bavarian General Jodl. He was very stiff and uncommunicative at first, but the need to express himself on the indictment soon asserted itself.

NOVEMBER 1. (*Jodl's Cell*)

"The indictment knocked me on the head. First of all, I had no idea at all about 90 per cent of the accusations in it. The crimes are horrible beyond belief, if they are true. Secondly, I don't see how they can fail to recognize a soldier's obligation to obey orders. That's the code I've lived by all my life. Thirdly, the guilt for atrocities in the East is suddenly reversed. How can the Russians sit in judgment on us for barbaric measures against Eastern populations? And then it says we enriched ourselves by looting our victims. Now that really floors me. Accuse me of giving the orders for the campaign against Holland, Belgium, Norway, Poland, if you will, but don't accuse me of profiting one nickel's worth from any of the actions. In fact, I was amazed when I used to hear how the Party officials were enriching themselves by exploiting our victories to their own advantage. I was a general, first and last."

When the conversation returned to the subject of atrocities, he threw up his hands. "These horrible things—they're utterly incomprehensible to me. It's impossible for me to understand what kind of beasts could have been in charge of those camps and could actually have done those things."

"Germans, of course; obeying orders, no doubt," I suggested.

"Germans, yes, but—. Tell me, man to man, did you ever know the Germans to be so bloodthirsty and brutal? I can't understand it. That's not a German characteristic. That's an Asiatic characteristic."

"The German people put up with active anti-Semitism like the Nuremberg Laws and Streicher's *Stürmer*," I remarked.

"I assure you that not a soul dreamed that any such measures were intended. And many people were nauseated by that porno-

graphic yellow journalist, Streicher. As you know, Goering finally
had him put on ice. No, the only thing that the people knowingly
fell for was the identification of Jewry with Communism, which
had a partially true basis in our revolution of 1918. But who could
have dreamed of such consequences?—It's absolutely horrible!"

──────────── VON PAPEN ────────────

Von Papen was the soul of politeness and courtesy except
when some slight irritation revealed the irritability of his 70 years.
In our interviews he revealed that he knew perfectly well that
Hitler was a liar and betrayer. He could never quite adequately explain why he kept working in the Hitler Government, however.

OCTOBER 30. (Von Papen's Cell)
    After his test, we discussed Hitler.
    "He was a pathological liar—that is obvious," said Papen. "I
can't figure him out exactly. I think he wanted the best for Germany in the beginning, but he became an unreasoning evil force
with the flattery of his followers—Himmler, Goering, Ribbentrop,
etc.
    "I tried to persuade him that he was wrong in his anti-Jewish
policies many a time. He seemed to listen at first, but later on I
had no influence on him." He went on to describe how he had
prevailed on Hitler to veto the Goebbels boycott of the Salzburg
Festival during his four years in Austria, 1934–1938. (Goebbels
wanted the festival boycotted because of the Jewish director,
Reinhardt.)
    Returning to his own role in Nazi politics, he stated: "Of
course, I knew that Hitler was guilty of bad faith in breaking the
Munich Pact. But what could I do?—Leave the country?—I
thought I might do some good by staying . . . I've been portrayed as an intriguing devil, as in the book Devil in Top Hat.—
But I can prove that I have always worked for peace. I am confident in American justice, and am glad to have the truth brought
to light through this trial. It's not so important what they do to
me—I'm at the end of my life. But this court has a higher mission to establish international justice."

—————————— THE PSYCHOLOGICAL TESTS ——————————

The psychological testing program was virtually completed before the beginning of the trial while the prisoners were still in
solitary confinement so that the validity of the results was safe-
guarded. Of the various tests given (Intelligence test, Rorschach
and Thematic Apperception personality tests), the simplest to
describe briefly, though not the most significant, was the Intelligence test.

I used my own German version of the American *Wechsler-
Bellevue Adult Intelligence Test*, eliminating and compensating
for those parts which are subject to cultural differences, like vo-
cabulary and general information. The test battery consisted of

A. *Verbal tests of memory and use of concepts*
    1. Memory span for number-series of increasing length.
    2. Simple arithmetic of increasing difficulty.
    3. Common sense questions.
    4. Concept formation by verbal similarities.
B. *Performance tests of observation and sensory-motor co-ordi-
    nation*
    5. Substitution Code Test (substituting digits for sym-
       bols).
    6. Object assembly (like jigsaw puzzles).
    7. Converting designs on colored blocks.
    8. Recognizing missing parts of pictures.

These tests have been well standardized for adults, giving a
good sampling of the abilities ordinarily associated with academic
intelligence. The IQ's were calculated according to the Wechsler-
Bellevue method which (unlike the Stanford-Binet) makes allowance for the deterioration of average intelligence with old age,
rather than assuming a constant level throughout adulthood. This
gave a fairer comparison of the IQ's of men of such widely di-
vergent ages. It should be borne in mind, however, that the effective intelligence of older men like von Papen, Raeder, Schacht,
and Streicher was 15–20 points lower than the IQ's indicated here
but their relative standing in their respective age groups is ac-
curately indicated.

| NAME | IQ | NAME | IQ |
|---|---|---|---|
| HJALMAR SCHACHT | 143 | ALBERT SPEER | 128 |
| SEYSS-INQUART | 141 | ALFRED JODL | 127 |
| HERMAN GOERING | 138 | ALFRED ROSENBERG | 127 |
| KARL DOENITZ | 138 | CONSTANTIN VON NEURATH | 125 |
| FRANZ VON PAPEN | 134 | WALTHER FUNK | 124 |
| ERICH RAEDER | 134 | WILHELM FRICK | 124 |
| DR. HANS FRANK | 130 | RUDOLF HESS (estimated)* | 120 |
| HANS FRITZSCHE | 130 | FRITZ SAUCKEL | 118 |
| BALDUR VON SCHIRACH | 130 | ERNST KALTENBRUNNER | 113 |
| JOACHIM VON RIBBENTROP | 129 | JULIUS STREICHER | 106 |
| WILHELM KEITEL | 129 | *On basis of retest after recovery. | |

Except for Streicher, the IQ's show that the Nazi leaders were above average intelligence (IQ 90–110), merely confirming the fact that the most successful men in any sphere of human activity —whether it is politics, industry, militarism, or crime—are apt to be above average intelligence. It must be borne in mind that the IQ indicates nothing but the mechanical efficiency of the mind, and has nothing to do with character or morals, nor the various other considerations that go into an evaluation of personality. Above all, the individual's sense of values and the expressions of his basic motivation are the things that truly reveal his character. The projective tests (like the ink-blot test) give some clues as to reaction-pattern, but a real study of character and personality requires prolonged close observation to reflect these values and motives.

However, a social movement as far-reaching and catastrophic as that of Nazism cannot be adequately analyzed and understood merely in terms of the individual character traits of its leaders. A realistic psychological approach requires an insight into the total personalities in interaction in their social and historical setting. The Nuremberg Trial afforded an ideal opportunity for such a study. The day-to-day record of the conversations and reactions of the Nazi leaders during the year in which their past record was legally on trial, and their whole system of values was psychologically on trial before the world, proved to be more revealing than the sum of all the tests could possibly be. We therefore turn to the combined historical and psychological record which constitutes the Diary.

## APPENDIX A.

### Statement of Individual Responsibility for Crimes Set Out in Counts One, Two, Three and Four

The statements hereinafter set forth following the name of each individual defendant constitute matters upon which the prosecution will rely *inter alia* as establishing the individual responsibility of the defendant:

### GÖRING:

The defendant GÖRING between 1932–1945 was: a member of the Nazi Party, Supreme Leader of the SA, ~~General in the SS~~, a member and President of the Reichstag, Minister of the Interior of Prussia, Chief of the Prussian Police and Prussian Secret State Police, Chief of the Prussian State Council, Trustee of the Four Year Plan, Reich Minister for Air, Commander in Chief of the Air Force, President of the Council of Ministers for the Defence of the Reich, member of the Secret Cabinet Council, head of the Hermann Goering Industrial Combine, and successor Designate to Hitler. The defendant GÖRING used the foregoing positions, his personal influence, and his intimate connection with the Führer in such a manner that: he promoted the accession to power of the Nazi conspirators and the consolidation of their control over Germany set forth in Count One of the Indictment; he promoted the military and economic preparation for war set forth in Count One of the Indictment; he participated in the planning and preparation of the Nazi conspirators for Wars of Aggression and Wars in Violation of International Treaties, Agreements and Assurances set forth in Counts One and Two of the Indictment; and he authorized, directed and participated in the War Crimes set forth in Count Three of the Indictment, and the Crimes against Humanity set forth in Count Four of the Indictment, including a wide variety of crimes against persons and property.

### RIBBENTROP:

The defendant RIBBENTROP between 1932–1945 was: a member of the Nazi Party, a member of the Nazi Reichstag, Advisor to the Führer on matters of foreign policy, representative of the Nazi Party for matters of foreign policy, special German delegate for disarmament questions, Ambassador extraordinary, Ambassador in London, organizer and director of Dienststelle Ribbentrop, Reich Minister for Foreign Affairs, member of the Secret Cabinet Council, member of the Führer's political staff at general headquarters, and General in the SS. The defendant RIBBENTROP used the foregoing positions, his personal influence, and his intimate connection with the Führer in such a manner that: he promoted the accession to power of the Nazi conspirators as set forth in Count One of the Indictment; he promoted the preparations for war set forth in Count One of the Indictment; he participated in the political planning and preparation of the Nazi conspirators for Wars of Aggression and Wars in Violation of International Treaties, Agreements and Assurances as set forth in Counts One and Two of the Indictment; in accordance with the Führer Principle he executed and assumed responsibility for the execution of the foreign policy plans of the Nazi conspirators set forth in Count One of the Indictment; and he authorized; directed and participated in the War Crimes set forth in Count Three of the Indictment and the Crimes against Humanity set forth in Count Four of the Indictment, including more particularly the crimes against persons and property in occupied territories.

### HESS:

The defendant HESS between 1921 and 1941 was a member of the Nazi Party, Deputy to the Führer, Reich Minister without Portfolio, member of the Reichstag, member of the Council of Ministers for the Defence of the Reich, member of the Secret Cabinet Council, Successor Designate to the Führer after the defendant Göring, a General in the SS and a General in the SA. The defendant HESS used the foregoing positions, his personal influence and his intimate connection with the Führer in such a manner that: he promoted the accession to power of the Nazi conspirators and the consolidation of their control over Germany set forth in Count One of the Indictment; he promoted the military, economic

A page from the author's autographed copy of the indictment. Goering's comment at the top of the page is: "The victor will always be the judge and the vanquished the accused."

# Trial Diary

## 1945-1946

# 1. The Prosecution Opens

## THE READING OF THE INDICTMENT

MORNING SESSION: *The grim catalog of Nazi crimes contained in the Indictment was read into the record. "Count One—The Common Plan or Conspiracy: . . . The acquiring of totalitarian control in Germany . . . Utilization of Nazi control for foreign aggression . . . Count Two—Crimes Against Peace . . . violation of international treaties, agreements, and assurances . . . "* \*

[In the prisoners' dock the tension relaxed as they began to realize that the opening session consisted merely of the reading of the Indictment, which they had already read. They sat silently with diminishing attention, some switching on the different translations on the earphones, others gazing around the courtroom to size up the judges, the prosecution, the reporters, and the audience.]

LUNCH HOUR: There was a general letting off of steam as the defendants met and shook hands and talked for the first time since captivity, some for the first time in their lives. They ate lunch right in the courtroom after it was cleared, buzzing with released tension about all sorts of things from power politics to physical needs.

Ribbentrop was arguing with Hess but getting nowhere, since Hess has no recollection of the world events recounted in the Indictment. Ribbentrop then remarked to me, "Why all this fuss about breaking treaties? Did you ever read about the history of the British Empire? Why, it's full of broken treaties, oppression of minorities, mass murder, aggressive wars, and everything." I asked him whether the crimes of past history should be the accepted pattern for international law. "Well, no, but I thought that as long as the atomic bomb has made war too dangerous for nations

—————————————————————
\**All trial evidence and proceedings are quoted or summarized in italics; everything else is "off-the-record."*

35

to resort to, they will settle their differences peacefully in the future anyhow—."

Here Hess pricked up his ears. "Atomic bomb? What's that?"

"The atom-smashing bomb," Ribbentrop tried to explain.

"What does that mean?"

Ribbentrop launched into an explanation of the atomic bomb again, and asked Hess whether he really couldn't remember any of the things they were talking about today.

As I watched the others eat, several of them remarked that the food was getting better. "I suppose we'll get steak the day you hang us," von Schirach grinned.

Streicher was sitting alone, still being snubbed by the others. As I passed him, he stood up to attract my attention. "You know, Herr Doktor," he said, trying to make small talk, "I was sentenced in this very room once before."

"Is that so? How many times have you been tried in your lifetime?"

"Oh, 12 or 13 times. I've had lots of trials. That's old stuff."

A little later Ribbentrop buttonholed me again. "You'll see. A few years from now the lawyers of the world will condemn this trial. You can't have a trial without law.—Besides, it's really not nice to let Germans denounce Germans as they will at this trial. —That will not make a very dignified impression, mark my word."

The colonel signalled to me to order them back to their seats. As von Schirach passed me, he said, "This is a bad day—not for you, but for us."

---

AFTERNOON SESSION: The reading of the Indictment continued:
"Count Three—War Crimes: . . . Murder and ill treatment of civilian populations . . . and prisoners of war . . . Deportation for slave labor . . . Killing of hostages . . . Count Four—Crimes Against Humanity: . . . Murder, extermination, enslavement . . . Persecution on political and racial grounds . . . "

The charges against the individual defendants and organizations were read, after the charges under the 4 counts of the Indictment had been completed.

[Ribbentrop suffered an attack of vertigo and tinnitus and had to be taken out of the courtroom. Later Goering told me that he was now sure that Hess was crazy, because he had said during the session, "You'll see, this apparition will vanish, and you will be Führer of Germany within a month."]

--------------------- November 21 ---------------------

## PROSECUTOR JACKSON'S OPENING ADDRESS

MORNING SESSION: *The defendants all pled "not guilty," some qualifying this with the additional phrase "—in the sense of the Indictment."*

*Justice Jackson then began his opening speech for the prosecution. He described the Party rise to power with the aid of its storm troop (SA) ruffians, who "terrorized and silenced democratic opposition and were able at length to combine with political opportunists, militarists, industrialists, monarchists, and political reactionaries." One month after Hitler's accession to power, the Reichstag fire was used as the pretext to get von Hindenburg to suspend the most vital guarantees of the Weimar Constitution and give Hitler dictatorial powers. Within a few months the labor unions were abolished and Robert Ley became the undisputed dictator of German labor. The Nazis put into effect their anti-Christian ideology by persecuting the various Churches, especially the Catholic Church, in spite of the Concordat signed with the Holy See. Pastor Niemoeller was thrown into concentration camp as a means of quashing opposition from the Lutheran Church.*

---

LUNCH HOUR: Nazi crimes against Christianity was the main topic of conversation among the defendants during the lunch hour.

"Crimes against Christianity!" Rosenberg remarked cynically. "Did you ever pay any attention to the Russian crimes against Christianity?"

I asked Ribbentrop whether his statement admitting knowledge and helplessness with respect to the Nazi persecution of the Church was as quoted. "Yes," he said, "I told them that it checks. There were several protests from the Vatican, and Hitler finally ignored them. There was nothing you could do about it."

"But that was our right!" Goering flared up in the middle of a mouthful. "We were a sovereign State and that was strictly our business."

Later Goering was heard to say to Funk: "Don't worry, you

were only taking orders from me. I'll take full responsibility for
the Four Year Plan." Funk grinned in sheepish gratitude.

——————————

AFTERNOON SESSION: Justice Jackson described the crimes against
the Jews, "The most savage and numerous crimes planned and
committed by the Nazis . . . The ghetto was the laboratory for
testing repressive measures. Jewish property was the first to be
expropriated, but the custom grew and included similar measures
against anti-Nazi Germans, Poles, Czechs, Frenchmen, and Bel-
gians. Extermination of the Jews enabled the Nazis to bring a
practiced hand to similar measures against Poles, Serbs, and
Greeks. The plight of the Jew was a constant threat to opposition
and discontent among other elements of Europe's population—
pacifists, conservatives, Communists, Catholics, Protestants. Socialists. It was, in fact, a threat to every dissenting opinion and to
every non-Nazi's life." As a result of the policy of discrimination,
then ghettos, then concentration camps and mass extermination,
60 per cent of the Jews in Nazi-dominated Europe were murdered
—or about 5.7 million Jews. "History does not record a crime per-
petrated against so many victims or ever carried out with such
calculated cruelty." Jackson cited Streicher as complaining that
Christian teachings stood in the way of the Führer's radical solution of the Jewish question in Europe and supporting Hitler's
program of extermination. Hans Frank made similar utterances in
his diary and speeches.

Justice Jackson proceeded to describe the specific actions undertaken in this program leading to extermination: the infamous
Nuremberg Laws of 1935; the well-planned "spontaneous" uprising of November 9-10, 1938; the instigated pogroms and mass
executions in the East from 1941 on; the sadistic cruelty, torture,
starvation and mass murder in the concentration camps—not to
mention such sidelights as "scientific experiments" like freezing
male victims almost to death and warming them back to life and
sexual intercourse with the "animal heat" of naked gypsies. "Here
Nazi degeneracy reached its nadir. I dislike to encumber your records with such morbid tales, but we are in the grim business of
trying men as criminals . . . Our proof will be disgusting, and
you will say I have robbed you of your sleep. But these are the
things that have turned the stomach of the world and set every
civilized hand against Nazi Germany."

——————————

During the intermission I overheard von Schirach asking Goering who had given the orders for the brutal wiping out of the Warsaw ghetto and such measures.

"Himmler, I suppose," Goering replied uncomfortably. Schirach shook his head and muttered, "Horrible!" then sat back grimly in his seat.

"These certainly are horrible things," I said as Goering turned around to me.

"Yes, I know," he replied, nervously looking around the courtroom. "—And I can see that the German people will be forever condemned by these brutalities. But these atrocities were so incredible, even in the smaller numbers that we heard about, that it was an easy matter to assure us that all such stories were mere propaganda. Himmler had his chosen psychopaths to carry these things out, and it was kept secret from the rest of us. But I would never have suspected him of it. He didn't seem to be the murderer type—. You're a psychologist, you ought to know.—I can't explain it."

---

*Justice Jackson continued with the crimes in the conduct of war: the murdering of PW's and hostages; the plundering of art treasures in occupied countries; the enforcement of slave labor and starvation; the war against civilian populations based on the "master race" ideology.*

*Finally, summing up the moral and legal aspects of the trial, he stated: "The real complaining party at your bar is Civilization. In all our countries it is still a struggling and imperfect thing. It does not plead that the United States, or any other country, has been blameless of the conditions which made the German people easy victims to the blandishments and intimidations of the Nazi conspirators. But it points to the dreadful sequence of aggressions and crimes I have recited, it points to the weariness of flesh, the exhaustion of resources, and the destruction of all that was beautiful or useful in so much of the world, and to greater potentialities for destruction in days to come . . . The refuge of the defendants can be only their hope that international law will lag so far behind the moral sense of mankind that conduct which is crime in the moral sense must be regarded as innocence in law. We challenge that proposition."*

——————— EVENING IN JAIL ———————

*Fritzsche's Cell:* (At the end of the afternoon session, Fritzsche had grown so pale, that Colonel Andrus inquired as to his health. Fritzsche said he was all right.) This evening I found him pacing up and down in his cell, obviously pale with anger. "I'm furious!" he exclaimed. "It's the intolerable hemming in between Scylla and Charybdis. The question of aggressive warfare on the one hand, and the disgraceful atrocities on the other. How dare they accuse us of a conspiracy with malice aforethought and of saying, 'Germany awake, Jew perish.' Believe me, I'm not just arguing for my life; I don't give a damn for it any more.—But don't use this giant legal apparatus just for propaganda. I plead not guilty to the charges as stated. But I am willing to recognize that I have made blunders, that I have been tricked and trapped by the Himmler murder machine, even when I tried to check on it . . . I don't give a damn about my life—but it's the disgrace, the awful disgrace!"

"You mean to say that you're prepared to die for Germany's mistakes, but not as a criminal who knowingly planned and committed mass murder?"

"Exactly. That's exactly it. And that's the way it is with the whole German people, concentrated in my little person as one of the symbols. Of course, somebody has to answer for it. But let us explain our position before the world, so that at least we won't die under this awful burden of shame."

I assured him that he would have ample time to state his position. He was quite surprised and relieved when told that there would probably be an adjournment between prosecution and defense, and that each one would have a fair chance to have his say. He was under the impression that steamroller tactics were going to be used to pin all the blame on them as instigators, and then simply place them before a firing squad with hardly a defense. I assured him that the Allied peoples would not tolerate such tactics, and that neither the judges nor the prosecution would be willing to face the public and history with such a record. He was genuinely relieved. He had thought they would be executed by Christmas.

———————

*Streicher's Cell*: I asked Streicher "as man to man" whether he didn't have some misgivings about having paved the way with *Hetzpropaganda* (rabble rousing) for the persecution and mass murder outlined in the afternoon session.

"I didn't pave the way for such things," he protested. "Why weren't there any murders from 1919 to 1934 if that's the case? That was all done by Himmler. I disapprove of murder. That's why I couldn't kill my wife and myself when we were in the Tyrol at the end of the war. I decided I would have to bear my cross."

"But why did you have to print all that sexual filth about the Jews?"

"Me—filthy?" he said with glaring eyes. "Why it's all in the Talmud. The Jews are a circumcized race. Didn't Joseph commit *Rassenschande* [race pollution] with Pharaoh's daughter? And what about Lot and his daughters? The Talmud is full of such things. They are crucifying me now," he said confidentially. "I can tell. Three of the judges are Jews."

"How can you tell that?"

"I can recognize blood. Three of them get uncomfortable when I look at them. I can tell. I've been studying race for 20 years. The body structure shows the character. I'm an authority on that subject. Himmler thought he was, but he didn't know anything about it. He had Negro blood himself."

"Really?"

"Oh, yes," he grinned triumphantly, "I could tell it by his head shape and hair. I can recognize blood."

Although insight and orientation were apparently normal, he gave me the impression for the first time that his fanatic bigotry was bordering on the paranoic.

---

# November 23

MORNING SESSION: *Major Wallis described how Hitler and Goebbels, after using propaganda successfully for "the conquest of the masses," used their propaganda machine "to prepare the ground psychologically for political action and military aggression." All educational, informational, and cultural activities were regimented under Hitler's control. Goebbels was in charge of official and*

Party propaganda. Rosenberg specialized in promoting racial and ideological policies, while von Schirach inculcated German Youth with Nazi doctrines.

LUNCH HOUR: Frank was telling some of the others how his wife had written that she had to send the children out to beg for bread. Suddenly he turned to Rosenberg. "Tell me, Rosenberg, was all this destruction and misery necessary? What was the sense in all that racial politics, anyway?"

Rosenberg remained silent, while Frank, Fritzsche, and von Schirach expressed despair over the ruin of the German nation, hinting that the racial policies were to blame. Finally Rosenberg said, "Of course we didn't expect it to lead to such terrible things as mass murder and war. I was only looking for a peaceful solution to the racial problem."

## ───────── November 26 ─────────

### PLANS FOR AGGRESSIVE WAR

MORNING SESSION: *Mr. Alderman read the fateful "Hoszbach document" recording a secret speech by Hitler, outlining his aggressive plans to Goering, von Blomberg, von Fritsch, Raeder, and von Neurath, on November 5, 1937. In discussing the various possibilities in his planned aggressions, Hitler stated in part (as recorded by his adjutant Hoszbach):*

*"German politics must reckon in part with its two hateful enemies, England and France, to whom a strong German colossus in the center of Europe would be intolerable . . .*

*"For the improvement of our military political position it must be our first aim, in every case of entanglement by war, to conquer Czechoslovakia and Austria, simultaneously, in order to remove any threat from the flanks in case of a possible advance westward . . . Once Czechoslovakia is conquered, and a mutual German-Hungarian frontier is obtained, then a neutral attitude by Poland in a German-French conflict could be more easily relied upon. Our agreements with Poland remain valid only as long as Germany's strength remains unshakeable . . . The Führer believes personally, that in all probability England and perhaps also France,*

have already silently written off Czechoslovakia . . . Naturally, we should in any case have to secure our frontier during the operation of our attacks against Czechoslovakia and Austria . . . If Germany profits from this war by disposing of the Czechoslovakian and Austrian questions, the probability must be assumed that England, being at war with Italy, would not decide to commence operations against Germany . . . In view of the information given by the Führer, Generaloberst Goering considered it imperative to think of a reduction or abandonment of our military undertaking in Spain."

LUNCH HOUR: Many expressed amazement at this document revealing Hitler's conception of power politics. Jodl said he had no idea of it at the time. One thing that impressed him about the document today was the overestimate of Italy's importance.

Seyss-Inquart likewise said he could never understand Hitler's evaluation of Italy. He had always called the Italians "small fry." In reference to the Hoszbach document he said, "If I had only known in 1937 that he had made such a statement, I certainly would have thought twice before playing along."

Von Schirach thought the document was "concentrated political madness."

Frank said, "Just wait till the German people read that and see the kind of dilettantism with which the Führer sealed their fate!"

Goering didn't like all this talk and broke it up with "Ach, fiddlesticks! What about the grabbing of California and Texas by the Americans? That was plain aggressive warfare for territorial expansion too!"

Ribbentrop, looking quite dishevelled, shook his head sadly when I asked him if he hadn't known about that statement of policy. "No, he never told me about it. I tell you again, Herr Doktor, if the Allies had given us half a chance on the Versailles issue, you never would have heard of Hitler."

Fritzsche admitted that the document threw a different light on the case. "Now I can see why there is a question of conspiracy, and I'll have to alter my own position to the indictment."

AFTERNOON SESSION: Mr. Alderman described the next step in Nazi planned aggression, after Austria and Czechoslovakia had been taken care of. A document by Hitler's adjutant Schmundt recorded Hitler's outright decision for aggressive war in another secret meeting on May 23, 1939, in the presence of Goering, Keitel, and Raeder. After speaking of Lebensraum, the document goes on to quote Hitler: "The national-political unity of the Germans has been achieved, apart from minor exceptions." (At this point Mr. Alderman interpolated, "I suppose those were in the concentration camps.") "—Further successes cannot be obtained without the shedding of blood . . . There is therefore no question of sparing Poland, and we are left with the decision: to attack Poland at the first suitable opportunity . . . If there were an alliance of France, England, and Russia against Germany, Italy, and Japan, I would be constrained to attack England and France with a few annihilating blows . . . Albeit under protest, Belgium and Holland will yield to pressure . . . "

Having made his preparations for war, Hitler called together his military leaders on August 22, 1939 at Berchtesgaden and explained that the war had to come in his lifetime and he was now ready to strike, as another document showed, "I will give a propagandistic cause for starting the war, never mind whether it is plausible or not. The victor shall not be asked, later on, whether we told the truth or not. In starting and waging a war, not the right is what matters but victory."

---

Toward the end of the day, Frank handed me a note describing an "Apocalyptic vision" he had had in the dock while listening to the last document. It was headed "Hitler on August 22, 1939," and ran as follows: "We sit opposite the court.—And silently the train of the dead goes endlessly by.—It is unbroken.—Pale and wan, without sound, in the dim yellow-gray light of eternity, this stream of misery flows on.—All, all surge on without pause, enshrouded in dim mist, whipped by the flames of mankind's agony —hither—thither—thither—on and on, and no end is in sight . . . The human beings torn from life in this war are the most gruesome booty of Death, raging in hate and destruction—youth and age, growth and existence, pride and humility . . . There they go—Poles, Jews, Germans, Russians, Americans, Italians—all nationalities, bleeding and wasting away. And one voice cries: 'This war must come, for only as long as I live can it come about!' Ah, what hast Thou suffered to come to pass, Almighty God!"

─────────── November 29 ───────────

## THE SHOWING OF THE ATROCITY FILM

AFTERNOON SESSION: *Goering, Ribbentrop, and Hess had a great laugh over the reading of Goering's telephone conversation with Ribbentrop on the day of Hitler's triumphant entry into Vienna, describing the whole thing as a lark, with birds twittering, etc. Then the hilarity in the dock suddenly stopped as Commander Donovan announced the showing of a documentary film on Nazi concentration camps as they were found by American troops.*

(Kelley and I were posted at either end of the defendants' dock and observed the prisoners during the showing of this film. Following are my notes jotted down during the showing of the film at about 1–2 minute intervals:)

Schacht objects to being made to look at film as I ask him to move over; turns away, folds arms, gazes into gallery . . . (Film starts). Frank nods at authentication at introduction of film . . . Fritzsche (who had not seen any part of film before) already looks pale and sits aghast as it starts with scenes of prisoners burned alive in a barn . . . Keitel wipes brow, takes off headphones . . . Hess glares at screen, looking like a ghoul with sunken eyes over the footlamp . . . Keitel puts on headphone, glares at screen out of the corner of his eye . . . von Neurath has head bowed, doesn't look . . . Funk covers his eyes, looks as if he is in agony, shakes his head . . . Ribbentrop closes his eyes, looks away . . . Sauckel mops brow . . . Frank swallows hard, blinks eyes, trying to stifle tears . . . Fritzsche watches intensely with knitted brow, cramped at the end of his seat, evidently in agony . . . Goering keeps leaning on balustrade, not watching most of the time, looking droopy . . . Funk mumbles something under his breath . . . Streicher keeps watching, immobile except for an occasional squint . . . Funk now in tears, blows nose, wipes eyes, looks down . . . Frick shakes head at illustration of "violent death"—Frank mutters "Horrible!" . . . Rosenberg fidgets, peeks at screen, bows head, looks to see how others are reacting . . . Seyss-Inquart stoic throughout . . . Speer looks very sad, swallows hard . . . Defense attorneys are now muttering, "for God's sake—terrible." Raeder watches without budging . . . von Papen sits with hand over brow, looking down, has not looked at screen yet . . . Hess keeps looking bewildered . . . piles of dead are shown in a slave labor camp . . . von Schirach watching intently, gasps, whispers to Sauckel . . . Funk crying now . . . Goering looks sad, leaning on elbow . . . Doenitz has head bowed, no longer watching . . . Sauckel shudders at picture of Buchenwald crematorium oven . . . as human skin lampshade is shown, Streicher says, "I don't believe that" . . . Goering coughing . . . Attorneys gasping . . . Now Dachau . . . Schacht still not looking . . . Frank nods his head bitterly and says, "Horrible!" . . . Rosenberg still fidgeting, leans forward, looks around, leans back, hangs head . . . Fritzsche, pale, biting lips, really seems in agony . . . Doenitz has head buried in his hands . . . Keitel now hanging head . . . Ribbentrop looks up at screen as British officer starts to speak, saying he has already buried 17,000 corpses . . . Frank biting his nails . . . Frick shakes his head incredulously at speech of female doctor describing treatment and experiments on female prisoners at Belsen . . . As Kramer is shown, Funk says with choking voice, "The dirty swine!" . . . Ribbentrop sitting with pursed lips and blinking eyes, not looking at screen . . . Funk crying bitterly, claps hand over mouth as women's naked corpses are thrown into pit . . . Keitel and Ribbentrop look up at mention of tractor clearing corpses, see it, then hang their heads . . . Streicher shows signs of disturbance for first time . . . Film ends.

After the showing of the film, Hess remarks, "I don't believe it." Goering whispers to him to keep quiet, his own cockiness quite gone. Streicher says something about "perhaps in the last days." Fritzsche retorts scornfully. "Millions? In the last days?—No." Otherwise there is a gloomy silence as the prisoners file out of the courtroom.

——————— EVENING IN JAIL ———————

We immediately went down to the cell block to talk to them individually. The first one was Fritzsche. As soon as we closed the door and started talking to him, he burst into tears and sobbed bitterly, "No power in heaven or earth—will erase this shame from my country!—not in generations—not in centuries!—" He shook with sobs and clenched his fists against his forehead, catching his breath only enough to say, "Excuse me for losing control—but I had to sit there and keep it in for a whole hour!" We asked if he needed any sleeping pills and he answered, "No, what's the use? It would only be cowardice to drug this thing out of my consciousness."

Von *Schirach* seemed fairly well composed, but said, "I don't know how Germans could do such things."

*Frick* made some feeble attempts at rationalization—"I suppose the disruption of communications in the last few months—the bombing and confusion—I don't know." Then he dismissed the subject and asked whether they weren't going to get their walk today.

*Funk* was depressed, and burst into tears as soon as we asked him how he was affected by the film. "Horrible! Horrible!" he repeated in a choking voice. When asked whether he would need a sleeping pill, he sobbed, "What's the use?—What's the use?"

*Streicher* admitted the film was "Terrible"—without any apparent feeling, then asked whether the guards couldn't be more quiet at night so that he could sleep.

*Speer* showed no outward emotional effects, but said that he was all the more resolved to acknowledge a collective responsibility of the Party leadership and absolve the German people of the guilt.

*Frank* was extremely depressed and agitated. As soon as we mentioned the film, he began to cry in abject shame and rage. "To think that we lived like kings and believed in that beast!—Don't let anybody tell you that they had no idea! Everybody sensed that there was something horribly wrong with this system, even if we didn't know all the details. They didn't *want* to know! It was too comfortable to live on the system, to support our families in royal style, and to believe that it was all right. You treat us too well," he said, pointing to the food on the table, which he hadn't touched. "Your prisoners and our own people starved to death in our camps.—May God have mercy on our souls!—Yes, *Herr Doktor*, what I told you was absolutely right.—This trial has been willed by God.—I was trying to be understanding with the others when we came together—but that's over—I know what I have to do . . . " He became more solemn with the last sentence. We asked if he needed anything to sleep. He shook his head. "No, thank you.—If I don't sleep, I can pray . . . " (There was no doubting his sincerity.)

*Seyss-Inquart* admitted: "It gets you.—But I can hold out."

Still trembling with emotion, *Doenitz* said half in English and half in German, "How can they accuse me of knowing of such things? They ask why I didn't go to Himmler to check on the concentration camps. Why that's preposterous! He would have kicked me out just as I would have kicked him out if he came to investigate the navy! What in God's name did I have to do with these things? It was only by chance that I rose to such a high position, and I never had a thing to do with the Party."*

We asked *von Papen* why he didn't watch the picture. "I didn't want to see Germany's shame," he admitted.

*Sauckel* was completely unnerved. His face twitched and he trembled from head to foot. He stretched out his fingers and cried, wild-eyed, "I'd choke myself with these hands if I thought I had the slightest thing to do with those murders! It is a shame! It is a disgrace for us and for our children—and for our children's children!"

*Schacht* was burning with indignation. "How dare they make me sit there with those criminals and watch a film on concentration camp atrocities! They know that I was an enemy of Hitler and ended up in a concentration camp myself! It is unforgivable!"

*Von Neurath* was rather bewildered, didn't have much to say. Simply pointed out that he wasn't in power when all this went on.

*Raeder* said that he had hardly even heard of concentration camps before. Just heard of three of them, when he made efforts to get some friends out.

*Jodl* was calm, but evidently moved. "It is shocking. Believe me —the shame of it all is that so many of the youth joined the Party out of idealistic motives."

*Keitel* was eating, having just returned from a conference with his defense attorney. He appeared to have forgotten the film until we mentioned it. He stopped eating and said with his mouth half full, "It is terrible. When I see such things, I'm ashamed of being a German!—It was those dirty SS swine!—If I had known it I would have told my son, 'I'd rather shoot you than let you join the SS.' But I didn't know.—I'll never be able to look people in the face again."

---

*Doenitz was not indicted on Count 4.

Hess seemed confused, kept mumbling, "I don't understand—I don't understand."

Ribbentrop had a visible tremor of the hands, and looked utterly bewildered. "Hitler couldn't even have looked at such a film himself.—I don't understand.—I don't even think that Himmler could have ordered such things.—I don't understand."

Rosenberg was even more nervous than usual. "It's an awful thing, even if the Russians did do the same thing—terrible—terrible—terrible—." I pointed out his responsibility in formulating Nazi *Rassenpolitik* (racial policy). "Oh, you can't explain it on the basis of *Rassenpolitik*," he answered defensively, "because so many Germans were killed.—This just weakens our whole defense."

As for Goering, he was apparently disturbed because it had spoiled his show. "It was such a good afternoon too, until they showed that film.—They were reading my telephone conversations on the Austrian affair, and everybody was laughing with me.—And then they showed that awful film, and it just spoiled everything."

--------------- November 30 ---------------

## LAHOUSEN'S TESTIMONY AND HESS'S MEMORY

MORNING SESSION: *General Lahousen, ranking surviving member of the Abwehr (counter-intelligence) testified today, making Ribbentrop, Keitel, Jodl, and many others squirm.* [His presence and testimony were apparently a shock to all the defendants, who learned for the first time of the resistance movement in the Abwehr, and heard one of their own generals denounce Hitler's aggressive warfare.] *Under direct examination of Colonel Amen, General Lahousen described how he had participated in an underground movement in the German Abwehr, led by his chief, Admiral Canaris. The purpose was to forestall Hitler's plans for an aggressive war, if possible, and failing that, to prevent its successful outcome or to do away with Hitler. He further described the roles of Goering, Keitel, and Jodl in planning with Hitler the* bombardment of Warsaw and extermination of the Polish intelligentsia, nobility, clergy, and Jews. To create an "incident" to provoke the planned attack on Poland, Himmler had obtained Polish uniforms, with which he dressed up concentration camp inmates and had them shot while "attacking" the Gleiwitz radio station, to make it look like Polish "aggression."

LUNCH HOUR: Goering was fuming. "That traitor! That's one we forgot on the 20th of July.* Hitler was right—the Abwehr was a traitor's organization! How do you like that! No wonder we lost the war—our own Intelligence Service was sold out to the enemy!" He was talking quite loud, half to me, but obviously announcing the "Party line" on Lahousen's testimony.

"Well, opinions may differ on that," I said, "but it seems to me it's only a question of whether his testimony was true or not."

"What good is the testimony of a traitor? He should have been busy giving me accurate reports on the results of our bombing missions instead of sabotaging our war effort. Now I know why I could never depend on him for accurate information. Just wait till I ask him that one question, 'Why did you not renounce your position, if you were convinced a German victory would be a tragedy?' Just wait till I get a chance at him."

Jodl took it all more philosophically. "If he was convinced of it, all well and good, but then he should have said something, and not betrayed his officer's honor. I know they are always asking me what I would have done if I had known of Hitler's plans. I would have said something, but I wouldn't have acted dishonorably."

"Well, it seems to me that there was a struggle between conscience and duty, and this man followed his conscience," I said.

"Oh, but you can't do such things. An officer must either follow orders or resign."

Keitel agreed, but was evidently disturbed about the damaging evidence. "That man was just reading from a prepared script! I'm going to tell my lawyer!" I told him I didn't think he was reading any prepared script, and anyway, it was a question of the truth of the testimony. He fell back on the "officer's honor" argument, without making much sense.

*During the purge following the attempt to assassinate Hitler on July 20, 1944.

I spoke to Lahousen again later, and he remarked, "Now they talk of honor, after millions have been murdered! No doubt it's unpleasant for them to have some one who can stand up and state these uncomfortable truths to their faces.—I've got to speak for those whom they murdered.—I am the only one left."

AFTERNOON SESSION: *In the afternoon session Lahousen stood up and parried all questions with dramatic vigor. He described how orders for mass murder of Communists and Jews were given and carried out in the war against Russia. This involved execution of both PW's and civilians by the SS, Gestapo, and special action groups. Mistreatment of prisoners resulted in epidemics, starvation, and cannibalism. Complaints were made to Keitel about conditions in PW camps, but the executions were under the jurisdiction of Himmler's RSHA,\* of which Kaltenbrunner was the head. Another little incident involved an order from Keitel to catch and assassinate the escaped General Giraud, at Hitler's wish. Lahousen and Canaris had sabotaged this order, and barely got away with it through a clever ruse exploiting the death of Heydrich. [In the mid-afternoon recess, Ribbentrop handed his attorney some questions but the latter said, "Let's not ask so many questions, he only throws them back in our faces with even more damaging information." "Well, leave out anything that you think might be damaging," Ribbentrop said nervously.]*

Early in the afternoon court adjourned for a special closed session to take up the matter of Hess's competence to defend himself. As the other defendants filed out of court, I struck up a conversation with Hess. I told him that he would probably be considered incompetent to defend himself, and that he would probably not be coming to court any more.—However, I said I would come down to see him once in a while in his cell. He seemed rather disturbed at this, and said that he thought he was competent to defend himself.

*Hess's defense counsel, Dr. Rorscheidt, started to argue to the Tribunal that Hess was not competent to defend himself, because of his amnesia. Suddenly Hess wrote a note and handed it to the guard to give to his counsel, but the latter ignored it. The prose-*

---

\*Security Headquarters which included the Gestapo and allied offices.

cution argued that Hess was competent to defend himself, since the psychiatrists had found him not insane. After about an hour and a half of this, Hess dropped a bombshell into the proceedings by declaring, "My memory is again in order. The reasons why I simulated loss of memory were tactical. In fact, it is only my capacity for concentration that is slightly reduced . . . Hitherto in conversation with my defense counsel I have maintained my loss of memory. He was, therefore, acting in good faith when he asserted that I lost my memory." The court adjourned in pandemonium.

When I saw Dr. Rorscheidt in the hall later, he was completely perplexed, not knowing whether his client was bluffing before or in court. When Kelley and then I saw Hess in his cell later, his memory was perfectly in order and he could answer questions about his imprisonment, his flight to England, his role in the Party and even his youth.

## December 1

Before court started, Kelley and I visited a few of the defendants in the cell block to tell them about Hess's sudden restoration of memory. Goering was at first incredulous, but then roared with delight at what he took to be Hess's joke on the court and the psychiatrists. He could not be sure whether the restoration of memory was genuine, but he just wished he could have been there to enjoy the scene and watch the judges' and prosecutors' faces.

Von Schirach greeted the news in pop-eyed amazement, then said, "Well, that's the end of scientific psychology." We told him to wait and see—there was no telling what surprises Hess's hysteria would spring next.

Ribbentrop was completely bewildered. "You mean Rudolf Hess—our Hess?—It is incredible!"

Up in the dock Goering asked Hess if he had really been faking, and whether he really remembered all the details about his flight to England. Hess related the details with relish, boasting about his skill in making the take-off, hedge-hopping, flying by instruments, and landing by parachute. "Yes, yes, I fly by instruments too," Goering said. "At what height did you jump?" Hess boasted that it was pretty low—about 200 meters. Goering gradually stopped enjoying the joke of Hess's "amnesia-faking," as he looked around the courtroom and saw that Hess was now the center of attraction. Hess was enjoying it immensely.

---

## December 1-2

## WEEK END IN JAIL

*Hess's Cell:* Hess is in quite a cheerful mood, very pleased with himself for having "fooled everybody." He said he could have done better on the psychological tests too, if he had tried harder —at least he could have worked a little faster. Retest on IQ test showed genuine improvement in memory span, and slight improvement on other parts of test, apparently attributable to better attention and effort, besides the practice effect of repetition. However, he still made some of the same mistakes and gave the same imperfect answers as previously, so his contention that he could have done much better does not stand up.

During the examination, I broached the subject of what Hitler said when he made his flight to England, to get his reaction to Hitler's declaration that he was insane. Hess bristled, "I don't know what he said, and I don't want to know!—It doesn't interest me!" Then he laughed apologetically for his brusque answer to the question. We continued with the tests, and later I remarked casually that I understood there were some streets that had been named after him. "Yes," he said, "the names were changed—even the hospital that was named after me." I asked him how he knew that, and he quickly tried to cover up. "Oh, I don't know for sure—I suppose so—it would have been logical under the circumstances."

Later I reminded him of what I had said before the hearing, (that he might not be coming back any more). "Yes, that's why I decided it was time to stop the game." (All of the foregoing gives a clue to his hysterical reaction to an idea which was catastrophic to his ego—rejected as insane by the Führer, he seeks refuge in amnesia, then snaps out of it to avoid the same rejection by his old friends.)

I asked him how he felt about the destruction of German cities. He didn't seem to know the details but had a typical rationalization-rejection reaction: "Oh, those old buildings—it was about time they were destroyed; they would have fallen apart in a short time anyway."

---

*Fritzsche's Cell:* Fritzsche said he had somewhat recovered from the condition of shock into which the film had thrown him. On Friday and Saturday he was too demoralized to give any thought to his defense. He confided that those were the first days in his life that he couldn't pray. He still looked quite depressed, and shook his head sadly when we referred to the film: "It went beyond my wildest imagination." He showed further interest in the IQ's and I told him who the first 6 or 8 men were on the list, and described the curve of mental growth and decline. We discussed the resistance to "Goering's front." He said even von Ribbentrop was not as sure to support Goering as Goering might think. Von Schirach was still vacillating, but he was sure that the film had had a devastating effect on the cynics.

"I wonder what Goering's game is now—what can he possibly say to such a thing?" Fritzsche asked.

"Apparently the film spoiled his act for a day," I answered, "but he has just given out a statement that he still supports the Führer, and apparently is still playing the game of martyr and cynic." Fritzsche just shook his head.

---

*Keitel's Cell:* Keitel was evidently suffering from loss of face after the damaging testimony of Lahousen. He looked very sheepish as he stammered his reaction without my having broached the subject. "I don't know what to say—that Giraud affair—well, I knew that was coming up—but what can I say?—I know that an officer and gentleman like you must be wondering—(*macht sich Gedanken*)—These are things that attack my very honor as an officer. —I don't care if they accuse me of starting the war—I was only doing my duty and following orders.—But these assassination stories—I don't know how I ever got mixed up in this thing . . . "

(He did not deny either story, but was quite evidently more concerned over the assassination plots against two members of the "honorable military profession" than his part in conducting a world war as damaging to his ego values.)

*Frank's Cell:* Frank was deep in meditation, but welcomed the visit. He referred to the "vision" he had jotted down and given to me in court the other day. "And do you know what followed that?" he said in a sort of mystic ecstasy. "It was too terrible to write down! Because then Hitler appeared in the vision—right there in court—and said, 'You have sworn faithfulness to me unto death—come!' Isn't that fantastic?"

He described this with such dramatic fervor and secretive confidence, that I almost suspected hallucination.

"You mean you were thinking about this in court?" I tested.

"Yes—that's the image that went through my mind that day, and it was so overwhelming, that I wrote it down—I thought it would interest you psychologically." (His manner of response dispelled any doubts about normal orientation.)

We went on to talk about the general reaction to the trial. "Do you know," he said, "they still don't see what is taking place. Take Goering, for instance. The other day we were about to take our walk together. He stopped and looked at me, waiting for me to walk around behind him to take my proper place at his left because he is the senior officer. Can you imagine that—even now, in this prison?—I just don't bother with him any more."

*Speer's Cell:* Speer was still cool and collected and quite reconciled to paying the death penalty for the collective guilt. He did not even seem depressed, but rather quietly contemptuous of the efforts the military leaders were making to save their necks, while all the more convinced himself that they share the guilt.

--------------------- December 6 ---------------------

## THE PLEAS TO AVERT WAR

MORNING SESSION: Mr. Griffith-Jones of the British delegation first described how Hitler and Ribbentrop talked of peace while planning war. Then he read the last-minute pleas from France and England in 1939 imploring and warning Hitler not to attack Poland.

On August 22, 1939, while Hitler concluded his Non-Aggression Pact with Russia and secretly gave his decision to the military leaders to attack Poland, Chamberlain wrote: "Whatever may prove to be the nature of the German-Soviet Agreement, it cannot alter Great Britain's obligation to Poland, which His Majesty's Government have stated in public repeatedly and plainly, and which they are determined to fulfil. It has been alleged that if His Majesty's Government had made their position clear in 1914, the great catastrophe would have been avoided. Whether or not there is any force in that allegation, His Majesty's Government are resolved that on this occasion there shall be no such tragic misunderstanding. If the case should arise, they are resolved, and prepared, to employ without delay all the forces at their command, and it is impossible to foresee the end of the hostilities once engaged." Chamberlain offered again to negotiate the Polish-German differences to avert war. Hitler's reply was more saber-rattling.

On August 26, 1939, French Prime Minister Daladier wrote: " . . . In so serious an hour, I sincerely believe that no high-minded human being could understand it, if a war of destruction was started without a last attempt being made to reach a peaceful settlement between Germany and Poland . . . I, who desire harmony between the French and German people, and who am on the other hand bound to Poland by bonds of friendship, and by a promise, am prepared, as head of the French Government, to do everything an upright man can do to bring this attempt to a successful conclusion." He also offered to mediate, and added, "You and I were in the trenches in the last war. You know, as I do, what horror and condemnation the devastations of that war have left in *the conscience of the peoples . . . If French and German blood should be shed again, as it was shed 25 years ago, in a still longer and more murderous war, then each of the two nations will fight, believing in its own victory. But the most certain victors will be destruction and barbarity."*

LUNCH HOUR: As the defendants filed upstairs for lunch, Frank said to me in a choking voice, *"Those were two letters!"*

At lunch Goering showed no signs of having been affected by the damaging evidence of Hitler's determination to wage war in spite of all warnings. He still harped on the subject of how the defense was being hamstrung in every possible way, and added, "Wait and see, they won't even let us give our final rebuttal."

Doenitz asked me why General Donovan had left Prosecutor Jackson's staff. "Yes," chimed in Goering with a malicious twinkle in his eye. "Why?" I said I didn't know. Doenitz started to say something about what he read in the paper, but Goering stopped him. It was obvious that they were referring to the comment in *Stars & Stripes* on the article in the *Army & Navy Journal* attacking Jackson for indicting "the honorable military profession," and giving that as the reason for General Donovan's leaving.

Downstairs Goering continued his cynical campaign by jibing at American social customs. He commented on the Negro officers he had seen in the balcony and speculated on whether Negro officers could command white troops, and wanted to know whether Negro officers were allowed to ride in trolley cars with white civilians.

AFTERNOON SESSION: *Mr. Griffith-Jones read President Roosevelt's cable of August 24, 1939, to Hitler, again offering to negotiate to avert war:* "To the message which I sent you last April I have received no reply, but because my confident belief that the cause of world peace—which is the cause of humanity itself—rises above all other considerations, I am again addressing myself to you, with the hope that the war which impends and the consequent disaster to all peoples may yet be averted." *Again he urged negotiation. Again he received no reply from Hitler.*

*On August 25, 1939, President Roosevelt wrote again:* "In his reply to my message the President of Poland has made it plain that the Polish Government is willing, upon the basis set forth in my message, to agree to solve the controversy which has arisen between the Republic of Poland and the German Reich by direct negotiation or the process of conciliation. Countless human lives can yet be saved and hope may still be restored that the nations of the modern world may even now construct the foundation for a peaceful and happier relationship, if you and the Government of the German Reich will agree to the pacific means of the settlement accepted by the Government of Poland. All the world prays that Germany, too, will accept."

Mr. Griffith-Jones continued to address the Tribunal: "But, my Lord, Germany would not accept, nor would they accept the appeals by the Pope which appear in the next documents!"

On August 31 the Pope wrote: "The Pope is unwilling to abandon hope that pending negotiations may lead to a just, pacific solution such as the whole world continues to pray for."

But the appeals were to no avail. Hitler had decided the war had to come in his lifetime. While Hitler, Ribbentrop, and Goering kept up a farce of pretending to negotiate, the Wehrmacht struck.

——————— EVENING IN JAIL ———————

Jodl's Cell: I noticed at lunch that Jodl wasn't eating with Keitel any more, so I visited Jodl in his cell this evening. We started talking about the day's evidence. He was quiet, but apparently profoundly disillusioned. "Realizing how we were betrayed is worse than the defeat.—I fought the war in the belief that it was inevitable and I was protecting my country.—To think that Hitler actually planned it and turned down the offers of peace.—I don't know what I would have done if I had known about it then—it's easy to talk after the fact—but it would have been a terrible conflict between conscience and duty. Perhaps it's just as well I didn't know it.—At least I fought with conviction and honor.—There are certain things that one cannot reconcile with an officer's honor—"

"Like assassination—" I interjected.

He hesitated a while, then answered very quietly: "Of course —that cannot be reconciled to officer's honor.—Keitel had told me that Giraud was under surveillance, and that the thing had later been turned over to the RSHA—but never a word about assassination. No—that is not honor. Oh, such things have happened in military history.—We determined that the King of Bulgaria was poisoned, you know.—But I never thought one of our own generals—" He looked at the floor.

"I notice you don't eat at the 'command table' any more," I said casually. "You know—Goering and Keitel's table—I call that the 'command table.' "

"Oh, did you notice that?" Again an evasive look.

"It just occurred to me today."

"Well, I don't want to hit a man over the head when he's down —especially when we're in the same boat.—I wouldn't even do that to Streicher."

(The conversation left no doubt that Keitel had lost face even among the military clique, and that Jodl had gone so far as to cut him quietly.)

————————— December 8-9 —————————

## WEEK END IN JAIL

*Goering's Cell*: Goering inquired about background of General McNarney, new Commanding General USFET—obviously interested in figuring the "angles," since he felt he had lost a good bet in General Donovan (especially after the garbled defense of the "honorable military profession," tied up by the *Army & Navy Journal* with Donovan's departure). I said I didn't know anything about General McNarney.

Goering said, "General McNarney made a big mistake in saying that all Nazis and Nazi-sympathizers should be reduced to common laborers. You'll drive the country to Communism." I said I didn't know about that, but we had to uproot the Nazi philosophy which had brought destruction to Germany and all Europe, and try to teach the German people to live together peacefully on democratic principles. "But democracy just won't work with the German people!" he said emphatically. "They're killing each other with hatred right now—the hypocrites. I'm glad I don't have to live out there any more—each trying to save his face and his neck by denouncing the Party, now that we've lost. Just take that photographer, Hoffmann, for example. I saw his picture in the paper sorting pictures to be used as evidence against us.—When I think of the money that man made on my pictures.—I won't exaggerate —at least 1,000,000 marks—at say 5 pfennig profit per picture.— And now he sorts pictures to incriminate me!—No, it's no use, democracy just won't work in Germany.—The people are just too selfish and hateful—they can't agree.—How can you have a working democracy with 75 parties?"

Later Goering remarked: "You know, Hess isn't normal.—He may have recovered his memory, all right, but he is still suffering from a persecution complex. For instance, he makes remarks about a machine having been put under his cell to drive him insane with the noise of the motor. I told him I hear the same motor under my cell. He keeps coming out with remarks like that.—I can't remember them all, but you might expect things like this: if the coffee is too hot, they are trying to burn him; if it is too cold, they are trying to upset him. He didn't actually say that, but that is the kind of thing he comes out with."

"You're having a hard time keeping your group in fighting trim, aren't you?" I suggested casually.

"Yes, at least I have to keep them from attacking each other."

"Well, the evidence is pretty damaging, don't you think?"

He evaded a direct answer, "Of course, it's not the prosecution's job to look for excuses on our side.—That's our job. But there are certain things they deliberately overlook—like the way a command gets changed on its way down the chain-of-command. For instance, as Chief of the Four Year Plan, I might say that foreign workers will be paid on the same basis as German workers, but they should have to pay higher taxes. Then the Finance Ministry writes a directive, then it goes to the Labor Ministry, and finally it turns out that the foreign workers are in some cases paying ⅘ of their salary in taxes. That doesn't mean that I said the foreign workers should starve."

I remained silent, and he knew he was evading my question, and I was waiting for an answer. Finally he said: "I still can't grasp all those things. Do you suppose I'd have believed it if somebody came to me and said they were making freezing experiments on human guinea pigs—or that people were forced to dig their own graves and be mowed down by the thousands? I would just have said, 'Get the hell out of here with that fantastic nonsense!' " He was dramatizing the hypothetical dialogue with such conviction, that I wondered whether it hadn't actually taken place. "It was all just too fantastic to believe! Why, if a couple of zeros had only been left off the figures the foreign radio gave, I might have thought it conceivable, but—my God!—that's the damnable thing —it just didn't seem possible.—I just shrugged it off as enemy propaganda." At that point he was called to see his defense attorney.

In the evening Chaplain Gerecke told me that Goering had said he would attend the chapel services to do the chaplain a favor— "Because as ranking man of the group, if I attend the others will follow suit."

---

*Frank's Cell:* Some more of Frank's soliloquizing: "Ah, yes, how old we are—how old Europe is—how old Germany is—past its prime. You know, barbarism must be a strong German racial characteristic.—How else could Himmler have gotten men to carry out his murderous orders?—And then sometimes I'm terrified at the thought that Hitler is only the first stage of a new type of inhuman being in evolution, which will end in destroying itself. Europe is finished.—And Hitler said, 'The war must come in my lifetime.' One man's madness, and a million people die! . . . Death is the mildest form of life. I am completely reconciled."

Later he turned to the evidence of the last couple of days showing how Chamberlain, Daladier, Roosevelt, and the Pope had implored and warned Hitler not to invade Poland. "Those pleas would have moved any human being to the depths of his soul. How can you explain that insensitivity psychologically? Can one speak of such a man as having feeling? What a pity for Germany! What a pity for the whole world!—And they called him an artistic soul—tommyrot! An artistic soul would have *melted* at those heart-rending pleas.—Oswald Spengler told me in 1933, 'It will last 10 years—we'll have the same lineup against us—then Germany, which led the rise of the West will be the cause of its decline.' " He went on to say that Oswald Spengler, Richard Strauss, Max Weber, and other German intellectuals were good friends of his. "I'll take their memory to the grave with me."

His final comment, coming back to the question of their own guilt was: "Ambition drove us on—all of us—me too. Don't tell the others I said that.—I'll say it in a different way at the trial."

---

*Ribbentrop's Cell:* He returned to the subject that was uppermost in his mind—the damaging evidence against him during the last two weeks. He was worried about Lahousen's testimony on his brutally anti-Semitic statements in support of Hitler's policy. "On that Jewish question—I never could have said what he said I did —Why I even introduced foreign Jews to Hitler in the early years. —I myself always thought the anti-Semitic policy was madness.— Naturally, in public I had to support Hitler in every way.—But statements like that—*ausgeschlossen!* [that's excluded]. Of course, I was one of his most faithful followers.—That is something that it is hard for you to understand.—The Führer had a terrifically magnetic personality. You can't understand it unless you've experienced it.—Do you know, even now, six months after his death, I can't completely shake off his influence?—Everybody was fascinated by him. Even if great intellects came together for a discussion, why in a few minutes they just ceased to exist and the brilliance of Hitler's personality shone over all.—Why, even at the discussions on the Munich Pact, Daladier and Chamberlain were simply overwhelmed by his charm."

"Really?"

"Why, of course—I experienced it myself." He went on to say that Himmler and Goebbels must have influenced Hitler to take more and more drastic anti-Semitic measures. "—And in the last few years, you know, there was simply no discussing the subject with Hitler.—I told you how I inquired about the Maidanek affair in 1944, and he simply said that was no affair of mine—just something between him and Himmler."

"Wasn't that enough to prove he was a deliberate murderer?"

Ribbentrop just shook his head and moved his hands in a feeble gesture of helplessness and confusion. After a brooding pause he mumbled something about "everybody was suffering from a mass psychosis—my lawyer tells me."

――――――――― December 10 ―――――――――

## THE AGGRESSION AGAINST RUSSIA

MORNING SESSION: *Mr. Alderman introduced evidence that the aggressive war against Russia had been planned by Hitler at least as early as December 18, 1940, under the code name of "Case Barbarossa." Hitler's directive stated, "The German Armed Forces must be prepared to crush Soviet Russia in a quick campaign before the end of the war against England . . . Preparations requiring more time to start are—if this has not yet been done—to begin presently and are to be completed by May 15, 1941 . . . Great caution has to be exercised that the intention of the attack will not be recognized." The directive was signed by Hitler and initialed by Keitel and Jodl. Other documents showed how Raeder and Goering were involved in planning the war in the subsequent months. Even philosopher Rosenberg saw a chance for putting his philosophy into practice with a plan for exploiting the conquered Russian territory for Lebensraum, and got himself appointed Commissioner for Central Control of the Eastern Territory two months in advance of the attack.*

――――――――――――――――

LUNCH HOUR: As they got ready to go up for lunch, Rosenberg said to me, "Just wait—in 20 years you'll have to do the same thing.—You can't escape these problems."

As Fritzsche took his place in line, he referred to the shift of populations in the East: "It's enough to make your hair stand up, the childish way these philosophic dilettantes played around with populations as if they were playing checkers."

Upstairs, as soon as Rosenberg finished eating he came over and wanted to continue the discussion. We had hardly started, when Goering, eager to keep the conversation under his aggressive control, shouted to us across the room, "Of course, we wanted to dissolve the Russian colossus!—Now you'll have to do it."

We stepped nearer, and I said, "Perhaps that's where you made your mistake."

When Fritzsche and some of the others indicated that they didn't see it Goering's way, he fell back on his usual last resort—humorous cynicism. "Ah well, you'll have the Russians on your hands one of these days, and it will amuse me to see how you handle it.—Of course, it's immaterial to me whether I'm watching from heaven or from the other place—the more interesting place." He laughed his usual hearty laugh. Some of the Goering clique laughed too, but only halfheartedly.

Later Fritzsche said, "I always said that our guilt in the war against the Western powers was about 50 per cent, because the Treaty of Versailles had a lot to do with it. But our guilt in the war against the East was 100 per cent.—It was reckless and uncalled for!"

After they assembled again in the prisoners' dock, Kelley brought Kaltenbrunner in for the first time. A coldness swept the prisoners' dock as if a freezing blast had come in through the open door. Kaltenbrunner had apparently thought he would get a royal welcome, and started greeting his fellow prisoners, more or less forcing Jodl, the nearest one to the door, to shake hands. But everyone was looking the other way. I told him to sit down in the front row between Keitel and Rosenberg. Both of his neighbors looked worried and preoccupied. Kaltenbrunner tried to strike up a conversation with his neighbors but they didn't seem to hear. Keitel leaned over and asked me to convey his regards to Major Kelley—obviously just making conversation to avoid having to talk to Kaltenbrunner. Frank kept his nose in his book, gritting his teeth. At one point when I was standing near him, he nodded in Kaltenbrunner's direction and said, "Look at that head.—Interesting, isn't it?" After a few minutes of this cold reception, Kaltenbrunner began to swallow hard, wiped his eye with his forefinger. When his defense attorney returned from lunch, K. held out his hand, but the attorney had casually clasped his hands behind his back. He spoke to him pleasantly, but did not shake hands.

Goering was watching all this rather discontentedly, seeing how all the photographers and reporters were directing their attention to Kaltenbrunner. The showman sensed a shift of the spotlight from his jovial cynicism to the more uncomfortable subject of the concentration camp atrocities.

"Why did they have to bring him in today?" he asked.

"This was the first day he could come after his attack," I answered.

"Do the doctors consider that man healthy?"

"Healthy enough to stand trial."

"If he's healthy, I'm Atlas. I don't see why they had to bring him in." He kept watching the photographers taking pictures of the newcomer, and looked around the courtroom to gauge the effect on the audience.

---

AFTERNOON SESSION: *Mr. Alderman continued to show how Ribbentrop advised his Axis partners to climb on the band wagon of the "New Order" by attacking the Allies. Italy's "stab in the back" against France, and Japan's against the United States followed. Ribbentrop kept urging Japan to attack Russia, but the Japanese apparently thought better of it.*

--------- December 11 ---------

## SHOWING OF NAZI FILMS

MORNING SESSION: The showing of Nazi films on their own rise to power brought a resurgence of the prisoners' old emotional reactions to their old symbols: speeches by Hitler, Goebbels, Hess, Rosenberg; pictures of the growing Wehrmacht; solving the unemployment problems; goose-stepping parades, *Sieg Heil*, etc.

Even Schacht's eyes were watery as he watched the scenes of reconstruction of Germany after Hitler's rise to power. Later he said to me, "Do you see anything wrong in solving unemployment?"

Fritzsche said, "At least it gives me the satisfaction of knowing that there once was a Germany worth working for—up to 1938."

Frank was greatly moved, but in a tortured sort of way. During the intermission he tried to say something without letting the others notice. "The laughter of God?" I asked.

"Ja, ja.—And that's the man that the German people set up as a tin god."

The film continued, showing how Hitler built up his war machine. The various branches of service rooted for "the home team." When the first planes appeared, Doenitz snickered, "Humph! Fliers!" Goering leaned back and whispered, "Psst! Lay off!" Later, when sailors were shown marching in a parade, Doenitz said, "Anybody can see that they're the best of the lot." "Not bad; not bad," Goering conceded. As the film went on, the Reichstag was shown laughing as Hitler read Roosevelt's letter asking for peace. In the dock, Goering laughed again.

---

LUNCH HOUR: Ribbentrop was completely overwhelmed by the voice and figure of the Führer. He wept like a baby, as if a dead father had returned to life. "Can't you feel the terrific strength of his personality?—Can't you see how he swept people off their feet? I don't know if you can, but we can feel it. It is *erschüt-ternd!*"

I remarked to Hess that he certainly looked inspired in the old days, and so did the whole people. "Yes, there's no denying that," Hess answered, grinning.

"Things have changed now, haven't they?"

"Oh, that's a passing phase—just wait 20 years." (Goering had previously told Hess that he was convinced that the German people would rise again—you couldn't keep them down.)

Goering showed some of the old cocky confidence. He said the film was so inspiring, he was sure Justice Jackson would now want to join the Party. I told him that the Reichstag's scornful and facetious reaction to Roosevelt's request to declare peaceful intentions was rather expensive laughter, since it resulted in the destruction of Germany. "Oh, but it was so funny," Goering said. "What interest do we have in conquering Palestine?* I had to laugh myself." He then used his usual tactics of turning the conversation to the aggression of the victorious powers. "After the United States gobbled up California and half of Mexico, and we were stripped down to nothing, territorial expansion suddenly becomes a crime. It's been going on for centuries, and it will still go on. Weapons change, but not human nature. Back in the stone age they just beat each other's brains out with clubs and then the

---

*President Roosevelt had drawn up a list of countries asking Hitler to declare that he would not attack any of them. Palestine had been included in this list.

live ones ate up the dead ones. That simplified the supply problem.—No ammunition, no rations, nothing." He laughed heartily,
then added, "I guess I would have made a meal for two, eh?"

---

AFTERNOON SESSION: *The Nazi film continued. The war and early
victories were portrayed.* [The generals and admirals gloated as
they saw themselves in their pristine glory. During the showing of
the courtroom scene trying the plotters of the July 20, 1944 assassination attempt, Goering and Ribbentrop kept whispering to Hess
to pay close attention—those were the traitors who planned to kill
the Führer.]

--------------- EVENING IN JAIL ---------------

*Goering's Cell:* Goering was still in fine fettle when I visited him
in his cell this evening with Kelley. "I could save the prosecution
a lot of trouble," he said. "They don't have to show films and read
documents to prove that we rearmed for war.—*Of course,* we rearmed!—Why, I rearmed Germany until we bristled!—I'm only
sorry we didn't rearm still more.—*Of course,* I considered your
treaties (just between us) so much toilet paper.—*Of course,* I
wanted to make Germany great! If it could be done peacefully,
all well and good; if not, that was fine too!! Why, my plans
against Britain were bigger than they suspect even now.—Just wait
till I get up on the stand and tell them—I'd like to see their
faces. I didn't want war against Russia in 1939, but I was certainly
anxious to attack them before they attacked us, which would
have come in 1943 or 1944 anyway." He was speaking freely and
expansively, enjoying the whole thing immensely.

"When they told me that I was playing with war by building
up the Luftwaffe, I just told them that I certainly wasn't running
a girls' finishing school. I joined the Party precisely because it was
revolutionary, not because of the ideological stuff. Other parties
had made revolutions, so I figured I could get in on one too.—
And the thing that pleased me was that the Nazi Party was the
only one that had the guts to say, '*To hell with Versailles!*' while
the others were crawling and appeasing.—That's what got me.
Naturally, Hitler was glad to have me because I had a great reputation among the young officers of the first World War.—After
all, I was the last commander of the Flying Circus, and quite a

drawing card for the Party.—Sure, I'll tell them I was willing to go to war to restore Germany's power.—But I just want to defend myself on one point where my honor is involved—I never gave any commands for the execution of those atrocities."

*Ribbentrop's Cell:* Still half moved to tears, Ribbentrop asked me if I hadn't felt the terrific power of Hitler's personality emanating from the screen. I confessed I hadn't. Ribbentrop talked as if he were again hypnotized by the Führer's figure. "Do you know, even with all I know, if Hitler should come to me in this cell now, and say 'Do this!'—I would still do it.—Isn't it amazing? Can't you really feel the terrific magnetism of his personality?"

## December 14

### EXTERMINATION IN POLAND

The momentary flair of Nazi inspiration which flickered up after the Nazi films was smothered completely by the devastating evidence of calculated mass murders brought out in yesterday's and today's sessions.

Before the session started this morning, Baldur von Schirach was still struggling to cling to the remnants of the Goering-inspired cynicism and skepticism with respect to the trial. "I doubt very much whether a German woman could have deliberately had lampshades made out of human skin," he said.

"Then it was done by a German man and she accepted it as a matter of course," I retorted. "What difference does it make?" Schirach sat back with a despondent look.

Keitel caught my eye and whispered *"Furchtbar!—Furchtbar!"* (terrible). He rolled his eyes and threw up his hands to indicate that he renounced the whole thing with horror.

MORNING SESSION: *Major Walsh read some excerpts of evidence on starvation and killing of Jews in Poland.*
*From Frank's diary: "That we sentence 1,200,000 Jews to die*

of hunger should be noted only marginally. It is a matter of course that should the Jews not starve to death it would, we hope, result in a speeding up of anti-Jewish measures.".

From SS General Stroop's report on the razing of the Warsaw ghetto: " . . . I therefore decided to destroy the entire Jewish residential area by setting every block on fire . . . Not infrequently, the Jews stayed in the burning buildings until, because of the heat and the fear of being burned alive, they preferred to jump down from the upper stories . . . With their bones broken, they still tried to crawl across the street into blocks of buildings which had not yet been set on fire or were only partially in flames . . . Their stay in the sewers also ceased to be pleasant after the first week . . . A great number of Jews who could not be counted were exterminated by blowing up sewers and dugouts . . . Only through the continuous and untiring work of all involved did we succeed in catching a total of 56,065 Jews whose extermination can be proved. To this should be added the number of Jews who lost their lives in explosion or fires."

___

During the intermission, Jodl shouted loudly and vehemently. "The dirty arrogant SS swine! Imagine writing a 75-page boastful report on a little murder expedition, when a major campaign fought by soldiers against a well-armed enemy takes only a few pages!"

I talked to Frank about those cold-blooded statements in which he spoke of letting a million Jews starve on the rations allowed. He admitted he had made such statements in his days of blind Nazi fanaticism, but had turned all his diaries and writings over to the American Military Government upon capture, so that the truth of the whole ugly episode could finally be brought to light, let the axe fall where it may.

___

Major Walsh continued reading documentary evidence of the extermination of Jews at Treblinka and Auschwitz. A Polish document stated: "All victims had to strip off their clothes and shoes, which were collected afterwards, whereupon all victims, women and children first, were driven into the death chambers . . . Small children were simply thrown inside."

While this was going on, Governor Frank was keeping a diary: On December 16, 1941 he wrote: "The Jews for us also represent extraordinarily malignant gluttons. We have approximately

2,500,000 of them in the Government General." On January, 1944, he wrote, "At the present time we still have in the Government General perhaps 100,000 Jews."

---

LUNCH HOUR: Hitler was the subject of conversation both at Frank's table and Goering's table. At the former, Hess and Ribbentrop had both raised the question whether Hitler had known about all those things. Frank scornfully replied that it would have been impossible otherwise. He insisted it was Hitler's direct command.

In the meantime, Keitel had apparently raised the issue at Goering's table as to whether the Führer shouldn't have stood by his followers and assumed responsibility for his commands. "Oh, but after all, think of his position," said Goering, trying desperately to stem the open defection in the ranks.

"Sure, the position of chief war criminal!" I said, standing between the two tables.

"Be that as it may, he was our sovereign. It would be intolerable for me to have him standing before a foreign court. You men knew the Führer. He would be the first one to stand up and say, 'I have given the orders, and I take full responsibility.' But I would rather die 10 deaths than have the German sovereign subjected to such humiliation." The others did not seem at all impressed by this dramatic loyalty.

Frank retorted across the tables, "Other sovereigns have stood before courts of law!" hurling open defiance at Goering for the first time since the trial started. His face was red with mounting rage. "He got us into this, and all that there is left is to tell the truth!"

Keitel, Doenitz, Funk, and Schirach suddenly got up and left Goering's table contrary to their usual custom, and Goering found himself sitting alone. To cover this up he rose and came over as if he had intended to continue the conversation with me. "You know," he said confidentially, "it is not my purpose to exaggerate my love for the Führer, because you know how he treated me at the end.—But, I don't know what to say—I think maybe in the last year and a half or so, he just left things to Himmler—"

"But they must have had a definite understanding; otherwise it would have been impossible for such large scale horrors to occur."

"I suppose Himmler must have reported so and so many deaths as inevitable or something like that—and in the war, with so many deaths on all sides—I don't know—." I walked away.

Schirach had joined Fritzsche, Speer, and Seyss-Inquart. After exchanging some wisecracks with me about the Hitler Youth getting older and grayer and wiser, Schirach said seriously: "But we're not going to live long enough to use our new-found wisdom. After today, it's all over. I wouldn't blame the court if they just said, 'Chop off all their heads!' Even if there are a couple of innocent ones among the 20, it wouldn't make a bit of difference among the millions who were murdered."

"I understand they read that Vienna speech of yours yesterday."

"Yes, that is the one we discussed at our first long talk." He shrugged his shoulders helplessly. "It is too late now."

The conversation shifted back to Hitler. "I told you I had the impression that he had gone crazy in '43," Schirach said to Fritzsche.

"I had that impression in '42," Fritzsche replied.

It was then time to return to the courtroom.

Downstairs Frank was openly lecturing the others on the necessity for telling the whole truth for the German people and the world to know. Rosenberg tried to hark back to the old tactic of Allied aggressions and how America was going to be faced with the same racial problem. He looked to Speer for moral support, but Speer laughed in his face with a sarcastic wave of the hand.

---

AFTERNOON SESSION: Captain Harris read further extracts from Frank's diary: "Poland shall be treated as a colony; the Poles shall be slaves of the Greater German World Empire." "We must annihilate the Jews wherever we find them, and wherever it is possible."

# December 15-16

## WEEK END IN JAIL

I made the rounds of all the cells again, getting the prisoner's reactions to the accumulation of evidence and to Hitler and the Party in view of recent revelations.

---

*Rosenberg's Cell:* Rosenberg was flabbergasted as usual, when Kelley and I asked him what he had to say. "Of course, it's terrible—incomprehensible, the whole business.—I would never have dreamed it would take such a turn.—I don't know.—Terrible!—on a scale like that, Hitler must have given the orders, or Himmler did it with the Führer's approval."

"What do you think of Hitler now?" we asked. "How do you feel about the Party program now that the results are in?"

Rosenberg was silent for about a minute. He twitched his hands, looked at the ground, shrugged his shoulders. Finally he said: "I don't know. I guess it just ran away with him.—We didn't contemplate killing anybody in the beginning; I can assure you of that. I always advocated a peaceful solution. I held a speech before 10,000 people which was later printed and distributed widely, advocating a peaceful solution.—Just taking the Jews out of their influential positions, that's all.—Like instead of having 90 per cent of the doctors in Berlin Jewish, reducing them to 30 per cent, or something like that—which would have been a liberal quota even then.—I had no idea that it would lead to such horrible things as mass murder.—We only wanted to solve the Jewish problem peacefully. We even let 50,000 Jewish intellectuals get across the border. Just as I wanted Lebensraum for Germany, I thought the Jews should have Lebensraum for themselves—outside of Germany. There was no use trying to send them to Palestine, because it meant moving 800,000 Arabs out of the territory with the help of British bayonets."

"Where did you think they could be settled for Lebensraum?"

"Well, I knew they were being transported to the East, and

understood that they were being set up in camps with their own administration, and eventually would settle somewhere in the East.—I don't know.—I had no idea that it would lead to extermination in any literal sense. We just wanted to take them out of German political life. A lot of the Jews expected drastic measures right at the beginning,· but when they saw that nothing was being done in that direction, some of them who emigrated came back. They thought, 'Well, even if we have to stay out of politics, we can still make a living.' The Party didn't take any drastic measures at first. But then conditions came about which simply took the matter out of my hands. The foreign Jewish-democratic press began hammering against the Party, and they forced the issue. And then there was the murder of von Rath.* Of course, you might say, Why didn't you treat that just as an individual crime? —I don't know.—Maybe so. It looked like the Jews' answer to Germany's treatment of the Jewish problem. That is when the reprisals started . . . I had nothing actually to do with the Nuremberg Laws. I just read them when proposed in the Reichstag, and naturally I couldn't stand up in the Reichstag and say 'I object!' That was out of the question."

---

*Streicher's Cell:* Still as unwaveringly fanatic as ever, Streicher seemed completely unaffected by the accumulation of evidence that had caused shame or at least embarrassment and defensive reactions in all the others. "Well, you know, I have to say what I believe," he insisted, when asked whether he would have altered his course if he had foreseen the consequences. "After all, the Talmud itself told the Jews to preserve their racial purity. Theodore Herzl, the Zionist leader, even said that wherever there are Jews there is anti-Semitism. The Jews are making a mistake if they make a martyr out of me; you will see. I didn't create the problem; it existed for hundreds of years. I saw how the Jews were pushing themselves into all spheres of German life, and I said that they should be pushed out. After all, if you read the Talmud, you will see . . . "

And so it goes, like the perseveration in an obsessive-compulsive

---

*Ernst von Rath, third Secretary of the German Embassy in Paris, was shot by a Polish youth of 17, Herschel Grynszpan, on November 7, 1938.

neurosis or an organic psychosis. There is neither sadism nor shame in his attitude; just a cool, apathetic obsessive quality.

---

*Speer's Cell:* Speer was calm and reasonable as usual. When asked what he thought of Hitler now, he replied, "The same as I thought in the last months of the war, only more so: a selfish destructive force that had no consideration for the German people. As I told you, I was through with him when he ordered the destruction of all German property and said the German people didn't deserve to survive if they couldn't win the war. But there have been some things that have amazed me in the trial. First, his speech in 1937 that 'war must come in my time.' Second, the evidence that the Polish 'incidents' were actually provoked by the SS, as Lahousen indicated. Third, the scope and secrecy of Himmler's murder system."

We then discussed German armaments, and he showed us the figures of the tremendous increase in production after he took over. He mentioned that he had advised the U. S. Strategic Bombing Survey on Japanese bottlenecks after the defeat of Germany. He admitted that our strategic bombing had his ministry worried during the war—especially the precision day bombing by the Americans. Coming to the subject of the atomic bomb, he said he knew we were working on it because we had some of their experts on nuclear physics and had certain required materials, but he didn't know anything about our progress. They were working on it too, "but we were still years from the goal." I told him that Goering had told me they were only a couple of months behind. "Oh, Goering—he doesn't know beans about science. He just liked to talk a lot. I had no sooner discussed the first experimental model of the jet-propelled plane, when he ran to Hitler and told him he would have 500 jet planes ready in 3 months—utter nonsense." He agreed that such wishful braggadocio may have helped support Hitler's belief in a miracle that would win the war.

---

*Funk's Cell:* Funk was depressed and whimpering as usual. "It is hardly bearable.—Germany is disgraced for all time.—Believe me, that is worse than any consequences of the trial [blubbers]. But do you think I had the slightest notion about gas wagons and such horrors?—I swear I heard about such things for the first time in Mondorf.—I only did what I could to prevent illegal acts. I prevented the surrender of the Belgian gold in French custody to Germany, because its ownership wasn't clear. I also prevented the devaluation of the franc during the occupation. By that act alone I saved France more money than all of the confiscated property was worth.

"The only accusation I can make to myself is, as I told you, that I should have resigned in 1938 when I saw how they robbed and smashed Jewish property. But even then, I understood that the Jews were supposed to collect damages according to law, for the destruction of their property."

---

*Schacht's Cell:* Still confident and chipper. "I guess the others are beginnnig to see what is in store for them. I have nothing to worry about—I just hope they keep moving and get it over with."

---

*Sauckel's Cell:* Sauckel was trembling as if I had come in to torture him. He immediately began to defend himself with trembling voice and wringing hands: "I want to tell you that I know absolutely nothing of these things, and I certainly had absolutely nothing to do with it!—It was just the opposite.—I wanted to make conditions as good as possible for the foreign workers."

"What do you think of Hitler now?"

"Well—it is hard to say.—We are of different opinions—whether Hitler knew about those things.—I just don't know. But there is no doubt that Himmler did those things, and they cannot possibly be justified. I just can't get it through my head how those things were possible.—About the misuse of foreign workers.—I am really not responsible for that. I was like a seamen's agency. If I supply hands for a ship, I am not responsible for any cruelty that may be exercised aboard ship without my knowledge. I just supplied workers to places like the Krupp works at Hitler's orders. I am not to blame if they were later mistreated.—Don't you see my point of view?—Those things are terrible, I grant you—of course."

---

*Von Neurath's Cell:* "Hitler was a liar, of course—that became more and more clear—he simply had no respect for the truth. But nobody recognized it at first. He was—how do you say it—a fascinating demagogue. Yes, he fooled lots of people. He must have done his conspiring with his little group of henchmen late at night. But I couldn't stay up so late. Sometimes he would call up at 1, 2, or 3 in the morning. That is probably when these secret discussions with Himmler and Bormann took place."

---

*Keitel's Cell:* Keitel said he was spiritually in bad shape "I am dying of shame.—It is disgraceful—horrible! I had at least counted on the honorable record of the Wehrmacht, but now the Wehrmacht too is disgraced. They had too many connections with Party organizations.—Like that horrible Warsaw ghetto affair. Imagine Stroop reporting 'The Wehrmacht engineers, in true comradeship of arms, gave faithful support to the SS in this undertaking, etc.' Why, I could swear the army commander who sent him those engineers didn't have the slightest idea of the dirty business they were intended for. I only wish that I had spent more time in the field. I spent too much time in Hitler's headquarters and when I went out I consulted the generals. I should have seen what was actually being done in the lower echelons.— But—what's the use?—It is too late now."

"What do you think of Hitler now? Do you doubt that he knew about or ordered those atrocities?"

"He must have done it. There is no doubt about it! It is clear to me now, why he always told me to keep hands off police matters. If anything came up, he said, 'That is none of your business —you're a soldier! Of course, I did not know that he was planning these horrible things and that Wehrmacht men were getting tied up with it. If I had known, I would have said, 'Mein Führer, here is where I draw the line! I object to having anything to do with such things! Please relieve me of my post.—If not, you will not find me alive tomorrow!' But I was never taken into his confidence . . . No, he spoke three entirely different languages: one for the Wehrmacht, one for the Party leaders where he discussed his real plans, and one for the Reichstag, which he used as a sounding board for the public.

"There were three main planks to his program which brought the eventual ruin and disgrace of Germany: the suppression of the Church, under the hypocritical motto, 'Every man must find salvation in his own fashion'; then the ruthless persecution of the Jews; and the limitless power of the Gestapo. These things are clear now . . . " Keitel made a gesture of a veil being taken away from his eyes, then a helpless shrug, "—but it is too late now."

As I took leave, he stood stiffly at attention as usual, but said in a whining tone: "Please let me talk to you once in a while, as long as I am not yet a sentenced criminal.—Don't despise me altogether.—Come around once in a while; it gives me a little moral support to stand this ordeal, just to be able to talk to someone."

---

*Goering's Cell:* I had a 2½ hour discussion with Goering, covering a wide variety of subjects from personal affairs to the Roehm blood purge in 1934. Goering's need to express himself during his confinement at the end of the week was very great. He wanted to show me something to back up what he had said about his efforts to prevent war with England up to the last minute.

"Just look—Ribbentrop will burst a blood vessel when he sees how I went around diplomatic channels." He showed me a book written by his Swedish intermediary, Dahlerus, describing in detail the secret efforts at negotiation between him and the British, saying he would bring this up at the trial.

He went on to expand on Germany's power politics vis-a-vis Britain, saying it wasn't Germany's policy to strengthen Japan at the expense of Britain. "In fact, we weren't very happy about the Japanese taking Singapore, since we knew that sooner or later it would come to a showdown between the European power and the Asiatic. There was no love lost between us and the Japs—that is clear.—But in time of war you have to get your allies where you can find them.—You can't look a gift horse in the mouth."

After a while we got around to discussing the effect of the past week's evidence. "Yes, I know.—It gets worse and worse, and it will keep on that way until we get up to tell our side of the story. But do you know what hurt me even more than the concentration camp film—bad as that was?—That short scene at the *Volksgericht* [People's Court] trial of those involved in the July 20th [Hitler assassination plot]—with that loud-mouth Freisler presiding. I tell you I just could have died for shame! I had heard that the *Volksgericht* was a crummy business, but it actually made me squirm, the way that judge howled at the defendants, who, after all, were German generals not yet proven guilty."

There seemed to be more discomfiture over this film than was accountable by his love of military decorum, or his possible identification with the position of defendant in a trial. Wondering about his possible guilt feelings in connection with the assassination plot, I introduced the question of his attitude toward Hitler at this point.

"After all the evidence of destruction and murderous guilt heaped on Germany's head by the Führer, I can't see why you would still want to support him even now. I should think the people would hardly appreciate that."

"Ah, then you do not understand the people as I do. If I were to back down now after the way I supported him, they would only have contempt for me. Who knows how things will develop in 50–100 years."

"He will probably be remembered as the most cruel and hateful monster of the 20th century."

"Yes, he could be cruel and hateful, but in another way. I just can't get it through my head that he really did those things. He was cruel and hateful to me for the last two years, as I've told you. In fact, he would scream about the inefficiency and uselessness of the Luftwaffe with such contempt and viciousness, that I would actually blush and squirm and preferred to go to the front to avoid these scenes.—You know, there wasn't much I could do once you had gained air supremacy.—But then he ordered me to be present at his staff conferences at GHQ just as if to say, 'Stand there and take it, damn you!' With that kind of viciousness!" He described this with such vehemence, that there was no doubt about the devastating effect it had on his pride, and my suspicion of his loyalty to the Führer grew. "Then, you know, he finally ordered me arrested and killed," he scowled.

"He probably suspected you of participation in the July 20 plot," I suggested. "Maybe Bormann said something—."

He gave me a peculiar look as he glossed over the remark quickly—almost too quickly. "Yes, I'm quite sure he was convinced of it at the end.—But I still cannot see how he was capable of ordering those mass murders.—I keep thinking—it is such a mystery—the whole thing—" He started to pace the cell, pressing his fists to his forehead, as if trying to get something through his head—a bit *too* dramatically, I thought.

"But he was obviously capable of ruthless cruelty—like the Roehm blood purge in 1934," I said.

At the mention of Roehm's name, Goering hit the ceiling. "*Roehm!* Don't talk to me about that dirty homosexual swine! That was the real clique of perverted bloody revolutionists! They are the ones who first made the Party look like a pack of hoodlums, with their wild orgies and beating up Jews on the street, and smashing windows! They set out to do right in the beginning what actually took place later under the pressure of war.—They would have given you a *real* demonstration of a bloody revolution! They were bent on wiping out the whole generals' corps, the whole Party leadership—all the Jews, naturally—everything, in one grand blood bath! What a gang of perverted bandits that SA was! It is a damn good thing I wiped them out, or they would have wiped us out!" The ruthless-gangster side of his personality stood clearly revealed as the jovial mask fell completely away, even as he strode up and down the cell in breeches, shirt, and bedroom slippers, gesticulating wildly, hatred flashing out of his eyes. "I made no bones about it. I went to that SA captain and said, 'Do you have any weapons?' 'Why no, *Herr Polizeichef*,' the swine says to me, 'none except the pistol for which you gave me a permit.' Then I found an arsenal in the cellar bigger than the whole armament of the Prussian police force! I just told my men to take the bastard out and shoot him. That was a gang of double-crossing cutthroats for you!—Do you think good old Hindenburg would have sent me a message of congratulation the next day, if he hadn't realized like a flash that I had averted a catastrophe?"

"Funny that Hitler should have built up his organization with the support of such hoodlums, if he really wanted law and order."

"Oh, he didn't realize it then, I suppose. We had to get rid of them to build up the Party and the State."

The guard asked him to hand over his mess kit for supper at this point. I got ready to leave.

"Well, we'll have plenty of time to talk things over some more before the verdict," I said.

"The death sentence, you mean," he said, returning to cynical bravado. "That doesn't mean a.thing to me—but my reputation in

history means a lot." Here he laughed slyly. "That is why I am
glad Doenitz got stuck with signing the surrender. I wouldn't
want my name attached to that thing in future history. A country
never thinks well of its leaders who accept defeat. As for death—
Hell, I haven't been afraid of death since I was 12 or 14 years old."

---

*Hess's Cell:* Hess had declined the opportunity to take his walk
in the afternoon, preferring to "lie down and think" instead.
However, he welcomed the visit. First he asked for retest on digit-
span—did 8 forward, 7 backward, showing even better concentration ability than immediately after his recovery.

"Can you follow the trial better now?"

"Yes, I can follow everything clearly now. It wasn't so clear at
first, after my memory came back, but it is clear now." There
was no apparent effort on his part to maintain the original version of "faking all the time." He seemed to accept the viewpoint
that it wasn't altogether simulation, though he obviously shied
away from any suggestion of mental disturbance. Asked what he
thought of the accumulated evidence, he said: "It is just incomprehensible how all those things came about."

"What do you think of Hitler now?"

"I don't know—I suppose every genius has a demon in him.
—You can't blame him—it is just in him." He continued to reflect on the idea, but was apparently unwilling to express himself
further, except to say, "It is all very tragic.—But at least I have
the satisfaction of knowing that I tried to do something to end
the war."

He expressed interest in the American form of government. I
described the legislative, judiciary, and executive system of selection, operation, and counterbalances briefly. He asked if the President could dissolve Congress at any time. I told him that was
impossible. Congress was subject to constant control by the elec-
torate by elections and expressions of opinion, and they were
fundamentally responsible to the people, whom they represented.

"National Socialism had a good idea behind it too," he said.
"—doing away with class differences and making the people
united."

"That may have been the idea given, but then you merely substituted a vicious system of racial discrimination which was far worse."

He agreed, with passive suggestibility, responding to the idea of the moment. "Yes, that is true. That worked in the opposite direction."

We then launched into a discussion of racial psychology, in which I showed that American psychologists and anthropologists had investigated the problem of racial differences extensively, and had found considerable evidence that so-called racial psychological differences usually turned out to be environmental differences, and that the theory of a master race was simply ridiculous. He agreed that the Nazis had probably "made a mistake" in their racial policies—Hess's belief as of Sunday, December 16.

When it was time to go to chapel, Hess again refused to go, saying that he had never had any use for religion before, and he wasn't going to weaken now just because he was on trial for his life.

─────────────── December 17 ───────────────

AFTERNOON SESSION: *Colonel Storey described the efforts of the Nazi Party to suppress Christianity. Hess's successor, Bormann, had laid down the Party line on Christianity to the Gauleiters in a secret decree, stating; "National Socialist and Christian concepts are irreconcilable. Our National Socialist ideology is far loftier than the concepts of Christianity, which, in their essential points, have been taken over from Jewry . . . All influences which might impair or damage the leadership of the people exercised by the Führer, with the help of the NSDAP, must be eliminated . . . " All Church denominations were harrassed; thousands of priests and ministers thrown into concentration camps.*

*In 1937 Pope Pius XI denounced Nazism for what it was, "the arrogant apostasy from Jesus Christ, the denial of His doctrine and of His work of redemption, the cult of violence, the idolatry of race and blood, the overthrow of human liberty and dignity."*

# 2. Christmas Recess in Jail

―――――――――― December 22 ――――――――――

## FRANK'S REMORSE

*Frank's Cell:* Frank was calmly smoking his pipe and smiled sweetly when I entered his cell.

"I've just had an argument with Ribbentrop. It's no use— these people simply do not understand the meaning of this trial. He tries to tell me the war was necessary and inevitable. Can you imagine that—after the proof that Hitler insisted on having it? —and the fat one is sore because I handed over those diaries— those 40 volumes. 'What's the matter with you? Why didn't you burn them?' he says to me. What does he know about truth and higher values? I remember how I thought it over when the enemy was closing in. They were begging me to burn the volumes before I was captured. I listened to some music as I thought it over. It was the Bach Oratorio, 'The Passion of St. Matthew.' When I heard the voice of Christ, something seemed to say to me: 'What? Face the enemy with a false face? You cannot hide the truth from God!' No, the truth must come out, once and for all. You know, I had an argument with the fat one at lunch the other day about whether Hitler should have stood trial for his actions. [See December 14.] Nobody seems to understand that there is nothing left but to tell the truth—except Seyss-Inquart—"

"―And Fritzsche and Speer?"

"Yes, Fritzsche and Speer too. It is such torture to sit through the trial.—Such horrible things are laid coldly before us and before the world—things we knew; things we didn't know; things we didn't want to know.—And one just sinks in shame—!" I looked him straight in the eye questioningly and the meaning of the shame became clearer as he went on. "—Oh, *ja*—the shame is devastating.—Such fine men, those judges and the prosecuting attorneys—such noble figures—the Englishmen—the Americans, —especially that tall fine Englishman.—And they sit on the opposite side, and I sit here among such repulsive characters as Streicher—Goering—Ribbentrop.—Ah, well," he sighed, "there is nothing that can be done about it . . . I am glad that you and Pater Sixtus, at least, still come to talk to me. You know, Pater Sixtus is such a wonderful man.—If you could say 'virgin' about a man, you would say it about him—so delicate, so sympathetic, so maidenly—you know what I mean.—And religion is such a comfort—my only comfort now.—I look forward to Christmas now like a little child.—You know, even if I sometimes wonder in my deepest subconscious, whether this belief in life after death is really only a fantasmagory—whether life doesn't essentially end in a cold grave—and bing! finis! then it is still good that one clings to the illusion to the very end.—Who knows?"

(This is the first time in two months that he has given any insight into the dynamics of his religious conversion, which had all the appearance of an utterly sincere repentance and remorse in his isolation before the trial.)

"I have such vivid dreams," he continued. "Sometimes I actually hear music. The other night I dreamt a selection from Bach's Violin Concerto.—So clear and so vivid!—It was wonderful!"

"Do you have any more sexual dreams?"

"No—not since that one I told you about—with the mountain and sea. I guess the impossibility of fulfilment has stopped it."

I returned to the guilt question. "I've been wondering, how could you have made those speeches and written those things in your diary, when you know that those things are wrong?"

"I don't know—I can hardly understand it myself.—There must be some basic evil in me—in all men. I'll be able to describe it better for you later.—Let some time pass—I'll write something for you to understand it . . . Mass hypnosis—that hardly explains it.—Ehrgeiz [ambition]—that had a lot to do with it.—Just imagine—I was a minister at 30; rode around in a limousine, had servants. I suppose I wanted to vie with the SS leaders.—But Hitler cultivated this evil in man.—Yes, that was really phenomenal.—When I saw him in that movie in court, and the building-up of the Party—I was swept along again for a moment in spite of myself.—I am such a responsive individual.—Funny.—One sits in court under the pressure of guilt and shame.—One racks his brains and seeks explanations, grasping at any straws.—Then Hitler appears on the screen.—You stretch out your hand—." Here he stretched out his hand and closed his eyes with a gasp, like a

drowning man grasping at a straw. "For a moment you are intoxi-
cated and think—maybe—. But then it passes—you open your
hand, and it is empty—utterly empty!—The stark reality of the
shame keeps mounting before you day after day in a very unemo-
tional courtroom.—God, what simpletons we are!

"And that is the way it was with all of us. Now we can see how
artificial that old inspiration was, seen against the cold background
of reason and the world's moral standards. But then we couldn't
see it. It was everywhere.—And as soon as one source of inspiration
wore off, another event, or speech, or victory reinforced the illusion.—Ah, well, it is too late. I am living on borrowed time now.
I can use it to cleanse myself before God. That Polish woman
who asked me what I would do if I should not be sentenced to
death.—I wanted to tell her—but I'll tell you—I'll end my own
life. This cannot go on.—Did I tell you a gypsy predicted in 1934
that I would not live to see 50? See that line on my hand? It does
end abruptly, doesn't it? Yes, she said there was something about a
big trial—which didn't seem strange, since I was a lawyer.—And
then she said I wouldn't live to see 50. Remarkable, isn't it?"

"By the way, why did you attempt suicide when you were captured?"

"Oh, that—. I cut myself here and here, you see. They treated
me pretty badly in the beginning—and then the whole catastrophe
with Hitler forsaking his people and everything going to pieces.—
I just couldn't stand it."

——————————— December 23 ———————————

## POWER POLITICS

*Goering's Cell:* Goering was in a philosophical mood and began to
speculate on the future of Germany and Europe. He reiterated
his view that there was an inevitable perpetual struggle of conflict-
ing interests in international power politics, that America had no
interest in Europe and therefore would withdraw eventually, leaving the continent the object of a showdown struggle between
Britain and Russia.

"Why is it necessary to have this endless conflict and hatred?" I asked. "Don't you think that nations and people can learn to cooperate finally—out of sheer interest in the survival of mankind?"

"No, there are simply too many people in the world," was the ready answer. Then he added half-jokingly, "—Or maybe science will develop a way of feeding the population of the world with nutrition pills, or something like that." Getting serious again, he continued: "The inescapable fact is that England has to maintain its balance of power on the continent or else dominate it directly. She has only a population of 45,000,000 to dominate an empire of 500,000,000. She has to maintain her lifeline through the Mediterranean, and prevent any one power from getting strong enough to threaten it. I wanted to convince England that it was to her interest to let us become the dominating power on the continent, and we would guarantee her a free hand in her empire. It was to our interest too to let her balance the Russian and Japanese threat. I told you we weren't too happy about the Japanese taking Singapore.—But anyway, England didn't want to see us controlling the continent. Now they've got to fight it out with the Russian colossus.—And I'm afraid that Britain is on the downgrade and Russia is just beginning to realize the dream of a Eurasian empire. England depends on a tenuous line of communications supported by a naval power which has already been weakened, while Russia depends only on an ever-expanding reserve of manpower. The decisive power is no longer on the sea, but in the air. Do you think Russia gives a hoot if the British Navy can shell a few seaports here and there? That won't stop Russia from dominating a Eurasian empire from France to China.—Just think of it—a total population of almost 1,000,000,000—about half the population of the globe.

"She may not even have to foment revolutions to gain this control. Germany is so impoverished now, that Socialism is a logical consequence. Stalin has been a temporizing influence in the Communist revolution. Even the Führer realized that. But, as he used to say, who knows what kind of a radical may come to control if Stalin should suddenly die?—I don't know; it may evolve peacefully. There is already an upper crust of logical candidates with power and influence.—Molotov, and all those fellows.—You know," he laughed, "there will always be an upper crust no matter what form of government you have, Communist or anything else.—The cleverest and strongest are bound to rise to the top—you can't kid me on that score." He was obviously vindicating himself, and quite pleased with the idea.

I made some comment about the desirability of arriving at an understanding with Russia. Goering reflected, but the idea of mutual understanding didn't appeal to him, "Don't forget that Russia is still as much a dictatorship as Germany was—and then you've still got the eternal problem of power politics. You cannot get around that."

"Perhaps we will get around it if reasonable government leaders try to work things out peacefully instead of forcing the issues the way Hitler did. You see the results."

"But there was absolutely no convincing the Führer once he made up his mind. You could have the most infallible proof, anything; he just wouldn't budge. That was the way it was on the Russian question. Once he had decided to attack, you just couldn't budge him . . .

"They ask me why I didn't turn against him, if I couldn't persuade him to take a more reasonable course.—Why, naturally, I would have been executed on the spot.—But aside from all that—the German people would never forgive me for that. As I've told you, it is not a question of dying but of my reputation in history. —And if I've got to die, I'd rather die as a martyr than a traitor. Nobody respects a man who turns against his own sovereign. Do you think the Russians had any respect for von Paulus? Do you think I had any respect for the Russian generals who co-operated with us? No, history sees things differently. Don't forget that the great conquerors of history are not seen as murderers—Genghis Khan, Peter the Great, Frederick the Great. Don't worry—the time will come when the world will think differently about all this, and the German people will see things differently too. They are tearing each other apart now, of course. They may even be denouncing us in their despair.—But all that will change. Just let them get a dose of your military government a little while longer. —Mistreatment, poverty, looting, unemployment.—They'll finally see who their real enemies are.—Just think of what I've said 5 years from now. They will be united in a hatred against you that will be something to behold. And that will give them strength for their comeback.

"You know, the Americans are amateurs at this game. They are so arrogant and naïve. We Germans made the same mistake. The English are much cleverer about these things.—They are older hands at it. There is a proverb, 'The German has a soft heart and a hard hand. The Englishman has a hard heart and a soft hand.' That is how they have kept their power. They beat the Boers, then used the soft hand, and had them fighting on their side 10 years later. They are doing the same now. They say, 'Sure, let the Americans be the jailers and the prosecutors. We just present our part of the case simply; we have a chief justice who is impartial and even sticks up for the defendants' rights now and then. Let the Americans take the aggressive part and earn the hatred of the Germans.' "

"I gather that you wouldn't have minded being an Englishman, if you could live your life over again."

"Next to my own people, I feel closest sympathy with the English.—There is something the English have that is lacking in the Americans. For instance, they respect a man's station. They would never call a general or marshal Mr. so-and-so, the way you people do. A general is a general, a title is a title. You Americans don't understand those things. The British do. Another thing: they wouldn't rush right into a country they had just conquered and try to set up a democracy overnight. They'd say, 'Well, in this country this will work; in that country it won't.' But you have only one idea. We made the same mistake—trying to sell National Socialism overnight in our conquered territories.

"Anyway, one thing is clear—Germany must rise either with the English or the Russians—and the Russians seem to have the upper hand.—They are clever too. Fritzsche tells me they kept asking about me. I didn't know they had so much interest in me. Maybe I would have been better off in their hands."

"Do you really think so?"

"Who knows? It's a toss-up. They might have liquidated me right away.—On the other hand—. Still, I couldn't have recognized Communism; I've been fighting it too long. I guess it would have depended on whether we could have worked out a deal."

---

*Ribbentrop's Cell:* Ribbentrop was nervously working on a pile of papers on his table. As soon as I entered he let forth a torrent of defensive pleas, speaking rapidly as if working against time to plead for his life:

"Do you think I really planned aggressive war, *Herr Doktor?* The prosecution presents such a one-sided picture. There are so many documents. I am sure the prosecution itself has sufficient documents to prove the opposite of what they maintain. They used to say that I advised Hitler that England wouldn't fight. Now they say just the opposite. There are so many angles to it. You know, I actually held up the march on Poland when England guaranteed her sovereignty.—This accusation of anti-Semitism: it is so absolutely against my nature. You can't put any stock in what that man Lahousen said. You can get any statements you want in this state of world psychosis and hate. You have the power and we cannot do anything about it—but it is so unwise to judge us in the midst of a war psychosis. It is not even wise for the Jews to express their hatred thus. I don't blame them a bit, you understand, but it is so unwise—"

"How do the Jews figure in this trial?"

"Oh, I know they have a certain power and influence.—There are so many Jewish bankers in New York. Haven't you heard of Kuhn-Loeb, and Felix Warburg?—But I am not anti-Semitic; not in the least. You mustn't pay any attention to Lahousen. Why, I had dealings with Jewish businessmen all the time. Just imagine a man who worked for 6 years—Lahousen, I mean—kept his office for 6 years saying he worked against Nazism all that time, when he could have gotten out of it somehow, if he really felt that way about it—and then gives verbal testimony out of his memory in the midst of all this war psychosis. You are a psychologist. No doubt you know about Lombroso's experiment on the reliability of testimony. He got 12 different versions of an accident from 12 different people."

His tune changed to whining in a low key. "Why can't the victors accept this as a historical tragedy that was inevitable, and try to work toward a peaceful solution?" he pleaded. "It is no use heaping hatred upon hatred. It will hurt you in the end, I assure you."

"Why didn't you and Hitler think of that before? God only knows the Allies didn't want war. Hitler whipped up all the latent hatred and aggression of the people, breaking treaties, violating neutrality, rejecting and betraying all attempts at peaceful settlement."

"Do you know, he never kept me informed on all the circumstances? Really. Most of those things you are referring to, I am finding out for the first time in the trial. And I am not so sure that that 1937 document is authentic.* I don't know. Anyway, I wasn't there. Von Neurath and von Fritsch were there. But all the persecution and atrocities are revolting to all of us, I assure you. It just isn't German. Can you conceive of me killing anybody? Now you are a psychologist. Tell me frankly, do any of us look like murderers? I can't conceive of Hitler ordering such things. I can't believe that he knew about it. He had a hard side, I know—but I believed in him with all my heart. He could really be so tender. I was willing to do anything for him. Himmler must have ordered those things. But I doubt if he was a real German. He had a peculiar face. We couldn't get along."

"Do you think it conceivable for Himmler to have done all that without Hitler's knowledge or approval, if not his direct command?"

"I don't know. I really do not know.—But don't forget we were in such a desperate situation after the last war. So much misery and unemployment. Germany needed Lebensraum. If you had given us a single colony, you never would have heard of Hitler."

Later the conversation turned to the atomic bomb and the conference for controlling it, which was now taking place in Moscow. I discussed the devastating effect of the bomb, its industrial potentialities, and its possibilities for the destruction or liberation of civilization.

"For heaven's sake," he said excitedly. "That means a complete revolution of civilization, doesn't it?—A complete revolution of all our concepts?"

"Yes. It throws all the old concepts of industry, international economy, power politics into the discard. Just imagine, if Hitler hadn't been so impatient, industrial atomic energy would have been harnessed gradually without using it first as a terribly destructive weapon. Germany would have had it as soon as anybody. In the face of its possibilities, Lebensraum would have ceased to be a major issue."

*The Hoszbach document. See trial note of November 26.

"Do you think so? My word! It is a terrific thought! It is beyond conception. This is an amazing thing you are saying, Herr Doktor! It is all so very amazing! I don't think I shall be able to sleep tonight."

## December 24

*Streicher's Cell:* Christmas eve finds Streicher no more inspired by Christian teachings than before. "The chaplain left some leaflets here for me to read, but I don't put any stock in that stuff. I'm quite a philosopher myself, you know. I've often thought about this business about God creating the universe. I always ask myself, if God made everything, who made God? You see, you can go crazy thinking about that. And all that stuff about Christ—the Jew who was the Son of God—I don't know. It sounds like propaganda."

He asked for the latest news of the world, and I told him that there was a three-power conference in Moscow for the control of the atomic bomb. I told him how atomic energy could bring about a far-reaching revolution in industry, politics, and even philosophy, making nationalistic politics and the whole question of Lebensraum outmoded. "You don't say!" he kept repeating, his eyes popping in amazement. "And how do you make these atoms?" I explained that one doesn't make atoms; it is merely a process for harnessing atomic energy, which is universal—but it was all obviously over his head. He asked if I couldn't bring some literature on it with pictures.

## December 25

### AGGRESSION IN RETROSPECT

*Goering's Cell:* The Christmas spirit is still the farthest thing from Goering's mind today. He insisted that the only reality was self-interest both among individuals and among nations. We thus got around to discussing the Munich Pact.

"Actually, the whole thing was a cut-and-dried affair," he began. "Neither Chamberlain nor Daladier were in the least bit interested in sacrificing or risking anything to save Czechoslovakia. That was clear as day to me. The fate of Czechoslovakia was essentially sealed in 3 hours. Then they argued 4 hours more over the word 'guarantee'. Chamberlain kept hedging. Daladier hardly paid any attention at all. He just sat there like this." Goering spread out his legs, slumped down on the cot, and bent his head with a bored expression. "All he did was nod approval from time to time. —Not the slightest objection to anything. I was simply amazed at how easily the thing was being managed by Hitler. After all, they knew that *Skoda* etc. had munitions plants in the Sudetenland, and Czechoslovakia would be at our mercy. When he suggested that certain armaments which were across the Sudeten border should be brought into the Sudeten territory as soon as we take it over, I thought there would be an explosion. But no—not a peep. We got everything we wanted; just like that." He snapped his fingers. "They didn't insist on consulting the Czechs as a matter of form—nothing. At the end the French delegate to Czechoslovakia said, 'Well, now, I'll have to convey the verdict to the condemned.' That's all there was to it. The question of a guarantee was settled by leaving it up to Hitler to guarantee the rest of Czechoslovakia. Now, they knew perfectly well what that meant."

---

*Keitel's Cell:* Keitel was grateful for the Christmas Day visit, and began to pour out his heart in confidence. "Please don't tell anybody else until this is all over—but I am convinced that Hitler's decision to attack Russia was a confession of weakness, and the Polish war was unnecessary!"

"Really?"

"Absolutely! I am now firmly convinced, and neither Goering nor Ribbentrop can dissuade me. But don't tell the others, or I'd rather keep my mouth shut.—When we couldn't get across to England—which was impossible because we didn't have enough ships—he just had to do something. What could he do? Take Gibraltar? We wanted to, but Franco was afraid to risk it. Sit tight? Impossible.—That was all England needed to starve us out sooner or later. And all the time the life blood of our Wehrmacht came from the Rumanian oil fields. Remember that, professor. Oil! That was the vital key to the whole situation. Without Rumanian oil we couldn't last a week.—And there was Russia; they could cut us off at any time. I think Hitler must have seen that we were actually in a desperate position. We were getting about 150,000 tons of oil a month from Rumania. We needed an absolute minimum of 300,000 to 350,000 tons a month to run a war. The 100,000 or so that we were getting from home production including synthetic was only a drop in the bucket. Why the Luftwaffe alone needed 100,000 a month. If we lost the Rumanian oil fields we were finished. Hitler knew that we just couldn't sit and wait. When it comes to strategy, he was smarter than either Goering or Ribbentrop, and of course I don't rate at all. The attack on Russia was actually an act of desperation, because he saw that our victory was only temporary, and Rommel's little shooting expedition in North Africa was of no consequence. Of course, he talked as if the Russian campaign was a sure thing, and our manifest destiny, and our solemn obligation. But now that I look back, I am sure it was just a desperate gamble."

"Do you really think so?"

Keitel put his forefinger to his forehead and winked, "Ja! I don't think he was so sure himself.—I mean inwardly, though he seemed convinced enough as far as one could tell. It was an act of desperation.—No one can talk me out of that. Neither Goering nor Ribbentrop.—But please don't tell them I said so. The Russian offensive was madness and the attack on Poland was provoked on our side."

"Yes, I remember—the testimony about the Polish uniforms and the Gleiwitz Radio Station." This struck a sensitive spot, and Keitel bristled.

"But I told Canaris—'Keep your hands out of that!'—I told him the Wehrmacht doesn't have to get mixed up in that kind of business. He could just say that he didn't have any Polish uniforms. Believe me, Herr Professor, I had no idea then what they were even planning, exactly. And we had absolutely no idea about the attempts of Chamberlain and Roosevelt to prevent the war in 1939. I had absolutely no idea! Hitler didn't give the slightest hint that the war was anything but inevitable.

"Ah well, that is fate for you.—I wanted to be a country gentleman.—But I must tell you one thing, *Herr Professor*, an American simply cannot understand our desperation after the Treaty of Versailles. Just think: unemployment, national disgrace. Let me say it bluntly in all honor—The Versailles Treaty was a *dirty shame!* And that is what every decent German had to feel. Just imagine ripping the heart out of Prussia to give Poland a corridor to the sea! No wonder it was easy to sell the people the idea that Poland was just being stubborn and selfish in denying us Danzig. Every decent German had to say, 'Down with the Treaty of Versailles, by any means, fair or foul!' "

"I think the Allies were perfectly willing to make reasonable concessions. If Hitler hadn't been dead set on war—."

"Yes, I know.—Well, it is all over now." He sighed sadly. "We all believed so much in him—and we stand to take all the blame —and the shame! He gave us the orders. He kept saying that it was all his responsibility. Then in all fairness he should have stood to take the blame too.—But please don't say anything about what I've told you to the others. I once mentioned it to Goering and he blew up, you remember."

"Hitler was certainly a destructive demon," I said, to test the extent of his renunciation.

"Yes, and a lucky one in the beginning. It would have been much better if Hitler hadn't gotten away with so much. Just imagine—we reoccupied the Ruhr with 3 *battalions*—just 3 *battalions!* I said to Blomberg, 'How can we do it with only 3 battalions? Suppose the French resist?' 'Oh!' said Blomberg, 'don't worry. We can take a chance.' And he got away with it!"

"I suppose one regiment of French troops would have thrown you right out," I said casually as I got up to leave.

Keitel made the gesture of flicking away a flea with his middle finger. "Why they could have chased us out just like that; and I wouldn't have been a bit surprised. But naturally when he saw how easy it was.—And then the Anschluss of all of Austria without firing a shot.—Well! So that is how one thing led to another.— Well, I thank you from the bottom of my heart for this Christmas visit. You are the only one I can really talk to. A most happy Christmas to you!" He snapped to attention and bowed from the waist.

# December 26

## HESS'S MENTAL STATE

*Hess's Cell:* Hess was working on his defense, and asked if the retest on the Rorschach couldn't be postponed until the resumption of the trial. He was very agreeable about the whole thing. I tried to get further details on his return of memory, following up previous conversations.

"By the way, after your lawyer told you that he was expecting you to be considered incapable of defending yourself, did your memory come back right after that? How did you feel the next morning? Did you wake up with a feeling that your mind was clear and did you then decide to tell them your memory was in order?"

"No, that all happened rather quickly, just before the beginning of the special session on my case."

"Then it was more the effect of my telling you that you might be considered *nicht verhandlungs-fähig* [unable to stand trial] just before the session?"

"Yes, that was undoubtedly it . . . By the way, there is something—maybe it is still an *idée fixe*—but I got a headache from eating crackers again yesterday." Here he pulled out a little cellophane wrapping of 10-in-1 ration crackers, and offered me one. "Would you be good enough to eat this and tell me if it gives you a headache? And this too." He then picked up a K-ration package of crackers and handed me one. I started to eat the two crackers, and he began to feel a little foolish. "Of course, it may be just accidental on account of my continuous stomach cramps. I wouldn't have given it any thought, but it happened twice."

"Are you getting along all right on your defense? Can you concentrate all right?"

"Yes, but I still get tired after a while. I cannot concentrate steadily; I have to rest every once in a while—either lie down or stop working for a minute. That is why I have to conserve my energy during this recess to work on my defense."

——————————— December 27 ———————————

*Hess's Cell:* Hess was lying in bed, resting. I told him the crackers did not give me any headache or ill effect. He then dismissed the subject with, "Well, then I suppose it must have been something else."

We talked a little about the trial. He admitted he was disillusioned about a lot of things that have come to light in the trial, which he did not know about during his imprisonment in England. I suggested that he must have been greatly disturbed by the turn of the war after America came in.

"Yes, that was quite a shock. When I flew to England I really was sure we would win," Hess reflected, without any show of emotion.

"But Hitler must have figured on the possibility of America joining even before the attack on Poland."

"Why? Just to go to war over Danzig?"

"No, as a necessary step to stop aggression. After all, the world couldn't just stand by and watch Hitler gobble up one country after another. We tried treaties—everything short of war. He should have known he wouldn't always get away with it as easily as with Austria and Czechoslovakia. You say you wanted peace. Didn't you try to dissuade him?"

Hess thought a while, then answered slowly, "Well—I'd rather not say right now."

Shortly thereafter he had another attack of cramps. He grunted in pain for a while and it subsided. Later he asked again if I had seen the press notices of his answers to the questions about the trip to England, which he had given to his attorney. I told him I hadn't but would let him know if I did.

———————

*Schacht's Cell:* Still in a cheerful mood, he regards his imprisonment as something which he has to put up with good-humoredly, as though the trial obviously wasn't meant for him.

"I at least tried to stop Hitler after I realized what he was up to . . . I consider Goering a born criminal. I can hardly look at him. You know, stealing is in a way even worse than killing; it shows a man's character. You can conceive of a crime of passion;

but stealing is so *low*." He made a contemptuous face. "Looting the treasures of occupied countries! Ugh! That is so contemptible. I could never get along with him; we always had differences. I know what kind of a man he is. Streicher is just a dope. He is hardly worth talking about. Keitel was a willing tool. He has it coming to him. You take a man like von Fritsch. He was a man. Obviously he stood up to Hitler on the aggressive warfare issue. You can see that now by the fact that his removal from office followed three months after that November 5, 1937 discussion."*

"Do you think his death on the battlefield was prearranged?"

"I can come to no other conclusion," replied Schacht.

We got around to discussing commerce and the Versailles Treaty. "Don't forget that what we tried to do in the beginning was not so bad. We had to have some basis for existence. The loans were actually no solution to our economy. They only provided your bankers with commissions. Even the Anschluss of Austria was more a liability than an asset. They have no national wealth. With Czechoslovakia and Norway it was a different matter. But I wanted a trade agreement, that is all. That is all that is necessary. We exchange our surpluses and everybody has more. People used to accuse me of reverting to a primitive barter system. What in the world could they expect? America has all the gold—stuck underground somewhere in Kentucky. That is the thing that doesn't make any sense. It isn't of any use to anybody, and the government even loses the interest on it."

"I assume there must be some purpose in storing the gold," I said.

"In wartime, perhaps. But if they keep hoarding it in peace, it makes no sense at all. Anyway, we were in no position to trade on the basis of gold. And the loans we got obviously could not be repaid, any more than the loans you are now making. J. P. Morgan got his commissions on them. Worse still were the loans between the Dawes and Young Plans. Those were the ones that Baker, Dillon Read, Lee Higginson, and some other New York bankers gave us. Those were just bad loans that we didn't want and couldn't repay. They only gave the bankers their commissions and our politicians something to play with."

---

*See trial note of November 26.

He expressed anxiety about his future after his expected acquittal, because his property had been looted by Germans as soon as he was arrested as a war criminal, and he doubted if Germany would have any more use for bankers. "Anyway," he added, good-humoredly, "I have only 12 more years to go. I shall die at 81."

"How so?" I asked curiously, not believing that he could be superstitious.

"Because we are a degenerating family. My grandfather died at 85, my father at 83, and I must die at 81, and my son at 79."

---

## December 28

## THE FÜHRERPRINZIP

*Rosenberg's Cell:* Discussing the *Führerprinzip,** he launched into another typical Rosenbergian piece of historical rationalization. The *Führerprinzip* had merely been abused, like many other great ideas in history. "The French Revolution was dedicated to the idea of *brotherhood*, but they ended in a blood bath in achieving it—and no one thinks of that now; the Catholic Church preached the doctrine peace on earth, good will toward men, but look at the mass murders in the Inquisition; Luther wanted an enlightened Reformation, but look at the bloody 30 Years' War with both Protestants and Catholics killing each other in the name of God. Would you hold Luther responsible for that war? You cannot hold us responsible for the atrocities that took place. That was not the original idea. Oh, I admit we all have a certain responsibility in building up a party that didn't work out well, and it should be abolished. But guilt in the sense of punishable acts —conspiracy, and all that—. That was at best Hitler, Himmler, Bormann, and maybe Goebbels.—But they are dead. We are not to blame. Himmler is the real culprit. He took advantage of the

---

*Führerprinzip, or "Leadership Principle," according to which the leader's word was law and civilians as well as soldiers were responsible only to their immediate superiors and ultimately to the Führer, to whom they owed unquestioning obedience.*

war measures to exercise his power of life and death for security
reasons, and then overreached himself."

"How did Himmler get into the racial issue anyway?"

"Oh, general experience—history—and some mysticism too, I
think. I doubt that he really understood the problem. That is
the real mistake we made: giving so much power to the police
chief. That is where the *Führerprinzip* went awry. It was intended
for perhaps 200,000 political leaders, not for a whole nation of
80,000,000. The people went in for idolizing Hitler and feeling
blind loyalty to him personally. That was not the original idea. I
even said in my speeches that this concentration of power was
only a wartime necessity. But that does not mean that the *Führerprinzip* was wrong."

Since Major Kelley was leaving for America, Rosenberg gave
him a note explaining why America would have to face the same
problems.

----------------- December 29-31 -----------------

## THE DACHAU WAR CRIMINALS

Visited Landsberg Prison near Munich, where the first 38 criminals sentenced to death at the Dachau war crimes trials are awaiting execution. The prison where Adolf Hitler wrote *Mein Kampf*
is now being used as the death house for those who murdered to
bring it to realization. Although built very much like the Nuremberg jail, the cell block presents an odd sight with two rows of
criminals' heads protruding through the portal openings of the
cell doors, talking and laughing to each other across the corridor,
making it look as if they were being pilloried before the execution,
and enjoying it. Bored GI's stand around playing with their car-
bines, comparing points for redeployment.

I interviewed about half of the criminals briefly and administered tests to 10 of them. They run almost the whole gamut of
intelligence, from dull-witted brutes like Viktor Kirsch to brilliant doctors like old Klaus Schilling, who killed hundreds of
Dachau inmates in malaria experiments. Dr. Schilling claims that

he was looking for an anti-malaria serum, but he isn't sure he achieved anything, because he couldn't get accurate reports on the causes of death. Himmler promoted these experiments because "Himmler was also impressed by the possibility of increasing the reputation of the SS if I succeeded. I didn't realize then that it was just his cheap gamble with human lives to improve his reputation, so that he could show he wasn't just a murderer, but a benefactor of science." Dr. Schilling remembered seeing the naked gypsies lying under blankets, waiting to be placed next to the bodies of men frozen to the point of death, to revive them, "—warming them back with 'animal heat' of the women—just sexual sadism!" His own experiments were more scientific.

The less scientific criminals claim that the killing at Dachau was done strictly on orders from above, and are indignant that they should be held personally responsible for it. The starvation was also an administrative matter beyond their control. Some sample explanations:

Josef Seuss, administrative assistant: "Yes, I saw the dead men who had been partly eaten in the transport of 1942 . . . What could I do? A soldier can do nothing but carry out his orders . . . We didn't know that Himmler was such a bastard—to take off and leave us here—" [blubbers in self-pity].

Walter Langleist, battalion commander, with thin-lipped, hard face, excessively polite, trying pathetically to show his officer's dignity in his rags and beard: "What could I do? I was just a little man. I didn't have much to do with it. Those things are done on orders from the big shots [Bonzen] . . . I am very disappointed in the verdict." [Eyes cigarette butt as he leaves; doesn't pick it up.]

Anton Endres, an overseer, a sadistic psychopath with a repulsive, cruel bony face, insensitive gray eyes and expression: "Himmler gave the orders, and if we didn't obey, we were killed. Now those big shots in Nuremberg don't want to know anything about it. They say they didn't order murder. What little guy would dare do anything without orders? They say it was all done behind their backs. It would be a dirty shame if they let the big shots who gave the orders get away."

Frank Trenkle, an overseer and executioner, acting very pathetic, subservient, helpless, with a woebegone expression: "I just did the shooting on command of Gauleiter Giessler. I couldn't prevent the atrocities.—I could only execute commands, or I would be stood up against a wall. The Führer and Reichsführer SS—they brought all this about and now they are gone.—Gluecks got it from Kaltenbrunner, and finally I got the orders to do the shooting. They can all pass the buck to me, because I was only a little Hauptscharführer* and couldn't pass the buck any further down the line, and now they say I am the murderer . . . I hope none of those bastards in Nuremberg get away with it. That would be a terrible injustice. They were the ones who gave the commands and knew all about it—and could have prevented it. I wish I was in Nuremberg—I'd like to tell them something." [Blubbers and picks up stepped-on cigarette butt as he leaves with guard.]

There seems to be something radically wrong with Rosenberg's *Führerprinzip.*

---

*Equivalent of a sergeant in the SS.

# 3. The Anglo-American Prosecution Concludes

## January 3, 1946

### SPEER DISRUPTS GOERING'S UNITED FRONT

MORNING SESSION: *Colonel Amen called former SD Chief Ohlendorf to the stand. Ohlendorf described how orders for mass murder were given and executed, and how he was given command of an action group to exterminate 90,000 Jews. He gave the gruesome details of mass shootings for men and gas-wagon extermination for women and children. It was all directly ordered by Himmler on behalf of the Führer, so he had to obey. [The effect on the defendants was generally depressing, as the inescapable reality and shame of mass murder was driven home by the unquestionable reliability of a German official who admitted participating in it.]*

LUNCH HOUR: At the end of the session Goering immediately tried to dismiss the testimony with "Ach, there goes another one selling his soul to the enemy! What does the swine expect to gain by it? He'll hang anyway." Funk tried to defend Ohlendorf feebly, saying he knew him as an honest and forthright worker in his ministry, and that there was no doubt that he was making a clean confession for the sake of establishing the truth. Several of the others also said that there was absolutely no question about the reliability of his testimony and Frank even expressed admiration for a man who signed his own death warrant to serve the truth. He turned to me at this and said, "I don't think one can call him a bad German for that; you know my position."

At the lunch table upstairs, Fritzsche was so depressed, he could hardly eat. Frick, however, remarked how nice it would be to be able to go skiing in this fine weather.

Fritzsche stopped eating and looked at me in desperation, then glared at Frick.

As they filed down for the afternoon session, Fritzsche whispered as he passed me, "Let's go skiing, doctor." He was pale with anger.

---

AFTERNOON SESSION: *During the cross-examination of Ohlendorf, Speer dropped a bombshell through his attorney, by asking whether the witness knew that Speer had attempted to assassinate Hitler in February, and had planned to deliver Himmler to the enemy to answer for his crimes. [This created a sensation among the defendants, who looked at each other in bewilderment while Goering began to boil and splutter invectives in his corner of the dock.]*

---

During the intermission Goering charged across the dock to Speer and demanded angrily how dare he make such a treasonable admission in open court and disrupt their whole united front! A heated discussion ensued, Speer virtually telling him to go to hell. Goering, amazed, hardly knew what to say. Seeking some kind of agreement he leaned over to Funk and said, "By the way, you are right about Ohlendorf." He retired to his seat and whispered his condemnation of Speer's "treason" to his more sympathetic neighbors, Hess, Ribbentrop, and Keitel.

---

*Later Colonel Brookhart called Gestapo man Wisliceny, who testified how he had seen the order from Himmler ordering the "final solution" of the Jewish problem, and definitely implicating Hitler as the originator of the order. Gestapo section chief Eichmann, in charge of "Church and Jewish Problems," had explained to him that "In this concept of final solution the planned biological destruction of the Jewish race in the Eastern Territories was meant . . . I told Eichmann, 'God forbid that our enemies should ever have the opportunity to do the same to the German people,' and Eichmann said I shouldn't become sentimental, that it was an order from the Führer and it would have to be carried out." This program started under Heydrich but continued under Kaltenbrunner.*

--------- EVENING IN JAIL ---------

*Goering's Cell:* Tonight Goering looked tired and depressed. "This was a bad day," he said. "Damn that stupid fool, Speer! Did you see how he disgraced himself in court today? *Gott im Himmel!*

*Donnerwetter nochamal!* How could he stoop so low as to do such a rotten thing to save his lousy neck!—I nearly died with shame! To think that Germans will be so rotten to prolong this filthy life —to put it bluntly—to piss in front and crap behind a little longer!—*Herrgott, Donnerwetter!*—Do you think I give that much of a damn about this lousy life?—" He faced me squarely with blazing eyes. "For myself, I don't give a damn if I get executed, or drown, or crash in a plane, or drink myself to death!—But there is still a matter of honor in this damn life!—Assassination attempt on Hitler!—Ugh!—*Gott im Himmel!!* I could have sunk through the floor! And do you think I would have handed Himmler over to the enemy, guilty as he was? Dammit, I would have liquidated the bastard myself!—Or if there was to have been any trial, a German court should have sentenced him! Would Americans think of handing over their criminals to us to sentence?"

He was called to see his defense attorney, and as we left the cell he reverted to his usual pose of jocularity for the benefit of the guards and any prisoners who might be listening.

---

*Speer's Cell:* When I entered Speer's cell he laughed nervously, "Well, the bomb exploded today.—I'm glad you came to visit me; it is going to be a little tough for me now.—It was a hard decision to make.—I mean, I had decided to do it a long time ago, but it was still hard to bring myself to it." He went on to explain that the only thing he regretted was not being able to make simultaneously his plea of sharing the common guilt of the Party leadership for supporting Hitler. "Here, let me show you—I have a draft of it, but we had to plead guilty or not guilty, and I pled not guilty to the charges as stated." He fumbled through the papers. "Of course, I'm a little nervous now.—Goering flew at me because I spoiled his united front.—Even Doenitz cut me, and you know we were good friends.—Here is the second page, anyway." He read the statement he had prepared for his plea, acknowledging the responsibility of the leadership for the catastrophe. He further explained in detail how he had planned to kidnap the 10 Party leaders, including Hitler, Himmler, Goebbels, Bormann, Keitel, Goering, and carry them in a plane to England, but the co-conspirators got cold feet at the last minute.

"Of course, they're all mad at me now," he said. "It shows that somebody *did* try to do something about it, instead of obeying that destructive maniac to the very end. I'm only afraid some crackpot will try to do something to my family now. You knew my stand from the very beginning. I have no illusions about my own life.—But it is the German people and my own family I am concerned about." I assured him that the German people were also disillusioned about the Nazi adventure, and wouldn't harm his family.

## January 4

MORNING SESSION: *The case against the General Staff and OKW (Supreme Command of the Wehrmacht) was presented.*

During the intermission, Jodl, red with rage for the first time, could be overheard saying to his attorney: "—Then those generals who are squealing on us as witnesses to save their damn necks ought to see that they are just as much criminals as we are, and just as liable to hang! They needn't think that they can buy themselves off by testifying against us and then saying they were only little clerks!"

LUNCH HOUR: Goering stopped in the middle of a casual conversation and pounded the table angrily: "Damn it! I don't care a hoot what the enemy tries to do to us, but it makes me sick to see Germans double-crossing each other!" Von Schirach got up and nodded to Goering, as if about to perform an errand for him. "Go and talk to that fool!" said Goering.

Out in the hall, I could see von Schirach walking up and down arguing with Speer. All I could hear was Speer saying, "—He was too much of a coward then—" as he passed.

## EVENING IN JAIL

*Speer's Cell:* Speer told me about the conversation with von Schirach. "He tried to tell me that I was disgracing myself and my good name in Germany, and Goering was furious and all that. I told him Goering should have been furious when Hitler was leading the whole nation straight to destruction! As the second man in the Reich, he had the responsibility of doing something about it, but then he was too much of a coward! Instead, he doped himself up with morphine and looted art treasures from all over Europe. I spoke sharply without pulling any punches. I guess they're all mad because I showed they didn't have to lie down and take it. You know, Goering still thinks he's the big shot and is running the show even as a war criminal. He even told me yesterday, 'You didn't tell me you were going to say that!' How do you like that?" He gave a little nervous laugh of relief.

---

## January 5-6

### WEEK END IN JAIL

*Schacht's Cell:* Schacht was playing his perpetual game of solitaire, sitting at the table in his fur coat because the cell was quite cold. I asked what he thought of the recent proceedings.

"Well," he laughed, "I guess Kaltenbrunner's goose is cooked. You know, I never really would have thought him capable of doing such things. Same with Ohlendorf. Did you ever see a more upright-looking man, a more straightforward, honest character? And he was principally a businessman—and suddenly he finds himself in charge of an action group with orders to murder 90,000 people! But how can a decent person bring himself to do such things? I've often wondered what I would do under similar circumstances. Suppose they came to me with such an order. Why, I would say 'Really—[Schacht gulps and stammers as he acts out the scene]—really—I am completely overwhelmed —I—I—didn't expect I'd have to do this sort of thing!' And then I would think it over a couple of hours, and finally I would say that is something I simply cannot do, and they could shoot me or arrest me or send me to the front, or anything they wanted to, but not that!"

"Well, Speer also refused to play ball with Hitler at the end.

and tried to assassinate him, as he brought out Thursday. It shows that you don't have to take everything lying down. What do you think?"

"Oh, Speer did that because Hitler was prolonging the war unnecessarily. But *I* was the one who first recognized him as a criminal. I made my first attempt to remove him in 1938." Schacht was apparently unwilling to let Speer take too much of the credit for wanting to kill Hitler. "I could see that he had absolutely no honor and was bent on a policy that was sure to end in catastrophe. I was just telling Hess about it on our walk this morning.—By the way, Hess is crazy. He's concocting some kind of a mystic notion about the whole thing. I mentioned that I could even understand killing under certain circumstances, but stealing and graft requires a basically vile character.—You know, what I told you about Goering. I also told him that I had supported the Führer until 1938 and then realized that he was a criminal; that I even made my first attempt to get rid of him after the von Fritsch affair.—That is how we got to talking about the whole thing.—Then suddenly he says to me mysteriously, 'Yes, I can explain all that—'—mind you, he had never heard of these things before—he suddenly says, 'Yes, I can explain all these things—Goering's enrichment, the Witzleben affair—everything —just wait and see!'—Can you imagine that? What a spectacle that is going to be when he gets up to give that final speech!"

---

*Goering's Cell:* Goering still deliberately ignores the evidence of mass murder and aggressive warfare, and picks on legalistic aspects of the trial.

"The case against the General Staff is awfully weak," he said, "I would like to see what your *Army & Navy Journal* has to say about that. The whole conspiracy idea is cockeyed anyway. We had a *Führerstaat.* In the last analysis, we had orders to obey from the head of the State. We weren't a band of criminals meeting in the woods in the dead of night to plan mass murders like figures in a dime novel . . . After all, the four real conspirators are missing: The Führer, Himmler, Bormann, and Goebbels—and Heydrich too; that's five. That Wisliceny is just a little swine who looks like a big one because Eichmann isn't here . . . "

He thought for a while, then continued: "That Himmler! I

just wish I could have him alone for an hour and ask him a few things. I tell this only to my closest confidants: If I had taken over I would have gotten rid of Bormann and Himmler; Bormann in five minutes, but Himmler would have taken a little longer—a few weeks maybe. I had two ways in mind: either invite him and his whole gang to a dinner and have a regiment of mine all set to get rid of them; or just jockey him out of power by splitting up the whole machinery and shoving him around with lots of titles but less and less power. The first thing I would have done would have been to separate the police from the SS. You see, Bormann was a nobody who was supported by the Führer and nobody else. But Himmler was too powerful to get rid of all at once."

I asked him again what he thought about the testimony that showed that Hitler himself had ordered the mass murders. His answer was an interesting revelation of his attitude towards the whole trial. "Ach, those mass murders! It is a rotten shame, the whole thing. I'd rather not talk about it, or even think about it.—But that conspiracy charge; Oho! Just wait till I get started on that! You'll see some real fireworks!"

---

*Ribbentrop's Cell:* He put aside his mass of papers, and said he would never get finished anyway, so he didn't mind being interrupted for a visit. Reflecting on the evidence to date, he said, "In the atrocities and persecution of the Jews our guilt as Germans is so enormous, that it leaves one speechless—there is no defense, no explanation. But if you just put that aside—really, the other countries all have a share in the guilt for bringing about the war. I kept telling all my British and French friends, 'Give Germany a chance, and you won't have Hitler.' That was before Hitler came to power, of course."

"Who were some of these British and French friends?"

"Oh, there was Cornwall-Evans, Daladier, Baldwin, Lord Rothermere—"

"Before Hitler's accession to power?"

"Well, no—I guess they were later—. But let me see—there was Sir Alexander Walker, Mr. Ernest Tennant, Lord Lothian, Lady Asquith—. There was the Marquis de Polignac, the Conte de Castiglione, de Brinon—all of this was while I was on business in England and France.—But the Versailles Treaty became more and more unbearable. The people crowded together under one strong leader like sheep in a storm. I was an observer on economic questions—as an expert on alcoholic imports and exports in making trade agreements, and I know how Germany was being strangled by the Versailles Treaty . . . How Hitler could have done all those things later, I don't know—I just don't know."

"You know, some of the others say they are sure he was crazy during the last few years. I think that there is no doubt that he was severely neurotic all his life."

"Oh, no, you can't say that—"

"I think it is almost certain. It is easy for a neurotic to act normal as long as he has everything his own way, and to convince others when he is so obsessed by his own ideas. But he could not stand frustration, and that is when his neurotic personality exploded and revealed the evil monster within him." I waited for the effect of this opinion on Hitler's most ardent believer.

"Well, it is true that he couldn't stand contradiction.—Do you know that since I contradicted him in 1940 I never had a calm discussion with him? I don't think anybody ever really had a heart-to-heart talk with him as man to man. Not a single one. I've asked lots of people. I don't think he ever really bared his heart to anyone.—I don't know—it is really hard to say.—And he replaced me as Foreign Minister in his will—I cannot understand it. It is an incomprehensible phenomenon, the whole thing . . . "

---

*Keitel's Cell:* Keitel started arguing "orders are orders" again.

"But don't you see, if Hitler ordered it, that was good enough for me. After all, I was only his office chief. That is the rotten part about the whole thing!" He now became heated. "I had *absolutely no command function!*—Even Goering tells me that any scrap of paper I sent him—just between us—he would use only for a certain purpose. I could only transmit commands from the Führer. To hold a man responsible without any command function—that is the most horrible injustice that there is in the world! That chart they presented in the courtroom—that gives a really false picture. I was not second in command. Here—I've prepared a functional chart that gives a much truer picture." He showed me a penciled diagram which showed Hitler in command and himself off to one side as Chief of Staff with other Oberkommandos under Hitler but not under him.

I told him it was a fatal mistake to believe in Hitler, to which he agreed. I then asked him what he thought of Speer's attempt to assassinate him. He balked at that.

"No, you can't do it that way. That isn't the right way; at least it isn't my way. There are certain things an officer cannot do." He paused and thought a while. "I can only say I was brought up in the Prussian officer's tradition to obey orders with honor and loyalty. God knows how honorable and immaculate and incorruptible the Prussian Officers Corps was!—A code of honor that was the pride of the nation ever since Bismarck, and had a fine tradition going back to Frederick the Great! Why, if an officer didn't pay a debt of 25 marks he was arrested and disgraced.— Why, it never occurred to me that Hitler had any other code—. The first thing you saw in his office was a marble statuette of Frederick the Great and paintings of Bismarck and Hindenburg."

"He certainly fooled you," I replied. "I have it on reliable authority that he intended to wipe out the 'old generals of the ice age who prate about their officers' code of honor and still don't have any conception of my revolutionary principles,' as he put it. He was going to get rid of them after the victory and put in his gang of SS cutthroats." I didn't tell him that my "reliable authority" was General Lahousen, the Abwehr chief, who put the finger on him a few weeks ago.

"Really?—Well, I don't know.—He did, did he? I would never have believed that, but after all I've heard and realized lately, I can believe anything . . . I can only say that I obeyed him in good faith, and now that I see where it has brought me, I can only say that my loyalty and faith have been betrayed!!" He pounded his fist on his knee and repeated the last word with hatred: "Betrayed—that is all I can say." Then he caught himself and said pleadingly, "Don't tell the others—I just had to get it off my chest. Standing trial with the others before a foreign court, there are certain things I cannot say.—Things I cannot say to anyone. —I hardly talk to the others. Believe me, I've had one hell of a time these last few years, and I am having an even harder time now struggling with my despair alone in this cell.—Goering said he knows what a hard time I've had during the war, and I told him he certainly didn't make it any easier; so he says, 'Don't worry, I'll stick by you now.'—The only one of them who understands me at all is Jodl.—But you are the only one I can tell what is in my heart because you are above all this, and not tied up with it.—And I can tell you that I suffer more agony of conscience and self-reproach in this cell than anybody will ever know. I believed in him so blindly.—If anybody had dared to tell me then any of the things I have found out now, I would have said, 'You are an insane traitor—I'll have you shot!' And that is how he exploited the loyalty of the General Staff. He couldn't use Roehm's gangsters, because they would have double-crossed him themselves. So he used us.—And now we sit here like criminals!"

As I rose to leave, he snapped to attention as usual and bowed from the waist.

---

*Hess's Cell:* After completing the retest, we talked casually about his "concentration"—our mutually understood term for his mental state and memory. He mentioned that he dreamed occasionally about his youth in Egypt, but could not give any specific examples. His parents, however, played a role. "I suppose that comes with age," he commented.

"Is the treatment here fairly satisfactory?" I asked.

"Oh, it is sometimes irritating, but I am getting used to it."

He was in a comparatively communicative mood, and we discussed his flight to England. He denied having flown there to see the King or to bring him to Germany. He said he merely wanted to see the Duke of Hamilton, who, he assumed, would communicate his proposals to the King. He admitted the suicide attempt and the suspicions of being poisoned. "It must have been an *idée fixe,* but it is really remarkable how an idea could be so fixed that even now it sometimes occurs to me, maybe it was true after all. But of course reason tells me that it couldn't be so."

I asked him about his "concentration" during the confinement in England, and how he reacted to the turn the war was taking. He thereupon spoke quite freely about his memory loss. "The first period of memory loss was really genuine.—I suppose it must have been the continual isolation, and the disillusionment also played a role.—But in the second period I exaggerated somewhat. It wasn't entirely loss of memory." He gave no indication of how these "periods" corresponded to the clinical data, and I had to avoid the appearance of examining him, in order to maintain rapport.

"And did that continue until you came here?" I asked.

"Yes."

"Do you remember the doctors who examined you here?"

"Not very well."

"We were sitting here on the cot, you remember? I was interpreting for the three American doctors who were standing there—a colonel and two civilians."

"Yes? I can recollect it only vaguely."

"They were all surprised when your memory came back."

Hess perked up at this. "Really? Did they discuss it later?"

"Oh, of course, we were all surprised."

"Well, if I hadn't actually had a period of real loss of memory before, I wouldn't have been able to exaggerate it so well. I wouldn't have known how to do it; there would have been no reference point."

"I understand. One can sort of suggest himself into it until it is a real memory loss that requires practically no voluntary effort."

"Yes, that is it," Hess agreed with the positiveness that distinguished insight from response to suggestion. "Sometimes one doesn't know whether it is exaggeration or not.—One simply does not remember, that is all."

"—And then too," I suggested, "this solitary confinement was hardly conducive to mental stimulation."

"That is true too. I suppose the contact with the others up in the court and on our walks was beginning to stimulate me after the trial started."

"Had you begun to recognize Goering and the others around you even before that special session?"

"Yes, a little, but everything really cleared up at once that afternoon after you spoke to me.—But I still get tired from thinking too much. Even now, for instance, the test and even just the conversation gradually tire me out, so I have to lie down." I told him he could lie down, and terminated the interview with the assurance that he could call on me for any help he needed.

─────────────── January 7 ───────────────

## PARTISAN WARFARE

MORNING SESSION: Colonel Taylor described measures taken to kill all captured commandos and partisan fighters in the conquered territories. He further showed how "the activities of the German Wehrmacht against partisans and other elements of the population became a vehicle for carrying out Nazi political and racial policies, and a vehicle for the massacre of Jews and numerous segments of the Slav population which was regarded by the Nazis as undesirable." An order by Hitler and signed by Keitel on October 16, 1941 stated: " . . . it should be remembered that a human life in unsettled countries frequently counts for nothing, and a deterrent effect can be attained only by unusual severity. The death penalty for 50–100 Communists should generally be regarded in these cases as suitable atonement for one German soldier's life."

A recent affidavit by Nazi General Heusinger stated: "It had always been my personal opinion that the treatment of the civilian population and the methods of anti-partisan warfare in operational areas presented the highest political and military leaders with a welcomed opportunity for carrying out their plans, namely the systematic extermination of Slavism and Jewry. Entirely independent of this, I always regarded these cruel methods as military insanity, because they only helped to make combat against the enemy unnecessarily more difficult."

─────────────────

LUNCH HOUR: Goering is becoming increasingly annoyed at the testimony and affidavits of the Nazi witnesses who are gradually putting the noose around the defendants' necks.

"It makes me sick to see Germans selling their souls to the enemy!" he fumed at lunch. Trying to give a face-saving explanation for discrediting testimony which was obviously reliable, he expostulated grandiloquently, "I just detest anything that is undignified!—Why, I didn't even make a single sworn statement in the interrogations, that is why they can't produce any of my statements in evidence." He began to laugh at his own cleverness.

"Not a single one! Haha! You don't have to swear to anything until you testify in court under oath.—Hess did it even better—he just 'couldn't remember.' Haha!—that was hot!—he couldn't remember until he was good and ready!" Those at his table began to smile, but didn't think it was so uproariously funny, since they all knew that everybody had his doubts about Hess's normality, and most of them had expressed those doubts to me.

"So they're bringing up Bach-Zelewski this afternoon," he remarked sarcastically after a while. Funk made some remark to the effect that that man Bach was a swine.

"At least the cross-examination ought to be interesting," I remarked.

"You won't see me bothering to ask such a swine any questions!" Goering answered. Then he turned to the audience in general, and said out loud, banging his fist on the table, "Dammit, I just wish we could all have the courage to confine our defense to three simple words: *Lick my arse!*—Götz* was the first to say it and I'll be the last!"

He repeated the proposed defense with great relish, telling how Götz had said it, how another general had said it, and how he would say it. Rosenberg and several of the others were beginning to enjoy the joke, and even the German PW mess attendants were laughing.

At this point I remarked "Ah, yes, war would be a great joke, if only so many people didn't die of it."

"Who gives a hang about that!" he said, brushing off the remark and still laughing. The German mess boys, however, suddenly stopped laughing . . .

---

AFTERNOON SESSION: *Under direct examination by Colonel Taylor, SS-General Bach-Zelewski, chief of anti-partisan forces in the East, described in detail how Himmler's SS murder-bands suppressed partisan resistance by mass executions and other terror methods. Himmler had explained the "purpose of the Russian campaign, which was to decimate the Slav population by 30 million, and in order to be active in this direction, a troop of low characters would have to be formed."*

---

*Götz von Berlichingen, 16th century warrier, hero of Goethe's play by that name.

Even upon cross-examination, Bach-Zelewski admitted that this mass murder was a direct outcome of Nazi ideology: "I am of the opinion, when for years, for decades, the doctrine is preached that the Slavic race is an inferior race and Jews are not even human, then such an explosion was inevitable."

During the intermission, Goering stormed and raged so that his place in the dock could hardly contain him. "Why, that dirty, bloody, treacherous swine!! That filthy skunk! Goddam, *Donnerwetter*, the dirty blankety-blank sonofabitch!!! He was the bloodiest murderer in the whole goddam setup! The dirty, filthy *Schweinehund*, selling his soul to save his stinking neck!! . . . "

Many of them were telling their attorneys to cross-examine with questions that showed what a bloody swine he was himself. Jodl was purple with rage. "Ask him if he knows that Hitler held him up to us as a model partisan-fighter!" he shot at his attorney. "Just ask the dirty pig that!"

Ribbentrop was sitting sadly silent, then looked up and said to me wearily, "You see what I mean?" He made a gesture with his hands indicating a clash from both sides, which was meant to indicate to me the pitiful spectacle of Germans denouncing Germans.

--------------------------- January 8 ---------------------------

## FROM "MEIN KAMPF" TO AUSCHWITZ

MORNING SESSION: Colonel Wheeler described some of the details of the persecution of the Christian religion and other religious sects; the imprisonment and killing of priests and ministers, the suppression of Church organizations, schools, and publications, Rosenberg was mentioned as the high priest of heathenism.

Mr. Elwyn Jones then prefaced the summary of individual charges against the defendants by citing "Mein Kampf," because "From 'Mein Kampf' the way leads directly to the furnace of Auschwitz and the gas chambers of Maidanek."

Wrote Hitler: "Germany will either be a world power or will not continue to exist at all. But in order to become a world power, *it needs that territorial magnitude which gives it the necessary importance today and assures the existence of its citizens." To realize this aim he had advocated the subjugation of inferior races to achieve Aryan supremacy, and scorned the "waving of olive branches and tearful misery-mongering of pacifist old women."*

*"Events have proved," concluded Mr. Jones, "in the blood and misery of millions of men, women, and children, that 'Mein Kampf' was no mere literary exercise to be treated with easy indifference, as unfortunately it was treated before the war by those who were imperiled, but was the expression of a fanatical faith in force and fraud as the means to Nazi dominance in all Europe, if not in the whole world."*

---

Lunch Hour: Before the afternoon session, Rosenberg cut loose again on the Russians and the Church. "The Russians have the nerve to sit in judgment—with 30 million lives on their conscience! Talk about persecution of the Church!—Why they are the world's greatest experts. They killed priests by the thousands in their revolution. They poured cold water on them and let them freeze—all kinds of things. They stripped the skin from the thighs of Czarist generals to imitate their red stripes . . . The persecution of the Church is a big question that goes back hundreds of years and there are several sides to the question.—Lord only knows how much blood has been spilled by and because of the Church.—Why are they getting so excited about a couple of little letters that some old women wrote, and introducing them in evidence?—Just because a Church paper gets suspended or some Church property is destroyed. Hundreds of papers and publishers have been bombed and ruined—the resources of half Europe can be destroyed, millions of people can die—but the dear old Church—oh, heaven forbid! That is holy!—It has been that way for a thousand years.—What intrigues hasn't the Catholic Church had with kings and cardinals and popes and wars—millions of people slaughtered—but the Church must remain holy and powerful and not pay any taxes! That is how they keep their power. They can undersell their products because they don't pay taxes, and with the profits they can overbid for acquiring more property since they don't have to pay taxes—so they keep acquiring more and more property and more and more power."

He went on: "Oh, I don't blame the Russians at all for trying to break the strangle hold of this clerical monster.—I have always been anti-Catholic.—But where do they get the nerve to sit in judgment on us as persecutors of the Church? That's all I say. Why all this fuss about something that has been going on for centuries all over Europe? If the Nazi Party overplayed its hand—all right, it is finished; abolish it. But why pick on us as criminals? That's my argument."

## January 10

### FRANK AND STREICHER

*Frank's Cell:* Frank's attorney startled those who knew Frank by asking whether the Vatican was helping the prosecution, and saying that in that case his client would have to leave the Church. Before court this morning I asked Frank what he meant by that. He explained that his attorney had misunderstood him. He merely wanted to know whether the Catholic Church, who should be far above all worldly affairs, was helping the prosecution, but he had not said he would leave the Church. He had merely said it would put all the German Catholics in a difficult position. "It was just another one of those times when I suddenly get startled [gasps] and jump right in . . . It is interesting to observe one's own reactions. It is as though I am two people.—Me, myself, Frank here—and the other Frank, the Nazi leader. And sometimes I wonder how that man Frank could have done those things. This Frank looks at the other Frank and says, 'Hmm, what a louse you are Frank!—How could you do such things?—You certainly let your emotions run away with you, didn't you?'—Isn't that interesting? I am sure as a psychologist you must find that very interesting.—Just as if I were two different people. I am here, myself—and that other Frank of the big Nazi speeches over there on trial.—Fascinating, isn't it?"

(Very fascinating, in a schizoid sort of way.)

MORNING SESSION: Colonel Baldwin summarized the proof of charges against Frank as Governor-General of Poland by reading excerpts from his own diaries: "Before the German people are to experience starvation, the occupied territories and their people shall be exposed to starvation . . . This territory in its entirety is the booty of the German Reich."—"I have not been hesitant in declaring that when a German is shot, up to 100 Poles shall be shot too."—"I am pleased to report to you officially, Party Comrade Sauckel, that we have up to now supplied 800,000 workers for the Reich."

Mr. Griffith-Jones then cited Streicher's speeches and writings as proof of his moral guilt in inciting to mass murder (from a speech in 1926): "For thousands of years the Jew has been destroying nations. Let us make a new beginning today so that we can annihilate the Jews." Pornographic pseudo-science: "The male sperm in cohabitation is partially or completely absorbed by the female, and thus enters her bloodstream. One single cohabitation of a Jew with an Aryan woman is sufficient to poison her blood forever. Together with the alien albumen she has absorbed the alien soul. Never again will she be able to bear purely Aryan children, even when married to an Ayran . . . Now we know why the Jew uses every artifice of seduction in order to ravish German girls at as early an age as possible; why the Jewish doctor rapes his patients while they are under anesthetic. He wants the German girl and the German woman to absorb the alien sperm of the Jew." Fantastic stories of ritual murder were also contained in the Stürmer.

---

LUNCH HOUR: At lunch Frank was beaming. "It was wonderful how the judge pointed out that one quotation was taken out of context—just marvelous! So fair!—so upright! It restores my faith in human nature. A thing like that really inspires me.—You know how I get these sudden emotional inspirations." Here he imitated the gasp of sudden astonishment which he had demonstrated both for his reaction to the Führer's image and to the mention of the Vatican. It seems to suggest a mixture of fear and admiration—the luring ambivalence toward the parental authoritative figure. "I still wonder how I could have said and done the things I did.—I was just too impetuous, I guess. Anyway, isn't it funny how the German mania for making complete records of everything works out? Now you have plenty of material for documents for the trial. Hahaha!"

"Are you sorry you handed over your diaries now?" I asked.

"No, not at all. God knows what I did, so mankind might as well know the whole truth too—all of it—the good and the bad. I have no illusions about my fate as I've always told you. Now only the truth remains."

The conversation then turned to Streicher, who was being avoided like the plague, since the revolting pornography and stupidity of his quotations was still fresh in everybody's mind. A few remarks were made to the effect that he never would have lasted even as a publisher, if Hitler hadn't supported him, and even Rosenberg ridiculed his pseudo-scientific approach to racial anti-Semitism.

Downstairs Streicher said to me, "A doctor wrote that piece about the breeding of the German race, and animal breeders have told me that it is so.—I didn't mean to insult anybody."

---

AFTERNOON SESSION: *Mr. Griffith-Jones showed that besides publishing a paper full of pornography, ritual murder, rape stories, and other lurid incitements to persecution of the Jews, Streicher found anti-Semitism profitable as Gauleiter of Franconia. Much of the proceeds from the aryanization of Jewish property failed to reach the Reich treasury. That was the ostensible reason for his removal from office in 1940, but the Stürmer continued to serve its purpose.*

---

In the intermission Goering said to Hess, "Well, at least we did one good thing: getting that prick kicked out of office." Hess agreed, saying it was hard to prevail upon the Gauleiters to agree. "But the really tough job was getting the Führer to agree," Goering said. "You can thank me for that." (He did not mention, however, that his real motive for getting rid of Streicher was a personal peeve over the latter's rumor-mongering that Goering's child must have been a test-tube baby because he didn't have what it takes. Benno Martin, the police chief of Nuremberg, and General Bodenschatz told me the inside story, and Streicher himself confirmed it.)

—————————— January 12–13 ——————————

## WEEK END IN JAIL

*Von Papen's Cell:* (The debonnaire white handkerchief in von Papen's jacket always looks a little incongruous with the OD shirt and pants which he wears on week ends.)

He asked about the UNO conference, but I had to admit I knew very little about it. The conversation turned to Hitler.

"In the beginning it was possible to insist on having your way with him," von Papen said. "Schacht and I were just talking about that.—You didn't have the impression then that you were dealing with a madman . . . I was going to say—later you couldn't reason with him at all. Take our departure from the League of Nations. Von Neurath and I tried to advise him against it. We didn't think he was convinced, so I followed him to his apartment in Munich, and argued for hours. I thought I had persuaded him. But the next morning he says to me as though inspired by a vision, 'No! I've thought it over during the night, and now I am absolutely convinced that Germany must go her way alone!'—And then there was simply no arguing with him any more. He became more and more that way.—Still, he seemed to be accomplishing so much without spilling a drop of blood—. Why, even Churchill wrote in 1937, 'If we ever lose a war, I hope we shall find a leader who will do so much to rebuild our country.' Can you expect less from a German, than Churchill himself was willing to concede to Hitler?"

"But couldn't you have seen from *Mein Kampf* what his intentions were? The anti-Semitism, the aggression, the seeds of hatred were all there."

"Oh, but who took *Mein Kampf* seriously, my dear professor? People write so many things for political purposes. I had my differences with him, but I never really thought he meant war until he broke the Munich agreement. He removed me from the Austrian post five weeks before the Anschluss, because he had decided not to go along with my evolutionary policy. But the Austrians seemed quite satisfied with that."

"Then why didn't you remain out of Nazi politics if you realized his aggressive intentions after breaking the Munich Pact?"

"Now that is an interesting question. What could I do? Leave the country and live as a foreigner? I didn't want that. Go to the front as an officer? I was too old, and anyway shooting isn't in my line. To denounce Hitler would of course simply have meant being stood against the wall and shot, and it would not have altered anything. The way it actually happened was this. I was out of public life for a year after the Austrian Anschluss. Then Ribbentrop calls me up and says, 'Herr von Papen, you will have to take the post in Turkey.' I come to Berlin and Ribbentrop says Germany is threatened with encirclement which will lead to war, unless Turkey is kept neutral, etc. etc. Well, I thought that I could at least keep that corner of Europe at peace, and that is what I did accomplish. When war did break out, what could I do?"

---

*Rosenberg's Cell:* I said I came to see how he was getting along on his birthday, and we got off to another discussion of his philosophy.

"National Socialism wasn't based on racial prejudice. We just wanted to maintain our own racial and national solidarity. I didn't say that the Jews are inferior. I didn't even maintain that they are a race. I merely saw that the mixture of different cultures didn't work—that is how Roman and Greek civilization went to pieces. The Jews wanted to maintain their identity as a people, and I say more power to them, but so do we. Look how the Jews were forced to be baptized in previous centuries. That is real racial prejudice and an incredible presumptuousness on the part of the Church.—The same thing with these Church missions today—the way this sect sends a mission to China, that one to Siam, and that one to Timbuktu or Swaziland. That is just damned arrogance and shows a real contempt for the rights of different groups to maintain their own culture. So what happens? The poor Chinks listen politely—" [Here he put his hands into the opposite sleeves of the field jacket he was wearing, imitating a bowing Chinese coolie.] "—they are Buddhists and Confucianists already, but they figure what-the-hell, a little Christianity won't hurt, and so they throw that in too, for good measure. Do you call that democracy?

"And what about that Open Door to China? Was it democracy to force a war on them so that England could corrupt 30 million Chinese with opium? Have you ever seen those opium dens? That is much worse than concentration camps. That is how millions of Chinese were spiritually murdered so that the Open Door for foreign trade could be maintained—and the various sects could keep sending missions. That is what I call racial prejudice with a vengeance!"

"But what about the democratic principle that people have to learn to live together and assimilate or live in mutual respect? New cultures always develop through the amalgamation of the old, and an artificial barrier to keep them separate is impossible in modern civilization."

"Maybe it will work out that way in America; I doubt it. It is only natural for the members of a group to feel a common bond and protect themselves and their identity."

---

*Speer's Cell:* He explained with amusement how the others were coming around now and accepting the fact that he had made an assassination attempt on Hitler's life. "It is typical of the hypocrisy of our whole system. Everybody had to pretend to be friendly to everybody else even if they were knifing each other behind their backs. I was the same as the rest in that respect. I visited Goering's birthday party, for instance, even when I was working furiously against him because of his reckless and neglectful policies. Here they all have to pretend to be faithful to the Führer and acted enraged when I made my admission; now they all act friendly again—even those who hate what I did. They haven't the guts to stand up and tell the truth. They must pretend to be loyal to each other at the trial, even though many of them cannot stand each other. It would be a good thing if they would drop their masks and let Germany see the rottenness of the whole system."

"I know. Goering uses his influence to maintain some semblance of mutual interest in the defense," I replied.

"That is true. You know, it is not a very good idea to let the defendants eat and walk together. That is how Goering keeps whipping them into line. It would be much better if they weren't intimidated from saying what they feel, so that the people will be rid once and for all of the last rotten remains of their illusions about National Socialism. There are Germans who have gone to America and become good democrats; why not here?—Of course, it will take some time."

"It will take forever, if they still cling to the illusion that Hitler meant well by the people."

"Exactly. They will think that all their present troubles are the fault of the conquerors, and that things were, after all, better under Hitler. That is what Goering would want them to feel, so that he will also be regarded as a hero. But I want to show the people that their present need and all the senseless destruction is directly the fault of Hitler. That is why I want to bring out the fact that I officially informed Hitler that the war was irretrievably lost in January, 1945, and that further resistance was a crime against the people." He showed me the outline he had written of questions he wanted to ask General Guderian to confirm that fact. "I was of the opinion even then that the best the people could hope for was a bare existence for the next 10 years under a generous victor. That is what the people must realize."

"Do you still accept a common responsibility of the Party leadership?"

"Absolutely, I shall say so in my final speech. Fritzsche and I have agreed to compare notes so that we don't duplicate each other. But somebody else must also take that stand to convince the people. Somebody the people respect. They respect me because they said 'he lives modestly.' That is also a reflection on our system. It was a miracle if a leading member of the administration lived modestly.

"As for Frank, he is a little whacky. He makes such grandiloquent mystic speeches, with his new Catholic conversion. He was always emotional. Anyway, his reputation is none too good. Even Fritzsche had none too good a reputation among the intelligentsia, because of his propaganda, though he is a fine fellow, and I know his lies weren't deliberate lies."

# 4. The French Prosecution

--------- January 17 ---------

## OPENING ADDRESS

MORNING SESSION: M. Francois de Menthon, chief French prosecutor,* opened the French prosecution with an impassioned denunciation of the Nazi aggression which had wounded France's national pride as well as her human and material resources:

"France, who was systematically plundered and ruined; France, so many of whose sons were tortured and murdered in the jails of the Gestapo or in their concentration camps; France, who was subjected to the still more horrible grip of demoralization and return to barbarism diabolically imposed by Nazi Germany, asks you, above all in the name of the heroic martyrs of the Resistance, who are among the greatest heroes of our legend, that justice be done."

Whereas Justice Jackson has outlined the planning and development of the Nazi conspiracy and Sir Hartley Shawcross has enumerated the various breaches of treaties, "I propose today to prove to you that all this organized and vast criminality springs from what I may be allowed to call a crime against the spirit, I mean a doctrine which, denying all spiritual, rational, and moral values by which nations have tried, for thousands of years, to improve human conditions, aims to plunge humanity back into barbarism, conscious of itself and utilizing for its ends all material means put at the disposal of mankind by contemporary science. This sin against the spirit, this is the original sin of National Socialism from which all crimes spring.

"This monstrous doctrine is that of racism:

"The German race, composed in theory of Aryans, purports to be a fundamental and natural concept. Germans as individuals do not exist and cannot justify their existence, except insofar as they belong to the race or Volkstum, to the popular mass which represents and amalgamates all Germans . . . The ideas and the bodily symbols of racism are an integral part of its political sys-

------
*M. de Menthon left right after his address to accept a political appointment in Paris. He was succeeded by M. Champetier de Ribes.

tem; this is what is called authoritative or dictatorial biology. The expression 'blood' which appears so often in the writings of the Nazi theorists denotes his stream of real life, of red sap which flows through the circulatory system of every race and of all genuine culture as it flows through the human body. To be Aryan, is to feel this current passing through oneself, this current which galvanizes and vivifies the whole nation . . . Let the individual go into himself and he will receive by direct revelation 'the commandments of the blood' . . .

"One reads in the 'National Socialist Monthly' (edited by Rosenberg) of September 1938: 'It is said that the body belongs to the State and the soul to the Church and God. It is not so. The whole of the individual, body and soul, belongs to the Germanic nation and to the Germanic State.'

" . . . True, this pseudo-religion does not repudiate the use of reason and of technical activity, but subordinates them rigorously, brings them infallibly to the racial myth . . . Anyone whose opinions differ from the official doctrine is asocial or unhealthy. He is unhealthy because in the Nazi doctrine the nation is equivalent to the race. The characteristics of the race are fixed. Any deviation from the spiritual or moral mould constitutes a malformation like a clubfoot or harelip . . .

"We are brought back, as can be seen, to the most primitive ideas of the savage tribe. All the values of civilization accumulated in the course of centuries are rejected, all traditional ideas of morality, justice and law give way to the primacy of race, its instincts, its needs and interests. The individual, his liberty, his rights and aspirations, no longer have any real existence of their own . . .

"Between the Germanic community and the degenerate population of an inferior variety of men there is no longer any other common measure. Human brotherhood is rejected, even more than all the other traditional moral values . . . Sacerdotal Judaism and Christianity in all its forms are condemned as religions of honor and brotherhood, calculated to kill the virtues of brutal force in man. A cry is raised against the democratic idealism of the modern era, and then against all internationals . . . This doctrine necessarily brought Germany to a war of aggression and to the systematic use of criminality in the waging of war . . . "

[In the dock Frank appraised the speech with a pleased air: "Ah, that is stimulating! That is more like the European mentality. It will be a pleasure to argue with that man! But you know, it is ironic—it was the Frenchman, de Gobineau, who started racial ideology!"]

─────────── January 19-20 ───────────

## WEEK END IN JAIL

*Streicher's Cell:* Sounding him out on any change of attitude since the British presentation of his case and the French denunciation of racism produced negative results. He is still as obsessed by anti-Semitism as ever, though he has lost just a little of his cockiness, now that the contempt of even the other defendants has become unmistakable. "Of course, the Jews are still a world power . . . Even the Catholic Church is only a tool of International Jewry," he ranted on. He explained how Christianity was being duped by Jewry, and Christ wasn't a Jew, he was quite sure. He then gave a very revealing illustration of how his own vulgar needs were projected on to the Jews:

"Do you know what the Talmud says about Christ? It says he was born on a dungheap—yes—and it says he was the son of a whore." His ugly face broadened into a lascivious grin. "Sure— that is right.—She was not married, and that story about getting the child from God. Now you know, if we are perfectly honest about it—it is true that according to that story she must have been a whore." His leer expanded into a laugh of self-satisfaction as he continued, "I agree with that myself—but naturally, when I used that for propaganda, I didn't say that. I just said, 'You see, Christians, what the Jews say about the Immaculate Conception!'" Streicher laughed at his own cleverness.

Inevitably, he harped on the subject of circumcision again. "Circumcision was the most amazing stroke of genius in history! Just think of it. It wasn't just for sanitary reasons or anything like that, you can be sure. It was to preserve racial consciousness. *Thou shalt always remember that thou art a Jew and shall have Jewish children with Jewish women!* Do you know what Heine said about circumcision? He said you can wipe away baptism, but you cannot wipe away circumcision.—Diabolical, isn't it?"

A quarter of an hour with this perverted mind is about all one can stand at one time, and the line never varies: World Jewry

and circumcision serve as the channels for projecting his own
lascivious thoughts and aggressions into a pornographic anti-
Semitism which could get official support only in Hitlerite Germany.

---

*Frank's Cell:* Slowly but surely, Frank is weakening on his violent
renunciation of Nazism, showing the same weakness of character
in his "guilt reaction" as he showed in following the Nazi lead.

"I begin to wonder now," he soliloquized, after the free communicative mood had been reestablished, "—just what should I
do?—Make my last stand with the Nazi leaders?—or renounce
them and give them their last kick down the stairs on the way out?
—It is hard to say."

I expressed surprise at this doubt, in view of his violent condemnation of Hitler and the whole Nazi system, and the shame
of it all, which he had often expressed. I reminded him of what
he said after he saw the atrocity film. "Oh, I have not forgotten
that," he hastened to assure me. "Believe me—it made a profound
impression on me.—I'll never forget that. But one must make his
exit somehow. Can I completely forsake my comrades? I don't
know.—Really, I am such an impressionable person—so responsive to my environment." He could guess what I was thinking,
and added, "I see that you don't argue with us so much any more,
but just observe us—that is much better. You can draw your own
conclusions anyway."

Frank's basic lack of integrity comes more and more to the
fore. First he reveals that his religious conversion is essentially
a hysterical conversion symptom of the guilt reaction, then even
his renunciation of Nazism turns out to be a pose which has to
be weighed for its ego value.

I asked him whether the discovery of his partially Jewish an-
cestry had anything to do with his enmity toward Hitler. He was
already growing vague on that subject, and answered rather eva-
sively.

---

*Hess's Cell:* Retest shows same extreme cognitive and affective con-
striction as during amnesia period. In addition, his failure to
remember ever having seen any of the cards shown today, as well
as a sharp decrease in digit span, indicate a probable relapse of

memory and concentration. This is supported by his introspective observation that his "ability to concentrate" has deteriorated in the last few days. It was noted in casual conversation that serious gaps were present in his recollections of the recent events at the trial. Thus he could remember that Bach-Zelewski had testified, but not Ohlendorf or Schellenberg, all of whom had testified at about the same time, and were fresh in the memory of all the other defendants. He remembered Bach because of Goering's cursing, which made the event more vivid. He also remembered the atrocity film, which was shown shortly before the restoration of his memory, and had apparently made a profound impression on him.

The fluctuation in his digit-span to date:

| 1 November | —5 forward; | 4 backward | Total: | 9 |
|---|---|---|---|---|
| 1 December | —8 " | 4 " | " | 12 |
| 16 December | —8 " | 7 " | " | 15 |
| 20 January | —5 " | 4 " | " | 9 |

Toward the end of today's session, I told him that I had shown him these cards before. He seemed quite shocked, and fell back on the cot in surprise, supporting himself on his elbows. "You don't say!—Did you really?" he whispered. I hastened to assure him that I did not expect him to remember them, since I originally showed them during his amnesia period, and these little incidents would not necessarily return to his memory as readily as the events of his life history. He accepted this explanation eagerly, and commented, "Actually, today is a particularly bad day—I can hardly concentrate at all, and I am not even working on my defense. I hope it goes away."

"It is understandable that the fatigue of these weeks of trial will impair your concentration. You needn't worry about temporary impairment. But you mustn't exaggerate it either of your own free will."

"No, I certainly do not want to do that. If I did this time, nobody would believe me after I had said I had deliberately faked my amnesia. I hope it doesn't stay this way." He then retreated to his characteristic guarded, withdrawn attitude, though apparently accepting my assurance that I would help him by continuing our interviews and exercises.

———————————————— January 22 ————————————————

LUNCH HOUR: Propaganda and the power of the press was again the subject of discussion among the Goering group. Goering and Rosenberg again agreed that every American trembled before the power of the press. Rosenberg sympathized with "—Poor Hearst. —Just because he published a few articles of mine and had his picture taken with me, his whole newspaper syndicate was almost threatened with bankruptcy, with boycotts and all—." I pointed out that that showed how public opinion could control the press in America, just as much as vice versa; that it further showed how repugnant any infiltration of Nazi influences was to the American public. Goering started to attack sensational yellow journals in America, but I pointed out that they never reached the depths of the Stürmer. Goering had no answer for that one, because he certainly did not want to defend Streicher.

———————

AFTERNOON SESSION: *M. Gerthofer gave a long detailed list of grievances against Germany for her economic exploitation of France during the occupation, causing starvation and financial ruin for France. This, M. Gerthofer explained, "is the application of the theories formulated in Mein Kampf, which had for a corollary the enslavement and then the extermination of the populations of conquered countries." Goering had said, "If famine is to reign, it will never happen in Germany."*

———————————————— January 26–27 ————————————————

## WEEK END IN JAIL

*Von Papen's Cell:* "Rosenberg happened to be walking with me in the exercise yard today.—I usually don't talk to him, because I have nothing in common with him, but we just happened to come out at the same time. We started talking about yesterday's evidence by the French—the tortures and the other atrocities.

And he says to me innocently, 'I don't understand how Germans came to do such things.' So do· you know what I said to him? 'I can understand it very well!' I said. 'You and your Nazi philos-· ophy and paganism and attacks on the Church and morality sim- ply destroyed all moral standards!'—It is no wonder that such barbarity resulted from it!"

---

*Ribbentrop's Cell:* I introduced Major Goldensohn, new prison psychiatrist. Ribbentrop began by reviewing his career, and ended with the usual confused ambivalence concerning Hitler.

He related how he returned from Canada in a coal-bunker at the outbreak of World War I, served as an officer, then married a champagne heiress after the war. He told with weak pleasure how he mingled with the "international clique" that met in Paris in the spring, wintered at St. Moritz, summered at the Riviera, Biarritz, etc. He did not enter into politics until 1932, when un- employment and inflation made business really bad. Aside from his own conceit and ambitious social climbing, he indicates his motives by saying that Hitler allowed him to continue maintaining an interest in his liquor business, and describing Hitler as a man who "only wanted a *reasonable capitalism.*"

The last time he saw Hitler was on April 23, 1945. When I asked him whether he had any indication at that time that Hitler intended to commit suicide, he said he was quite sure then that Hitler intended to die in Berlin. "He didn't actually say so, but it was obvious. That was the first time he ever mentioned an im- pending defeat. In fact, only six weeks earlier he had said that we would still 'win by a nose.' He had never said a word about losing the war before. You didn't dare suggest it. But this time I was able to ask him what he wanted me to do if it came to the point of surrender. He said I should try to remain on good terms with Britain.—He always wanted that, you know."

Hitler is still a "puzzle" to Ribbentrop, and he expresses his confusion (the confusion of a frustrated opportunist who can neither rationalize his position nor admit his guilt) in a most inane manner. "I cannot understand it. He was a vegetarian, you know.—He could not bear to eat a dead animal and he called us *Leichenfresser* [corpse eaters]. I even had to go hunting secretly because he disapproved of it. Now how can a man like that order mass murder?"

According to Ribbentrop, Hitler became rigid and fixated in his ideas only toward the end. One eye showed a cloudiness and strabismus after the assassination attempt. His hands and face in the last couple of years were so pale as to give the impression that there was no blood in his veins. He was getting no sleep, and practically living on Dr. Morel's injections.

In explanation of why he did not dare argue with Hitler, he related the incident in 1940 when he threw a fit in a temper tantrum. "You know I had a terrible experience when I had an argument with Hitler in 1940, and I was never able to have an argument with him since. It was over some trivial thing—I forget what. I disagreed with him violently and threatened to resign. But he got red in the face and screamed and then had some kind of attack. He fell into his chair and said, 'Look what you are doing to me! You are driving me to distraction. Now I've got a roaring in my ears and I am sick. Suppose I should get a stroke. Do you want to ruin Germany? I am the only one who can lead Germany in these dangerous times, and you will ruin her by upsetting me this way!' So I promised never to resign or oppose him again."

---

*Hess's Cell:* Still apathetic, withdrawn, and somewhat secretive . . . As for the trial, he wasn't listening very attentively, he said, because the French talk so much and so much of it is repetition. He admitted that he didn't remember all of what had gone before, but the others had told him that most of it was repetition. He still could not understand what had brought the atrocities about. From his attitude, I gathered that the current apathy and beginnings of real and ostensible memory failure were part of the negativistic pattern of reaction to the final smashing of the ideology which had supported his ego, and now faces him with an intolerable choice between accepting a share of the guilt of Nazism or rejecting his Führer. He will probably end by hysterically rejecting reality again, and converting it into some unpredictable functional disturbance, either amnesia or paranoia, or a mixture of these and other symptoms and behavior.

—————————————— February 2 ——————————————

## GOERING ON "COMMUNISTS"

*Goering's Cell*: Visited him early in the afternoon with Goldensohn. He spoke in his usual expansive and uninhibited style. Now that the French were winding up their case, he was anticipating the Russian prosecution as directed particularly at him. He felt that the Russians would be especially hard on him, because he was the most violent opponent of Bolshevism.

"Oh, I think Rosenberg would dispute that title," I replied. But Goering insisted that he deserved the title of chief Communist-baiter because he expressed his opposition in deeds, not merely in words, and he knew there were many things the Russians would never forgive him for.

He began to relate with relish how he had persecuted Communists as soon as Hitler came to power. "Why, as police chief of Prussia I arrested thousands of Communists. That is why I set up the concentration camps in the first place—to keep the Communists under control. Then I intercepted funds they sent to the Spanish Loyalists, and then there was the munitions shipment to Barcelona—hah! They'll never forgive me for that!" Here he laughed with the malicious glee of a little boy who had put a tack on teacher's chair. "They had paid for a shipload of arms to a neutral country destined for Loyalist Spain, but I had my men among the crew that loaded the ship, and I sent a shipload of building bricks with only a layer of munitions on top. Haha! They'll never forgive me for that one." Goering's fat laugh resounded in the bare cell. I said nothing, and finally it was time to go to chapel service. As we left the cell, I told him that I did not want to interfere with his prayers, because Lord knows, he needed them. He laughed again and said sarcastically, "Prayers, hell! It's just a chance to get out of this damn cell for a half hour."

After the chapel service I saw Chaplain Gerecke in Goering's cell, still trying to inspire him with some feeling of repentance. (He told me later that Goering had said he just couldn't accept the religious teachings, and he hoped that his wife would have the courage to kill herself and the child rather than live this way.)

---

## February 7

### IDEOLOGY AND LOOT; HESS'S MISSION

MORNING SESSION: *M. Mounier of the French delegation began to wind up the French prosecution with a summary of Rosenberg's role in the Nazi conspiracy. He attacked his "anti-scientific obscurantism which mixes the physiological traits of man with the concept of nations; the neo-paganism which aims to abolish what twenty centuries of Christianity have brought to the world in the way of moral rules of justice and of charity; this myth of the Blood which tends to justify racial discrimination, with its consequences of slavery, massacre, looting, and the mutilation of human beings. I shall not dwell . . . on what we consider a hodgepodge with philosophic pretensions . . . "—because Rosenberg's Weltanschauung was amply expressed in deeds, including the looting of art treasure from the Rothschilds in France.*

*M. Mounier went on to describe the roles of Sauckel and Speer in recruiting slave labor from France; Goering's looting of French art treasures and failure to prevent the shooting of captured Allied airmen while allowing Luftwaffe experiments with human brains*

---

LUNCH HOUR: Fritzsche and Speer showed that Goering's stealing of art treasures was really the damaging accusation in German eyes. "They didn't even mention the worst part of it," Fritzsche pointed out, "—that he even *sold* the stuff he stole.—But that Frenchman who presented the case did a really good job—much more effective than name calling, and he cleverly left the word for it up to the court to decide."

"You see," added Speer, "how can there be any talk of a united front among the defendants when that man has disgraced himself like that?"

Goering came over after lunch while I was reading the paper to some of the others, looked over my shoulder. He started to

wisecrack about having a grudge against the brain-doctors. The
others walked away to avoid the pretense of joking with him, and
Goering expressed great interest in the day's news.

AFTERNOON SESSION: *Mr. Griffith-Jones (British) presented the
case against Hess. It was to. Hess that Hitler dictated Mein
Kampf during his detention in the Landsberg fortress in 1924.
Later, as deputy of the Führer he had one of the most influential
positions in Germany. He signed decrees persecuting the Jews and
churches; supported rearmament; helped organize a foreign fifth
column with the Auslands Organization (organization of Germans abroad), participated in plans for aggression against Czechoslovakia and Poland. Finally he flew to England on May 10, 1941,
to offer them peace on Nazi terms. "He gave his reasons . . .
that he was horrified at the thought of a long war. England could
not win, and therefore she had better make peace now. He said
the Führer entertained no designs against England. He had no
idea of world domination, and he would greatly regret the collapse
of the British Empire." Hess was willing to let the British off easy
if they would give Germany a free hand in Europe and against
Russia, but of course, they would have to get rid of Churchill.*

[The other defendants felt partly amused and partly disgraced
by the naïve and presumptuous gesture by Hess in offering the
British peace on his terms. During the presentation, Goering repeatedly turned to Hess and asked him if he had really said that.
Hess nodded that he had.]

At the end of the session, Goering, hardly able to control his
own scorn at Hess's attempt to meddle in diplomacy, slapped him
on the back in mock congratulation and encouragement for a
good try. After they had gone down in the elevator, the others expressed themselves. Von Papen, von Neurath, Fritzsche, Schacht,
and Funk literally threw up their hands in expressions of disgust
and desperation at "such stupidity . . . such childish naïveté
. . . that was what Hitler called a political leader . . . " All except Schacht believed that Hitler had not sent him on that mission, and that it was an irresponsible dramatic gesture. Fritzsche
mentioned that the flying ace, Udet, had testified at the time that
an ME-110 plane couldn't land in Britain under those conditions,
and that Hess had probably landed in the Channel.
"Yes," commented Funk wryly, "all the insane. drunk, and

childish are protected by God." He did not specify under which heading he classified Hess. "But seriously, it is not funny—it is disgraceful—it shows what irresponsible people ruled Germany. There is a point at which things stop being funny and become disgraceful."

——————— EVENING IN JAIL ———————

*Von Papen's Cell:* Von Papen reiterated his opinion of the stupidity of Hess's mission to England, and ridiculed his childish attempt at diplomacy. Like Goering, he said that he himself could have contacted the British at a moment's notice through a neutral power, if there was any real negotiating to do. In general, his attitude was that fools rush in where angels fear to tread—and that, by further implication, included that fool Ribbentrop.

# 5. The Russian Prosecution

---------------------------- February 8 ----------------------------

## OPENING ADDRESS

Goering looked rather depressed as I pointed out that the court-room was full for the first time in weeks, to hear the chief Russian prosecutor, General Rudenko, make his opening address. "Yes, they want to see the show," he said scornfully. "—You will see—this trial will be a disgrace in 15 years."

---

MORNING SESSION: *General Rudenko began the prosecution by the Russian delegation with an impassioned condemnation of the fascist invaders. " . . . The defendants knew that cynical mockery at the laws and customs of war constituted the gravest crime. They knew it, but they hoped that the total war, by bringing victory, would also secure their immunity. But victory did not arrive on the heels of their crimes. Instead came complete and unconditional surrender of Germany, and with it came the hour of grim reckoning for all the outrages they committed . . .*

*"When entire regions of flourishing countryside were turned into desert areas, and the soil was drenched with the blood of those executed, it was the work of their hands, of their organization, their instigation, their leadership. And just because the masses of the German people were made to participate in these outrages, because . . . the defendants for years had poisoned the conscience and the mind of an entire generation of Germans by developing in them the conceit of 'the chosen,' the morals of cannibals and the greed of burglars, can it be said that the guilt of the Hitlerite conspirators is any less great or grave? . . .*

*"The criminal conspiracy aimed at the establishment of a 'new order' in Europe. This 'new order' was a regime of terror, by which, in the countries seized by the Hitlerites, all democratic institutions were abolished and civil rights of the population were abrogated and those countries themselves were plundered and rapaciously exploited. The populations of those countries, and of Slav countries first of all, were subjected to merciless persecutions and mass extermination. Russians, Ukrainians, Belo-Russians,*

135

Poles, Czechs, Serbians, Slovenes suffered more than others. The conspirators failed to achieve their objectives. The valiant struggle of the peoples of democratic countries, led by the coalition of the three great powers—The Soviet Union, The United States of America, and Great Britain—resulted in the liberation of the European countries from the Hitlerite yoke. The victory of the Soviet and of the Allied armies destroyed the criminal plans of Hitlerite conspirators, and liberated the people of Europe from the terrible threat of Hitlerite domination."

---

LUNCH HOUR: (During the address Goering and Hess took off their headphones as a gesture that the address was not worth listening to.) When I asked Goering why he hadn't been listening, he said that he knew in advance what the Russians were going to say, but he was amazed to hear them talking about Poland—he had caught that word when General Rudenko mentioned aggression against various countries. "I did not think that they would be so shameless as to mention Poland," he said.

"Why do you consider that shameless?" I asked.

"Because they attacked at the same time we did.—It was all a prearranged affair."

Hess said he didn't have to listen to foreigners slandering his country. (A significant repetition of his statement with regard to his amnesia on the second day of the trial.) I pointed out that even if he disagreed, it was necessary to hear what they had to say, in order to prepare his own defense. "That is a matter that concerns only me," he retorted.

After lunch Goering started in again on the theme of how shameless it was of the Russians to mention the violation of human rights. "I wonder if they will have the nerve to mention that in their newspapers," he said to Fritzsche.

"No, that is not the kind of stuff they like to print in Russian newspapers."

Here von Schirach laughed, "Why, when they mentioned Poland, I thought I'd die."

As I joined the conversation, Fritzsche mentioned that one thing the Russians brought up which he had not known about, was the extermination camp behind the German lines, in which Russian women and children were exterminated in a pit, and no buildings to mark the site. Goering retorted that all the atrocities the Russians were bringing up were Russian atrocities which they were blaming on the Germans.

"You will have a hard time proving that the Russians murdered their own citizens to blame you for atrocities," I said.

"How do you know what I can prove?" Goering snapped back fiercely. Fritzsche also asked him what he meant by that. "I saw the official reports and pictures myself!" he bellowed.

"Where are they?" Fritzsche asked.

"In Geneva!" Goering roared, becoming increasingly furious over the needling he was getting.

"Oh, but that Geneva report is an entirely different matter," Fritzsche explained, as if Goering didn't know it. Goering kept fuming and splattering invectives in all directions.

At this point Rosenberg came to Goering's support with: "Everything they say about Nazi atrocities you can say about the Communists."

Goering calmed down long enough to take another tack. "It's all right—as I've always said, the world is round, and turns around, and some day the tables will be turned—"

I expressed the opinion that Germany's day of ascendancy was past, and it was now a question of preserving the peace and re-building what Hitler had destroyed, but not for any dreams of empire.

"What do you mean by that?" Goering demanded.

"I mean that the day of German world power and aggression is past."

"I hope you don't have to see that day," he retorted threateningly.

Fritzsche caught him up on that. "No, I agree that Germany's day of power is past, and I am even opposed to encouraging the people ever to risk regaining it!" Von Schirach agreed, timidly.

"But I happen to be a patriot nationalist!" Goering challenged.

"I think I have some patriotism too—and some sympathy for the German people besides," Fritzsche replied. "That is why I don't want to see my people led back into such a mad adventure ever again." Von Schirach nodded.

"Oh, you're chicken-hearted little boys. What do you know about patriotism. *Chicken-hearted*, that is what you are! Phooey!" Goering dropped some more scornful remarks, and then it was time to go down to the courtroom. As he passed me, Goering gave the parting shot, "I believe the German people will rise again!"

---

AFTERNOON SESSION: [As the Russians continued with evidence of German aggression and atrocities, Goering still tried to look bored.]

General Rudenko continued: "Together with the chief prosecutors of the United States of America, Great Britain, and France, I charge the defendants with having prepared and carried out a perfidious attack on the peoples of my country and on all freedom-loving nations.

"I accuse them of the fact that, having initiated a world war, they, in violation of the fundamental rules of international law and of the treaties to which they were signatories, turned war into an instrument of extermination of peaceful citizens; an instrument of plunder, violence, and pillage . . .

"Now, when as a result of the heroic struggle of the Red Army and of the Allied Forces, Hitlerite Germany is broken and overwhelmed, we have no right to forget the victims who have suffered. We have no right to leave unpunished those who organized and were guilty of monstrous crimes.

"In the name of the sacred memory of millions of innocent victims of the fascist terror, for the sake of the consolidation of peace throughout the world, for the sake of the future security of nations, we are presenting the defendants a just and complete bill which must be paid. This is a bill on behalf of all mankind, a bill backed by the will and the conscience of all freedom-loving nations. May justice be done."

--------- EVENING IN JAIL ---------

*Fritzsche's Cell:* I dropped in on Fritzsche in the evening.

In the course of the conversation I mentioned Goering's accusation that Roosevelt had forced the war on Germany. To my surprise Fritzsche said that he had discussed that with Goering and Ribbentrop. I asked him what brought that up.

"I was only explaining why I had said so in my radio speeches. Naturally at that time I did not know anything about Hitler's deliberate plans for aggressive war. I only knew that Ambassadors Bullitt and Biddle were giving other countries assurance that America would support them."

"You mean that America would not stand by and see Hitler conquer all of Europe. If Roosevelt did that, you may be sure it was a desperate attempt to prevent war, not precipitate it. God knows he tried everything possible—pleading, conceding, threatening. Hitler obviously simply could not be appeased, and Roosevelt must have realized that the only language he could understand was the threat of force. It was clearly Hitler's intention to make and break treaties, and attack one small country after another until he was strong enough to attack the big powers."

"That is what I realize now—but then I did not.—I thought he was threatening Germany.—But Goering must have misunderstood me. I must sound him out."

----------------- February 9–10 -----------------

## WEEK END IN JAIL

*Von Schirach's Cell:* (Von Schirach's attitude of remorse before the trial has completely disappeared since he came under Goering's influence again in the first weeks of the trial. The essential moral weakness of this narcissist has been clearly shown in the manner in which he has subdued his indignation at the "betrayal" of German Youth by Hitler, under the influence of Goering's aggressive cynicism, nationalism, and pose of romantic heroism. Attempts to sound him out on his reactions to trial evidence during the past two months have produced only evasive and half-hearted responses. His original intention to write a denunciation of "Hitler's betrayal" to leave behind with me after he is executed, fizzled out, in spite of efforts by Major Kelley and myself to encourage him to write it. He has acted as Goering's messenger to lay down the "Party line" to recalcitrant defendants like Speer, and has not had the courage to speak up in Goering's presence in lunchroom arguments. The arrest of his family has given him an additional grievance to focus his attention on mistreatment and "guilt" on the part of the Allies—a welcome substitute for his own guilt, sedulously cultivated by Goering. After yesterday's argument in

which Goering impatiently attacked both Fritzsche and von
Schirach as "young weaklings" while he was by implication a more
heroic nationalist, I decided the time was ripe to make another
attempt to draw out von Schirach.)

He offered me the "soft chair" he had rigged up on his cot with
blankets, as usual, when I entered his cell, and immediately turned
to the subject of the arrest of his family. He showed me the letter
General Truscott had written the Tribunal, apparently as a result
of the request I instigated, explaining why von Schirach's family
had been arrested. He tried to pooh-pooh the "excuses" for the
arrest and criticize the mistreatment of Germans by the Allied occupation forces. I told him, after reading the letter, that it seemed
to me to be perfectly in order, that such security measures were
reasonable and necessary so soon after the war, especially during
the trial, and that he knew perfectly well that his family was not
being mistreated, would not be exterminated, as the Gestapo
would have done.

The sharp tone of my answer made him wince and take a more
apologetic defensive stand. He did not mean to criticize the
Americans so much as the Russians (I told him to pay attention
in court and he might find out why the Russians were so "incon-
siderate" now). He certainly did not approve of the war against
Russia, and does not even agree with Goering that the war with
Russia was inevitable. He merely suspects that there was collusion
in the attack on Poland. He criticized Ribbentrop for his double-
dealing policy, which brought about first an understanding and
then a war with Russia. The conversation then shifted to Ribbentrop.

"I told him the other day," von Schirach continued, "that I
don't want to argue with him now, but I have always and still do
oppose his foreign policy. 'If you were for an understanding with
Russia,' I told him, 'how could you participate in an aggressive
policy against Russia?' He said that Hitler was afraid Russia
would attack us."

"I think Ribbentrop was a rank opportunist who did anything
Hitler wanted him to do."

"Well, he didn't act that way then. He went around with the
utmost arrogance, talking about his foreign policy, his clever statesmanship, his (and Hitler's) credit for leading Germany to great-

ness. Now he says he was not responsible for all of that—he only did Hitler's bidding. I suppose he probably did get his orders from Hitler in private and then went strutting around cackling about his brilliant decisions on foreign policy.—I never thought much of him, but I did wonder whether I was wrong when he succeeded in pulling off the Russian Non-Aggression Pact.—It is funny how he got into diplomacy in the first place.—No one had ever heard of him, and all of a sudden he turned up as an important man in the Foreign Office—practically overnight. I asked people who he was, when he suddenly started figuring in foreign negotiations, and they just said, 'That is von Ribbentrop—he is a very important man.'—But what von Ribbentrop?—What was his background?—Where does his influence come from?—It was all a mystery.—All I could determine was that he had placed his house in Munich at the disposal of foreign representatives for negotiations, and all of a sudden he became a leading diplomat."

"He doesn't really belong to the nobility, does he?" I asked. "I assume there's something phony about von Ribbentrop."

Von Schirach smiled maliciously. "Why, no, he doesn't really belong—we've always smiled about that."

I followed up on this remark by mentioning that it had always struck me that there was something phony about the way he was constantly bragging about his connections among the rich and titled aristocracy of western Europe.

Von Schirach's smile expanded into frank delight. "So you really fished out Ribbentrop as a phony, did you? He is a phony, you know. He got himself legally adopted by some branch of a remote von Ribbentrop family—the same name as his—after the first World War—but his father was just Lt. Colonel Ribbentrop. Once somebody addressed his father as von Ribbentrop, and he said deliberately, 'My name is Ribbentrop.' He did not want to support his son's pose as a phony nobleman. That is why I wondered who he was and what family he came from—because we all knew each other, and our father's regiments, and all that.—I found out the real story, but of course we didn't dare discuss it openly, because it was strictly legal and he was backed by Hitler, even though we knew he didn't really belong. It isn't generally known. But you can really tell the difference can't you?—That is most interesting."

It was most interesting as a reflection on von Schirach's sense of values too. He had evidently always opposed Ribbentrop as an upstart pretender more than for his dangerous foreign policy. In spite of his pretense at wanting to abolish class distinctions among German Youth, he still felt himself identified with those born to lead. But his passive character required a strong leader to identify himself with. Hitler supplied this, but Goering supplemented it by adopting the pose of the Junker-officer which helped draw the aristocratically-inclined like von Schirach. Although the damning evidence produced in court makes him feel that Hitler has betrayed him, it is evident that his willingness to renounce Hitler will depend on the forcefulness of the personalities influencing him now, more than his own sense of moral indignation.

I rose to leave. Characteristically, he asked me not to tell anybody what he had said about Ribbentrop.

---

*Speer's Cell:* I showed him a copy of a book on Speer as the Führer's leading architect. This prompted a discussion on Hitler's plans and taste in architectural construction, and his accomplishments in utter destruction. He confirmed what Hitler's physician Dr. Brandt had said about Hitler's plans for grandiose construction as originating from his beer-hall putsch days. He compared Hitler's taste to Napoleon's. The latter went through several stages: *Jacobin, directoire, empire,* reaching its height in ornateness and pretentiousness in the empire period, just as the empire collapsed. Hitler's preferred style was always like Napoleon's empire period, but Speer managed to restrain him in the early years, preferring simple classical lines. But Hitler's pretentious and grandiose taste became more and more insistent as his power rose to domination and disaster. This was evident when he ordered a resumption of construction after the French victory. I suggested that if the pretentious, ornate style represented destructive ambition, Hitler must have had it from the very beginning, because his own taste remained essentially unchanged from the early days onward. Speer agreed.

He thumbed through the pages of photographs of the Reich Chancellery and boulevards in Berlin, the plans for the supertremendous amphitheatre to eclipse the amphitheatre of Athens, the Autobahn bridges, the Stadium in Nuremberg, and other works completed and destroyed, or never completed, and sighed with genuine regret—"It is a pity, though, that so much of this had to be destroyed—."

I agreed. "Behind Hitler's pretense of a passion for constructive planning there lurked a destructive mania which revealed itself in destroying all it had built."

"—And that isn't all—" Speer controlled his bitterness. "He ended in destroying not only all he had built, but much of what Germany had built up painstakingly for the past 800 years!"

"When did you first realize that you were dealing with a destructive demon?"

"When the Rundstedt offensive failed, and I told him it was time to quit. You see, I had been fighting my doubts for some time and doing my best to back up the war effort with production. Finally, I was told that the Rundstedt offensive was our last try to turn the tide. I doubted if it would succeed, but I thought: Well, at least I'll squeeze out all the production I can to back it up, and if it fails, then at least we will be through once and for all. But when it failed, and I told him in January that it was no use, he said we would continue anyway. Then I knew he was bent on utter destruction of the German nation rather than surrender his power—you know the rest of the story."

I showed him some of my own photographs of beautiful German countryside around Garmisch-Partenkirchen, etc.—Germany as it was before Hitler; and then by contrast some photographs of lines of German prisoners (destroyed manpower), the ruins of Munich (destroyed cities), a dynamited bridge (destroyed architecture), and murdered prisoners in Dachau (destroyed culture and national prestige). He grew more and more grim as he looked at the pictures.

Finally he banged his fist on the cot and exclaimed in one of his rare emotional outbursts: "Some day I would just like to cut loose and give a good piece of my mind about the whole business, without pulling any punches! I would just like to sit down and write one final blast about the whole damn Nazi mess and mention names and details and let the German people see once and for all what rotten corruption, hypocrisy, and madness the whole system was based on!—I would spare nobody, including myself.— We are all guilty. I ignored the bare truth too!"

I asked him whether he wouldn't care to write a short summary. He said he would feel freer to do it after the trial was over.

---

*Frank's Cell:* Still wavering, Frank expressed his ambivalence toward Goering: "I don't know what to think about Goering—he can be so charming at times—really!—But how could he steal those treasures for himself in war time, with the people in such desperate straits?—That is what I cannot understand."

We went on to discuss the ruthless ambition and two-sidedness of many of the Nazi leaders. I quoted from Goethe's Faust, "Zwei Seelen wohnen, ach! in meiner Brust—" ("Two souls dwell, alas, in my breast!") He finished the quotation and went off on the desired theme of split-personality in one of his expansive, introspective monologues:

"Yes, we do have evil in us—but do not forget that there is always a Mephistopheles who brings it out. He says, 'Behold! the world is wide and full of temptation—behold! I will show you the world!—There is just a little triviality of handing over your soul!' . . . " He became more and more expansive, dramatizing his speech with all the appropriate gestures, waving his arms to behold the world, and rubbing his fingers like a miser asking for the triviality of a soul in payment. "—And so it was.—Hitler was the devil. He seduced us all that way." ·

The metaphor of seduction must have stirred something deeply latent within him, because it perseverated, and he returned to it after the conversation had gone off on another tangent. "You know, the people [Volk] are really feminine.—In its totality, it is female. One should not say das Volk [neuter], one should say die Volk [fem.]—It is so emotional, so fickle, so dependent on mood and environment, so suggestible—it idolizes virility so—that is it."

It was interesting that he was using the same terms of describing the Volk as he had used in previous conversation to describe himself. "And it is so ready to obey—" I suggested further, with obvious reference to the German Volk.

"That, yes—but not merely obedience—surrender [Hingabe]—like a woman. You see? Isn't it amazing?" He burst into explosive laughter as though tickled by projection into a lewd joke. The identification was unmistakable. "—And that was the secret of Hitler's power. He stood up and pounded his fist, and shouted, 'I am *the man!*'—and he shouted about his strength and determination —and so the public just surrendered to him with hysterical enthusiasm.—One must not say that Hitler *violated* the German people—he *seduced* them! They followed him with a mad jubilation, the like of which you have never seen in your life! It is unfortunate that you did not experience those feverish days, *Herr Doktor*—you would have a better conception of what happened to us.—It was a madness—a drunkenness."

Later he returned to the subject of his diaries, after discussing the "evil Frank." "I gave those diaries so that I could rid myself once and for all of the other Frank.—Those three days after Hitler committed suicide were decisive—the turning point in my life. After he had led us on and set the whole world in motion, he simply disappeared—deserted us, and left us to take the blame for everything that had happened. Can one simply disappear after all that, and wipe one's footsteps out of the sand, leaving no trace?— One realizes at a moment like that how insignificant one is— 'planet bacilli,' as Hitler used to call mankind."

This talk is the most revealing one I have had with Frank thus far. He reveals spontaneously the latent homosexuality, which, in addition to his ruthless ambition and lack of scruple, drove him to follow and identify himself with the Führer with a passionate enthusiasm that beclouded all reason and legal or humane concepts of human rights. When the evil genius who justified his existence passed out in an orgy of blood, destruction, and shame, he dissociated himself from this intolerable picture of his ego, went into a religious ecstasy, renounced the world and his evil self as well as the evil figure who seduced him; but left his diaries behind, because complete extinction was intolerable to his ego and the evidence of his guilt also served a masochistic need.

───────────── **February 11** ─────────────

## GENERAL VON PAULUS TESTIFIES

LUNCH HOUR: I showed newspapers at lunch. Jodl blew up at the headline, "HESS FLEW TO ENGLAND ON HITLER'S ORDER" in the Nuremberg paper. "That is a dirty lie! I never in my life saw a man in such a fury as when Hitler heard that Hess had flown to England. He was in such a rage he was fit to be tied!"

"Why?" I asked.

"Because he was afraid the Italians would think he was negotiating peace behind their backs and leaving them in the lurch. He was mad as hell!"

Jodl and Keitel then started talking about von Paulus' expected testimony this afternoon. "Of course, those generals are just talking now to preserve their own existence," Jodl assured me.

"Do you mean that they were forced to testify under pressure?"

"No, but they realized that they would never return to Germany regardless of whether Germany won the campaign or not, and they had to decide to make their peace with the Russians."

"But couldn't von Paulus have decided that Hitler was destroying Germany in a reckless adventure, and considered himself absolved of his oath of loyalty to Hitler?"

Here Keitel flared up. "Then he should have taken that stand *before* he was captured!—He should not have accepted his iron cross, his promotions to Colonel-General and Field Marshal, his sword, and other decorations, and keep sending messages of loyalty to the Führer—*that* is my viewpoint.—I always stuck up for him with the Führer. It is a shame for him to be testifying against us."

"He swore loyalty to the Führer right up to the last minute," Jodl put in "—even after his position was hopeless."

Suddenly Doenitz popped up. "They cost us the lives of thousands of German women and children, by causing defection in the ranks."

I couldn't follow Doenitz' argument. "I thought it was the unnecessary prolongation of the war that caused the unnecessary loss of life."

"No, it was the undermining of morale by their disruptive propaganda. If we had collapsed in January, there would have been still more loss of life. At least I made an orderly peace." It was an obvious *non sequitur*, and Speer looked at me, knowing I knew his views about the needless slaughter and destruction since January 1945. He did not want to rebuff his friend, Doenitz, in open discussion, however.

Fritzsche caught up the propaganda angle, and showed his friendship for von Paulus, "It wasn't von Paulus who directed that propaganda campaign anyway."

"I am not talking about von Paulus. I mean that Seydlitz group. They were preaching out-and-out treason," Doenitz insisted.

---

AFTERNOON SESSION: *In the afternoon, von Paulus testified that Germany had prepared its "criminal attack" on Russia at least as far back as September 3, 1940, according to his own knowledge, thus violating its Non-Aggression Pact with Russia. He also denounced the "irresponsible policies" of Hitler, and implicated Keitel, Jodl, and Goering in the plans for aggressive war and the senseless sacrifice of German lives.*

---

During the afternoon intermission, the military section blew up in an uproar, and they argued with heated invective with their attorneys and each other. "Ask that dirty pig if he knows he's a traitor! Ask him if he has taken out Russian citizenship papers!" Goering shot at his attorney.

Raeder saw me watching and shouted at Goering, "Careful! The enemy is listening!"

Goering kept right on shouting to his attorney, and there was real bedlam around the prisoners' dock. "We've got to disgrace that traitor!" he roared. Keitel was still arguing with his attorney, and Raeder passed him a slip with the same warning.

At the other end of the dock, the attitude was more sympathetic toward von Paulus. "You see," said Fritzsche, "that is the tragedy of the German people right there. He was caught between the devil and the deep blue sea." Von Neurath, Seyss-Inquart, and Schacht also made sympathetic remarks about von Paulus.

"The military section seems to think he is a traitor," I said.

"Nothing of the sort," said Funk gloomily, "it is a human tragedy."

———————————— February 12 ————————————

## THE ATTACK ON RUSSIA

Before the opening of the morning session for the cross-examination of von Paulus, there was an air of tense expectancy in the prisoners' dock. Hess jerked a smile at me, to show that there were really no hard feelings over yesterday's quarrel.

While the defendants sat in glum expectancy, Keitel suddenly laughed. To my inquiring glance, he answered, "The thought just went through my mind—if that plan had only materialized—. Von Paulus was supposed to take Jodl's place—in that case he would be sitting here now."

———

MORNING SESSION: The 'cross-examination took place before a courtroom crowded to standing room for the first time in weeks. [As I expected, the questions designed to show that Hitler was Commander in Chief came from Keitel's attorney. It was surprising, however, that the questions attacking von Paulus' personal honor came from Dr. Sauter, attorney for von Schirach and Funk, since these two were the least concerned with the Russian campaign. Apparently Goering has prevailed upon his two weak table-companions to take the lead in defaming a German general so that he would not have to do it himself.] Von Paulus had to admit he helped plan the attack on Russia in spite of their Non-Aggression Pact. Jodl, however, tried to trap him into admitting that having helped to prepare the plans for the attack himself, he knew about the strength of the Russian troop concentrations (alleged) on the German border. Von Paulus said he did not remember the details.

———

During the morning intermission Goering sneered out loud: "He doesn't remember!—Hess, do you know you've got a competitor? [shouts to Jodl] *Generaloberst*, did you get that? Hess has a competitor. The witness doesn't remember. Haha!—Making believe he didn't know.—Where does he get off, anyway?—Why, he was the expert on Russian troop strength."

"Sure, he was," Jodl agreed. "He was the expert in drawing up the plans. But he didn't fall into my trap. He couldn't say that the Russian forces were weak, because then I would have confronted him with his own report. He couldn't say they were strong, because then he would embarrass the Russians. He just said he didn't know. But *I* know. Just wait till I get up and give the whole story."

Ribbentrop, who had been sitting silent and depressed throughout all this, later said to Goering and then to Jodl, "That man, von Paulus, is finished—he has disgraced himself."

"Of course," Jodl agreed. "He is all washed up—but I cannot say I blame him too much—he has to save his own neck."

It is somehow ironic to hear the defeated and disgraced Nazi war criminals, facing death, pass judgment on von Paulus, as if deciding that they would not hire a man like that for the next war.

———————————

LUNCH HOUR: In the lunchroom discussion, Speer, Fritzsche, and von Schirach showed sympathy for von Paulus, although von Schirach echoed some of Goering's arguments about von Paulus' own participation in the plans for the Russian attack and estimate of Russian strength.

Fritzsche described how he had witnessed von Paulus' desperate struggle on the horns of a dilemma—whether to use his meager reserves to support the hard-pressed troops in the North, or hold them for the encirclement he was planning from the South. "I know what terrible despair he experienced at the time.—And just imagine what a tormenting position he was in—to have this assignment to take 200,000 German souls into the jaws of hell—and then to wonder what the purpose of the whole thing was."

————— EVENING IN JAIL —————

*Ribbentrop's Cell:* This evening I visited von Ribbentrop in his cell in order to get some expression on the Russian aggression. I put the questions to him rather directly, after commenting that von Paulus had made a strong impression in labeling the Russian campaign a "criminal attack." Ribbentrop hemmed and hawed, and finally came out with, "Well, maybe history will show that Hitler was right and I was wrong."

"How do you mean?"

"I was always for a rapprochement with Russia. Hitler thought we would be attacked sooner or later.—Maybe he was right."

"But you had a Non-Aggression Pact. Wasn't the attack actually a criminal breach of faith on your side—to say nothing of the reckless gamble with human lives?"

"Well, the problem is very difficult—very difficult. History will have to decide.—You must regard these things in proper perspective.—It is not so easy to understand. I wanted to arrive at a peaceful understanding with the Russians. Do you know what I planned? I wanted to include them in our three-power pact, and make it a four-power pact."

"A four-power Anti-Comintern Pact, including Russia?" I asked.

"Well—er, no. The Anti-Comintern Pact ceased to operate as such as soon as we made our pact with Russia.—But I wanted a free hand to deal with England for all emergencies."

"To wage war?"

"No, we wanted a peaceful solution—a counterbalance to England's balance-of-power politics. They were constantly oppressing us.—Just imagine going to war over Danzig—such a world catastrophe, just to prevent Germany from getting a piece of territory that belonged to it—because Britain was afraid Germany was getting too strong."

"Oh, come now, you know perfectly well it wasn't over a little piece of territory. It was just the last straw in a series of aggressions and broken pacts which had already violated the peace of Europe and the sovereignty of peaceful nations. If you wanted peace, why did you break the Munich Pact? England certainly conceded more than enough to appease German demands. Did Hitler intend to break it even while he was signing it?—Or did he decide to break his word later?"

"Oh, Hitler didn't break the Munich Pact!"

I looked at him incredulously. He didn't even seem to be joking. "How in the world do you figure that? You swallowed all of Czechoslovakia even after you were handed over the Sudetenland and made it clear to the whole world that Hitler's word was worthless, and German aggression knew no bounds."

"Oh, but Czechoslovakia was a state that had been merely created by the Treaty of Versailles. Anyway, Hitler made a Protectorate out of Czechoslovakia.—I'll admit he exerted some pressure on Hacha . . . Legally we did not break the Munich Pact."

The sheer bare-faced hypocrisy of this man is incredible.

---

## February 15

MORNING SESSION: *The Russians continued with German atrocities, and mentioned excerpts from Frank's diary and other utterances which show that he was directly tied up with atrocities in Poland.*

---

LUNCH HOUR: After lunch, Fritzsche said he was actually physically ill, when I asked him why he was sitting alone so depressed at the table, while the others were talking and walking as usual. He clearly meant it as a "psychosomatic" complaint in reaction to the statement attributed to Frank, that Hitler would be pleased to know that another 150,000 Poles were dying! "And the people believed so earnestly in their cause—sacrificed themselves so unselfishly, with such patriotic self-denial and discipline.—And on top we had these selfish, ambitious brutes—these—ah, well—."

Down in the dock after lunch, Goering was saying something about insisting on reading in court the whole document that had just been put in evidence. "What? The *whole* document?" Raeder asked. It was apparently a very voluminous one.

"Sure, why not?" There was a suggestion of filibuster in all this. "We've got plenty of time. Either we make no defense at all— which is all right with me, since then they will disgrace themselves —or—"

"There, you see?" Hess interrupted, suddenly looking up from his book. "Then you come around to just what I have always said."

"Aha!" Goering laughed. "Hess is a man of principle. He won't

say a word.—Not even to us. By the way, Hess, when are you
going to let us in on your great secret?" Doenitz and Raeder were
grinning. They did not mind my listening as long as the joke was
on Hess.

"Yes, Hess, how about it?" Ribbentrop joked.

"Won't you let us in on it during the recess?" Goering continued, teasing, "I make a motion Hess tell us his big secret during
the recess. How about it, Hess?"

"Uh-huh—I am agreeable to everything," Hess grunted, bury-
ing his nose in his book again. It was obvious that he had no
intention of departing from his secretive attitude.

I mentioned that the Russians were expected to show an atrocity
film on Monday.

"*Ach*, what the Russians show!" Goering scoffed uneasily.

Ribbentrop promptly parroted the Rosenberg line of attack:
"Haven't you heard about how the Americans slaughtered the
Indians? Were they an inferior race too?—Do you know who
started concentration camps in the first place?—The British. And
do you know why? To force the Boers to give up their arms."

"Those atrocity films!" Goering continued. "Anybody can make
an atrocity film if they take corpses out of their graves and then
show a tractor shoving them back in again."

"You can't brush it off that easily," I replied. "We *did* find
your concentration camps fairly *littered* with corpses and mass
graves—I saw them myself in Dachau!—and Hadamar!"

"Oh, but not piled up by the thousands like that—"

"Don't tell me what I didn't see! I saw corpses literally by the
carload—"

"Oh, that one train—"

"—And piled up like cordwood in the crematorium—and half-
starved and mutilated prisoners, who told me how the butchery
had been going on for years—and Dachau was not the worst by
far! You can't shrug off 6,000,000 murders!"

"Well, I doubt if it was 6,000,000," he said despondently, apparently sorry he had started the argument, "—but as I've always
said, it is sufficient if only 5 per cent of it is true—." A glum silence
followed.

In the evening before they went back to the cells, I read to them the new order prohibiting communication in the prison, and restoring the solitary confinement except in court. They took it in silent anger.

---

# February 16-17

## WEEK END IN JAIL

*Schacht's Cell:* Schacht was furious over the new ruling. He actually screamed as he worked himself into a frenzy over his treatment in prison: "It is disgraceful!—*shabby!!*—The colonel can do with us what he likes, but I do not envy him his power! . . . This shows treatment by people who have no tradition and ho culture —it is *contemptible!!*" His contemptuous reference to the Americans was the Goering line probably transmitted by his table companion Raeder. His fury disclosed a good deal of feeling otherwise concealed under a shell of hurt innocence. "I assure you I don't *want* to talk to most of those people!—criminals like Goering, Rosenberg, Ribbentrop, Keitel, Streicher, Frank—but there are a few gentlemen I *do* enjoy talking to:—decent people like von Papen, von Neurath.—But how dare they treat us in such a highhanded manner!—Don't forget that we were a *Kulturvolk* from way back.—What Hitler did was a crime against *our culture!*—But don't forget what desperate straits the Allies drove us into. They hemmed us in from every side—they fairly strangled us! Just try to imagine what a cultured people like the German people has to go through to fall for a demagogue like Hitler.—Just try to imagine: a people that led the culture of Europe ever since the Dark Ages, with great figures like Goethe, Schiller, Kant, Beethoven—the most outstanding figures in every field—music, literature, art, philosophy—"

"Didn't the French have a fairly respectable culture too?" I put in edgewise.

"Oh, the French!" he retorted with chauvinistic contempt. "In a small court circle, perhaps—but even that was the influence of

the Germans.—Just imagine what a cultured people like ours has
to go through to be dragged to such desperation.—And think of
what a demon it was who seized upon the desperate plight of the
German people to abuse their faith in such a criminal way.—Don't
worry, I'll have plenty to say about that.—And the German people
were *so willing* to do anything for peace.—We were *so modest* in
our demands.—All we wanted was some possibility for export, for
trade, to live somehow—."

"You mean the Weimar Republic?"

"Yes, of course.—And to every little suggestion the Allies said
NO! We asked for a colony or two—anything for trading possibilities—out of the question! We asked for a trade union with
Austria and Czechoslovakia, and they said NO! We pointed out
that Austria had voted 90 per cent for union with Germany.—They
said nothing doing.—But when a gangster like Hitler comes to
power—oh, my, take all of Austria; remilitarize the Rhineland—
take the Sudetenland, take all of Czechoslovakia, take everything
—we won't say a word.—Why, before the Munich Pact Hitler
didn't even dare dream of getting the Sudetenland incorporated
into the Reich.—All he thought he *might* get was a measure of
autonomy for the Sudetenland.—And then those fools Daladier
and Chamberlain drop the whole thing in his lap.—Why didn't
they give the Weimar Republic *one-tenth* that much support?—
They wouldn't give us one damn little crumb!!—And because I
finally tried to build up some economic security without the Versailles Treaty to *avoid* a catastrophe, and sabotaged the war measures and finally tried to kill that maniac—they threw me into jail
like a CRIMINAL!!" He screamed so that the whole jail must
have heard it. "—With the most *disgraceful, undignified,* SHAME-
LESS treatment!! Even in concentration camp I didn't have to
sweep out my own cell and be forced to face this way or that way
so that I couldn't sleep!" He sat biting his lips and quivering with
emotion, his face flushed. After a while he said apologetically,
"Well, I am sorry, but if you want to know my reaction, there it
is.—I will have nothing more to do with any American institutions.
I will not even attend chapel any more."

---

*Goering's Cell:* Dejected and tremulous like a rejected child, he
asked why they were being punished this way. He guessed rightly

that his ridiculing, domineering attitude had something to do with it. "Don't you see—all this joking and horseplay is only a comic relief. Do you think I enjoy sitting there and hearing accusations heaped on our heads from all sides? We've got to let off steam somehow.—If I didn't pep them up, a couple of them would simply collapse." His manner was subdued and apologetic.

I told him that I knew he felt he had to act differently before the others than he did in his cell. I was sure that he was probably hiding a lot of shame behind his bravado. He did not take exception to any of this, exhibiting the closest thing to humility he has displayed in any of our talks, although it was undoubtedly partly calculated.

"Of course—a psychologist understands those things," he conceded. "But the colonel is no psychologist.—Don't you think I reproach myself enough in the loneliness of this cell—wishing that I had taken a different road and lived my life differently—instead of ending up like this?" This sounded very much like the sentiment he expressed in his letter to his wife in October 28. It was quite a far cry, however, from the cocky self-confidence and heroic loyalty to the Führer he expressed on all other occasions, especially for the benefit of the press.

I told him they would probably also be separated during the lunch hour. He begged me to intercede with the colonel to let them at least talk during the lunch hour, and did not conceal his anxiety over being cut off completely from holding the whip over the defendants.

---

*Speer's Cell:* Speer expressed satisfaction with the new regulation that separated the defendants in the jail even during the exercise period. "It comes at a critical time too—just when some of them are beginning to become a little uneasy over Goering's dictatorship, and he is beginning to put on the real pressure. He got hold of Funk in the exercise yard a couple of days ago, and told him to reconcile himself to the fact that his life was lost and the only question now was to stand by him and die a martyr's death—and he needn't worry, because some day—even if it takes 50 years—the German people would rise again and recognize them as heroes, and even move their bones to marble caskets in a national shrine."

We both laughed. "I don't suppose the marble casket was any inducement to poor little Funk," I said.

"No, he is not quite the martyr type.—And then Goering approached von Schirach, and said the same thing loud enough for me to hear.—A *marble casket,* can you imagine? Now we all joke about the marble casket." (Fritzsche had just described the same incident with the same comments, and had said that he told Goering that the peace of Europe was more important than a marble casket.) "Poor Funk is all worried about it.—Even von Schirach isn't too keen on this martyrdom, when you get right down to it. But Goering knows his goose is cooked, and needs a retinue of at least 20 lesser heroes for his grand entrance into Valhalla."

"You mean he actually doesn't want anybody to survive him who knows what a thief and criminal adventurer he was, and spoil his chances for a heroic legend to be built around him?" I asked.

"No doubt. He knows what most of us think about him, even though most of them are afraid to say so. It is amazing what a tyranny he exercises over the rest. The other day von Papen told his attorney to say something slightly damaging to Hitler. Goering flew at him with 'How dare you!' and so on—the way he did to me —and poor old von Papen actually trembled. It is a good thing we are being separated now. In fact, even I will have less reluctance to say what I have to say."

Reflecting further on the marble casket, Speer added: "You know, this martyr line is actually a double-cross on his own original line.—At first he told them not to worry, because they would probably only be exiled to some island.—Then he was afraid they would talk too much to save their own necks, and show up the guilt of the leading Nazis, and so he switched to the marble casket line, to make them think that they had nothing to gain by telling too much of the truth—especially about himself."

---

*Frank's Cell:* Frank said the new ruling did not bother him at all —in fact, he was glad to have a little peace of mind instead of the constant *Quatsch* (tommyrot) they were talking in the lunchroom and during their exercise period. His attitude was more sober, and one could sense the slowly returning asceticism and expiation of guilt in his manner. The damaging quotations from his diary were still fresh in mind, and he undoubtedly preferred the enforced solitude to the necessity of explaining constantly why he surrendered the diaries, though he was probably not asked very much why he said those things. He relapsed into his introspective mood with the usual ambivalence: "Ah, I am a unique specimen —a very peculiar sort of individual.—Hah!" He burst into his high-pitched laugh, "—have you ever seen a specimen like me? Extraordinary, am I not?—to say such things.—Ah, but we are all robbers, we Germans. Don't forget that German literature began with Schiller's *Die Räuber* [*The Robbers*].—Has it ever occurred to you?"

Since he was really soliloquizing, he didn't wait for my answer, but continued to remark how evil mankind was fundamentally. I asked him to tell me frankly what he had in mind when he wrote that Hitler would compliment him if he told him that he had killed 150,000 Poles. He said that such a statement was a reflection on Hitler. "Just imagine—a man who would say 'nice work!' if you told him that you had murdered 150,000 people. Naturally, that does not mean that I actually did it.—You must believe me, *Doktor*—this is like a deathbed confession—I am facing death, and I say it only to you and to the priest—I never gave orders for mass murders nor for the shooting of hostages. Even the prosecution has not tied me up with any act of murder.—But the things I *said!* That is enough. I am glad I gave up my diaries because it shows how a man under the diabolical influence of Hitler comes to say such things entirely out of keeping with his character.—Horrible!—Repulsive!"

He went off into some remarks about his unhappy married life, referring to his wife as a woman who was too old for him physically and spiritually, but he did not dwell on this subject.

---

*Von Schirach's Cell:* Von Schirach expressed amazement at Frank's diary excerpts. He was such a brilliant speaker and lawyer —had defended Hitler so brilliantly in the "*Völkischer Beobachter*" cases, had such an amazing knowledge of music and art and literature.—It was simply astounding that such a man could make such statements of outright acquiescence in mass murder.

In the matter of the new restriction, he readily accepted any explanation that it was Goering's fault, and I pointed out that even he and Doenitz were falling into the pattern of undignified courtroom behavior. He felt impelled to apologize for Goering. "You cannot change him. You know how expansive and impulsive fliers are anyway. He is even more so—and he had a great reputation. He himself realizes that he is a great historical character, and that his greatness depends on the very fact that he sticks to his role to the very end." But Goering's looting—well, that was a "chapter in itself."

In the course of the discussion he mentioned that he had gradually come to the conclusion that the Roehm purge was a put-up affair between Himmler and Hitler, to get Roehm out of the way and keep Hitler in power. At the time he had accepted the explanation that Roehm was about to foment revolution, but now that he understands the true ruthlessness of Hitler's and Himmler's characters, he was convinced that it had been a falling-out among gangsters, and a dark secret between them, which accounted for Himmler's hold on Hitler. Roehm's execution was plain murder of a political rival. The homosexual business was a poor excuse, because everybody knew about it before, and there was no need for such a furor about it on this occasion. Then too, the number of announced executions was about 60—it turned out to be about 200 murders.

——————— GOERING LOSES HIS AUDIENCE ———————

Colonel Andrus asked me to draw up a new seating arrangement for the defendants at lunch, separating them into 5 rooms with 4 in each, and Goering separate in another room. I drew up the following arrangement, bearing in mind the attitudes, dominance and submissiveness of the various defendants, with a view to defeating Goering's attempt to obstruct justice by terrorizing the defendants into supporting Hitler and the Nazi myth, and staging a martyr's appeal to the "persecuted German people":

1. ("Youth Lunchroom") SPEER, FRITZSCHE, von SCHIRACH, FUNK (the purpose being to let Speer and Fritzsche wean the other two away from Goering's influence, and to give even von Schirach a chance to declare that Hitler had betrayed German Youth and that racial policy was Germany's catastrophe).

2. ("Elders' Lunchroom") von PAPEN, von NEURATH, SCHACHT, DOENITZ (the purpose being to give the old conservatives a chance to denounce Hitler and Ribbentrop by encouragement from Schacht, and letting Doenitz get some of their influence so that he isn't kept in conflict with "Offiziersehre").

3. FRANK, SEYSS-INQUART, KEITEL, SAUCKEL (the purpose being to take Keitel away from Goering and let him get a sample of Frank's impassionate denunciation of Hitler, guilt displacement and confession. In general a group which would not communicate much and would on occasion show some consciousness of their guilt).

4. RAEDER, STREICHER, HESS, RIBBENTROP (the intractable Nazis who would not be apt to talk to each other even if allowed, because of Streicher's presence and Hess's secretiveness, Raeder's security-consciousness, Ribbentrop's frustration—keeping them neutralized).

5. JODL, FRICK, KALTENBRUNNER, ROSENBERG.
6. GOERING.

──────────── **February 18** ────────────

LUNCH HOUR: There were signs of disgruntlement as they were sent to the various rooms to which they had been assigned. Goering was furious over being put in a small room by himself, and complained of the lack of heat and daylight, though it was obvious that his anger was really due to his frustration over losing his audience. Frank said he was quite pleased with the arrangement. Schacht was still indignant, but stressed that there were no hard feelings toward me personally. Speer looked pleased. The others in his room did not seem to mind. Ribbentrop and Raeder sat with a hurt look, feeling humiliated at being forced to eat in the same room with Streicher. Hess was enjoying the "persecution," strutting up and down his room with a gait that was almost a goose-step. Most of the rest appeared satisfied with the explanation that it was Goering's fault.

As they filed down to the courtroom, Goering stood by the door trying to catch their eyes as they passed, to make them sneer with him at their treatment by the Americans, but they all avoided his glance, with the exception of Raeder and Hess. Being brought down to the dock last, he still tried to stir up sympathy for the "persecution," but they were not in a very sympathetic mood.

AFTERNOON SESSION: [As the Russian prosecution proceeded with the details of murder and mutilation of women and children, Goering slumped in his seat and looked defeated, even though he was not listening much.]

## ———————— EVENING IN JAIL ————————

In the evening I visited several of the defendants to get the re-action to the "new order," now that they had experienced the whole change.

*Speer's Cell:* "I see you put Funk and von Schirach with me and Fritzsche," Speer laughed. "Obviously we two will sooner or later win those two over to taking a forthright stand against Hitler."

"As long as I had the placement to decide on," I replied, "I de-cided to do it in a way which serves the interests of bringing out the truth and defeats the attempts of Goering to obstruct justice by terrorizing weak individuals."

"That is absolutely true. Goering was exercising a kind of moral terror among the defendants. He was even bargaining with testi-mony. Did I tell you, he went to Schacht early in the trial and told him he could give him favorable testimony that Hitler was dissatisfied with his co-operation on rearmament. But after that stuff came out in the trial about Schacht saying Goering was a fool in economics and had no business being put in charge of the Four Year Plan, he told Schacht nothing doing on that testimony. And that is how he bargained everywhere."

"I think von Schirach and Funk can actually make their de-fense more unencumbered, now that they are with you and Fritzsche rather than at Goering's table," I replied. "I was going to put Doenitz with you too."

"No, it is better this way, because even I feel a little inhibited when Doenitz is around."

*Frank's Cell:* Frank said he was glad that the noisy nonsense of joint lunch and exercise was over, and that he could now have his peace. "You cannot stand before your fate and try to keep up comradeship. I was glad to meet some of these people at first, because I had not gotten to know them before.—But at a time like this a man needs peace and meditation. Now at least I can go on my walks alone and think and pray and meditate.—They kept talking such eternal nonsense out there all the time—*defense, defense* —never a word about our *guilt!*—no conception of the tragedy of mankind. Did you read Pastor Niemoeller's recent speech? The people are disturbed because he said they talk too much about their hardships and not enough about their guilt. He is right. Some of the others may complain about this new restriction in prison, but I find it a blessing. I have gotten so used to the Franciscan life, that I find this actually a blessing.—The quiet lunch today, the peaceful walk in the yard, meditating—it was wonderful."

## ———————— February 19 ————————

## RUSSIAN ATROCITY FILM

LUNCH HOUR: Most of the defendants have quickly reconciled themselves to the solitary lunch arrangement, but Goering is still incensed over it, the more so because he can see the indifference and rejection of many of the defendants, rather than sympathy for his isolation. The Goering tyranny is apparently at an end, and he does not like it one bit. He kept complaining about the coldness and artificial light in his room.

AFTERNOON SESSION: *The Russians presented their atrocity film, a horrifying document of mass murder even more terrible than the one presented by the Americans.* [I stood at Goering's end of the dock and watched the prisoners in the semidarkness during the showing of the film.

Goering is tickled at the false start, as the film starts upside down and has to be readjusted; he covers his laugh with his hand, but looks around to see if the audience is laughing . . . The film starts again] . . . *It shows the acres of corpses of Russian PW's murdered or left to starve in the fields where they had been cap-*

tured; the torture instruments, mutilated bodies, guillotines and
baskets of heads; bodies hanging from lamp-posts, found upon recapture of towns where the Gestapo had been active; the ruins of
Lidice; women weeping over their dead—mass burial services;
raped and murdered women, children with heads bashed in; the
crematoria and gas chambers; the piles of clothes, the bales of
women's hair at Auschwitz and Maidanek . . . [Goering keeps
pretending to read a book through all this, yawning in boredom,
occasionally making a sarcastic remark to Hess and Ribbentrop.]

--------------- EVENING IN JAIL ---------------

*Goering's Cell:* I went down to the cell block with Major Goldensohn to get a sampling of the reactions. Goering readily gave
"reasons" why he did not consider the Russian atrocity film worth
looking at: "First of all, a film that they made is no proof, just
looking at it from a legal point of view. They could just as easily
have killed a few hundred German PW's and put them in Russian uniforms for the atrocity picture—you don't know the Russians the way I do. Secondly, lots of those pictures were probably
taken during their own revolution, like the baskets of heads.
Thirdly, those fields covered with bodies.—Why, such pictures are
easy to get any time in a war. I've seen thousands of bodies myself. And where did they get the *fresh* corpses to photograph?
They couldn't have come right in ready to take pictures. They
must have shot those people themselves." He was eager to appear
perfectly satisfied in dismissing the whole thing with this preposterous propaganda line but threw in a sop to our moral sensitivity.
"Of course, as I've always told you, it is enough if only 5 per cent
of all the atrocity stories are true, from all that has already been
presented before—but I do not put any stock in what the Russians
bring.—They are blaming their own atrocities on us."

More interested in the restriction against talking to the others
at lunch and exercise, he quickly changed the subject. "Just because I am the No. 1 Nazi in this group doesn't mean I am the
most dangerous.—Anyway, the colonel ought to bear in mind
that he is dealing with historical figures here.—Right or wrong,
we are historical personalities—and he is nobody." He repeated his
reference to Napoleon's jailer, who had to write two volumes justi-

fying his treatment of Napoleon while he was imprisoned, and the British themselves condemned him for it.

___

*Frank's Cell:* Frank was still projecting his guilt on to Hitler and the whole human race. "Can you imagine a man cold-bloodedly planning the whole thing? At some moment Hitler and Himmler must simply have sat down and Hitler gave him orders to wipe out whole races and groups of people.—I try to picture the scene.—I cannot.—It was a turning point in human history. Is it the beginning of a final horrible phase of human evolution, or is it the end of one?—It is horrible. What could they have been thinking of?"

I asked him what he could have been thinking of himself, when he permitted the mass transportation of Jews to concentration camps. He said he just didn't think of anything—did not think of the consequences.

___

*Schacht's Cell:* Schacht said he was playing solitaire just to quiet his nerves. He had refused to watch the film on German concentration camps, but this was atrocities in the East. I failed to get the distinction . . . He said it was a disgrace not only for Germans but for all mankind that such atrocities could have taken place. He reminded us again that he had been thrown into concentration camp himself.

"After this trial is over, it would be much smarter if you let us Germans track down and sentence the guilty parties. I assure you the judgment would be much more severe than you would make it.—It is a disgrace against Germany. You can sentence the guilty leaders. But only Germans could track down every last murderer who gave such orders or executed them."

___

## February 21

### FRITZSCHE BREAKS DOWN

LUNCH HOUR: Fritzsche was sitting depressed in his corner of the "Youth" lunchroom, not joining in the discussion which the others indulged in, using my presence as an excuse to circumvent the no-communication rule. After the prisoners went back to the dock, I saw Fritzsche struggling to avoid crying, and he put on his dark glasses to hide his eyes, although the bright lights were not turned on. I went over to say something, but he shook his head to signify that I should not make him talk. I noticed him again during the afternoon intermission, and he was still evidently choking back tears. I handed him a note saying that if he didn't feel well, I could have him sent back to the cell. He wrote in answer: "It will only attract more attention.—But I am at the end of my rope.—I shall have to stick it out today."

——————— EVENING IN JAIL ———————

*Fritzsche's Cell:* After the showing of the film on the destruction of Russian cities and cultural monuments, I went down to meet Fritzsche in his cell. He was pale and miserable, his facial muscles taut with effort to prevent bursting ino tears. He spoke haltingly, choking with every phrase. "I have—the feeling—I am drowning in filth—whether theirs or ours—it is immaterial—I am choking in it—."

I asked him whether the Russian atrocity film had affected him that way. I could feel the cot shaking as he choked his silent crying.

"Yes—that was the last straw—. I have had the feeling—of getting buried in a growing pile of filth—piling up week after week—up to my neck in it—and now—I am choking in it—." I remarked on how easily Goering was taking it all and simply brushing off the Russian atrocity evidence with easy propaganda slogans. He cursed Goering as a "thick-skinned rhinoceros" who was disgracing the German people. " . . . I cannot go on.—It is a daily execution."

I told him I would have the German doctor give him a sleeping pill and see Major Goldensohn about having him excused from court tomorrow.

## February 22

## RESISTANCE TO GOERING STIFFENS

LUNCH HOUR: In the Elders' lunchroom I started another discussion about the sins of aggressive war and the guilt of the Nazi leaders, to see how the separation was affecting the attitudes of von Neurath, von Papen, Schacht, and Doenitz toward Hitler and Goering (since they did not identify themselves as "Nazi leaders"). Schacht came over and took the aggressive lead as expected.

"They were gangsters! I recognized that already in 1937. The only leading statesman who saw the danger even earlier was Roosevelt!" Goering was pacing the hall outside, taking his 8-minute walk, and was cocking a surreptitious ear at the door, stopping in the doorway on purpose to stretch himself. Schacht noticed it, and so did they all, but he kept right on in spiteful glee. "—And turning the economy of Europe topsy-turvy—destroying the peaceful economy I tried to build up—deliberately plunging into war —looting, corruption, reckless destruction—that was the kind of leadership our country had, my dear Dr. Gilbert." This preview of Schacht's defense was interesting because of its open call to arms against Goering's and Hitler's leadership. Doenitz sat taking it all in, watching Goering posturing at the doorway, trying to make his presence felt.

Von Papen and von Neurath got up enough courage to blame Goering for their respective indictments, not quite loud enough for him to hear, but loud enough for Doenitz to hear. "You know the forceful Anschluss was really his fault too," von Papen said.

Von Neurath smiled. "The same goes for the Czechoslovakian affair—the fat one was responsible for that too—it was all his fault." The three old men grinned with satisfaction at the open agreement on putting the blame "where it belongs," and not being kept under Goering's moral pressure to support Hitler and blame the Allies for everything.

—————————— February 23-24 ——————————

## WEEK END IN JAIL

*Speer's Cell:* Speer repeated that the new order made him feel much freer to plan his defense according to his original intentions. It is apparent that the consciousness of Goering's isolation and the breaking up of the "united front" has removed the sole obstacle to his willingness to denounce Hitler and the whole Nazi State for the fraud that it was. He said he hoped that the German people would realize that it was Hitler and not the Allies who were to blame for their present misery.

"When I think back of how black things looked to me last March and April—when I realized that Germany would be lucky if it could exist on a bare subsistence level for the next ten years—. And now things are comparatively quiet—there is no starvation, bridges are being rebuilt—. All I had hoped for was that the German people would not starve to death.—I even told Doenitz after the Armistice, when he wanted to oppose an Allied Military Government, that we ought to be glad we didn't have to take the responsibility for ruling Germany in the desperate straits in which the prolonged war had left it."

"Goering wants to tell the people that the Nazi leaders tried to save Germany, but their enemies insist on exterminating her. I guess his last heroic gesture will be to sow the seed for another final catastrophe."

"That is why I told von Schirach that if Goering wants to play hero, he should have done it before, instead of doping himself up and collecting loot. As far as the Nazi leaders are concerned, they ought to be glad that the Allies are saving Germany from the mass starvation and ruin that Hitler forced the country into. Do you know how you could have discredited Nazism once and for all? Just by letting our administration stay and rule Germany. All you had to say was, 'Go ahead, try to govern yourselves; you made your bed, now lie in it.—We won't interfere, but it is not our responsibility to feed you. You started it; now finish it.'—Why, Germans would simply have starved by the million."

"You can say all this at the trial," I replied.

"I will—and as an expert in production, I can bring it out quite clearly, and I think the people have respect for my opinions."

He commented that the indications of Goering's line of defense given by his attorney did not sound like such heroic stuff either, and he thought that even thàt pose might fall flat. The proposed witnesses like Goering's former associates in the Air Ministry, Milch and Bodenschatz, knew him too well to have too much to say in support of Goering.

I commented that a common feature of the militarists' defense was a blind insistence on the principle that orders were orders, and they were not too deeply concerned with matters outside of their individual chain-of-command.

"I don't know how you feel about it," I said, "but I am convinced that if there is to be peace in Europe, German militarism must be wiped out." Speer agreed.

He seems sincere in his present anti-militaristic, anti-Hitler convictions, however belated and materialistic these convictions may be.

"How could you play along with a monster like Hitler so long?" I asked.

"I must admit that was weakness on my part," Speer replied. "I don't want to make myself any prettier than I am. I should have and actually did realize it sooner, but kept playing at this hypocritical game until it was too late—well, because it was easier. I know, for instance, that I could have and should have taken my stand of opposition at least as early as the 20th of July 1944. But even though I was on the list of post-assassination ministers, I didn't actually take any part in the plot. But anyway, after the plot failed and my name was revealed to be on the list, then at least I should have said, 'I do think we are pursuing a reckless policy!' and I should have insisted on a showdown, or something, or tried another plot, which I did later anyway. But I just wriggled out of it, and said I couldn't help it if the assassins had put down my name for their cabinet, and I still supported Hitler. That was the kind of weakness and hypocrisy I accuse myself of, because I had begun to realize even then that Hitler was playing havoc with German lives and resources; but I put the thought away. It was too dangerous. It is easy to rationalize things—patriotism in war, and all that. That is my guilt, and I don't deny it."

In the course of the conversation he mentioned that Goering
had tried to seize the government in April. I asked him whether
this was the occasion on which Goering was invited to take over
the government. We did not seem to understand each other, until
it became clear that Goering had lied to me in saying that he had
been requested to take over the government. Speer was present
with Hitler and Bormann when Goering's telegram arrived, and
he remembered distinctly that there was no indication of any
previous telegram having been sent Goering authorizing him to
take over the government. That was why Hitler was in such a rage
over the uncalled-for approach on Goering's part. Goering had
merely acted on the theory that Hitler was cut off from the possibility of exercising his authority, and wanted to make himself boss.

"Then Hitler had some reason to suspect Goering of trying to
pull a fast one," I suggested.

"Naturally. I even accused him of it in Mondorf, because I
didn't want to tip my own hand as a would-be Hitler assassin.
Later he got sore because I accused him of treason, while I had
plotted against Hitler myself."

The most interesting part about this revelation to me is the easy
convincing manner in which Goering can lie and distort facts to
Americans who do not know the inside story, and attempt to keep
the whip hand over the defendants to prevent the truth from leak-
ing out.

———

*Ribbentrop's Cell:* I entered Ribbentrop's cell and started the
conversation with some offhand remark about how hard he was
working on his defense.

"It is very difficult to prepare a defense under these circumstances," he answered. "—Very difficult, indeed.—You see they
have even denied us the three-week recess we asked for.—It is
very difficult.—There are so many documents—."

"By the way, how did that Russian Non-Aggression Pact actually come about? Was it a sudden inspiration, or was it under consideration for a long time? I can hardly imagine that it was a long-
standing policy to arrive at an understanding with Russia, when
you had the Anti-Comintern Pact."

"Well, it was a comparatively sudden thing; it all happened
within a couple of months. It was my idea, you know.—I always

approved of co-operation between Germany and Russia." He passed right over the inconsistency of these two statements. "You know, I was not an ideological fanatic like Rosenberg or Streicher or Goebbels.—I was an international businessman who merely wanted to have industrial problems solved, and national wealth properly preserved and used. If Communism could do it—all right; if National Socialism could do it—all right too." His materialistic opportunism is thinly-veiled to say the least. He maintains a pose of social broadmindedness and statesmanship, but there is hypocrisy implicit in virtually every sentence. "It is these social problems and industrial crises which bring about wars—it wasn't merely a quarrel over Danzig [cf. Feb. 12].—But really, England could have prevented the war by merely saying one word."

"What word?"

"*Do it.*—That is all.—If they just told the Poles to do it—the whole war would have been avoided. Our demands were so reasonable.—It wasn't necessary to go to war over it."

Again the old line. I asked him whether the Russian Non-Aggression Pact hadn't actually been concluded merely to have a free hand in waging war against Poland.

"No, you cannot say it was as simple as that.—We wanted a peaceful solution with Poland.—You must remember that in diplomacy things are not so simple.—It is all very complex—very difficult—very difficult."

"No doubt.—Anyway, why couldn't you at least keep your Non-Aggression Pact with Russia? It seems to me that was your last fatal blunder, aside from the moral issue."

"Oh, I was in favor of keeping the peace with Russia all the time. After all, the pact had my signature on it.—Yes, I was strongly in favor of peace with Russia—right up to March, 1941. I felt we *could* do business with Russia . . . When I first went to the Winter Palace, what did I see but a painting of Czar Nikolaus with his peasants—which shows that even the Communists themselves revered a Czar who worked for the good of the people, and I told Hitler about it, and I said that the Communist revolution is in a stage of reasonable evolution, and that we could arrive at an understanding with them."

"If that was so, why did you attack them?" We've been on

this merry-go-round once before, but I was giving it another fling.

"Well, the war guilt does not lie entirely on one side.—I believe that Hitler feared just what has, after all, actually taken place." He seemed to have a bright idea.

"And what is that?" I asked.

"The destruction of Germany," Ribbentrop beamed, as if he had proven his point with a *reductio ad absurdum.*

"Wasn't that all the more reason to avoid war instead of precipitating it?"

He weighed the argument in confused silence for a while, wondering where he had left the loophole. Finally he sighed weakly, "Well—history will have to decide that."

"History will decide that Hitler was the most terribly destructive maniac of modern times."

"Oh, he was hard, perhaps, but not cruel. Himmler was the cruel one. He must have gone insane in the last few years. I believe he must have talked Hitler into it."

"How do you mean?"

"Well, Himmler had the cruelty of a schoolmaster—a man who makes up his mind pedantically, and cannot be swayed by any human considerations—"

"That is what most people realize now about Hitler. The two must have understood each other very well."

Ribbentrop was greatly relieved when the guard told him it was time for chapel services.

---

*Sauckel's Cell:* Still tremorous and anxious, his line of defense is essentially unchanged: He only did his duty by the Fatherland in time of war. He was under the impression that the foreign-Bolshevistic-Jewish-capitalistic world had forced the war on Germany, but of course he realizes now that it was all propaganda. He spoke about how he idolized honest work, how terrible the inflation and unemployment had been, and how decently he had tried to treat the foreign workers in Germany, how good a Christian he was, etc.

"I still cannot see how you can reconcile dragging millions of foreign citizens out of their homes to work in Germany with your Christian principles or any standards of morality and human rights."

"Well," Sauckel stuttered nervously, "—you must realize it was war—and we had gone through a lot already, and I was given this assignment which I could not refuse—and besides, I did everything possible to treat them well.—Here, I have the books which show what my policy was: [reads] 'A well-fed worker is a good worker.' etc. . . . —Those terrible things that happened in concentration camps.—I had absolutely nothing to do with those things . . . "

---

*Goering's Cell:* Somewhat frustrated in his aggressive cynicism and domination of the environment, he is now striking the pose of the misunderstood affable humanitarian. He scraped his mess kit with bread and pleaded between mouthfuls, "Really, professor—there is something you have got to understand. I am not a callous monster who has no use for human life. It is not that atrocities make no impression on me.—But I have seen so much already—the thousands of maimed and half-burnt bodies in the first World War—the starvation—. And in this war, the women and children burnt to death in air attacks. It is all right for Fritzsche to break down over the films so that he has to stay out of court—but all he had to do during the war was read an announcement over the radio that Berlin or Dresden has suffered another terror-attack and so-and-so-many people died. But I went and *saw* the corpses—sometimes still burning—because I was *Luftfahrtminister* [Air Minister]. I don't have to see a film to be horrified."

"I should think you would have had your belly full of war and destruction from the first World War and not relish a repetition of those horrors."

"Why, yes, of course, but don't forget it did not depend on me. I did everything I could to stop it.—I told you how I even negotiated behind Hitler's back.—And I am sure that Hitler would have been willing to get what he wanted without war—if he could get it cheap, so to speak."

"But *did* you do everything you could? Did you revolt? Did you assassinate him? Did you even resign? Anything would have been justified if you really wanted to avert such a catastrophe."

"Well, now, let us even assume that I had resigned—something which was, of course, completely irreconcilable with an officer's honor and patriotism. But let us assume that I had. Do you think that would have changed anything? Not a damn bit.—Then Kesselring or Milch or Bodenschatz or somebody else would have become Chief of the Luftwaffe, and things would have gone on just the same. Or let us say that he gave an order and I countermanded it. Do you think anybody would have paid attention to me? Why, Hitler wouldn't even have bothered having me shot. He would simply have said 'Poor Goering, don't pay attention to him, he is just a little sick in the head.' Don't you see? Such things were simply unheard of."

I told him that I thought it was all well and good for him to take whatever stand he pleased in court, but the others had an equal right to defend themselves as they saw fit. This brought the heroic actor out of him quite frankly.

"Ah, but you mustn't value life too highly, my dear professor. Everybody has to die sooner or later.—And if I can have the chance to die as a martyr, why so much the better. Do you think everybody has that chance? If I can have my bones put in a marble casket that is, after all, a lot more than most people achieve.— Of course, it may not even be my own bones. It is the same as Napoleon and Frederick the Great—the French have robbed their graves a dozen times—or like the pieces of wood from the True Cross. I've always said that if you put all the pieces of wood from the 'True Cross' together you could build a forest—hahaha! No, it may not even be my own bones—but it is the idea behind it."

---

*Hess's Cell:* Hess complained of continual stomach cramps and disturbance of his sleep by the guards. He did not know whether it was *intentional* disturbance (stuttered over word *intentional*, as if afraid to reveal his delusions of reference and persecution). He was not sure whether the colonel alone was behind it, or somebody else higher up. The stomach cramps and disturbance of sleep were interfering with his concentration. He was not bothering much with his defense, but he was preparing his final rebuttal speech, and he needed his concentration for that. I asked him whether he considered this an interference with his defense.

"Well, maybe the opposition considers this disturbance necessary to reduce my concentration ability.—I cannot imagine any other purpose." He said it with his usual apathetic seriousness, making slight gestures and shrugs of the shoulder to allow room for a reasonable doubt, so that it would not be thought he was paranoic, if it was not in fact so. That is the extent of his reality testing. It does not prevent him from seriously entertaining such ideas, however.

I asked him about Ohlendorf, Bach-Zelewski, Lahousen, witnesses whom every defendant remembered only too well, who had testified about the mass murder program of the Nazis. Hess tried to recall them, but their names had only become vaguely familiar, and he seemed to be confused about it all. He remembered the Russian atrocity film, shown 3 days ago, but was vague about the American atrocity film, shown almost 3 months ago. He remembered von Paulus who testified 2 weeks ago, fairly well. I checked with him again on the duration of the trial, and he still thought it had been running 6 months. I told him it had started November 20, and then he computed it to be 4 months. (Actually 3 months.)

In summary, the present state of his memory seems to be: fairly good memory for events of the past week or two, but substantial dimming-out of even significant events for the past few months and earlier.

Before the interview was terminated, he complained once more about his stomach cramps and the continual disturbance at night. "I still cannot see what sense the noise at night has unless it is to interfere with my concentration on purpose.—Otherwise it makes no sense." I told him I would look into it.

---

# February 27

## SURVIVORS TESTIFY ON EXTERMINATION

MORNING SESSION: *A surviving Jewish resident of Vilna told how all but 600 of the 80,000 Jewish residents of Vilna were exterminated by special commandos, and babies, including his own, were killed at birth. Colonel Smirnov then continued to describe*

from documents, experiments on concentration camp inmates, the
wholesale murder of sick people in hospitals, etc.

Then a woman prisoner from Auschwitz, Severina Shmaglev-
skaya, described the treatment of women and children there.
Babies born in camp were taken away immediately and never seen
again. She demanded with suppressed bitterness, "In the name
of all the women of Europe who became mothers in concentration camps, I would like to ask German mothers, 'Where are our
children now?'" [Several of the defense attorneys bit their lips.
As she went on to describe how Jewish children were thrown alive
into the crematorium furnaces during the rush season of 1944, most
of the defendants lowered their heads. Funk turned his back on
Streicher and leaned sickly on the back of the bench. Frank
flushed; Rosenberg fidgeted. Goering solved the problem as usual
by taking his earphones off. Hess hadn't even been listening.]

------

LUNCH HOUR: At the end of the session, before going to lunch,
Doenitz' naval attorney, Dr. Kranzbuhler, asked him, "Didn't
anybody know anything about any of these things?" Doenitz shook
his head and shrugged sadly.

Goering turned around. "Of course not.—You know how it is
even in a battalion—a battalion commander doesn't know anything that goes on in the line. The higher you stand, the less you
see of what is going on below." I could hardly have thought of a
more damning argument against the military hierarchy, but
Goering, in his militaristic perversion, thought he had given a reasonable explanation.

After they went up to lunch Goering started to complain to
me that he had been seated in the cold room again. I did all I
could to restrain myself.

"Why don't you listen to the evidence?" I asked.

"Because I don't have to listen to the same stuff a thousand
times," he grumbled nervously.

In each of the other five lunchrooms, everybody was quietly
eating his lunch, and after looking at me, showed no desire to
start a conversation. I went over to Jodl and asked him whether
he thought it was possible that nobody knew anything about any
of the things mentioned today. Kaltenbrunner was sitting in the
next corner.

"Of course, somebody knew about it," Jodl said quietly. "There was a whole chain-of-command from the Chief of the RSHA down to the people who executed those commands."

I then walked over to Kaltenbrunner. "I suppose you didn't know anything about these things either."

"Of course not," he whispered. "The people who did are all dead.—Hitler, Himmler, Bormann, Heydrich, Eichmann—"

"Did those few people have the sole knowledge and responsibility for the murder of millions of people and the burning of children alive?"

"Well, no—the people who actually participated in it did—. But I had nothing to do with it."

"Even as Chief of the RSHA?"

"Concentration camps were not my responsibility. I never found out anything about any of this."

In the Elders' lunchroom the old men shook their heads. Doenitz buried his nose deeper in his paper. Only Schacht had the courage after a few minutes of uncomfortable silence to hark back to the subject of how he had tried to stop the radical tactics of the Nazis early in the regime. He said that he had protested against the Gestapo methods, the persecution of the Jews, etc., always giving the excuse that it was "bad for business," because Hitler would not even listen to any other reason. The American Ambassador had acquainted him with Roosevelt's proposal that armaments be limited to that which a man could carry on his back. He had urged Hitler to support the proposal, but Hitler had told him it was impractical, and anyway, he should stick to his own business.

In the Youth lunchroom, I made some more remarks about nobody knowing anything about anything, and about the propagandists who blithely advocated getting rid of the Jews then saying they had nothing to do with the persecution and finally the extermination. Fritzsche tried to explain that the propaganda line as he knew it was merely to separate the Jews. I pointed out that this was the first step to mass murder. He flushed and showed signs of breaking down again.

---

AFTERNOON SESSION: *A former inmate of Treblinka extermination camp described how the sorting out and extermination of victims took place—10 minutes after arrival for the men; 15 minutes for*

*the women, because their hair had to be cut off first. A fake rail-*
*way station had been set up to make the arrivals think it was only*
*a stop-over on their "resettlement" journey.*

———————————— **February 28** ————————————

LUNCH HOUR: In the Elders' lunchroom Doenitz warned that the
Germans must have the feeling that they are being treated justly,
if they are to be won over to co-operating with the Allies. "Don't
forget that the Germans themselves are the first to resent the betrayal by their leaders." It is interesting to note that Doenitz
has finally come around to the betrayal theme in open discussion,
showing the effect of separation from Goering. "I must say, I was
furious over the idea of being dragged to trial, in the beginning,
because I did not know anything about these atrocities. But now,
after hearing all this evidence—the double-dealing, the dirty business in the East—I am satisfied that there was good reason to try to
get to the bottom of the thing." It certainly sounded quite different from the Doenitz who had pronounced the indictment "typical American humor" in the beginning.

They then began vying with each other in apologetic defensive
explanations of their previous attitudes toward the trial. This was
probably partly for my benefit as an American officer whose opinion might be of some consequence, but had the effect of autosug-
gestion and social suggestion in bringing out the latent anti-Hitler,
anti-Goering resistance.

"I have no objection to the trials," Schacht declared. "It is
only my *treatment* as a prisoner.—I have no objection to the trials
at all. I think the Nazi leadership *should* be exposed!"

"I am perfectly willing to accept my year of imprisonment as
my sacrifice to the cause of exposing the Hitler regime to the German people," von Papen contributed. "The German people must
see how they have been betrayed, and they must also help to wipe
out the last remains of Nazism."

"We can also say that in the trial," Schacht urged.

"Yes—of course," the other three agreed.

"And the vengeance of the decent Germans will be much
sharper and more thorough than anything the Allies could do,"

Schacht continued. " . . . But I must say, Roosevelt was the only one who saw the Hitler administration for what it was from the very beginning, and he was the only one who never sent a representative to a single Party meeting—not one."

Doenitz took out a paper he had been saving in his wallet, with a quotation from a Roosevelt fireside chat on April 17, 1938. "Here—even Roosevelt knew that the Germans abandoned democracy only because of their state of desperation." He read the statement, quoting Roosevelt as saying that some nations have left democracy because of their confusion, desperate straits, and lack of leadership.

"Yes, Roosevelt was the only one who really saw what we were heading for," Schacht repeated.

I mentioned a remark Goering had made to the contrary. "*Ach,* what that fat one says!" Schacht exclaimed. "You don't have to pay any attention to that! That blustering windbag is liable to blame anyone but himself!"

"Yes," von Papen agreed, "he can shoot his mouth off about anything, but it won't help him."

"All he is good for is smashing windows," von Neurath added with a contemptuous grin.

──────────── March 2–3 ────────────

## WEEK END IN JAIL

*Ribbentrop's Cell:* He was working on his defense papers as usual, looking disheveled and confused, and I resumed our discussion on the Russian pact and attack.

I said that some people speculate on the theory that the Russians and Germans had prearranged the partitioning of Poland at the time of the signing of the Non-Aggression Pact.

"No—that is not so," Ribbentrop said with his usual lack of conviction. "You know, diplomacy is not as simple a matter as it sometimes seems.—Of course, the possibility of a war with Poland was recognized and discussed at that time.—But the pact was signed in absolutely good faith by Hitler and me. There are, of course, those who claim that the Russians purposely entered into the pact to serve their aggressive purposes.—I do not know about that, but that is what some people say."

"But I thought that the pact was your idea—."

"Well, yes—." He puffed on his pipe, fishing for a rationalization of the inconsistency. "But the Russians made the first move —that is certain." He puffed some more. "Yes, they have their ways of doing these things—that is certain." (One can almost count the expressions of hypocrisy by the number of times he says "that is certain.") "Why should people think it was a prearranged affair?" He asked me.

"Because they think it looks suspicious that Russia and Germany partitioned Poland without any serious disagreement on the matter."

"Oh, but the Russians grabbed their part of Poland after the war was won—that is certain." He kept puffing on his pipe, and made no further attempt to show how this justified his denial. I began to have the distinct feeling that he had become demoralized to the point of not caring how clumsily he lied or what sense his statements made.

He continued to discuss the great power of the Russians. Tito is a Comintern man; Franco is on the spot in Spain, and that means Juan Negrin will come to power—another Moscow man. "Russia will surely rule all of Europe and Asia.—But maybe it is for the best—I do not say it is all wrong. Such a change must come about—that is certain. They are a tremendous power. I don't know how England will protect itself against this power. Or the Americans either."

---

*Von Papen's Cell:* He had been reading a translation of an article on militarism from the *Saturday Evening Post,* which had been printed in a German newspaper. He was slightly disappointed at my not bringing any newspapers, because if he should ever be freed, he would want to be informed on current affairs.

"Yes, especially if you want to enlighten the people on the sins of the Nazi leadership," I remarked.

"Exactly. That is the main problem. As this article says, militarism destroys the independence of the individual.—It violates

Christian teachings of the dignity of man."

"—And maintains illusions of heroism and a hypocritical code of honor and fair play—like the assassination order from Keitel, the looting and highway robbery of Goering—the completely amoral code which recognizes no law but 'orders are orders!' "

"You are absolutely right, *Herr Doktor*," von Papen said emphatically. "And don't you think it will be even more effective when a German tells that to the people?"

Von Papen began to work himself into a frenzy over the militarists, his face taking on a Mephistophelean expression, as it always does when he bares his teeth and twists his eyebrows. "—This evil suppression of individual freedom of thought—this contempt for everything that does not agree with the militaristic concept of rigid attention before superior officers!—This degradation of human dignity!—The perversion of the youth!—The people must be re-educated—entirely re-educated! I think that the propagandists who spread and encouraged this worship of militarism are more guilty than anybody else! Goebbels said, 'We must use the tactics of the Catholic Church to hammer our ideology into the German Youth.' But how in heaven's name can we compare this evil ideology with the moral precepts of the Christian religion?—Why, the Nazi ideology was the very antithesis of everything that was moral or worthy of the dignity of man!"

We went on to discuss the broader issues of solving the economic problem by some kind of social control, without restricting the freedom of the individual as a dictatorship did, but rather for the sake of liberating the individual to enjoy life according to his inclinations and capabilities. He said he would like to express some of these ideas at the trial, but was afraid that the court might confine him to answering questions about the charges against him.

Later in the day I brought back yesterday's newspaper for him to read. I pointed out the article quoting *Pravda* as saying that the Vatican was still pro-Nazi and mentioning von Papen's Concordat with the Pope as the beginning of the policy.

"Well—of course, the Russians must maintain their anti-Church policy—but actually, the Pope did not support Hitler. I had decided that since these radical elements came into power, it was high time to settle the question of Church rights legally. The Pope agreed with me.—We merely arranged an understanding on the questions of education of youth, Church property, etc. I favored a similar understanding with the Protestants too—but actually the chief resistance to the Nazis came from the Catholics. The Protestants were so divided, they had no control over their people, and they were in no position to take a united stand against the Nazis—except for Pastor Niemoeller, and a few others. I do not mean that they offered no resistance, but the Catholic Church was certainly not pro-Hitler."

"No, I am sure there was no love lost between the two. Himmler, Hitler and Bormann certainly showed their hatred, and I understand they planned to wipe out the Church hierarchy after the victory." (I was using information I had gotten from Lahousen.)

Von Papen nodded in acquiescence. "—I was also disappointed in Goering. I thought that since he came from a different circle—his father was a high official in the Kaiser's court—I assumed he was brought up with a certain amount of moral scruple and would oppose Hitler's radical policies.—But instead, I saw how he kept praising Hitler to the skies in his Reichstag speeches, and offering no protest whatever against the excesses." Goering was apparently right in saying that Hitler was glad to use him because of his following among the Junker-officer group.

"I did what I could," von Papen continued. "I even told the King of Sweden he ought to use his influence to convince Hitler of the falseness of his anti-Semitic policy. I have requested a questionnaire be submitted to him to confirm this."

---

*Von Neurath's Cell:* He was smoking the second of the two cigars I had given him on his birthday, and welcomed me into his cell. In anticipation of his defense, he reviewed his disagreement with Hitler over the Hoszbach speech, and went on to describe his part in the Munich and Czechoslovakian affairs. When Chamberlain had offered to come and discuss the Sudeten question to avert war, he went to urge Hitler to do so, even though he was no longer Foreign Minister. He virtually had to force his way in to see Hitler, and succeeded in inducing him only by virtue of his assurance that Mussolini was in favor of such a pact. Then Hitler said, "All right, if Mussolini is in favor of it, I am willing to listen." Von Neurath put through the telephone connection to Mussolini, and an understanding was reached. When Chamberlain and Daladier

came, he greeted them, and later asked Daladier whether they
shouldn't consult the Czechs on the Sudeten issue. (I had asked
him why that had not been done.) "So, do you know what
Daladier says to me?—This really should not be repeated too loud.
—He says, 'The Czechs will just have to carry out what we decide.' That is the way it was.—But after the pact had been signed,
he got a little worried about it, and said, to me, 'I suppose I'll get
stoned for this when I get home.' I told him that he could be sure
he would be greeted with jubilation when he came home, for having averted a war. And that is the way it was. Both he and Chamberlain were greeted with wild jubilation because everybody
believed that the peace of Europe had been saved."

---

*Hess's Cell:* He complained again that the severe stomach cramps
and disturbance of his sleep by the guards were diminishing his
concentration power. "Don't the others have the same trouble?"
he asked. I said that Ribbentrop and some of the others were also
having a little trouble of that sort. It was noteworthy that he
blocked on simple words and had difficulty expressing himself,
sometimes having to give up an idea altogether because he could
not find the proper words. Sometimes I had to supply a word. The
words on which he blocked were not necessarily emotionally-toned
or difficult. He said that he was having difficulty following the
trial now, because the abstract legalistic arguments (on the guilt
of the Party organizations) were too hard to follow. Sometimes
he finds his mind wandering and suddenly realizes that he has not
been paying attention.

I tested his recall of the main witnesses, and found that he had
not only forgotten the witnesses as of a week ago, but had already forgotten von Paulus as well, showing progressive partial
amnesia for events more than two weeks old. When I mentioned
von Paulus, he asked whether he had not appeared as a witness,
because his name sounded vaguely familiar.

"Can you recall anything about him?" I asked.

"I don't know—it seems to me that his name is somehow familiar in connection with being a witness"

"Don't you remember what he said?"

"No.—I cannot say that I do."

"Do you remember your flight to England and all the circumstances surrounding it?"

"I remember why I went, but not the details. Did I ever remember them before?"

"Yes, your memory was very clear two weeks after it returned. Now look here, Herr Hess," I adopted a professional tone, "I must help you refresh your memory. I want you to write down everything you can remember about your flight to England. Then we can compare it with the written interview you gave the press.—Do you remember that?" He did not. "Well, I will help you refresh your memory about your flight to England. Then I will refresh your memory about the witnesses.—You don't want to get up on the stand and say you don't remember, when they ask you questions about the testimony, do you, especially after you said you were simulating your amnesia?"

"No—no—."

I told him I would come back later in the day. After I left the cell, he promptly set about writing down his recollection of the flight to England. I also noticed that he had to lie down and think things over in the middle, and later continue writing. I returned to his cell about three hours later, and he had just finished a 300-word description of his flight and some of the circumstances surrounding it, but failing to mention many of the details he had previously recalled. I told him I would come back some other time with a list of questions to see how much more he remembered, and would see him weekly to keep refreshing his memory. "Of course, none of the others have to know about this," I added. The idea appealed to him.

──────────────── March 6 ────────────────

## CHURCHILL'S SPEECH

As they filed into the courtroom in the morning, the Reichstag fire was still the subject of sensational interest. (A news story had appeared over the week end, attributing the 1933 Reichstag fire

to Goebbels and Goering.) Ribbentrop asked some of the others
if they had heard about it, and everybody started talking about
it, since Goering was not yet in the dock. Schacht said again that
he had known about it all the time. Fritzsche said he had been
told at the time that the Communists had done it, and he never
questioned it. Jodl grinned, not at all averse to seeing the Luftwaffe chief openly discredited, and von Papen kept shaking his
head sadly. Frick was about the only one who refused to believe
the story, or at least entertain its plausibility, and claimed that
the Party did not need a Reichstag fire for propaganda purposes,
because they already had a majority, so the whole idea was silly.
The discussion stopped when Goering entered the dock, but he
seemed to sense an ever more strained coolness.

---

LUNCH HOUR: If Goering needed a change of subject to occupy
their attention, it was supplied by today's headline, "UNITE TO
STOP RUSSIANS, CHURCHILL WARNS AT FULTON."

"Naturally, I told you so," Goering said as he went up to lunch.
"It has always been that way. You will see—I was right.—It is the
old balance of power again." He continued when I dropped in on
him at lunch. "That is what they get for trying to balance us
off against the East. They could never make up their minds
whether to balance us off against the East or the West. Now
Russia is too strong for them, and they've got to counterbalance
her again." I asked him whether he thought that England had
made the Munich Pact as an invitation to expand eastward toward
Russia through Czechoslovakia. "Why, naturally," he said, as if
it was the most obvious thing in the world. "But then they got
afraid that Germany would be too strong. Now they've got Russia to worry about." He seemed to feel that it served Churchill
right for not allowing Germany to expand eastward without
hindrance from England.

In the Elders' lunchroom, von Papen read the headline, then
said, "*Donnerwetter, nochmal,* he is outspoken, isn't he?"

The others gathered around and von Papen began to read the
article aloud. "There!" declared Doenitz with some satisfaction,
"—now he is going back to his old line."

"Naturally, he welcomed Russia's help when he needed it,"
von Neurath observed, "but it is still the British Empire first and

last. He shouldn't have conceded so much to the Russians at Teheran and Casablanca."

"Yalta! Yalta!" Doenitz corrected. "That was the time. He didn't have to give in so much to the Russians when it was obvious that Germany was going to lose the war anyway. Now they've got the Russians in Thüringen.—That is what I wrote Eisenhower when I was still alive.—If they wanted to have a pro-Russian policy, all right—but if they did not want such a policy, they would have to make certain changes."

"Of course, it is only words now," von Papen observed. "Probably just a warning."

"Yes," Schacht suggested, after listening to the argument, "I suppose that the British Labor Party cannot very well say those things, so they tell Churchill to say it." The others thought that was probably the explanation, hinting that regardless of party, the empire must be preserved, and the Labor Party merely wanted Russia warned not to force a showdown over British policies in the East.

# 6. Goering's Defense

## THE FIRST DEFENSE WITNESS

This morning Goering was brought up early to have his picture taken. Obviously nervous, he did not take the delight that he has formerly taken in being photographed. As the courtroom began to fill, I remarked that he was at least going to play to a full house. He looked around, but was too nervous to take any satisfaction in the fact that he was the center of attraction again, especially since the context of my remark obviously did not imply an admiring audience. Hess remarked that he had just heard that his secretary had declined to appear as a witness. "Naturally," Goering remarked, "Why would a woman want to come into this hostile atmosphere. I would never subject a woman to this."

MORNING SESSION: [As Dr. Stahmer began his defense, Goering sat fidgeting very nervously, his hands trembling as he tried to write some notes, but he finally gave up writing and folded his arms akimbo; then changed his pose every minute. One could sense an intolerable strain in his being forced to face cold reality with cold facts, before a world that was too embittered by war and murder to appreciate bravado and horseplay.]

The first witness, Goering's adjutant, Bodenschatz, testified to the Luftwaffe's unreadiness for war in 1939 and Goering's attempts to negotiate with England behind Hitler's and Ribbentrop's back to avert war with England at that time. He also testified to the fact that Goering had taken many of his friends out of concentration camp. He attempted to show in various ways that his chief was just a peace-loving man. Prosecutor Jackson played havoc with his testimony upon cross-examination, revealing that Goering's motives may not have been so creditable as alleged, emphasizing his knowledge of unjustified arrests in concentration camps, his knowledge of plans for aggressive war, and in general tripping up the witness in a maze of uncertainty and self-contradiction.

LUNCH HOUR: As the courtroom cleared at the end of the morning session, Seyss-Inquart's attorney said to me, "Your American attorneys have a good deal of experience in cross-examination, and it is obvious that Mr. Jackson is one of the best."

At lunch many of the defendants expressed a malicious satisfaction at the way Mr. Jackson had made a monkey out of Goering's first witness. Jodl, who has no great love for Goering's code of conduct anyway, expressed a frank delight at the morning's proceedings. "That was a good show," he laughed. "That Bodenschatz was never a great brain anyway, but he sure didn't help Goering's case any. Your man Jackson is a clever prosecutor. I'd like to tangle horns with him myself."

In the Elders' lunchroom, Schacht was brimming over with joy at Goering's discomfiture. "The fat one is sure taking a beating so far!" he chortled. "Your Prosecutor Jackson is certainly a brilliant cross-examiner. Even when he is not sure what he will find, he beats on each bush to see if a rabbit jumps out—and sometimes it does." (Later Fritzsche claimed credit for that metaphor.) "It will be a pleasure to match wits with him." He called the score: 1 to 0 favor the prosecution.

The general effect on the Elders, however, was to make them somewhat concerned over their cross-examination. Von Papen, Doenitz, and Schacht agreed that the best technique in taking the stand was to talk without notes and answer the questions spontaneously, telling nothing but the truth, because the prosecutor could trip up anybody who tried to camouflage the truth.

Hess was still bellyaching about his bellyache, and Ribbentrop complained that he was by no means ready with his defense.

Goering was not very happy. "Well, now, really, that poor fellow has been through so much.—I wasn't sure if I should use him as a witness, but he is so loyal, he wanted to say a good word for his chief.—But wait till he [Jackson] starts on me—he won't have any nervous Bodenschatz to deal with . . . Anyway, I must say I am flattered. The chief of the prosecution himself has to cross-examine my witness." He nervously scraped his mess kit with a piece of bread, obviously neither amused nor flattered. I took out a cigarette and offered him one, knowing that he rarely smoked cigarettes. "Yes, today I think I'll take one," he said, taking one with trembling fingers. He went on to protest weakly against the unfairness of holding against him utterances he had made "in the heat of battle," and quoted equally "reckless" statements by General Doolittle and Lord Fisher.

────────── March 9-10 ──────────

## WEEK END IN JAIL

*Goering's Cell:* Goering was lying in bed with his clothes on, waiting for his attorney to call him. I told him that I had arranged for him to go to court early during the days of his defense, so that he could talk to his attorney, as he had requested, and that the defense finally having gotten under way, I was curious to see what the defendants had to say about their crimes. He propped himself up in bed on his elbow and said in a quiet, earnest voice: "—But there is just one thing I want you to know—really—you can believe it or not—but I must say in dead earnest—*grausam bin ich nie gewesen!* [I have never been *cruel*].—I'll admit I've been *hard*— I do not deny that I haven't been bashful about shooting 1,000 men for reprisals, or hostages, or whatever you please—but cruel —torturing women and children—*du lieber Gott!* that is so far removed from my nature—. Maybe you will think it is pathological of me—but I still cannot see how Hitler could have known about all those ugly details. Now that I know what I know, I wish I could just have Himmler here for 10 minutes to ask him what he thought he was pulling off there.—If only some of the SS generals had protested—."

"Then how can you condemn a man like Lahousen, who knew what was going on and did everything he could to sabotage this tyranny?"

Again the nationalist in him spoke louder than ever the alleged humanitarian: "Oh, but that is different—betrayal to the enemy—no, not that!—One could start a revolution, try an assassination even, anything—naturally running the risk of having one's own head chopped off.—That is anybody's privilege.—I even took that risk myself in 1923 in our putsch. I could easily have been killed instead of getting wounded.—Don't forget there is a difference between *Landesverrat* and *Hochverrat*." I asked him to explain the difference. "*Landesverrat* is treason of the Fatherland to a foreign power—there is nothing more shameful than that. *Hochverrat* is simply treason against the head of the State—that is a different matter."

"Considering that your little revolution—or beer-hall putsch, as we call it—was actually treason, I am surprised that you and Hitler got off so easily."

Here he laughed with the old foxy laugh. "Aha, naturally! Don't forget it was a Bavarian court and the Bavarians themselves were in cahoots with us, because they wanted to pull their own brand of revolution. Of course, what they wanted was separatism from North Germany, and a kind of Catholic alliance with Austria—but we Greater Germany patriots wanted just the opposite. So we strung them along with the idea of getting rid of the present government first and letting us get in—but naturally we had no thought of breaking up Germany for their Catholic alliance. Anyway, they couldn't afford to be too hard on us, because they also wanted to see the Weimar Republic overthrown."

The afternoon coffee had just been handed in by the guard and he sat up, thoughtfully dunking his bread in it, and swallowing both noisily.

"Well, you've had an interesting life," I observed.

"Yes, it has been interesting all right. I suppose if I had it to do all over again, I would avoid certain mistakes.—But what difference does it make? We don't have much to say about our fate. The forces of history and power politics and economics are just too big to steer. It stands to reason that England wished with all her heart that Germany would fight Russia so that she could keep her power and her empire, and it also stands to reason that the Russians therefore did not mind if we fought the Western powers." Again he grinned slyly. "You know, if I could just get hold of the good Sir David Maxwell-Fyfe over a glass of whiskey some night and have a heart to heart talk with him, I bet he'd have to admit that the British wished with all their heart that we would fight Russia.—Well, that's the way it is—the forces of history, overpopulation, and everything else determine the course of events. It doesn't matter who comes to power—it is an inescapable chain of events."

This historic fatalism is apparently his favorite ego-saving device, conveniently subordinating the moral issues to geopolitical forces. Otherwise social events are essentially the unfolding of a Greek tragedy, and he can at least take satisfaction in being one of the leading actors, rather than a member of the chorus.

---

*Frank's Cell:* Frank is becoming so absorbed in his own abstractions, that he is not even reacting with normal interest to the trial. When I asked him what he thought about Goering's defense, he waved it off as just running its normal course. "—But the court is no longer a God-willed court," he assured me, as though the change was objective rather than subjective. "If I were to give you my reaction again, I would not say it is a God-willed court. The Russians have no business in this court. Why, how dare they sit in judgment!"

He turned to the book he was reading. "I have been reading about the 30 Years' War, when the Catholics and Protestants slaughtered each other, and finally all of Europe was embroiled in the extermination of the German population.—And finally the Protestants and Catholics decided there was no reason why both couldn't preach the word of God." Again the high-pitched hysterical laugh.

"And now Germany has just gotten through another blood bath with a new kind of fanaticism," I observed. "Don't you think people will ever learn?"

"Ah, no," he sighed profoundly, "there is a curse on mankind. The lust for power and aggression is too strong."

It was an expert opinion, anyway.

---

*Ribbentrop's Cell:* Still tired and confused, Ribbentrop had nothing to say about Goering's case. I asked him what he thought about Goering's assertion that he had negotiated behind his back to reach an understanding with England. He shrugged his shoulders. "There were lots of things I did not know." He complained wearily that he would never have his defense ready in time.

---

*Von Papen's Cell:* Von Papen scoffed at Goering's defense. "Ach, he can defend himself from now till doomsday, but he will never explain away all he has done.—The court ought to stop wasting time and say 'Next case!' "

---

*Hess's Cell:* Lying in bed this afternoon, daydreaming, Hess did not at first know what I was talking about when I said I had come to review the matter he had written about last week. It was only after I prompted him, that he recalled that he had written down some details of his flight to England. Questioned on what he had written, he could only remember that he had undertaken the flight to arrive at an understanding with England to avoid bloodshed, and that he had hurt his leg in landing. Upon further urging, he could recall that he spoke to Sir John Simon. That was all, I then asked him whether he did not remember having broken his leg another time. He did not remember. I described the incident of the suicide plunge, but he evidently did not recall it. I asked him whether he recalled anything about difficulty with his food. He did not recall. Sealed packages? No. Does he have any suspicions about his food now? Yes, sometimes he thinks there is something in it that causes his stomach cramps. He did not remember any suspicions about the food in England. Did he have any trouble with his memory at that time? He could not recollect.

I then went on to test his recollection of the main witnesses of the trial, discussing the matter casually, to avoid the appearance of an actual test. The results were as follows:

General Lahousen, Ohlendorf, and Schellenberg—no recollection.

General von Paulus—name vaguely associated with trial.

General Bodenschatz—recalled as witness for Goering who appeared "within the last few days," and said he had burned his hands and lost some of his hearing during the assassination attempt against Hitler; did not recall any of testimony, and was startled when I told him that Bodenschatz had appeared only yesterday.

---

*Von Schirach's Cell:* Von Schirach felt embarrassed at the flop Bodenschatz had made, and wondered what he was supposed to prove anyway. He asked me whether Goering would be asked about his looting and other such uncomfortable questions. I told him I did not know.

Suddenly he asked me, "By the way, what is the matter with Hess?"

"Why do you ask?"

"Well, I must tell you something. About two weeks ago I discussed two questions which he was supposed to answer for me on the witness stand. The next day he told me he had the answers, knew all about it, and even remembered the date in question. So the day before yesterday I asked him about those two questions again, and he didn't even know what I was talking about . . . I looked at him and said, 'But Herr Hess, we discussed it only 8 days ago and you even remembered the date!' 'I am terribly sorry,' he says, 'but I simply cannot remember. Try as I may, I simply cannot keep my memory intact.' Now, what do you think of that?"

I said I knew that something like that was going to happen.

"Well, then I better not ask him any questions. It would certainly look funny if I ask him for testimony in court, and he says he does not remember."

--------- March 12 ---------

MORNING SESSION: *Goering's adjutant, the younger von Brauchitsch, Paul Koerner, his State-Secretary in Prussia, and Field Marshal Kesselring testified.*

[Of greater interest in the morning and luncheon discussions, however, was the headline, "MOSCOW CALLS CHURCHILL 'WARMONGER,' SAYS HE SEEKS TO SABOTAGE UNO." Goering giggled, "The only Allies who are still allied are the 4 prosecutors, and they are only allied against the 20 defendants." He rubbed his hands and chuckled with satisfaction.

"That's right," Doenitz said. "Churchill was always anti-Russian —that is what I have always said."

"Of course, I knew that all the time," Goering repeated.

Ribbentrop shook himself out of his depressed and confused lethargy just long enough to say, "Yes, it is just as I said—isn't it?"]

LUNCH HOUR: At lunch Ribbentrop asked to see the paper again. After reading the Churchill article again, he said, "There, you see, it is as I've always told you. The Russians are a strong power— very strong. Now England is worried, and America will lose interest and leave Europe. Don't you see, you will leave Germany at the mercy of the Russians. Why did you enter the war?"

"Why did you start it?" I retorted. "If you were afraid of the Russians, why didn't you keep your Non-Aggression Pact with Russia? Why didn't you keep the Munich Pact? Why was Hitler such a liar?"

At this point Hess suddenly jumped out of his corner, tightened his beltless pants' waist, and strode toward me, his sunken eyes flashing. "Herr Doktor, would an American officer stand for having a German call his dead Chief of State a liar?"

"Naturally not—because he wasn't a liar."

"Then I must ask you to refrain from saying that about our Chief of State," he snapped.

"I am quoting your own diplomats," I replied.

Hess strode back to his corner and sat down. Raeder stopped his pacing up and down long enough to tap Hess on the shoulder and say, "You are perfectly right. I didn't hear it, but you are right."

In the Elders' lunchroom, the discussion on the Churchill controversy took another turn. Von Papen took a conciliatory tone about the whole Churchill controversy. "Oh, it will cool off.—But it is just as well that somebody gives the Russians a warning that they cannot do what they please."

When I suggested that Hitler's cardinal mistake was the attack on Russia, Schacht corrected me with, "No, the cardinal mistake was attacking Poland in the first place."

"Yes," said Doenitz, "the guilt lies in starting the war. Once the war starts, an officer has no choice but to do his duty." (Doenitz has finally found a position which reconciles his own honor with his obedience to Hitler in spite of his guilt.)

"Speaking about cardinal mistakes," Schacht continued, "declaring war on America was the most catastrophic madness a statesman could possibly have made. I warned him about America's production potential."

"The 'statesman' in the next room doesn't seem to know that Germany declared war on us. He just asked me why we got into the war anyway," I remarked.

"Statesman!—Why, that scatter-brained idiot!!" Schacht sneered. "That is proof of Hitler's ignorance of foreign affairs."

"Statesman!" von Papen echoed. "Nitwit!"

The conversation then turned to the problem of solving the world's economic problems without war. Schacht objected to State Socialism, because it deprived the individual of freedom, initiative, and competition. He did not object to Socialism as such. All I could get out of it was that he seemed to favor "capitalistic Socialism."

---

## March 13

### GOERING TAKES THE STAND

Went down to see Goering in his cell before he came up to court, today being the day that he was likely to take the stand himself. There were signs of nervous tension in the slight tremors of his hands and the jerkiness of his facial expressions, and he began to rehearse his role as martyred nobleman about to enter the stage for the last act:

"I still don't recognize the authority of the court—I can say, like Maria Stuart, that I can be tried only by a court of peers." He smiled a little.

"Well," I observed, "that may have been all well and good in the days of royal sovereignty, but the issues at stake here go to the root of civilized existence."

"Nevertheless, anything that happened in our country does not concern you in the least. If 5 million Germans were killed, that is a matter for Germans to settle; and our state policies are our own business."

"If aggressive warfare and mass murder are nobody's business and not punishable offenses, then we might as well reconcile ourselves to the extermination of civilization right now!"

Goering shrugged his shoulders. "Anyway, bringing the heads of a sovereign state before a foreign court is a presumptuousness which is unique in history."

---

AFTERNOON SESSION: *In the afternoon session Goering started his personal defense on the witness stand. He began with a factual description of his background and decorations, his meeting with Hitler, his role and his motives in helping to build up the Nazi Party. He told how he took over the Storm Troops (SA) and whipped them into shape, how he participated in the beer-hall putsch. He became Nazi member of the Reichstag in 1928, President of the Reichstag in 1933, and helped Hitler to become Reich Chancellor in 1933. He also set up concentration camps in Prussia to intern Communists.*

-------- EVENING IN JAIL --------

*Goering's Cell:* He had returned his supper untouched, and was sitting on his cot, smoking his big Bavarian pipe. He admitted that he was too excited to eat tonight. "You must realize that after being imprisoned for almost a year, and sitting through this trial for 5 months without saying a word in court, it was really a strain for me—especially the first 10 minutes. The one thing that annoyed me, dammit, is that I could not keep my hand from shaking." He held out his hand. "There, you see, it is steadier now."

He was in a rather serious mood, seeking small consolation in his cynical fatalistic views. He called man the biggest *Raubtier* (beast-of-prey) of all, because he has the brains for large-scale destruction, while other beasts-of-prey merely kill to eat when they are hungry. He was sure that wars would become more and more destructive—it was all fate. There was an air of *Götterdämmerung* in the ill-defined space of the darkened cell. (He had told the guard not to turn on the light.) One could almost fancy him saying his lines to the echoes of Wagner's music.

*Speer's Cell:* I dropped in on Speer, and interestingly enough, he said that he was moved in spite of himself by Goering's speech, because it was obviously his swan song, and symbolized in a way the tragedy of the German people. "Seeing him so serious and stripped of his diamonds and decorations, making a final defense before a tribunal, after all the power, pomp, and bombast, it was really *erschütternd!* [gripping]."

Note: During the day, Ribbentrop's attorney took me aside and asked me if I had noticed anything strange about Ribbentrop lately. I said I thought he was slowly approaching a nervous break-down. He confided in me that he had been noticing for the last few weeks that he was actually suggesting himself into situations that were not so, and assuring him that he had not been at meetings which he had actually attended, so that half of his proposed defense was nullified on the lawyer's investigation. He had also done irrational things like addressing a letter to the Tribunal offering to be tortured to death for his unwitting allowance of such abominable atrocities. I said I thought this was all the outcome of a weak, suggestible character's frustrated ambition and pangs of conscience. He remarked that he was certain Ribbentrop was a gullible tool, but was not sure whether Ribbentrop or his wife was the more ambitious. He said he would give me more details of psychological interest after the defense is finished. He is obviously fishing for the possibility of a plea of insanity, although he admitted there was no question of Ribbentrop's responsibility for his actions.

---

## March 14

### GOERING STRUTS AS HESS AND RIBBENTROP WILT

Before the morning session started, I told them that von Blomberg had died last night. Keitel shook his head sadly. Goering, who was talking to his attorney, quickly turned around in the middle of a sentence, and said to Keitel, "We are all convinced that a man of honor has died," and then continued the sentence to his attorney. That was the official 5-second eulogy for former Field Marshal von Blomberg, once Commander in Chief of the German Wehrmacht.

I told Hess that von Blomberg had died. It did not register.—"So?"—I asked him if he knew who Field Marshal von Blomberg was. "One of our generals—" he answered, vaguely. I then told him that Haushofer and his wife had committed suicide. He said he remembered that a man by the name of Haushofer was supposed to give testimony for him, but he did not know anything

else about him. Neither by word nor expression did he give any
indication of having any recollection of the famous geopolitician
who was supposed to have inspired his flight to England. Von
Schirach was sitting behind him leaning forward intently, while I
was questioning Hess. He gave me bewildered looks as it became
obvious that Hess's memory for past events was indeed virtually
gone. After a while, Hess made one of his rare unsolicited remarks,
"I hope none of my other witnesses leave me in the lurch by
preferring death."

Then he looked around the court and remarked that it was almost full. I said it would probably be even fuller when he got up
to testify. He asked me why. "Because you created the major
sensation at the beginning of the trial," I said. That did not seem
to register either.

"Really?—How?" he asked.

"Don't you remember anything about the question of your
memory coming up early in the trial?" He shook his head. He had
already forgotten that he had forgotten to forget.

Ribbentrop came to court today without a tie and his collar
unbuttoned, his eyelids drooping, his left cheek twitching—an
even more bewildered expression on his face than usual: the picture of confusion and depression. There was considerable raising
of eyebrows when I called the former German Foreign Minister's
attention to the fact that he had come to court without a tie. He
replied wearily that his collar was too tight. I sent for the tie and
told him he could wear it without buttoning his collar. The impropriety was certainly not due to ignorance of form on the part
of the formerly proud emissary to the court of St. James.—Perhaps
it was an unconscious feeling that the noose was tightening around
his neck, and he was not ready to come to court, now that he had
actually seen the first Nazi defendant take the stand.

---

MORNING SESSION: Goering took the stand again and continued to
tell how he helped the Nazi Party build up its political and military power, including his version of the Roehm blood purge,
and the moves to keep the Church out of political and military
life—although some clergymen, unfortunately, had to be sent to
concentration camp in the process. [As he tried to justify the anti-
Semitic laws on the basis of the hostility the Jews had shown
toward the Nazi regime, many of the defendants hung their heads.

Funk covered his eyes and cried. Aside from that, the defendants listened with rapt attention and many signs of approval.] *He continued his recital of how the Party solved unemployment, rearmed, annexed Austria, for all of which he accepted a major share of the credit and responsibility.*

LUNCH HOUR: At lunch Goering asked me expectantly, "Well, how was it? You cannot say I was cowardly, can you?" he said proudly.

"No, I cannot say that. You took the responsibility for certain things that you should take the responsibility for. But that is only the beginning. How about aggressive war?"

"Oh, I'll have plenty to say about that too."

"And atrocities?"

He lowered his eyes. "Only insofar as I didn't take the rumors seriously enough to investigate them—." The last few words were swallowed. I read some of the day's headlines, and then sent him down to see his attorney, as prearranged.

In the other lunchrooms, the attitude was generally approving. Even Schacht said that everything Goering said was right, except for his attempt to show that the anti-Semitic measures were in any way justified. Doenitz expressed surprise that Goering had shown such sober self-control.

"That is the Goering of the early days," von Papen said, "—when he was still reasonable. But he said that 'outside of his charming personality, von Papen contributed nothing to the Party.' I must tell the court that I not only did not contribute, but tried to take away."

Fritzsche said that Goering described the early years of the Party exactly as it was, and he could refer to it in his own defense.

Von Schirach admitted that his heart was in his mouth while Goering was talking. I told him that I had actually observed that he swallowed and burped in gastric nervous tension.

Hess said that he could understand what Goering was trying to put over, but it was hard to follow because it was too much of a strain of concentration and he did not remember any of the background.

Rosenberg and Jodl said they agreed in general, but would have differences to explain. Rosenberg started a harangue on race,

*Kultur*, and *Lebensraum*, this time citing the Chinese desires to settle in Australia . . .

Down in the dock after lunch, Doenitz said, "Biddle is really paying attention. You can see that he really wants to hear the other side of the story. I wish I could meet him after the trial."

---

AFTERNOON SESSION: *Goering testified to his role in the Czecho-slovakian affair, the Polish and Norwegian campaigns. In the course of his testimony he commented that independence of opin-ion among the military leaders was unthinkable. "Perhaps this is the way to avoid wars in the future, if you ask every general and every soldier whether he wants to go home or not; but not only in the leadership of this state but in any state of the world the mili-tary formula is clearly defined."*

---

During the afternoon intermission Doenitz encouraged him to "shame the prosecution by giving a sample of decency and honor" in his manner of testifying.

Goering turned around. "Yes, I was really glad to get that word of honor to Czechoslovakia* straightened out, once and for all."

Doenitz repeated what he said, to make his meaning clear, shaming the prosecution with decency and honor.

"And good memory too," Goering added, making a scornful face at Hess as he got up from the dock to take his place again at the witness stand.

Someone asked Hess if he really was having trouble remember-ing things. He said he was. They told him he has got to remember. "I wish I knew how." Hess sighed feebly.

--------- EVENING IN JAIL ---------

*Goering's Cell:* In the evening, Goering was puffing his Bavarian pipe again, relaxing. "Yes, it is quite a strain," he admitted. "—And it is all out of memory. You would be surprised how few cue words I have jotted down to guide me.—As far as Hess is con-cerned, I must admit you have me licked. His memory is definitely shot, and I don't believe any more that he was faking in the first

---

*His assurance to Czechoslovakia that it would not be attacked at the time of the Anschluss, which, he explained, applied only to that occasion.

place. He even admitted a couple of weeks ago that he really had suffered amnesia in England, and said it wasn't all fake here either —just as you always said. On that score I am thoroughly convinced. God, what a farce it is going to be when he gets up to testify!"

──────────────── **March 15** ────────────────

LUNCH HOUR: Goering went down early to talk to his attorney, Dr. Stahmer, and his conversation was overheard by the guard.* Dr. Stahmer wanted to know whether he should bring up the matter of a certain meeting or contact with Himmler. Goering hastily rejected it. "No, no, thank God that hasn't come to light yet—I don't want to hear a thing about that."

He mentioned that he had had a little run-in with Rosenberg, because the latter apparently wanted him to say more about the anti-Semitic issue and the confiscation of art treasures. "I told him he will have to do that himself; I've got to think of myself at a time like this."

Commenting on the judges, he thought that Judge Lawrence was getting tired and wanted to go back to drink whiskey in London. He thought Judge Parker was a reasonable gentleman, and had given him a friendly look as he left court this morning.

Surveying the Hitler policy, he repeated that Hitler had tried to do too much too fast; and that he tried to force in 10 years what might have been achieved in 100 years, because he was afraid that anybody who came after him might not have the energy and persistence to see it through. Goering thought that the Danzig Corridor problem, for instance, could have been solved peacefully with a little more patience.

─────────────────

AFTERNOON SESSION: *Goering attempted to "explain" the attack on Yugoslavia, the bombing of Warsaw, Rotterdam and Coventry.*

─────────────────

*From this point on I always had 2 or 3 members of the court guard who could understand German report to me all overheard conversations. The word "overheard" hereafter refers to such reported conversations. I wish to express my indebtedness to Pfc. Beyer, Pfc. Conrad, Cpl. Albrecht, Sgt. Ohler, and Sgt. Gruener.

*He admitted discussing the plan to attack Russia as early as the fall of 1940, but he had advised Hitler to put it off until they had attacked Gibraltar, and to try to turn Russia against England.*

──────────── March 16-17 ────────────

## WEEK END IN JAIL

*Frank's Cell:* Frank was in a positive phase of his ambivalence toward Goering. "The one thing that pleases me about Goering is that he takes the responsibility for what he has done.—Of course, he dodges around the issue of those paintings—haha!—He is trying to get around that.—I did not send him a single one from Poland . . . It is going to be interesting when Jackson gets up to cross-examine him. Haha! The representative of Western democracy and Goering, the 'Renaissance figure.'—But I must say, I am pleased at the way Goering is conducting himself.—If he had only always been that way.—I told him today in jest, 'It is too bad you weren't thrown into jail for a year a few years ago!' Hahaha!" His sentences were interjected with the sharp, high-pitched hysterical laugh that is beginning to characterize his speech more and more. "Haha!—Now Goering finally has his wish—standing up at last as the No. 1 spokesman for the National Socialist regime—what's left of it!—Hahaha—hahaha! . . . "

───────────

*Von Schirach's Cell:* Von Schirach was very pleased with his hero. He thought it would be political madness to sentence him, because he is so popular, even in America, "—and now you can see why he was so popular." He thought Ribbentrop was far more guilty for the war. He pointed out that Goering had testified that he wasn't even in Berlin when the Munich Pact was broken, and it was clearly indicated that Ribbentrop was the man who influenced Hitler at the time, or at least acquiesced.

───────────

*Von Neurath's Cell:* Von Neurath was pleasantly surprised at Goering's line of defense, especially his taking the responsibility for many of his actions. It was more like the Goering of the early days, before he got puffed up with his vanity and ambition, corrupt and licentious living, etc.

His thoughts also turned to Ribbentrop as contemptible by comparison, and the reason was obvious. Ribbentrop was a four-flusher, not even a real nobleman. All von Neurath knew about his "nobility" was the fact that a lawyer had come to him to ask how he could collect the sum that Ribbentrop had promised to pay for his adoption to get his title. He felt Ribbentrop was also a pathological liar, like his master, Hitler. He had heard from the director of a sanatorium that Ribbentrop had been a patient there (in Dresden) in 1934. The doctor told him that he had to throw Ribbentrop out because he considered him a psychopath—a liar, irresponsible in his behavior—and even suspected him of abnormal sexual practices. With Hitler he was an "arse-licker."

---

*Speer's Cell:* Speer admitted that Goering was making a good impression on most of the defendants and defense attorneys, but assumed that Jackson would show him up when the cross-examination started. He was anxious to have Goering's heroic pose of loyalty and integrity stripped to its corrupt reality. "Why, when I last saw Hitler and the question of Goering's succession came up over that telegram, Hitler spoke with contempt that he always knew Goering was corrupt and disloyal.—Just imagine that—*always knew it*—and kept up the hypocrisy of keeping him as his true, loyal supporter! And now a corrupt coward like Goering —I could tell you about his private air raid shelters, and the soft life he led while Germany was in agony—a coward like that wants to play the hero. That's what burns me up!" However, he was satisfied with the freedom that was being given Goering to defend himself, so that Germans would never say that he was railroaded, and would realize that what was brought out of the trial was not a one-sided story.

---

*Funk's Cell:* Funk conceded that Goering and Schacht were strong personalities "—but the rest of us—I assure you I don't have the" stuff for heroism. I didn't then and I don't now. Maybe that is the trouble.—But I often wonder what I would have done if I had known these things before. I don't think I would have lived through it." He then began to blubber. "—But those atrocities— that remains a permanent shame.—No matter what Goering or anybody else says—no matter what sentences are pronounced— this systematic mass murder of the Jews remains a disgrace for the German people which they will not live down in generations!"

---

*Goering's Cell:* Goering was very tired from the strain of the past three days' testimony. His defense being almost completed, he was already moodily brooding over his destiny and speculating on his role in history. Humanitarianism had become a thorn in his side, and he cynically rejected it as a threat to his future greatness. The empire of Genghis Khan, the Roman Empire, and even the British Empire were not built up with due regard for principles of humanity, he expostulated with weary bitterness—but they achieved greatness in their time and have won a respected place in history. I reiterated that the world was becoming a little too sophisticated in the 20th century to regard war and murder as the signs of greatness. He squirmed and scoffed and rejected the idea as the sentimental idealism of an American who could afford such a self-delusion after America had hacked its way to a rich Lebensraum by revolution, massacre, and war. He clearly would tolerate no maudlin sentimentality to crab his entrance act into Valhalla.

---

*Rosenberg's Cell:* Rosenberg was impressed by Goering's defense, but said that much had yet to be explained about the looted treasures, libraries, etc. Rosenberg's thought for today: the Russians are whipping up all the colored races against the white race, and that is why Churchill is worried about the British Empire.

---

# March 19

## GOERING'S "STAR WITNESS"

MORNING SESSION: *Goering's chief witness, the Swedish engineer Dahlerus, began to testify how he had mediated Goering's efforts*

to arrive at an understanding with England to "prevent" war over
Poland. Dr. Stahmer tried to show that it was simply a matter of
reaching an agreement on Danzig and the Corridor. It soon became clear that the testimony showed merely how intent Hitler
was on war, and the big unnamed question loomed over the whole
proceeding: If Germany wanted to make a real attempt to avoid
war, why didn't the Foreign Minister negotiate?

LUNCH HOUR: At lunch the Elders were contemptuous of the
whole business. Schacht resumed his hostile attitude toward
Goering, after telling me that the score was about even. Von
Neurath called this amateur diplomacy "dilettantism without parallel."

Von Papen agreed emphatically. "Dilettantism is absolutely
right!—But that is the way German diplomacy was carried on
under Hitler.—A Swedish businessman! You can see how much
influence we elder diplomats had in that regime!"

As usual, Schacht showed that his own egotism was at the bottom of his indignation. "I had just come back from India myself.
I offered to negotiate, but all I got from Ribbentrop was 'Thank
you for your letter.' So there you are—a man of experience and
knowledge—after all, I had some knowledge of the situation—
must have nothing to do with the affair, but a foreign small-fry
businessman is given the job of negotiating with Great Britain by
that other expert statesman."

Seyss-Inquart sized up the whole situation as follows: "It is a
wonder the British took him seriously at all. You see, after he
established contact, they said, 'All right, contact has been established, now let us see the representative of the German Government.'—And when they saw that nothing further came of it, they
knew that it was not a serious intention expressed by the head of
the German Government.—Yes, it is a wonder that Lord Halifax
took it seriously at all."

Ribbentrop was sitting despondent in his corner of another
lunchroom. When I asked him what he thought of Dahlerus'
testimony, all he could say was, "Well, there were lots of things I
did not know."

As they filed down to the courtroom after lunch, Fritzsche said to me, "You will see—this defense witness will turn out to be a prosecution witness."

---

AFTERNOON SESSION: [Fritzsche was right.] *Under skillful cross-examination by Sir David Maxwell-Fyfe, the entire defense value of Dahlerus' testimony collapsed, and the witness actually ended up by denouncing the hypocrisy of the whole gesture. In the course of the cross-examination, Dahlerus testified how Goering had warned him that Ribbentrop was trying to sabotage the negotiations, even planning to have his plane crash.* [As this came out, Ribbentrop exploded in the dock. Goering had predicted that Ribbentrop would split a gut over the testimony, but he apparently did not anticipate this revelation of his own back-biting intrigue.] *The prosecution further elicited testimony out of Dahlerus' book (the one Goering had read in his cell), showing how Hitler was in a frenzy to build "U-boats! U-boats! U-boats! . . . and I will build airplanes! airplanes! airplanes!—and I will exterminate my enemies!!"—right in the midst of the alleged peace negotiation, while Goering did not turn a hair.*

[Goering fumed in the dock, pulling at the telephone cord until it looked as if he would break it, and the officer of the guard, had to pull the cord out of his hand and tell him to behave himself.] *It was brought out that Dahlerus had gained the impression that the Führer was abnormal, Goering was in a crazy state of intoxication, and Ribbentrop a would-be murderer—that the whole German Government including Goering had apparently had no serious intention of avoiding war, but only of getting British acquiescence to the rape of Poland. He even identified the map Goering had given him, showing the parts of Poland the Nazis wanted as their next price for peace. Finally, Dahlerus testified, in spite of defense counsel's overruled objections, that "had I known what I know today, I would have realized that my efforts could not possibly succeed."*

---

As court adjourned, there was a general feeling among the defendants that Goering was all washed up. Some of the overheard remarks:

Frick: "Stupid of him to bring that witness; he should have known the prosecution would get hold of that book."

Speer: (smiling) "Goering's luck is *ausgespielt*—all gone—all gone."

Funk: "Disgraceful—disgraceful!"

Ribbentrop (to Kaltenbrunner): "I don't know whom to trust now."

When I came to tell Fritzsche he was right, Speer said that this trial would be the White Book of future German administrations to show how criminal the Nazi administration was. Von Neurath was contemptuous of the fat one who beat his chest about being a leader and bowed to the ground before the Führer. Schacht announced the latest score: 2 to 1 favor the prosecution.

---

## March 20

## GOERING'S CROSS-EXAMINATION

MORNING SESSION: *A nip-and-tuck word duel between Goering and Prosecutor Jackson. In spite of Goering's evasive tactics, it was established that Goering was responsible for supporting anti-Semitic decrees. In spite of his claim to being a moderating force in the Jewish question, he had to admit participating in the taking over of Jewish-owned business and property as director of the Four Year Plan, proclaiming the Nuremberg Laws as President of the Reichstag, levying a fine of a billion marks on the Jewish population, ordering Himmler and Heydrich to settle the elimination of the Jews from German economic life. After the riots of November 9–10, 1938 he declared to Heydrich, "I wish you had killed 200 Jews and not destroyed such valuable property." He had then turned the destruction of Jewish property to the profit of the insurance companies and the government.*

---

LUNCH HOUR: At lunch Fritzsche said he was now surprised that Goering had interceded on Goebbels' behalf, when Goebbels was in the dog house with Hitler over his philandering, and was about to be ousted. The incident of Goering's quarrel and apparent opposition to Goebbels occurred only 8 weeks before Goering interceded for Goebbels. With typical naïveté, Fritzsche drew the conclusion that Goering must have done it out of chivalry toward an opponent. The more plausible explanation that Goering really did not want to get rid of a strong anti-Semite who suited the Nazi program of looting Jewish property, apparently did not occur to him.

Funk tried to explain the necessity for putting the aryanization of Jewish property on a legal basis, after the reckless excesses of hoodlums who smashed thousands of Jewish store windows in the "spontaneous" uprising at Goebbels' instigation.

"That is almost more disgraceful," I commented, "—putting robbery on a legal basis and giving it official sanction."

"Oh, I don't justify it in the slightest—the whole policy was wrong—I do not mean that—it was entirely unjustifiable."

---

AFTERNOON SESSION: *Funk's concern over the legality of organizing Jewish property became understandable as Prosecutor Jackson continued to present documentary proof that Funk as well as Heydrich were involved in Goering's plan for the elimination of Jews from economic and public life and their segregation in ghettos. Then came Goering's looting of art treasures from occupied countries, by the trainload. Goering insisted he was only building an art collection for the future cultural interest of the State. He had similar rationalizations for his use of PW and slave labor, confiscation of food and property in occupied territories.*

---

During the intermission there was general agreement that it was not a very proud spectacle to have one of their statesmen trying to explain how he came by 50 million marks worth of art property while Germans were being exhorted to undergo sacrifices for their "ideals."

---

However, at the end of the day, Goering was apparently quite proud of his performance, and told the others, "If you all handle yourselves half as well as I did, you will do all right.—You have to be careful—every other word can be twisted around."

After he went down, Speer remarked scornfully to Seyss-Inquart, "Well, even Hermann made some bad slips; he needn't be so pleased with himself."

"All that talking isn't going to do him any good," Seyss-Inquart replied coolly. "They have it all in black and white."

## March 21

MORNING SESSION: *Sir David Maxwell-Fyfe made Goering sweat over the murdering of British RAF officers who had escaped from the Sagon PW camp and handing Russian PW's over to the Gestapo. Goering quibbled and denied responsibility. [Fritzsche pointed out during the intermission that the really damaging part of the testimony was that Goering turned the administration of PW camps over to someone else, after the Sagon incident, rather than insisting on changing the system.] Goering had to be asked several times by the court to stop evading direct answers to questions. Sir David continued to make Goering squirm over the hypocritical intrigue in connection with his attempt to "prevent war" by his negotiation behind Hitler's back, while acquiescing in Hitler's aggressive plans.*

AFTERNOON SESSION: *At the beginning of the afternoon session, Sir David asked Goering whether he still maintained his loyalty to the Führer in the face of all these murders. Goering replied that he did not approve of the murders, but maintained his loyalty in difficult times as well as in good times. Pressed further about atrocities, he weakly maintained that he did not think the Führer knew the extent of them, and he himself certainly did not. He had merely known about a few instances of extermination and "certain preparations."*

## March 22

### EGOTISM, LOYALTY, AND BIGOTRY

MORNING SESSION: *Goering's defense ended on a note of anticlimax as General Rudenko terminated his brief cross-examination and the French prosecutor said he had nothing further to add. On re-examination, the court ruled that they were not interested in any further speeches, and the defense counsel brought his examination to an abrupt end.*

──────── EVENING IN JAIL ────────

*Goering's Cell:* When I visited Goering in his cell, to see what he had to say after the completion of his defense, he made an outright bid for applause for his performance.

"Well, I didn't cut a *petty* figure, did I?" he asked for the third time.

"No, I cannot say you did."

"Don't forget I had the best legal brains of England, America, Russia, and France arrayed against me with their whole legal machinery—and there I was, alone!" He couldn't help admiring himself, and paused for a moment to do so. He then expressed satisfaction with the court's ruling that the others did not have to go over the history and program of the Nazi Party again, since he had been given free reign to do so once and for all. Yes, he was quite satisfied with his figure in history. "Why, I bet even the prosecution had to admit that I did well, didn't they? Did you hear anything?" The test of his medieval heroism was admiration by the enemy. I shrugged my shoulders.

He then began to go over the two days' defense in detail. Being cut off from making more speeches at the end was slightly frustrating. He said he had wanted to tell the court that he accepted the formal responsibility for the anti-Semitic measures, even though he did not know it would lead to such horrible excesses. I told him that he could say that in his final speech anyway, but what was more important was whether he considered that policy correct.

"Nein, um Gotteswillen!—After what I know now?—For heaven's sake, do you think I would ever have supported it if I had had the slightest idea that it would lead to mass murder? I assure you we never for a moment had such things in mind. I only thought we would eliminate Jews from positions in big business and government, and that was that.—But don't forget they carried on a terrific campaign against us too, all over the world."

"Do you blame them? It is understood that they would not accept this persecution lying down."

"That is the trouble. That is the mistake we made," he admitted.

He agreed that it would have been better not to have started the persecution altogether. He had just never considered it important one way or the other.

He returned to the more pleasant topic of his duel with the prosecutors. "That guy Rudenko was more nervous than I was, that's a sure thing. Hoho! but he pulled a boner when I slipped in that one about the Russians transporting 1,680,000 Poles and Ukrainians to Russia. Instead of saying, 'We are not interested in your accusations,' he said, 'You do not have to bring up Soviet actions.'—'Actions,' he said. Hoho! I bet he gets a hot wire from old Joe on that one! He sure fell into it!—I also gave him a good dig when he asked me why I didn't refuse to obey Hitler's orders. I answered 'Then I certainly would not have had to worry about my health.' That's the technical terminology for liquidation in a dictatorship. He understood me, all right."

I then broached the subject of loyalty again, to get more of a revelation on this point in his system of values. "By the way, I noticed that you gave Sir David the same answer you gave me on your loyalty to the Führer. Of course, you didn't answer his question directly."

"I know, that was a very dangerous question. Somebody else might have been trapped by it. He asked me, 'Do you still seek to justify and glorify Hitler after you know he was a murderer?' That was a tough one—a very dangerous one. I told him that I did not justify him, but kept my oath, in hard times as well as in good times."

"Yes, and then I remembered what you had said about being impressed by figures in history who kept their loyalty even in difficult times. Do you remember any examples?"

"Oh, yes, that impressed me even as a little boy.—You know the story about the Nibelungen—and how Hagen killed Siegfried because Günther wished it. And then Krimhilde demanded revenge from her three brothers. But they said to Hagen, 'Nay, though thou art our enemy, we must bow to thy loyalty to thy king.'—I can see it now—how they held their shields before him and said they would protect him against any attack for what he did in loyalty to his king." I didn't get the analogy to this loyalty to the Führer, unless he was trying to convey that even Goering's enemies should respect his loyalty, even if it condoned murder.

He then launched into a tirade on the homosexuality of the Catholic clergy, to show that his anti-Catholicism also had some basis. "Did you ever see one of their seminaries? There are 14, 15, 16, and 17-year-olds from all over the world, and you can see at 10 paces that they are selected pederasts. It stands to reason. You cannot go against human nature. When we arrested their priests because of homosexuality, they hollered that we were persecuting the Church.—Some persecution!—We had to pay them close to a billion marks a year in taxes anyway.—But that Catholic clergy—don't you think I know what goes on behind drawn curtains in those confessions, or between the priests and the nuns.— The nuns are 'brides of Christ' you know.—What a setup!" There was an obvious streak of Streicher-like lewd bigotry in all this, that had not been revealed before. It was interesting only in view of his pretended sympathetic interest in the Catholic Church when the Catholic chaplain came around to see him at lunch yesterday.

He mentioned off-handedly that he did not think America would get away with its Negro problem so easily. This was apparently recently borrowed from Rosenberg, indicating the Nazi fear lest they die without leaving behind some heritage of racial hatred somewhere, to prove in a macabre sort of way that they were right after all.

---

*Speer's Cell:* (Went to test out the effect on the opposition.) Speer felt that all in all the prosecution had succeeded in penetrating Goering's heroic armor. "It is all well and good for him to claim loyalty to the Führer in grandiloquent terms, but when they pin him right down to take the blame for specific crimes, what does he do? He says he made intrigues behind Hitler's back, he didn't know about this, he disagreed with that. I had to laugh.— He was claiming opposition to Hitler almost as much as I was, after bawling me out for it. Yet he maintains the pose of the loyal servant to the very end. It is just a lot of words.—He knows perfectly well they can't hang him for *saying* he is loyal, but he dodges responsibility wherever he can, when they pin him right down to facts. And when he can't dodge it, he comes out bravely and says, 'Yes, I take full responsibility!'

"You know, when Jackson cross-examines Goering, you can see

that they just represent two entirely opposite worlds—they don't even understand each other. Jackson asks him if he didn't help plan the invasion of Holland and Belgium and Norway, expecting Goering to defend himself against a criminal accusation, but instead Goering says, Why yes, of course, it took place thus and so, as if it is the most natural thing in the world to invade a neutral country if it suits your strategy.

"Anyway, it is remarkable how he held up under the strain. Your prison discipline has certainly had a sobering effect on him. You should have seen him in the old days.—A lazy, selfish, corrupt, irresponsible dope addict. Now he cuts a dashing figure, and the people admire his nerve. I hear from my attorney that they are saying, 'That Goering is quite a guy [Mordskerl]'—But you should have seen him before. They were all corrupt cowards in the country's hour of crisis. Why do you suppose Goering wasn't in Berlin, to stand by his beloved Führer? Because it was too hot in Berlin when the Russians closed in. The same with Himmler. But not one of them gave any thought to sparing the people any more of this madness. You know, I get furious again every time I think of it.—No, none of them must go down in history as the least bit worthy of respect. Let the whole damn Nazi system and all who participated in it, including myself, go down with the ignominy and disgrace it deserves!—And let the people forget and start to build a new life on some sensible democratic basis."

## March 23

### FRAU GOERING

I visited Frau Emmy Goering at the house in the woods of Sackdilling near Neuhaus, to which she had retired with her daughter and niece after her release from custody. They are living in rather primitive circumstances (no running hot water or heat). She is a rather handsome woman of 45, well-poised, though somewhat emotional, especially in the present circumstances. I gave little Edda some chocolate, and Frau Goering sent her out to play while we talked. As the child left, she said, "Can you imagine that madman ordering that child shot?"

Then she told with bitterness how they had been arrested on Hitler's order, and how they were supposed to be shot because Hitler suspected Goering of disloyalty. She had been furious over this colossal injustice. "My 7 weeks detention were uncomfortable, of course—but I assure you what I have put up with the last few months is nothing compared to what we went through when Hitler ordered Hermann and his family arrested and shot. My husband was beside himself with fury, to think that Hitler could suspect him of disloyalty. He stormed and raged so much, accusing Hitler of ingratitude in such vicious language, that I was afraid the guard would shoot him on the spot. I begged him to forget that he had heard it. The guard said he would forget it, but he felt that my husband was right. Disloyal! God knows what my man sacrificed out of loyalty to the Führer! He lost his health, his fortune, and his first wife as a result of that putsch in 1923. He supported Hitler in everything. He helped him to power. And in gratitude all he got was an order for his arrest and assassination. —And my own child too! When we heard that Hitler had committed suicide, Hermann said bitterly that the unbearable part of it was that he could never tell him to his face that Hitler had wronged him."

"It is amazing to me," I said, "that he should persist in maintaining his loyalty even now, in view of all that has happened, and in view of the fact that all the world knows Hitler was a murderer. Doesn't all this relieve him of his oath of loyalty?"

"Of course! Of course!" She wrung her hands. "Oh, if I could only speak to him for 5 minutes! Just for 5 minutes!"

"The only thing I can imagine," I suggested, "is that he says it just for spite in front of a foreign court."

"That is it! That is exactly it! I know just exactly how he feels about it—so that for God's sake, one man at least will stand up and say, 'Yes, I supported the Führer, here I am—do with me what you please!' It is so disgraceful to us to see how many Germans are saying they never really supported Hitler, that they were forced into the Party, there is so much hypocrisy, it is sickening! And he wants to show that he at least is not back-tracking like a coward." (Her niece started serving tea.)

"But it puts him in an unfortunate light. He is actually con-doning Hitler's policies even now. Isn't there a limit to this *Nibelungentreue* [Nibelungen loyalty]? He owes it to himself and the German people to clarify the guilt."

"Of course!—The German people must know!" both women declared emphatically. Frau Goering's eyes welled up again. "Oh, God! If I could only see him again!—Just for 10 minutes!" There was desperation in her voice, and a sense of the futility of his "heroic" gesture, however understandable from his point of view. "I can see how he has just made a rightabout face, after seeing how many Germans were renouncing their allegiance to the Führer, and showing fear before the conqueror. He hated Hitler for what he did.—But he is so fanatic on the issue of loyalty. That is the one thing in which we cannot agree.—A man who would murder my child!—" She choked up, and hatred blazed in her eyes.

"Hitler must have been insane!" Frau Goering blurted out. "Did you speak to Dr. Morel? He must have known! He attended him daily."

"I did speak to Dr. Morel. He did seem worried about the ac-cusation that his injections had had a bad effect on Hitler. But he was not a psychiatrist, and I gather he was rather a quack. Any-way, he seemed to be going insane himself."

"I should think he would! A doctor who attended him every day should have been able to see that there was something wrong with the man. I could see it myself! He was not normal!"

"If a psychiatrist had declared Hitler abnormal—" I suggested, "I suppose he would have been shot."

"Oh, but then my husband would have taken a stand. Then his oath of loyalty would not have bound him any longer. He could not have trusted the fate of the German people to such a man. —But his loyalty—*loyalty*—" She actually gagged at the word. "God, what a difference there would have been for Germany if he had become Führer before the war. There would have been no war; there would have been no persecution. You know my hus-band. He is not a man obsessed by hatred. He only wanted to enjoy life and let other people enjoy it. Hitler was another type of character. Just rigid determination to go straight toward his goal without rest or compromise.—He was not that way in the beginning. He must have gone insane toward the end.—Dr. Morel must have known. Isn't there something wrong with a man who never rests, never laughs, and goes around holding his arm like this—?" She crooked her right arm as if holding it in a sling, imitating the functional lameness that Dr. Brandt had described to me as most likely a hysterical symptom.

Going on with the subject of atrocities after tea, while Edda was not present, she told how she had asked Himmler to let her go and see Auschwitz concentration camp, because she had received so many letters saying that things were not quite as they should be. As the first lady of the land she wanted to be convinced that everything was in order. Himmler wrote a polite letter, but told her not to meddle in things that were no concern of hers. She told me that of all the thousands of letters she got requesting favors, not one said anything about mass murders in concentration camps. She could only assume that the Gestapo had been screening her mail in some way.

Speaking of Goering again: "It is such a pity that I can do nothing to help him. He has been so good to me. And now I am so helpless. I don't even know my way around to take care of the things we need to exist now.—He always protected me from all those things." I called AMG to help her get the clothes that had been packed away when she was taken into custody.

I went away with the impression that Goering's protected lady fair was thoroughly enamored of her dashing knight, and had been kept in an ivory tower, the better to admire her hero's exploits and sterling character. The rude awakening that her hero had been serving a murderous lord did not succeed in shattering her illusions about her husband. On the trip back to Nuremberg I speculated on the possibilities of confronting him with the emotional appeal of his wife to abandon his misguided "loyalty," and to test the impact of her aroused motherly and humanitarian instincts on his medieval heroic sense of values and conceit.

## March 24

## CHIVALRY

*Goering's Cell:* I brought Goering the letter from his wife and the postcard from his child. He did not want to read them in my presence, but asked me how they were. I described the circumstances and the conversation.

"We talked a lot about your loyalty to Hitler, and how he ordered you arrested and shot at the end—and little Edda too," I told him.

"Oh, I don't believe any more that Hitler himself sent that order. That was the work of that dirty swine, Bormann." Suddenly his face grew grim. "I tell you, *Herr Doktor,* if I could have that pig alone in this cell for just 5 minutes, and leave that portal closed—there would be no need to try him, I assure you!" His teeth and fists were clenched. "I would strangle the sonofabitch with my bare hands!—And not alone because of what he did to me—but all that dirty double-crossing conniving with the Führer!" He laughed off his momentary fury, but I noticed that his right fist remained clenched for another 5 minutes without his awareness, while he went on talking.

"Yes, that question Sir David asked me," he continued, "—that was a dangerous question—the most dangerous question in the whole trial." He repeated Sir David's question about maintaining loyalty to a murderer, and his own answer. "—You see, I did not glorify him, and I did not condemn him. I merely reserved my judgment in that situation—you understand."

"That is what I thought—you did not want to say what you really thought before a foreign court."

"Naturally—and in addition to that, I wanted to set my people an example that loyalty was not dead."

At this point I put it to him. "Your wife was rather desperate about your blind loyalty to the Führer, after all the misery, and the orders for murder. She said, 'Oh, if I could only see him for 5 minutes!'" He watched me dramatize it, and got the significance.

His reaction was an indulgent smile. "Ha, yes, I know.—She can influence me in lots of things, but as far as my basic code is concerned, nothing can sway me on that. She could have her way in the household, in getting me to do lots of things for her, but when it comes to these basic things in a man's life, it is not a woman's affair."

That was the answer to my question. Goering's medieval egotistical sense of values is complete down to the "chivalrous" attitude toward women, which conceals its narcissistic purpose behind a façade of condescending protective indulgence and allows no womanly humanitarian values to interfere with that purpose.

Goering leaned on his elbow at the other end of the cot and brooded, mumbling half to himself: "No, my people have been humiliated before. Loyalty and hatred will unite them again.— Who knows but that in this very hour the man is born who will unite my people—born of our flesh and bones, to avenge the humiliation we suffer now!"

# 7. Hess's Defense

## HESS DECIDES NOT TO TAKE THE STAND

*Hess's Cell:* Hess said he has decided not to take the stand in his own defense, because he did not want to be subjected to the embarrassment of not being able to answer questions the prosecution would ask. He insisted this was his own decision, but I know that Goering and Dr. Seidl have urged him not to take the stand.

We went over the same material as last week in casual conversation. He had no real recollection of the Party's rise to power, his flight to England, the psychiatric examination, the atrocity films, or star witnesses like General Lahousen, Ohlendorf, General von Paulus. He remembers that Goering has been "testifying endlessly —but I couldn't tell you about what at the moment, even if you beat me."

In an attempt to get his reaction to the idea of simulation, I said, "Supposing someone asked you, How do we know you are not simulating your loss of memory? What would you say?"

"Simulating?—Well, I would say, Why should I simulate?—And then, well, how can I prove it?" Further questioning around this theme did not bring forth the slightest suggestion of familiarity or defensiveness on this subject, either by word or gesture or expression.

*Digit span:* 4 forward, 3 backward.

## HESS'S WITNESSES

Before the morning session started, as Goering learned that Hess would not take the stand and Ribbentrop was out sick, he announced smugly, "Well, I cannot conduct everybody's defense; I can only conduct my own. I cannot give everybody my nerve or my guts—or even give them a swift kick in the arse to make them perk up.—Hahahaha!"

Dr. Sauter, Ribbentrop's former attorney, said sarcastically to von Schirach, "Well, now, isn't that strange!—Ribbentrop is sick on the day his defense is supposed to begin.*—What an unfortunate coincidence! Now isn't that just too bad!—Just like Ribbentrop! He drove me crazy with his double-talk! First he had to have this Gauleiter as an absolutely indispensible witness—then he decided after all the trouble in getting him that he'd better not have him after all. First he would say he said so-and-so at a meeting, and then he would say he wasn't even there.—I am glad I washed my hands of the whole thing!"

MORNING SESSION: *Hess's first witness was Ernst Bohle, who tried to show that his Auslands Organisation (for German Bunds in foreign countries) was not really a fifth column. Mr. Griffith-Jones of the British prosecution made mincemeat of that argument by forcing him to admit that the Germans in foreign countries sent him intelligence reports on foreign activities during peace, and helped the invaders when they entered conquered territory.*

LUNCH HOUR: Schacht gave his opinion of that man Bohle: "*That* was the politician whose grocery clerks and bootblacks became *Landesleiter*, [German Bund leaders in foreign countries]—experts on foreign affairs. And a man like me was ignored on Indian and British affairs! I had made a study of the situation; but no, some little punk of a butcher boy under Bohle was the only one who was supposed to report on India! The prosecution should have asked me.—I could tell them how Bohle used his organization to give Hitler false information on the foreign situation!"

Von Papen also had it in for Bohle. "That was the man who made my life miserable.—He did everything he could to get me out of the way."

*It was expected that since Hess wasn't taking the stand, his defense would be finished in a few hours and Ribbentrop would take the stand in the afternoon. Dr. Sauter had originally taken over Ribbentrop's defense, but asked to be relieved of this assignment early in the trial.

Goering bragged, "I could have handled that Englishman! I would have told him, 'Of course we had spies in foreign countries —so what! . . . Anyway, I told Hess that they were not showing his witnesses the same courtesy as they showed mine—they are using only second-string prosecutors to cross-examine his witnesses, not the big chiefs."

In the Youth lunchroom there was general agreement that Hess's witness was not doing him much good.

AFTERNOON SESSION: *Bohle's cross-examination was concluded and the only other witness, Stroelin, was also cross-examined. There was little of consequence in the afternoon's testimony.*

——————— EVENING IN JAIL ———————

*Ribbentrop's Cell:* Ribbentrop was still depressed and complained about his numbness and *Willenslähmung* (laming of the will). He could speak a little more easily, but mumbled like a man facing the gallows, his senses dulled by prolonged anxiety. "Yes—I know—nobody is even interested in the trials any more. If they shoot us, or exile us—nobody in America will care—nobody in England or France will care—only maybe some Germans will care a little bit.—I did not want them to hold the trial. I begged them not to hold the trial.—I even wrote Jackson that I would subject myself to the verdict of an American court—that I and a few others would rather take the whole responsibility than have a trial like this—Germans denouncing Germans. It is not very nice —believe me, *Herr Doktor*, it is not very nice . . . "

——————— **March 26** ———————

MORNING SESSION: *Hess's defense continued with the reading of documents. The court adjourned over the relevancy of opinions on the Versailles Treaty.*

LUNCH HOUR: This precipitated a general discussion on the Versailles Treaty as soon as I entered each lunchroom.

Schacht and von Papen pointed out that America had never

ratified the Versailles Treaty because it betrayed Wilson's 14 Points. Doenitz again flattered Biddle: "He understands that very well—he is sharp. He has quick perception." Schacht repeated that there never would have been a Hitler if it had not been for the Versailles Treaty.

Jodl expressed the same sentiment, when I started to talk to him. "That is the only reason why the Wehrmacht and the Nazi Party were able to get along at all. Otherwise they were always at each other's throats." Rosenberg popped out of his corner; so did Kaltenbrunner.

"Oho!" said Rosenberg. "Of course, they don't want to discuss Versailles. Even the Americans refused to sign that thing, because it stank. Wilson had drawn up his 14 Points so carefully, and then when the time came to make the peace treaty the French laid their secret treaties with Poland and all the rest on the table, and said that's what they were fighting for, and that's that—the 14 Points were thrown into the wastebasket."

"Does all of that have anything to do with justifying aggressive war and crimes against humanity?" I asked.

"Oh, no—it only explains how the whole thing came about."

"There never would have been a Hitler except for the Versailles Treaty," Kaltenbrunner echoed, and Rosenberg agreed.

---

AFTERNOON SESSION: *The court ruled that debate over the Versailles Treaty was irrelevant, and Dr. Seidl brought his defense of Hess to a close with the remark that because of Hess's attitude toward the court (not recognizing their authority) he would not take the stand.* [It is not generally known that Hess had intended to take the stand until a couple of days ago, and has gotten cold feet because of his loss of memory. Today I determined that all he could remember about yesterday's proceedings was that Bohle had testified, but he had already forgotten Stroelin.]

# 8. Ribbentrop's Defense

## ——————— March 26 (Cont.) ———————

## THE FOREIGN OFFICE

AFTERNOON SESSION: *Ribbentrop's first witness was Dr. Steengracht, his State-Secretary. In Ribbentrop's defense he testified that there were about thirty offices and organizations meddling and overlapping with the Foreign Office; that anybody who had ever had a pleasant breakfast in a neighboring country considered himself an expert on foreign affairs and was accepted as such by Hitler; that there was constant wrangling over authority, requiring Ribbentrop to spend 60 per cent of his time in bureaucratic jurisdictional disputes; that Hitler was not amenable to the influence of experts and reasonable men; that the highest governmental officials were constantly at odds with each other, and, in general, the whole government was in a rotten mess.*

At the end of the day, scorn and contempt was expressed for Ribbentrop and his defense from one end of the dock to the other. Goering asked Dr. Horn if he had any more questions to ask that stupid witness. Dr. Horn said that the witness was not answering the way he expected him to. Ribbentrop said he had not told him to say all those uncomplimentary things about Hitler and the government.

At the other end of the dock there was open contempt.

Von Papen and Schacht threw up their hands. "Now you see it! That was the Foreign Office."

Fritzsche said, "And just imagine German soldiers going to war, confidently thinking that there is a competent Foreign Minister and a responsible administration that would not send them to war unless it was necessary."

Funk muttered, "Disgraceful! Disgraceful!—the whole thing!"

———————————— **March 27** ————————————

MORNING SESSION: *Colonel Amen tied Dr. Steengracht all up in knots on cross-examination, and the witness ended up by making a very sorry spectacle of himself, his chief, and the whole Nazi Government.*

———————— EVENING IN JAIL ————————

*Schacht's Cell:* I dropped in on Schacht in the evening to get his reaction. He gave it quite bluntly. "Ugh! Such a washrag for a Foreign Minister!—and look at the people he had working for him!—Such a good-for-nothing, stupid weakling! Why, Hitler and Goering were brutal criminals—all right, that is something.—But that Ribbentrop—why he wasn't good enough to be a bootblack! He wants to show he was not a typical Nazi. No, of course not; he only did everything Hitler wanted him to, but he was no Nazi. Ugh! It makes me ashamed of being a German—the kind of people we had running the government. What kind of characters are Frank, Rosenberg, Streicher, Keitel—" He spat each of the names out with contempt. "You can even see the difference between Keitel and Jodl. But the generals are really the most to blame. I really cannot understand that militaristic mentality. Hitler says, 'Let's go to war!' and they all click their heels and say, 'War? Why yes, indeed, naturally, let's go to war!' Take General Halder, for instance. He did not have any use for Hitler. He was going to help me kick him out in 1938. Then Hitler says we are going to war, and all of a sudden Halder snaps to and says, 'War? Oh, yes, fine, anything you say.'—Never a thought about the reasons, the alternatives—nothing."

——————————

*Ribbentrop's Cell:* Ribbentrop was just a tired old man awaiting death. He spoke in a subdued monotone. "Ah, well, it makes no difference.—We are only living shadows—the remains of a dead era—an era that died with Hitler. Whether a few of us live another 10 or 20 years, it makes no difference. What could I do anyway, even if I were released, which, of course, will not happen. The old era died with Hitler—we do not fit into the present world any more. On April 30th I should have taken the consequences. Yes, it is a great tragedy—a great tragedy, that is certain. —What can one do now?" He thought it was not very nice of Mr. Dodd to say he was only nervous yesterday. (It was only a "laming of the will"—he had told me so himself.)

--------------------- March 28 ---------------------

## THE SECRET PACT

MORNING SESSION: *Ribbentrop's former secretary, Fräulein Blank, testified in his behalf. The court recessed over the admissibility of a question with respect to a secret treaty with Russia.*

----

While the court was deliberating, Goering said to Ribbentrop, "It's all right; you can depend on your witness. A woman is always braver than a man."

"Is that a dig at me?" Ribbentrop asked, smilingly.

"Oh, no, I mean in general."

Everybody commented on the secret clause which was supposed to have accompanied the Russian-German pact. It was generally taken for granted that the secret clause was the advance partitioning of Poland before the German attack. Speer, who had suspected it all along, said, "History is history, there is no use hiding it." Most of those around him agreed.

Jodl was grinning like a fox. "So now they want to hide the fact that there was a secret treaty. They cannot do it. I had the advance demarcation line right among my plans and planned the campaign accordingly . . . The war would probably never have been risked if Hitler didn't have this agreement in advance. But once he had this agreement in his pocket, he said, 'Now I can risk it.' Because our Eastern front was secured."

Frank and Rosenberg enjoyed themselves over the anticipated Russian embarrassment. Frank laughed out loud. "Hah! There you see the real conspiracy. If there was any conspiracy, it was between Hitler and the Russians. The Russians ought to be sitting here in the prisoners' dock with us!"

Seyss-Inquart remarked, "Now I finally see who was running the Foreign Office. It was Fräulein Blank." The others laughed.

It was finally decided to allow the question.

---

LUNCH HOUR. At lunch, Fritzsche, in high spirits, gave a radio commentator's version of the incident. "The defense counsel asks her if she knew about any secret treaty.—She knew of one with Russia.—The whole courtroom pricks up its ears.—The Soviet prosecutor objects.—The court recesses.—They decide the question may be asked. The suspense is terrific. Finally the question *is* asked.—At last the world will know about the secret treaty with Russia.—Yes, she knew it was in an envelope marked *secret*.—That is all.—You should have seen Biddle's face drop.—Hoho, what a let-down for the whole court! It was priceless!"

Everybody felt rather let down about it. Doenitz, who has taken to watching Biddle's every move and gesture, said, "You could see that Biddle wanted that thing brought out, and he was disappointed when it didn't come out . . . But he has a sense of humor. Did you notice that when Miss Blank said her chief never approached her in 10 years he gave Parker a nudge?"

Schacht had noticed it. "Yes, that is the old American humor."

Ribbentrop was worried because the prosecution had not cross-examined his witness. "Is that good or bad?" he was overheard asking his attorney. He was given assurance that there was nothing to worry about.

Goering understood the gesture perfectly well. "Of course the purpose of the prosecution was to show that they did not take the testimony of his secretary seriously. It was clever of them, and a chivalrous gesture at the same time. I would have done the same thing."

"Ribbentrop was rather miffed at your saying that women are more courageous than men," I said.

"Yes, he knew perfectly well what I meant. He hasn't had the guts to bring up the matter of the secret clause deciding in advance the demarcation line in case of an attack on Poland. *In case* of an attack, mind you. At that time it was not certain. I know all about it. Jodl knows about the map, but Ribbentrop and I know all the details. I left it for him to bring it up. If he's too chicken-hearted to do so, I'll bring it up myself in my final plea at the very latest, you can count on that."

——————— **March 29** ———————

## RIBBENTROP TESTIFIES

MORNING SESSION: *Ribbentrop gave a weary recital of pre-war conditions, the Party's rise to power, the difficulties of the Versailles Treaty, the rearmament question, the Anti-Comintern Pact, the Munich Pact, etc., contributing nothing to information already generally known. He had to be urged several times to get on with his story.*

———————

LUNCH HOUR: At lunch Schacht imitated him, hunching his shoulders and saying in a stupid, sleepy voice, "—So I went to London—and Mr. X. Y. met me at the train—and then I went and changed my clothes—." He straightened up and said contemptuously, "—And that is the Foreign Minister of Germany speaking!"

Von Neurath was equally contemptuous. "You can just see by the way he talks that he did not have the faintest conception of foreign affairs when he took over the Foreign Office. And yet at that time he puffed himself up as the big expert."

"That's right!" von Papen interjected with a sour face. "Not the remotest conception!—You can see from the way he talks about the Munich Pact and the Anti-Comintern Pact. The man simply did not know what he was doing!"

The Anti-Comintern Pact touched on von Neurath's tender spot. "Yes, he does not say why he was the one to sign the Anti-Comintern Pact,*—because I refused to!! I knew it was dangerous business.—But he slavishly did everything Hitler wanted him to,

———————

*Von Ribbentrop had negotiated the Anti-Comintern Pact of 1936 in his capacity as Minister Plenipotentiary at Large. He became Foreign Minister only two years later.

even sticking his nose into things that were none of his business. As Ambassador to England he should have absolutely minded his own business in this matter. Instead he went out of the way to give the British a deliberate slap in the face by signing this pact while he was still ambassador there. Naturally the British had no use for him after that."

"The most flagrant violation of diplomatic usage you can imagine!" von Papen scowled. "—And such stupid. dangerous dilettantism!—And such abject servility to Hitler—ready to sign anything any time, the moment Hitler even thought of it, or before, if possible." He repeated the incident of the threatening letter to Turkey which Ribbentrop was about to send because Hitler had suggested it. Ribbentrop had said there was absolutely no swaying the Führer on the point, but von Papen quickly made Hitler change his mind.

Doenitz had been listening and finally spoke up. "I don't think that Hitler was so dull as not to have seen through his stupidity, but I imagine he purposely kept such a man as his Foreign Minister, so that he could run the show himself."

"Yes—Ribbentrop and his 'connections'," Schacht resumed. "He signed the Anti-Comintern Pact with Japan because he had connections with the Japanese, and he got connections with the Japanese by signing the pact.—That's the way that four-flusher did things.—Without the remotest conception of what he was doing."

Goering evaluated Ribbentrop's performance as a performance. "He's boring the court stiff," he told me without concealing a little malicious amusement at Ribbentrop's expense. "I told him, if he wants to get away with that long spiel he has got to make it interesting—the way I did. After all, the judges and the reporters want something interesting to listen to, or they just don't pay any attention."

Ribbentrop was quite disturbed over the repeated prodding to get on with his story. "Why does Mr. Biddle try to hurry me?" he asked. "Is he nervous?"

I sent him down early to talk to his attorney. The guard overheard him upbraid Dr. Horn for making motions and signals to drop the details and get on with it. "Now don't interrupt me!—And don't coach me!" he repeated.

"I am just trying to get you to get to the point," Dr. Horn explained. "You see how impatient the court gets."

"Well, why is Biddle so impatient?"

"He is waiting for you to get to the secret Russian pact. That is what they are all waiting for."

Ribbentrop said there was nothing important in that secret clause, and he didn't see what they were all getting so excited about. He hoped they wouldn't get to it this afternoon, because he would rather sleep on it over the week end. Dr. Horn said they probably would get to it this afternoon, and coached him on how to put it—very simply, just describing what the Russians were supposed to get and what the Germans were supposed to get. "All right! all right! Don't coach me!" Ribbentrop repeated impatiently.

As a final admonition, Dr. Horn told him not to talk so much about Hitler—and not to say anything at all about Roosevelt. He also advised him to talk without notes, because his papers would not help him when the prosecution started in on him.

---

AFTERNOON SESSION: [As soon as Ribbentrop started again, Goering told his neighbors that Ribbentrop's defense was a flop. When Ribbentrop came back for a few minutes during the intermission, Goering told him he was doing fine. As soon as he went back on the stand, Goering said, "I don't understand why Hitler made him an SS Gruppenführer—the weakling!"]

Finally the prearranged partitioning of Poland in a secret clause to the Non-Aggression Pact with Russia was disclosed. But by this time it was an anticlimax. He then described the slight delay in the attack on Poland after the British guarantee of Poland; the Führer's "proposals" which he had read to Sir Neville Henderson, but had been forbidden to give him in writing; the attack because Poland was being "insolent," and the Führer's willingness to negotiate after he had conquered Poland.

---

## March 30

MORNING SESSION: Ribbentrop completed his direct examination, telling how he and Hitler did not like war, how they broke pacts,

*only with the greatest regret, and how he himself lost a couple of
nights' sleep over the invasion of the neutral Low Countries.*

———————— March 30–31 ————————

## WEEK END IN JAIL

*Ribbentrop's Cell:* When I visited him in his cell in the afternoon, he complained that he was physically and mentally exhausted. "There is a limit to every man's endurance.—In fact, I
reached my limit in 1943.—I really should have resigned then.—
The doctors talked to Hitler about it. But he would not hear of
it.—I can hardly think straight now.—The end of the war finished
me.—It was terrible.—I kept going to my house outside of Berlin,
and I saw the thousands of wounded veterans retreating, and the
refugees fleeing by the thousands, streaming westward before the
Russian advance." He said that his nerves just cracked with the
German collapse, and by the time he was interned in Mondorf,
in May, he was already suffering memory difficulty. It is so hard to
concentrate and make things clear now.—Why don't they let him
speak? Why do they always interrupt? He has to show what his
own attitude was to these things, and in order to do that he has
to explain the historical background, and . . . Ah, well, they had
let him say 30 per cent of what he wanted to say, and that would
suffice.

I reminded him that he had denied the secret clause in the Russian Non-Aggression Pact, partitioning Poland, in our conversation
four weeks ago. Instead of telling me that he had reserved his
testimony for the witness stand for diplomatic reasons, as von
Papen might have done, or simply pointing out politely that it
was none of my business, as Goering might have done, he first
denied having denied it, and then said it was not the way I said it
was. "You see, Russia and Germany felt entitled to regain land
that they had lost in the last war—that was all.—It was perfectly
natural. Russia is a great power.—Hitler had great admiration for
Stalin. He was only afraid some radical might come in his place."

He did not see why the prosecution had resorted to such unfair mudslinging to besmirch his character. "Why are they trying to make an anti-Semite out of me? They know I couldn't have said those things." I reminded him that Paul Schmidt, Hitler's interpreter, had confirmed his statement to the Hungarian Regent Horthy that the only two solutions for the Jewish problem were extermination or concentration camps. "Ah, no, he didn't, did he? I didn't get it all—it is so hard to concentrate.—But I could not have said such a thing. It is so entirely contrary to my character." It occurred to me that perhaps he did not recall it very clearly, partly because he had parroted Hitler's sentiments thoughtlessly in the first place, hardly realizing what he was saying, and because he was now blocking and rejecting such damaging facts anyway, thus making the lying easier.

The prosecution was also "maligning" his integrity in making an issue out of his 6 houses. "—Is it a crime for a statesman to have money and property?—Don't your statesmen have money and property too?—Didn't Roosevelt live in a big White House? It is a symbol of the government, isn't it? Well, it was the same with me. I lived in the big house Hindenburg used to occupy, and it cost a lot of money to keep it up. The Führer wanted it that way, and so did the people. I can even understand Goering's art collection. The leaders of the State have to have a certain style of living to impress foreigners. That is understandable, isn't it?" I thought that Goering's looting was understandable, all right, but not excusable. "Well, anyway, the prosecution should not smear my character like that. History will take a different view of the matter.—And the German people will not believe them. I know what my people think of me. I have only tried to help them."

---

*Von Neurath's Cell:* Von Neurath had a different view of Ribbentrop's reputation among the German people. "You will not find another official who is held in lower esteem than that man Ribbentrop," he commented spontaneously, as he put aside the washing of his handkerchiefs in his cell. "Some of the people in the dock are surprised at the extent of his stupidity and the shallowness he is showing in court—but to me it is an old story.— I had to put up with that nonsense for years—just a lot of gab and no sense. He still lies. He said he was my State-Secretary before

he became Foreign Minister. But he wasn't. Not for a single minute. Hitler wanted it, but I flatly refused. He actually did more
harm than is evident in court with his stupid meddling."

---

*Frank's Cell:* Frank was quite condescending about "that poor fish
—what do you expect?—He is so untutored and so ignorant. He
can hardly even talk German straight, let alone show any understanding of foreign affairs.—Really, I had trouble following his
grammar. I hope the translators can make some sense out of his
statements for the transcript.—Why, I don't see how he could
have sold champagne, at that rate, let alone National Socialism.
Haha! Hahaha!—Really, I can only pity him. It was not that
poor simpleton's fault that he did not know anything about foreign affairs. But it was a crime on Hitler's part to make that man
Foreign Minister for a nation of 70 million people. That shows
you the real weakness of a dictatorship. It cannot stand criticism.
Hitler surrounded himself by such fawning, ignorant yes-men to
give himself an artificial appearance of strength."

---

*Goering's Cell:* Goering was in a subdued, reflective mood, sitting
out the intermission before his last entrance on the stage, while
the supporting cast spoke their lines. He was not at all satisfied
with Ribbentrop's performance. He shook his head slowly and
commented disapprovingly: "What a pitiful spectacle!—If I had
only known, I would have gone into our foreign policy a little
more myself.—I tried so hard to prevent him from becoming Foreign Minister—but believe me, it is no pleasure to see how right I
was—people saying, 'What kind of a Foreign Minister did you
Nazis have anyway?' It makes our foreign policy look so stupid.
He was always fighting over questions of authority and prestige.
History could go to pot, but he had to have his authority recognized. He was always jealous and suspicious of me, and would ask
me if I was trying to be Foreign Minister. I told him, 'No thanks,
I still prefer to be second man in the State.' I know that he pulled
one dirty trick that was probably decisive for history." I asked
him what this decisive event was. "—A meeting with Churchill,
that I was supposed to have.—He blocked it—it was supposed to
take place 2 or 3 days before the war broke out.—I didn't find out
until later . . .

"He wasn't always so stupid and weak—but I realize now more than ever that he was concealing a lot of ignorance behind that arrogant front . . . Oh, God, it is sad—very sad! I don't give a hoot how Kaltenbrunner explains his role in the RSHA, or how Rosenberg defends his philosophy, but our foreign policy—that is something that reflects on the whole administration.—What a calamity!"

---

*Von Papen's Cell:* Von Papen was full of his usual contempt for Ribbentrop. "Ach, there's no use letting that fool talk any more —he has convicted himself already.—They might as well go on with the next case . . . Just imagine the casual way he passed off such a catastrophic event as the declaration of war against the United States!—'Well, they are already shooting at our U-boats, so we might as well declare war.'—That was Hitler's Foreign Minister!—God, the criminal dilettantism with which that man gambled away a Reich!" He was apparently referring to Hitler, for taking the advice of stupid men like Ribbentrop instead of seasoned diplomats like himself. "He thought he was being smart with that Russian Non-Aggression Pact and the partitioning of Poland, but I think he just played right into Stalin's hands with that smartness. When Stalin saw that Hitler intended to attack Poland to get what he wanted, he thought, Well, if that's the way the wind blows, and nobody wants to stop him, all right, I might as well cut myself a piece of cake.—And what about Goering? If instead of that stupid amateurish move with Dahlerus, he had taken the whole cabinet and gone straight to Hitler and said, 'Look here, if you insist on going to war, we refuse to play along!' —Then Hitler would have had to back down.—But with no serious opposition, he just thought he could get away with anything . . . "

———————— April 1 ————————

## RIBBENTROP IS CROSS-EXAMINED

MORNING SESSION: *Ribbentrop was cross-examined by Sir David Maxwell-Fyfe. By means of evasion, self-contradiction, re-interpretation, irrelevant argument and analogy, straddling of issues, "diplomatic language," and a good deal of hemming and hawing, Ribbentrop sought to deny or sidetrack the damaging documentary evidence against him: that he had helped Hitler exert threats of force to bring about the Anschluss and the seizure of Czechoslovakia; that he had carried out the diplomatic preparations for the attack on Poland, knowing that it meant war with England, etc. Even Jodl had noted in his diary that the Foreign Minister was playing a dangerous game.*

LUNCH HOUR: Discussing the cross-examination in the Elders' lunchroom, Schacht excitedly sawed the air with his hand, emphasizing the crux of the whole case: "—It all boils down to this: he knew that there was going to be war over Poland, and he did nothing to prevent it!—That is the simple crux of the matter— all the rest is hot air!"

Von Papen recalled how Hitler had put the pressure of a military threat on the Austrian Chancellor Schuschnigg. At a crucial point of their conference at Berchtesgaden on February 12, 1938, he screamed, "K E I T E L!!" so that he could be heard all over the building. Keitel came running, out of breath, but was just told to sit down in a corner. The gesture had worked to intimidate Schuschnigg. But von Papen and Schacht were both of the opinion that no threat was necessary, because Schuschnigg knew perfectly well that 80 per cent of the Austrians were in favor of the Anschluss. What Schuschnigg objected to was the domination by the Nazis. Schacht recalled what a timid man he was, when he met him in concentration camp.

Seyss-Inquart was enjoying Ribbentrop's ignorance of history. As I walked past him in the other lunchroom, he whispered with an artful smile, "Pssst! Don't say anything now, but I suspect our

Foreign Minister of not even knowing that the Bulgarian question refers to the Treaty of Trianon."

Dr. Horn was overheard briefing Ribbentrop for the afternoon session: He told him to refer any further questions on Jodl's diary to Jodl, and any orders signed by Keitel to Keitel. On the anti-Semitic issue, he should point out that he never made a statement such as Goering's cynical remark that it would have been better to shoot an additional 200 Jews than to destroy so much property. To the latter, Ribbentrop declared, frightened, that he would not dare to say anything against Goering, because he was still a powerful man.

---

AFTERNOON SESSION: *Ribbentrop continued to deny aggressive intentions. The cross-examination reached the depths of the ridiculous when Ribbentrop denied exerting any intolerable pressure on Hacha to surrender Czechoslovakia in violation of the Munich Pact. "What further pressure could you put on the head of a country except to threaten him that your army would march in, in overwhelming strength, and your air force would bomb his capital?" Sir David wanted to know. "War, for instance," Ribbentrop answered innocently, as the whole courtroom roared. Ribbentrop also denied following a deceptive policy of outwardly friendly relations with England while fomenting a coalition against her, until Sir David presented him with a document signed by him, setting forth precisely that policy to Hitler. Ribbentrop kept quibbling about documentary evidence that he had said "Britain would leave Poland coldly in the lurch" in case of an attack; that he had expressed satisfaction after the war started, because he, too, thought the problem should be solved in the Führer's lifetime; that he had urged Japan to attack England.*

---

During the afternoon intermission, Keitel, Goering and Jodl discussed the march into Poland. They had held up the march on the 24th of August, declaring a 5-day postponement on the 25th, and another 24-hour postponement on the 30th, because they were waiting for word of concession to their demands. Then they attacked on the 31st.

Later Keitel said to me: "You see, nobody wants to believe Ribbentrop when he says he did not know about the advance military preparations.—But that is the way it was. Hitler told him one thing and then told us another thing. He lied to each of us in turn." Jodl was listening and anyone could have overheard him. This is the kind of sentiment he never dared express outside of his cell while he was under Goering's influence.

## April 2

MORNING SESSION: *The French prosecutor, M. Faure, cross-examined Ribbentrop, tying him up in knots on his anti-Semitic statements and policies. Ribbentrop had apparently been very active in advocating deportation of Jews from occupied and satellite countries to concentration camps. Ribbentrop protested he was not an anti-Semite but was only obeying the Führer.*

During the morning intermission Hess showed a rare burst of emotional reaction to the testimony. "It is disgraceful and undignified, the way they treat a man on the witness stand! I would never submit to that!" He apparently remembered that he had not taken the stand, but not why. Dr. Seidl and Goering explained to him that he had not been put on the stand because he had lost his memory. Hess suddenly calmed down and began rubbing his forehead and making helpless gestures with his hand. "Oh— is that so?—I do not remember that—." Dr. Seidl assured him, however, that he had made the proper explanation to the court, namely, that it was on account of Hess's attitude toward the court that he did not put him on the stand. "Yes?—What attitude?" Dr. Seidl explained that Hess had said he did not recognize the court. Hess rubbed his forehead. "Oh—did I?"

"Yes, yes," Goering added impatiently. "I said that myself in the beginning.—Then you said it too." Hess shrugged his shoulders. Goering waved his hand in disgust to Raeder behind Hess's back.

AFTERNOON SESSION: *Colonel Amen cross-examined Ribbentrop briefly, using his previous interrogations to tie him up in self-contradictions. Under cross-examination by General Rudenko, Ribbentrop claimed that the attacks on Czechoslovakia, Poland, Yugoslavia, Greece, and Russia did not constitute aggression, ex-*

*actly.* [There was a general feeling among the defendants that Ribbentrop was finished. Goering was heard to lean over to Raeder and say, "Ribbentrop is all washed up." Nevertheless, with his usual hypocrisy, he told Ribbentrop that he was doing fine at the end of the morning session.]

--------- EVENING IN JAIL ---------

*Ribbentrop's Cell:* When I came into his cell in the evening, he looked even more shabby than usual. His shirt was not properly buttoned up or tucked into his baggy pants, his cell was a mess and he was a mess as he sat munching a piece of bread. He asked a number of plaintive questions, rhetorical and otherwise. "Why did the French prosecutor try to stamp me as an anti-Semite?— It is so contrary to my views, and they know that. If I was an anti-Semite at home, I would not be afraid to say so.—I asked Hess what made Hitler so violently anti-Semitic, but he did not know . . . Can you understand my loyalty to Hitler?—I suppose some people cannot understand that.—Tell me frankly, what do you think of my case?" ¯

"I think that as a result of your blind loyalty to Hitler you have gotten yourself into a situation from which you cannot extricate yourself.—But I especially cannot understand why you cannot renounce him now, when all the world knows he was a murderer."

"Can't you?—No, Americans don't seem able to understand that. We Germans are peculiar people; we are so loyal. People don't seem able to understand that."

"No, nobody can understand it."

"Well, I do not know. What would I have done if I had known all about those terrible Jewish murders—"

"You did know about it when the whole world learned of the Maidanek extermination camp."

"Oh, yes—but then it was too late anyway.—I wonder what I would have done if I had known in the beginning, I mean.—I don't know. I could not have opposed him. I would have had to commit suicide.—That would have been the only way. Can you understand that?"

"No, I would certainly have denounced him as a murderer, and if that was impossible, I would have felt it my solemn duty, as a last resort, to kill him myself."

"Oh, no! I simply could never have thought of that. I could never have brought myself to do it."

"Why? Would it have been like killing your own father?"

"Yes, something like that.—And because he became for me the symbol of Germany.—I told you, after we saw the Nazi film in court, if he came to me now, I simply could not renounce him.—I might not *follow* him any more, but *repudiate* him—no, I just could not do it. I don't know why."

# 9. Keitel's Defense

## KEITEL TAKES THE STAND

MORNING SESSION: [As Keitel took the stand, Jodl shifted position in his seat and fumbled his papers nervously. Doenitz tapped nervously on the dock.] *Keitel blinked and wiped his eyes as he told how he tried to do his duty for 44 years and was convinced that the mass of German soldiers acted in good faith and loyalty. There was a sense of earnest pleading in his voice, as he explained that he had no command function and only transmitted Hitler's commands.* [Doenitz, Raeder and Jodl departed from the impassive immobility which they had maintained throughout virtually the whole trial, including the atrocity evidence, and showed some signs of emotion by their facial expression and occasional use of handkerchiefs for surreptitious blowing the nose and wiping the face.]

———————————————

LUNCH HOUR: At lunch Jodl admitted that he was moved, but hesitated to say much about it. "Is it the idea of seeing the Chief of the OKW [High Command] taking the stand before a military tribunal?" I asked.

"Yes, that is it.—To think that it has come to this.—It is certainly something we did not deserve."

"Well, if you didn't then at least you have a chance to tell all the world whose fault it was," I said. He agreed that that was the only consolation. He had already told me that there was nothing he had desired more passionately all his life than this opportunity to tell the world the truth about the German leadership.

Doenitz reserved comment except for the remark, "He is an honest man."

"Yes," said von Papen, "an honest man without a mind of his own. But anyway, an honest man."

"Sure," said Schacht sarcastically, "an honest man, but not a man at all."

237

Goering could still think only of the fact that he was the only important man on the bench. "I've already told the court he had no command function, but I suppose he has to say that himself. The poor devil, he really had nothing to say.—In his case, I can almost understand it when he says, 'Why isn't Hitler here to answer for these things?' Lots of people don't even belong here. I never even heard of Fritzsche before. Where does little Funk fit into this? He only took orders from me. Even Kaltenbrunner wouldn't be here if Himmler were here—"

"But you belong here, don't you?" I said.

"Sure, I would consider it an insult if they had overlooked me."

──────────── April 4 ────────────

MORNING SESSION: *Keitel continued his testimony by relating his disapproval of the attack on Poland because of inadequate preparation, his surprise at the lack of intervention from the West, and his misgivings over the attack on France.*

During the morning intermission Goering was overheard telling the others how they could have wiped out France in 14 days, if his and Hitler's plan to attack immediately after the conquest of Poland had materialized. Dr. Horn asked why they didn't follow through. Goering said it was only the weather that tied up the Luftwaffe. Raeder added that if the winter attack had succeeded, they could have polished off England in the spring of 1940. Goering said it would have taken only 5 airborne divisions to knock out England in the spring if France had already been licked. During the winter Hitler had told him that they now had the choice of trying to beat England on English soil, or waiting until the English came over to France.

LUNCH HOUR: As Keitel returned to the dock before lunch, Goering said to him, "I would have been glad to confirm your *Schlappheit* [weakness] over the attack on France. Why didn't you tell me you were going to say that? I would have been glad to confirm it in advance."

"I know, I know," Keitel answered, not insensitive to the concealed sarcasm, in spite of Goering's slap on the shoulder in congratulation for his performance. "I am just telling the facts as they were."

At lunch Keitel repeated to me that he was only telling the facts as they were, let the chips fall where they may. His lunchroom-mates, Seyss-Inquart and Frank, made encouraging remarks, but Sauckel still remained silent and timid as a mouse—he probably has orders from Goering to be careful of what he says in my presence.

In the Elders' lunchroom, Schacht had the most to say about Keitel's defense of following orders from Hitler, and always trying to be an upright soldier. "It sounds upright, and all that, but it doesn't change the guilt one iota. What if he did follow orders from Hitler and nothing else? There is no law in the world that compels me to commit murder." He then related a story he had heard in concentration camp. The man's cousin was a captain in the German Army, who was going to evacuate 70 PW's to Corps, but a higher officer told him that no prisoners were wanted, and he should "get rid of them." He refused and said he would evacuate them according to normal procedure. The commanding general then came down himself and ordered him to get rid of the prisoners. When the captain refused, the general said, "Do you realize what the consequences are for disobeying a direct order from your commanding officer?" The captain said, "Yes, I realize it fully, and I hereby flatly refuse to obey your order, and will take the consequences." He then turned to his lieutenant and said, "I hereby order you to evacuate these prisoners safely to Corps, and authorize you to use your weapons if anybody tries to stop you, and I hold you personally responsible to me for their safe arrival." The prisoners were evacuated, and nothing more was heard of it. Nothing happened to the captain.

"There!" said Schacht. "There is no law that forces a man to commit murder, but most of the military simply do not have the guts to refuse. I refused. I drew the line at going to war. And that is what I am going to say. I am sorry I cannot spare Keitel and the others the embarrassment, but I must show that they *did not have to obey* that maniac, Hitler!"

Von Papen was reading today's paper and expressed pleasure at the understanding reached between Russia and Iran. He thought that perhaps Churchill's speech had contributed to an understanding after all, because it showed that the Russians could not go too far without arousing criticism. "You see, sometimes plain talk is the best thing. Just imagine what a little plain talk would have done in 1938. Supposing after the breaking of the Munich Pact Chamberlain had put his foot down with the help of the other democracies and said flatly, 'Hitler has broken his solemn pledge, and we hereby break off diplomatic relationships with Hitler's government, and refuse to deal with Germany until it gets an honest leader!' Why, if they had done that, Hitler would have collapsed in a matter of days! It would have forced a showdown and the people simply would not have stood for it. As it was, the whole thing was glossed over, and one thing led to another until a war was inevitable." He went on to show how much was built on bluff, according to Keitel's own testimony today.

───────── EVENING IN JAIL ─────────

*Speer's Cell:* When I saw Speer in his cell this evening, he was considerably depressed and expressed great concern over the turn the trial was taking. The defendants were getting away with their poses of upright loyalty, the court was cutting off the prosecution from asking questions of political and psychological interest. He was disturbed that Goering and Keitel were not being unmasked for their failure to spare the people unnecessary death and misery, but were being allowed to use the trial as a means of making a graceful exit as loyal nationalists. "One judges individuals and movements by their last moments. It would have been better to let Nazism end on a note of collapse and corruption and the basic rottenness and disgrace of the whole thing, as it did at the end of the war, instead of adding another final chapter that gives some of the leaders a chance to make fine speeches and make a good appearance in history, and make the people think there was something good in it after all." He was worried that at this rate his own line of attack would fall flat. I have never seen him so depressed.

In the prisoner's dock of the Nuremberg courtroom twenty-one indicted Nazi leaders await their sentences. Left to right, first row: Hermann Goering; Rudolf Hess; Joachim von Ribbentrop; Wilhelm Keitel; Ernst Kaltenbrunner; Alfred Rosenberg; Hans Frank; Wilhelm Frick; Julius Streicher; Walther Funk; Hjalmar Schacht. Back row: Karl Doenitz; Erich Raeder; Baldur von Schirach; Fritz Sauckel; Alfred Jodl; Franz von Papen; Artur Seyss-Inquart; Albert Speer; Konstantin von Neurath; and Hans Fritzsche.

Results of one day's work in the concentration camp at Weimar, Germany.

GOERING    STREICHER

HESS    KALTENBRUNNER

VON RIBBENTROP    FRANK


KEITEL    ROSENBERG

Von Ribbentrop testifies on the witness stand under the screen on which atrocity films were shown.

Allied prosecutors Robert H. Jackson, American, and Uri Pokrovsky, Assistant Prosecutor, of Russia, listen to the sum-up speeches. Justice Jackson, in his summation, said, "They have been given the kind of a trial which they, in the days of their pomp and power, never gave to any man. . . ."

The Palace of Justice, site of the trials, in Nuremberg, Germany.

A twenty-four-hour watch was put on each cell in the Nuremberg Prison after Robert Ley, one of the defendants, committed suicide.

SAUCKEL   FRITZSCHE

FRICK   JODL

—Photo from European

**SCHACHT    SEYSS-INQUART**

**DOENITZ    VON PAPEN**

—United Press International Photo

—United Press International Photo

Allied judges sit beneath the flags of their respective nations. Left to right, rear: A. F. Volchkov and I. T. Nikitchenko, of Soviet Russia; Norman Birkett and Geoffrey Lawrence, President of the Court, of Great Britain; Francis Biddle and John J. Parker, of the United States; and M. Henri Donnedieu de Vabres and M. Robert Falco, of France.

Three of Hitler's yes-men were found not guilty and were acquitted. Colonel B. C. Andrus, in charge of the Nuremberg Prison, presents letters certifying freedom to (left to right) Hans Fritzsche, Franz von Papen, and Hjalmar Schacht. Eleven others were declared guilty and sentenced to death by hanging; seven received sentences of from ten years to life imprisonment.

# ──────────── April 5 ────────────

## A POINT D'HONNEUR

*Keitel's Cell:* I saw Keitel in his cell before going up to court in the morning. He said he was going to take up the matter of handling of prisoners and the Giraud assassination affair. Even though the latter was a comparatively minor matter in the whole complex of aggressive war and mass murder, it was a point d'honneur, and he had to make some explanation. Canaris had misrepresented the thing, and so had Lahousen in his testimony. Anyway, he thought, Canaris was a shady character. He is now convinced that it was Canaris who tipped off the Dutch to grab the German courier who came to Holland to tip off the German Ambassador that Holland was going to be invaded. The Dutch police were waiting for him at the border, thus preventing the Dutch queen from getting a formal announcement of the invasion through the German Ambassador. The other point of officer's honor that he thought was already cleared up was the matter of his loyalty to a man like Hitler. "I've already told the court that I have been loyal to Hitler, but he never trusted me, and never told me the truth."

─────────────

MORNING SESSION: *Keitel explained that he had only general supervision and direction of prisoner camps under his jurisdiction, and that he did have a serious quarrel with Hitler over handing over the escaped British fliers to Himmler, knowing perfectly well it meant murder. He then gave an explanation of the Weygand and Giraud affairs (after mentioning briefly that he had nothing to do with Rosenberg's looting expeditions and never got a pfennig's worth of loot out of it—a subtle dig at Goering). [The military section leaned forward and watched Keitel intently as he gave his testimony on these points, as if it was the high point of the whole defense.] Keitel explained that he had merely transmitted an order for surveillance of Weygand and the recapture or voluntary return of Giraud. [He ignored the fact that Canaris*

had told him assassination was not in their line and he should give
the job to Heydrich.]

---

LUNCH HOUR: The explanation satisfied the military clique, and
Keitel was welcomed back to the dock virtually with open arms.
The honor of the Wehrmacht had been exonerated. The murdering of British fliers, the "special treatment" of Russian prisoners
all faded into the background—Keitel had not violated the code
by trying to assassinate a fellow-general. Doenitz slapped him on
the back and said, "Great work!" Keitel said he was glad he had
a chance to explain that Giraud affair finally. Doenitz assured him
that he had explained it perfectly. Goering concealed his annoyance over the reference to the looting, and also congratulated him.

Up in the lunchroom Doenitz said, "You see how a man can be
put under a thoroughly unjustified suspicion in a trial like this?
That man Lahousen was a louse. Those espionage men are all that
way. And Keitel has to wait four months before he can clear his
reputation. That's what burns me up about this trial."

Goering commented on Keitel's technique. "He is using a different approach. He is answering each and every one of the
charges directly to forestall the cross-examination. I merely gave
my general line and then dug in for the attack."

I told him it might have been better to face the issue squarely
and recognize the fact that Hitler was a murderer. A currently
reported newspaper interview with his wife bore the headline
"FRAU GOERING CALLS HERMANN 'TOO FAITHFUL'
TO HITLER." I showed it to him, and summarized her repetition
of the story of Hitler's order to murder the family, just as she had
told it to me. "Oh, well," he said, "that's all right. She is a woman
—that's what women are for. People will understand that." We
went on to discuss the matter, but struck a snag again over the
killing of women and children. Goering said he could even go so
far as to conceive of the murdering of Russian prisoners, Jews,
political enemies, but he just could not get it through his head
that Hitler had deliberately ordered the murdering of women and
children. That was the only thing about which his "sense of
chivalry" gave him any real misgivings.

I pressed the matter further, suggesting that in spite of his good
judgment of character, he did not understand psychopathology.

(He has accepted this ever since Hess's relapse of amnesia proved I was right.) Hitler and Himmler were psychopaths, I suggested, even though they could speak very nobly in polite society. He agreed that must have been the case with Himmler, but wrestled with the thought of applying it to Hitler. Again he seized his forehead as if trying to squeeze out an image of how Hitler could have done it. I suggested the picture: Hitler, obsessed by anti-Semitism and incapable of countenancing opposition or moderation, finally told Himmler, "Get rid of them—I don't care how—I don't want to hear any more about it!" Goering thought a moment, apparently visualizing the scene, then declared that that was the way it probably had come about.

I pursued the matter of his attitude toward the collapse of Nazism. He recalled the decision to surrender to the Americans in preference to the Russians or British, although they were all approximately equidistant from his castle near Berchtesgaden after his rescue by his parachute regiment. He admitted he was very bitter against Hitler at the time, and quite ready to co-operate with the Americans. "You could have had Germany cheap then. Most of the leaders would have been glad to co-operate—and even the war crimes trials would have been handled better with our co-operation . . . But after you kept me prisoner and put me on trial as a war criminal—well . . . " Obviously, the deal was supposed to include chivalrous treatment of a defeated war lord, and putting *him* on trial as a war criminal was simply not cricket. He would have been glad to co-operate in liquidating the murderers of women and children, but under the present circumstances would maintain his loyalty to the Führer.

───────────── April 6 ─────────────

## KEITEL IS CROSS-EXAMINED

MORNING SESSION: *Sir David Maxwell-Fyfe cross-examined Keitel. He presented a letter that Keitel had written to Colonel Amen before the trial, explaining that he was only a soldier and that Hitler* was responsible for the terroristic and illegal measures. [As the letter was read, Goering turned around to Doenitz contemptuously and said, "The little weakling." A little while later he said, "The little white lamb, he had nothing to do with the Party!—Why, if he hadn't been in sympathy with National Socialism he wouldn't have lasted a minute!"] *The cross-examination continued with sharp rebuke for the killing of captured saboteurs, the reprisals against families of Allied volunteers, the shooting of escaped prisoners and other violations of international law. Keitel could only admit that these things had taken place and that he had signed such orders in spite of his personal misgivings.*

[When he came back to the dock Goering asked him angrily why he hadn't retaliated by saying something about the Allies' treatment of saboteurs. Keitel retorted in annoyance, "There is still time for that." Goering replied, "But *this* was the best time to bring it up, and you bungled it!!!" Keitel sat back in angry silence. Goering, still fuming, continued, "That document did not specify anything about the mothers being shot!—Why don't you *read* the documents they hand you?!" Keitel did not answer or even look at him and continued to sit in stony silence. As the routine business of proposing witnesses and documents by the attorneys continued, Goering cursed the stupid attorneys, cursed Keitel's weakness, cursed the prosecution and everything around him.]

--------------------- April 6-7 ---------------------

## WEEK END IN JAIL

*Keitel's Cell:* I visited Keitel in his cell with Major Goldensohn after the morning session. Keitel reviewed the cross-examination repeating many of the questions and answers. Finally he observed, "I could only tell them the way things were. The only thing that is absolutely impossible for me is to sit there like a louse and lie —that is absolutely impossible! I would rather say, 'Yes, I did sign it.'" He waved his fist in his characteristic gesture, apparently reacting to Goering's needling on his failure to evade responsibility or minimizing the crime by using clever evasive arguments.

"—As I said in the beginning, whether it is guilt or the working of fate, it is something that one cannot say; but in any case it is impossible to let the subordinate take the blame and deny one's own responsibility."

It was clear that this was his main argument for making Hitler take the blame for him, just as he had to take the blame for things done on his order. I put the question bluntly, "Do you feel then that Hitler was the real murderer?"

"Yes, of course!" he replied emphatically with a wave of both fists, "—but that doesn't mean that I too should be branded a murderer! I can only say that I passed on his orders. As Sir David Maxwell-Fyfe gave me the opportunity to say, there were many things that I did not approve of—the shooting of hostages, the mistreatment of Russian prisoners, the shooting of escaped British fliers . . . but what could I do? I might have committed suicide but then somebody else would have come in my place anyway. I thought I would prevent the worst things even if I did not prevent much that was bad."

*Doenitz' Cell:* Doenitz was very annoyed at Keitel's cross-examination. The honor of the Wehrmacht was being discredited after all. "I would have answered those questions quite differently. He is too weak. As long as he did go so far as to sign those orders he could at least have said that the Russians did just as much and worse." I pointed out that, since Hitler attacked Russia and started the war in the first place, one could hardly blame the Russians for hating Germany and taking sharp measures to repulse the enemy on their soil. Doenitz then fell back on the usual argument, "Well, I guess Hitler felt that Russia would attack us sooner or later anyway."

*Ribbentrop's Cell:* Ribbentrop was not particularly concerned about Keitel's testimony, but was still worried about the impression he himself had made in court. One thing that still bothered him was the fact that Mr. Dodd had said he was not sick but only nervous. "In the protocol it says that Mr. Dodd told the court that I was nervous. Did you tell him that? That is not fair." I pointed out to him that I was not the medical officer and that anyway a nervous condition was indicated. He then asked me what people were saying about his case and what I thought of it.

"Well, they say it is too bad you followed Hitler so slavishly," I told him.

"Oh, they can say that, but I wonder what they would say if Hitler himself would appear in court. I bet they would all be amazed. People who seem so impressive now would shrink in size, even Sir David Maxwell-Fyfe.—Believe me, I saw how it always happened that way, even Chamberlain, Daladier and the rest of them. People were terrifically impressed by him."

He also thought it was unfair that people blamed him for the use of "diplomatic language." "Have you ever played poker? You know how it is—you can't win a hundred dollar pot for a nickel; you have to gamble all the way. If I knew that Hitler wanted to wage war and it was my job to try to solve the problem diplomatically, I could not tell Ciano that Hitler is only fooling because then that report would go to all of the capitals of Europe and nobody would want to negotiate and then there would be war . . . As I said, it was better to tell Hacha that Hitler meant business than to have war." The laughter in the courtroom over that part of his testimony apparently still stung him.

"You mean it is better to threaten war than to wage it," I suggested, offering a logical explanation of the point. He agreed. "But, when they call your bluff you have war anyway, don't you? —and threatening war is gangsterism anyway, isn't it?" He mumbled something about diplomacy being very difficult to understand but diplomats understand such things.

---

*Jodl's Cell:* Jodl recalled that he was also furious over the killing of the English fliers. "—A sheer, willful, utterly unjustified crime! —I knew that was one thing we could never justify.—From then on I knew what kind of man Hitler was.—I bucked him at every turn on such matters, because I knew that Keitel was no man to stand up against him. But the order to kill the escaped British fliers—there was absolutely no justification for that—just the sheer, arbitrary, wilful fury of Hitler against Keitel for not preventing prisoners from escaping. I knew that that was something we could never explain. In fact, when the British called for Keitel after the Armistice, I told him it was on account of that affair."

"The killing of the 50 escaped prisoners and the assassination plot against Giraud seem to disturb the military men more than the whole murder program that exterminated millions of Jews and other ideological opponents," I commented.

"Yes, of course—that concerns our honor vitally. We had nothing to do with the other thing. It will be shown conclusively that we had nothing to do with that."

He went on to explain how Hitler had disrupted the entire basis of the officers' code of honor and fair play in war which had been handed down through the centuries. Hitler brought with him a new radical capricious will which did not fit into their world —the world of von Hindenburg, von Neurath, etc. Even Goering understood the old officers' code and frequently had his way with the Führer on such matters.

"How do you explain, then, that Goering still maintains his pose of loyalty to the Führer?" I asked.

Jodl smiled. "Well, in his case, of course, he is in it so deep, as one of the leaders who brought the Party to power and loudly proclaimed his loyalty to the Führer for 20 years, he might just as well stick it through . . . But the rest of the old officers' set were opposed to Nazism from the very beginning. We only played along because he was legally chosen Reich Chancellor. But it is funny, in the last two or three years of the war, Goering simply disappeared from time to time, going hunting, living his soft life in his various castles, collecting his art treasures—he just couldn't be depended on for anything."

---

*Speer's Cell:* Speer was of the opinion that Keitel was being more honest than Goering. He not only said that he assumed responsibility for orders he signed, but admitted that they were crimes and that he knew that he would have to suffer the consequences. Goering, on the other hand, had loudly proclaimed his loyalty to the Führer knowing perfectly well that the court could not hang him for that, but defended himself in every possible way on criminal counts. He resorted to many and diverse means of evading and belittling the issues, depending on his skill in rhetoric and argumentation. To the accusation that he had said it would have been better to kill another 200 Jews rather than to destroy so much property in 1938, Goering had merely reacted by brushing it aside as a "temperamental utterance." On the issue of killing the 50 British fliers, he had emphasized his own absence at the time and his violent disapproval of the act. In planning aggressive war, he tried to show that he had tried to avoid it by negotiation through Dahlerus, even though the prosecution soon showed this up to have been an insincere move. He even sought credit for such trivial things as refusing to report the name of a Luftwaffe officer who had interfered with the lynching of Allied fliers.

Speer still has some misgivings about the way Goering has gotten away with the pose of a loyal patriot, but feels that the trial is succeeding in any event in proving the guilt of the Nazi leadership.

## April 8

## CRIMINAL ORDERS

MORNING SESSION: *Sir David Maxwell-Fyfe continued with the cross-examination of Keitel, pinning him down on the execution of the 50 British fliers and the plans of aggression against Czechoslovakia and Poland.*

*The cross-examination was concluded with Keitel's statement that, if the generals had known before [what Hitler was up to], they would have fought against him. Then Mr. Dodd got Keitel to admit that he had knowingly transmitted criminal orders from Hitler. In re-examination by his attorney, Keitel repeated that they might accuse him of weakness and guilt but not of disloyalty or dishonesty. [Goering scowled and cursed under his breath through all of this.] To Justice Lawrence's inquiry, Keitel was not able to indicate that he ever made any effective protest in writing against any of Hitler's policies.*

LUNCH HOUR: When Keitel returned to the dock, Goering was again overheard upbraiding him for his frank answers to such dangerous questions. "You don't have to answer so damn directly! You should have said you were a good soldier and were obeying orders loyally! You don't have to answer that criminal business.— The question itself doesn't matter so much as the way you answer it. You can dodge around such dangerous questions and wait until they hand you one you have a good answer for, and then sail into it!"

"But I can't make white out of black!" Keitel retorted in annoyance.

Goering insisted, "You can always get around such questions until they hand you what you want. They are bound to sooner or later!" Keitel did not answer.

After they had gone up to their respective lunchrooms, Keitel said to me. "There, I put it just as I told you. I answered the questions honestly—even that one Mr. Dodd put to me. He asked me if I admitted that I had transmitted criminal orders. I said 'Yes.' What else could I say? Let them judge it as they will—it was the truth. Of course, if I wanted to get technical about it, I could have said that paragraph 47 in our military law specified that it was a crime to execute orders that are given with criminal motivation. I did not execute such orders—I merely transmitted them. But after all, that is only a legalistic technicality and there is no use trying to dodge the issue on such petty argumentation."

—————— April 9 ——————

## COLONEL HOESS OF AUSCHWITZ

*Hoess's Cell:* Examined Rudolf Hoess, 46, commandant of the Auschwitz concentration camp, who has recently been captured, in anticipation of Kaltenbrunner's defense.

After completing his test, we discussed briefly his activity as the commandant of the Auschwitz concentration camp from May, 1940, to December, 1943, which camp was the central extermination camp for Jews. He readily confirmed that approximately 2½ million Jews had been exterminated under his direction. The exterminations began in the summer of 1941. In compliance with Goering's skepticism, I asked Hoess how it was technically possible to exterminate 2½ million people. "Technically?" he asked. "That wasn't so hard—it would not have been hard to exterminate even greater numbers." In answer to my rather naïve questions as to how many people could be done away with in an hour, etc., he explained that one must figure it on a daily 24-hour basis, and it was possible to exterminate up to 10,000 in one 24-hour period. He explained that there were actually 6 extermination chambers. The 2 big ones could accommodate as many as 2,000 in each and the 4 smaller ones up to 1500, making a total capacity of 10,000 a day. I tried to figure out how this was done, but he corrected me. "No, you don't figure it right. The killing itself took the least time. You could dispose of 2,000 head in a half hour, but it was the burning that took all the time. The killing was easy; you didn't even need guards to drive them into the chambers; they just went in expecting to take showers and, instead of water, we turned on poison gas. The whole thing went very quickly." He related all of this in a quiet, apathetic, matter-of-fact tone of voice.

I was interested in finding out how the order had actually been given and what his reactions were. He related it as follows: "In the summer of 1941, Himmler called for me and explained: 'The Führer has ordered the *Endlösung* [final solution] of the Jewish question—and we have to carry out this task. For reasons of transportation and isolation, I have picked Auschwitz for this. You now have the hard job of carrying this out.' As a reason for this he said that it would have to be done at this time, because if it was not done now, then the Jew would later exterminate the German people—or words to that effect. For this reason one had to ignore all human considerations and consider only the task—or words to that effect." I asked him whether he didn't express any opinion on the subject or show any reluctance. "I had nothing to say; I could only say *Jawohl!* In fact, it was exceptional that he called me to give me any explanation. He could have sent me an order and I would have had to execute it just the same. We could only execute orders without any further consideration. That is the way it was. He often demanded impossible things, which could not be done under normal circumstances, but, once given the order, one set about doing it with his entire energy and often did things that seemed impossible. For example, the building of the dam on the Weichsel River in Auschwitz which I estimated would require three years; he gave us one year in which to finish it and we did."

I pressed him further for some reaction to the enormity of what he was to undertake. He continued in the same apathetic manner: "At the moment I could not oversee the whole thing, but later I got some idea of its extent.—But I only thought of the necessity of it, as the order was put to me." I asked him whether he couldn't refuse to obey the orders. "No, from our entire training the thought of refusing an order just didn't enter one's head, regardless of what kind of order it was . . . Guess you cannot understand our world.—I naturally had to obey orders and I must now stand to take the consequences." What kind of consequences? "Why, that they will have a trial and hang me, naturally." I asked whether he didn't consider the consequences at the time he started the job. "At that time there were no consequences to consider. It didn't occur to me at all that I would be held responsible. You see, in Germany it was understood that if something went wrong, then the man who gave the orders was responsible. So I didn't think that I would ever have to answer for it myself."

"But, what about the human—?" I started to ask.

"That just didn't enter into it," was the pat answer before I could finish the question. I asked him whether he didn't think he would hang for murder as soon as he started it. "No, never."

"When did it first occur to you then that you would probably be brought to trial and hanged?"

"At the time of the collapse—when the Führer died."

---

LUNCH HOUR: Goering had said he wanted to know how it was technically possible to murder 2½ million Jews. I explained it to him during the lunch hour, just as Hoess explained to me this morning: each of the gas chambers could accommodate up to 1500 or 2000 persons; the killing was easy but the burning of bodies took all the time and manpower. Goering felt extremely uncomfortable at the realization that it was no longer possible to deny the extent of the mass murders on the basis of the technical incredibility of the numbers. He wanted to know just how the order was given. I told him that Himmler had given it to him directly as a Führerbefehl (order from the Führer).

"He is just another German being loyal to the Führer," I commented.

"Oh, but that has nothing to do with loyalty—he could just as easily have asked for some other job—or something," Goering speculated. "Of course, somebody else would have done it any-way."

"What about killing the man who ordered the mass murder?" I asked.

"Oh, that is easily said, but you cannot do that sort of thing. What kind of a system would that be if anybody could kill the commanding officer if he didn't like his orders? You have got to have obedience in a military system."

"If I am not mistaken, millions of Germans are sick of this obedience and blind loyalty among their leaders. I think they would have preferred a little less loyalty to the permanent shame that loyalty to the Führer has brought them. There is an article on the trials in yesterday's *Nürnberger Nachrichten* with the headline 'Blind Obedience without Conscience.' You ought to read it and see what the people think of your blind obedience, and Ribbentrop's and Keitel's."

"Ach, what the American-controlled newspapers print now does not mean a damn." He nevertheless seemed disturbed over the idea that this was what the German people were reading and agreeing with nowadays.

--------------------------------- April 10 ---------------------------------

## RUSSIAN PRISONERS

MORNING SESSION: *General Westhoff was cross-examined on the treatment of Allied prisoners. The session ended with some questions about the authenticity of a document.* [As the court adjourned Jodl sprang up and shouted at his attorney, red-faced with rage, "Goddammit, why don't you tell them to ask somebody who knows! Why do they beat around the bush asking an amateur legalistic questions! Of course thousands of Russian prisoners came in transports frozen to death!—so did our own soldiers! There were train-loads and fields full of starved and frozen soldiers! Why don't they ask me? I could tell them and give them a belly-full!"]

LUNCH HOUR: At lunch he continued to explain what he was so excited about. "It burns me up as a soldier to see these damned lawyers picking around the technicalities of a document, when every soldier who fought on the Eastern front remembers what a horror and a nightmare that winter of 1941 was.—Of course thousands of prisoners died of starvation and cold! The Russians had been putting up last-ditch resistance in spite of cold and starvation, living on roots and the human flesh of their dead comrades. —I could show you pictures of it with pieces chewed off the thighs—and they died like flies!—Why, they were half dead when we captured them; but so were our own soldiers! We were fighting in 45° below—even the cylinder blocks in our trucks cracked in that cold, in spite of the anti-freeze.—Hospital trains arrived with carloads of frozen soldiers both Russian and German.—It was horrible!—horrible!—It was a nightmare we'll never forget! Fighting in a wilderness of space and snow—the Russian space is beyond conception.—And now these damned lawyers ask stupid questions about the initials on a document!—It is enough to make you explode!—Why don't they read about Napoleon's retreat from Moscow?! Ours was even worse!"

He went on for several minutes describing the torture of the first winter offensive and the subsequent retreat. Kaltenbrunner, Frick, and Rosenberg pricked their ears from their respective corners. I could only comment, "I guess Hitler didn't figure on that when he broke the Russian Non-Aggression Pact." Jodl gave me a knowing look but didn't say anything.

The references to the Russian campaign must have started Frank on another flare-up of Hitler-denunciation. He harangued his neighbors in the dock after they came down from lunch: "It was the most criminal madness in the history of the German Reich!—He thought he could simply grab off Russia with one sweep of the hand, just as he did Czechoslovakia." He made the appropriate gesture with his gloved hand. Then, seeing me, he added: "Imagine throwing the fate of a nation of 70 million against the endless space of Russia with its 180 million population! —just because of the iron will of one man!"

Goering was overheard discussing the evidence with Doenitz and Raeder. Doenitz wondered whether Keitel really knew all that was going on concerning the treatment of prisoners. Goering leaned over and whispered, "Listen, children. Just between us, I think he did." He then changed the subject and spoke loudly about the German court stenographers, and how much more innocuous the testimony looked in the transcript, so that Keitel would not suspect what he had just said behind his back.

Keitel, feeling himself on the spot with respect to Westhoff's testimony on the killing of the British fliers, said to Jodl, "You know how it was—it was all arranged between Hitler and Himmler."

# 10. Kaltenbrunner's Defense

## KALTENBRUNNER TAKES THE STAND

*Kaltenbrunner's Cell:* I visited Kaltenbrunner in his cell before we went up for the beginning of his defense. He seemd to be in good condition except for a little hesitation in speech. As expected, he hinted at his defense along lines of evasion of formal responsibility of concentration camps. "That organizational chart of the RSHA—I will be able to demolish that myself in a few minutes."

"But what about the mass murders?"

"That is just it. I can prove that I had nothing to do with it. I neither gave orders nor executed them. You have no idea how secret these things were kept even from me."

"Frankly, I doubt if many people can believe that you, as nominal Chief of the RSHA, had nothing to do with concentration camps and knew nothing about the whole mass murder program."

"But that is because of newspaper propaganda. I told you when I saw the newspaper headline 'GAS CHAMBER EXPERT CAPTURED' and an American lieutenant explained it to me, I was pale with amazement. How can they say such things about me?—I told you I was only in charge of the Intelligence Service from 1943 on. The British even admitted that they tried to assassinate me because of that—not because of having anything to do with atrocities, you can be sure of that."

I asked him whether he was going to bring Hoess as a witness. He said he was not sure; it depended on whether the attorneys felt it would help his case and could throw light on the whole issue. He said that his attorney, Dr. Kauffmann, was a very conscientious man and had hauled him over the coals much more mercilessly than even the prosecution might be expected to. He seemed rather afraid of the forthright direct examination that he expected from his attorney. He said that Dr. Kauffmann didn't understand his case very well (apparently covering the fact that his attorney was not very happy about his proposed evasive defense).

---

MORNING SESSION: *Dr. Kauffmann began Kaltenbrunner's defense with affidavits by Mildner and Hoettl, two other Gestapo officials, testifying that Kaltenbrunner was a nice man and that he was not Himmler's right hand man, but simply a weak stooge, because Himmler did not want a rival for his power such as Heydrich had been.*

*Kaltenbrunner then took the stand and started his personal defense with an explanation of his nationalistic motives as an Austrian, his moral purpose, his loyalty, and his ignorance of concentration camps. To be sure, he was Himmler's second-in-command as formal head of the RSHA, but he was only supposed to be in charge of the intelligence service, and therefore could not know anything.* [Goering was overheard telling Doenitz; "Just listen to that—tsk! tsk!" Doenitz answered, "He ought to be ashamed of himself."] *Recalcitrant slave laborers were only sent to "labor education camps."*

---

LUNCH HOUR: Fritzsche commented, "Yes, he is trying to make himself out as someone who could not hurt a fly; I am surprised his attorney even lets him use that line.—But after all, Dr. Kauffmann has a hell of a case."

Schacht showed his impatience. "They ought to ask him just one question: 'Were you the superior officer or weren't you?' What's the use of beating around the bush about whether he signed this or that order, or whether a subordinate signed it for him and showed it to him? It is his responsibility to know what is going on."

Later Fritzsche said bluntly, "He is lying."

I made a remark to Schacht that Kaltenbrunner seemed to be another "loyal German."

"Never mind. I'll have plenty to say about that loyalty business when I get up," Schacht retorted emphatically.

Speer nodded, "Yes, you can depend on it; there will be a lot said about that from this end of the dock."

Before the afternoon session started, Frank said to me, laughing,

"Well, it seems that I am the only guilty one in the dock—everybody is so innocent!"

Rosenberg started saying something about the prosecution blocking questions for the defense of his philosophy. He said he merely wanted to show that he was not the creator of the ideas in the Nazi ideology, but had forerunners even in French philosophy. I told him that the trial could not degenerate into a debate over the history of philosophy and anti-Semitism of the past century. Thereupon Rosenberg retorted, "Yes, of course, then it just becomes an Inquisition against an ideology, with no argument on the subject!"

"How do you mean, Inquisition?" I asked. "You are being given every reasonable opportunity to defend yourself."

Frank bristled with clenched teeth, looking daggers at Rosenberg. "He means an Inquisition like the Roman Catholic Church —don't you, Rosenberg?" Frank glared at Rosenberg, who looked the other way. That brought the argument to an abrupt end, and the two sat in stony silence looking away from each other, waiting for the afternoon session to begin.

---

AFTERNOON SESSION: *Colonel Amen first produced counter-affidavits of the same Mildner and Hoettl who had testified that Kaltenbrunner was a nice man, stating that Kaltenbrunner was, in fact, responsible for transmitting orders for exterminations and the shooting of Anglo-American commandos. Kaltenbrunner quibbled about the chain-of-command, tried to evade the issue, and finally said he had protested to Hitler and Himmler about these measures. He denied responsibility for concentration camps and everything else he was charged with, shifting the blame to Himmler, Heydrich, Mueller, and Pohl, his superior, predecessor, and subordinates in the Gestapo setup.*

---

## April 12

---

MORNING SESSION: *Colonel Amen proceeded to cross-examine Kaltenbrunner, presenting him with documents, inconsistent statements, and direct accusations, calling forth a constant series of flat denials, even of his own signature on the documents. Kaltenbrunner maintained the position that even as Chief of the In-*

*telligence Service under Himmler he knew nothing about the atrocities in his own organization.* [Sauckel frequently muttered, "Ach, you devil—you swine—"]

———————————————————

LUNCH HOUR: The other defendants expressed their contempt and skepticism throughout the entire cross-examination and, at lunch, Raeder, Doenitz and Seyss-Inquart remarked that it was stupid of him to try to deny everything because it stands to reason that he must have known something about something when he was the nominal chief of the organization. Speer tried to explain Kaltenbrunner's denials as "prison psychosis." He thought that Kaltenbrunner had actually talked himself into a misconception of his entire role in the RSHA and had blocked out many things that had actually taken place.

"But, for heaven's sake, can one believe that he didn't know anything about anything?" Fritzsche protested. "—and that he seriously disagreed with Himmler even in 1943?—Why, if he did, he never would have lasted until the end of the war.—They would have liquidated him in a minute."

Von Schirach's attorney asked him if he should ask Kaltenbrunner any questions. "Don't bother," von Schirach admonished him. "He can't help himself; how can he help anybody else?"

————————— AFTERNOON IN JAIL —————————

*Colonel Hoess's Cell:* After completing today's test, Hoess said: "I suppose you want to know in this way if my thoughts and habits are normal."

"Well, what do you think?" I asked.

"I am entirely normal. Even while I was doing this extermination work, I led a normal family life, and so on."

"Did you have a normal social life?"

"Well, perhaps it is a peculiarity of mine, but I always felt best alone.—If I had worries I tried to work them out myself.—That was the thing that disturbed my wife most.—I was so self-sufficient. I never had friends or a close relationship with anybody— even in my youth.—I never had a friend. And in company, I was sometimes present, but not spiritually. I was glad when people enjoyed themselves, but I could never participate with them."

"Did that ever bother you?"

"No, never—even now, while I was in the farm, hiding, I felt best when I was alone with the horses in the field."

"In hiding, yes, but before?"

"Yes—I was always alone.—Of course, I loved my wife, but a real spiritual union—that was lacking."

"Did you notice it and did your wife notice it?"

"Yes, I did, and so did my wife. My wife thought I wasn't satisfied with her, but I told her it was just my nature, and she had to be reconciled to it." I asked him about the sexual relationship. "Well, it was normal—but after my wife found out about what I was doing, we rarely had desire for intercourse. Things looked normal outwardly, but I guess there was an estrangement, now that I look back . . . No, I never had any need for friends—I never even had any real intimacy with my parents—my sisters either. It only occurred to me after they were married that they were like strangers to me.—I always played alone as a child. Even my grandmother says I never had any playmates as a child."

Sex never played a great part in his life. He could take it or leave it—never felt the urge to have or continue a love affair, although he had momentary affairs now and then. Married life also —very rarely showed any passion. Claims he never even felt the desire to masturbate and never did.

I asked him if he had ever considered whether the Jews whom he had murdered were guilty or had in any way deserved such a fate. Again he tried patiently to explain that there was something unrealistic about such questions because he had been living in an entirely different world. "Don't you see, we SS men were not supposed to think about these things; it never even occurred to us. —And besides, it was something already taken for granted that the Jews were to blame for everything." I pressed him for some explanation of why it was taken for granted. "Well, we just never heard anything else. It was not just newspapers like the Stürmer but it was everything we ever heard. Even our military and ideological training took for granted that we had to protect Germany from the Jews . . . It only started to occur to me after the collapse that maybe it was not quite right, after I heard what everybody was saying.—But nobody had ever said these things before; at least we never heard of it. Now I wonder if Himmler really believed all that himself or just gave me an excuse to justify what he wanted me to do.—But anyway, that really didn't matter. We were all so trained to obey orders without even thinking that the thought of disobeying an order would simply never have occurred to anybody and somebody else would have done just as well if I hadn't . . . Himmler was so strict about little things, and executed SS men for such small offenses, that we naturally took it for granted that he was acting according to a strict code of honor . . . You can be sure that it was not always a pleasure to see those mountains of corpses and smell the continual burning.—But Himmler had ordered it and had even explained the necessity and I really never gave much thought to whether it was wrong. It just seemed a necessity."

In all of the discussions Hoess is quite matter-of-fact and apathetic, shows some belated interest in the enormity of his crime, but gives the impression that it never would have occurred to him if somebody hadn't asked him. There is too much apathy to leave any suggestion of remorse and even the prospect of hanging does not unduly distress him. One gets the general impression of a man who is intellectually normal but with the schizoid apathy, insensitivity and lack of empathy that could hardly be more extreme in a frank psychotic.

——————————— April 13-14 ———————————

## WEEK END IN JAIL

*Kaltenbrunner's Cell:* Concerning his own denial of his signature on a couple of documents, he said it was possible that he may have signed them, but he did not recognize the signature and he signed so many things—. The prosecution really had not given him time to study those documents. I asked him when he learned about the mass murders which he claimed to be ignorant of in the beginning. This brought forth another evasive answer.

"That is a typical American question—you want to make things exact. It is not as simple as all of that. I cannot say I found out about it on any particular date; all I can say is that, as soon as I learned things were not being done according to law—after all, I am a lawyer—I protested to Himmler."

"It couldn't have been a very effective protest," I commented.

"You Americans, like Colonel Amen, seem to think that our whole RSHA was nothing but an organized gang of criminals," Kaltenbrunner protested.

"I must say that impression does exist."

"Then how can I defend myself against such prejudice?" Kaltenbrunner wanted to know.

---

*Speer's Cell:* Speer has decided that Kaltenbrunner is not suffering from "prison psychosis"—he is just lying. He has probably made up his mind to deny everything and then to figure out as good an explanation as he can. Speer is not so worried any more about the other Nazis making too good an impression. Ribbentrop, Keitel and Kaltenbrunner have made bad impressions as Nazi leaders, and Goering's attitude can now be seen as a pose in the light of the criminal irresponsibility of the whole system. He thinks that Kaltenbrunner will make an especially bad impression among the German people because in saying that he knew nothing he implies that his subordinates are guilty. The SS men will be especially incensed at this because their whole tradition was loyalty to their superiors who were supposed to bear the responsibility for any orders given.

---

*Rosenberg's Cell:* Rosenberg thought that "Kaltenbrunner was really not as bad as Heydrich.—He has a very difficult case.—But, of course, I don't blame the court if they don't believe what he says."

He was nervously anticipating his own defense and said that he would not try to enter into debate on his philosophy, because the court was apparently not interested in it. I then asked him whether apart from all of the legal considerations he did not have some misgivings about his anti-Semitism.

"Well, that depends on how you look at it. Naturally, after all that has taken place, I must say that it is horrible how things have turned out, but you can't tell those things in advance. You see, even in 1934 I made a speech calling for a *chivalrous* solution of the Jewish question . . . I assure you no one ever dreamed that it would result in mass murder."

---

*Schacht's Cell:* "Really, if I were a judge, I would be quite embarrassed. How can a man lie under oath like that? I haven't the slightest doubt that the judges don't believe him. Neither do I. Neither does any one. Now he might have said, 'Look, gentlemen, believe it or not, I signed these things without paying much attention, and naturally I must take the consequences. As for the rest, I was responsible for what went on and it was my duty to know. How much I knew is now an academic question and I don't see the point in arguing about it.' Something like that might have been understandable. But these flat denials and lies—ugh! Really it makes us all very uncomfortable because it throws a shadow over all of us. You can see the difference between him and Keitel. Keitel at least told the truth."

As for his own case, he felt it would be a sensation, and thought that the prosecution should withdraw the indictment against him after he and his witnesses take the stand.

---

*Von Papen's Cell:* Von Papen looked at me and shook his head and laughed as soon as I entered the cell. After a while he said, "Well, I suppose there is no doubt that Kaltenbrunner was not as bad as his predecessor, Heydrich; but, after all, who can believe that he knew nothing about these things?—Denying everything, even his own signature on documents—." Suddenly Von Papen laughed again. "—And I see that even the Chief of the Security Police was trying to be a Foreign Minister at the end, negotiating with a neutral power. It really would be funny if it were not so tragic."

---

*Frank's Cell:* Kaltenbrunner's perjured defense has thrown Frank back into his passion for guilt confession and denunciation of Hitler. As soon as I entered his cell, he threw up his hands painfully and cried, "*Ach, Du lieber Gott!*—Did you hear how he sat there and said he didn't know anything about it? Did you hear that, *Herr Doktor?* He sat there and *swore* in *cold blood* that he did not *know* about *any* of these things!" He emphasized each word as he spoke, and then covered his eyes as if in shame. "Does anything like that happened in my organization, I could have the body believe that man? Can anybody believe him? I know the judges don't believe him. Why, I myself went to Himmler to demand an explanation for all the atrocities that the world was talking about and then of course he lied to me—but Kaltenbrunner certainly knew about it. He even stooped to claiming treason—did you hear it? He says that he negotiated with neutral powers because he knew the war was lost—and yet he persecuted thousands of Germans for defeatism; threw them into concentration camps.—I know what a hell of a time I had getting one of my own officials out, and now he makes himself out to be a defeatist himself. If it was true, it was even a worse crime—because the leaders made our soldiers—fine young German men—made them keep fighting and dying to the bitter end past all hope. I asked Keitel how many soldiers died in the war. He said 2½ million.—Just imagine—they kept spilling young German blood, and now they say they didn't even believe in the possibility of a victory since 1943.—God Almighty!—and then he flatly denies being Krüger's [police chief in Poland] superior when they read him that excerpt out of my diary. He glared at me and denied it, and later he said I would have to deny it too. But it would be perjury if I denied it. It was a fact. Why did he have to deny it?

"No, God forbid that I should get up and make such a lying spectacle of myself. No, I am now more glad than ever that I turned in my diary. The others have reproached me for it, but I am glad.—Millions of Germans have died through the guilt of the system and now when their own necks are involved, they sit here and lie and try to conceal the truth.—I don't think even Goering was so truthful.—And Ribbentrop—what a pitiful spectacle!—Keitel—well, at least he told the truth. But that Kaltenbrunner —tell me, does anybody believe him? What is your opinion?"

"Everybody seems to agree that he was lying," I answered.

"Of course he was; it was awful. It just knocked me off my feet. I tell you I am now absolutely resolved to follow the line I intended to in the beginning.—Today is Palm Sunday and I swore by the Crucifix that I would tell the truth and expose the sin as my last act on earth, let the chips fall where they may.—But I would just like to ask you, please stick up for me if the others attack me.—Of course, it makes no difference what they think.— I have sworn and I will go through with it, and even if my religious conviction is only a dream—I need it to give me strength and nothing will sway me.—But you know how the others are when we sit there talking in the prisoners' dock, and I want you to support me."

"Well, I see you have come around to your original position again. I noticed you were wavering."

"Well, you must understand how it is. It is such a strain to sit there for months under this constant burden of guilt with others around you under the same strain, and one looks for ways out and gets consolation from the others, and then I am such a weak person—."

"Goering is only trying to confuse the whole issue of guilt and make a grandstand play as a German hero and to get everybody to support him," I remarked.

"I know—and he never supported me. He could have done something to help me when Hitler deprived me of my SS rank for criticising him—but Goering didn't move a finger.—And now he wants me to support him and the whole system.—No, I can see that fate has put me here to expose the evil that is in us all. God grant that I keep my strength to do it and not weaken again. You must support me, Herr Doktor. I will do what I have to do, but all I ask is a little moral support—and then before it is all over, if you will perhaps pay a friendly visit to my family to see that they do not suffer for what I have done . . ."

--------- April 15 ---------

## COLONEL HOESS TESTIFIES

MORNING SESSION: *In the morning session, Colonel Hoess testified to the murder of 2½ million Jews under his direction at Auschwitz. It was all done at Himmler's direct orders as a Führerbefehl [Führer's order] for the final solution of the Jewish problem. [He gave his testimony in the same matter-of-fact, apathetic manner as he had related it to me in his cell.] The Jews arrived in large train transports from all countries. Those capable of working* were sent to the labor details, and the rest, including most women and all young children, were sent to the extermination chambers immediately. Children who were hidden under the dresses of their mothers to escape notice were torn from their mothers and sent to the gas chambers. Gold teeth and gold rings were extracted from the corpses after gassing and the melted gold was sent to the Economics Ministry. The women's hair was packed in bales for commercial use.

[The defendants listened to all of this in gloomy silence. Frank, in spite of the revival of remorse which he professed to me yesterday, was overheard using some of the stock Nazi defensive rationalizations in a conversation with Rosenberg, within hearing of Kaltenbrunner, during the morning recess. "They are trying to pin the murder of 2,000 Jews a day in Auschwitz on Kaltenbrunner—but what about the 30,000 people who were killed in the bombing attacks on Hamburg in a few hours?—They were also mostly women and children.—And how about the 80,000 deaths from the atomic bombing in Japan?—Is that justice too?" Rosenberg laughed. "Yes, of course—because we lost the war."]

---

LUNCH HOUR: At the end of the morning session after the point of the persecution of the church had been raised in the examination of a witness, Neubacher, Frank suddenly relapsed into his denunciation of the Nazi Party. Sauckel said he didn't see why the Church had to be dragged into this because the Church was not being persecuted, at least not in his district.

Frank flared up, "It certainly was! . . . In Bavaria it was definitely persecuted!—I know for a fact that the SS men threw the nuns out of the convents and took them over for billets.—I know that for a fact from my own observation in Bavaria and it was probably that way all over Germany!—And the Nazi Party is to blame for it all! They absolutely persecuted the Church!" He then glared at Rosenberg and turned away with clenched jaw.

At lunch there was a depressed silence in all of the lunchrooms, and they sat for the most part in their own corners even reluctant to take advantage of my presence to start a conversation as they otherwise invariably did. Only one comment could be elicited from Goering* and later from Doenitz. The comment was virtu-

---

*Goering was born in Bavaria but identified himself with Prussianism when talking to Prussian militarists, since he got his military training in Prussia.

ally identical and seemed to have been agreed upon by them in the dock: Hoess was not a Prussian but quite obviously a southern German; a Prussian could never bring himself to do things like that.

Frank said to me with some feeling: "That was the low point of the entire trial—to hear a man say out of his own mouth that he exterminated 2½ million people in cold blood—. That is something that people will talk about for a thousand years."

I mentioned something about obedience to *Führerbefehl* and the *Führerprinzip*. Keitel defended himself. "But you see, I brought it out very clearly that as far as the generals were concerned, if we had known what criminal acts Hitler was planning and executing as we know now, we would have refused to go along."

Rosenberg, who was due to take the stand this afternoon, commented nervously that it was a dirty trick to put Hoess on just before his case, because it naturally put him in a very difficult position to defend his philosophy.

Naturally.

# 11. Rosenberg's Defense

## ROSENBERG TAKES THE STAND

AFTERNOON SESSION: *Rosenberg started defending his philosophy with the usual merry-go-round of abstruse historical rationalizations. He had to be interrupted frequently by the court, the prosecution and even his own defense counsel and told to get down to cases. Rosenberg had always been in favor of a chivalrous solution of the Jewish problem and helping their emancipation by moving them out of Europe to develop their culture on the soil of Asia. To be sure, 12,000 German Jews had died at the front in World War I, but there had to be "an understanding" just the same.*

At the end of the day he rebuked his attorney for interrupting him, and his attorney tried to argue that the court was not interested in the history of philosophy. Rosenberg turned to me and said, "Well, if they just want to make it a criminal trial, why don't the prosecution stick to criminal acts instead of attacking my ideology?"

## PROPAGANDA

*Colonel Hoess's Cell:* Tracking down the source of the anti-Semitism which made him feel that Himmler's explanation for the extermination of the Jews was right, I asked him how he got his anti-Semitic views. He said that he read Goebbels' editorials in *Das Reich* every week for many years, as well as his books and his various speeches; Rosenberg's *The Myth of the 20th Century,* and some of his speeches; and, of course, Hitler's *Mein Kampf,* as well

267

as hearing and reading most of his speeches. In addition to these authors, there were the ideological pamphlets and other educational material of the SS. He read Streicher's *Stürmer* only occasionally, because it was too superficial. (He noticed that those of his subordinates who had been in the habit of reading the *Stürmer* were usually men of narrow outlook.) Goebbels, Rosenberg, and Hitler gave him more food for thought. All of these writings and speeches constantly preached the idea that Jewry was Germany's enemy.

"For me as an old fanatic National Socialist, I took it all as fact—just as a Catholic believes in his Church dogma. It was just truth without question; I had no doubt about that. I was absolutely convinced that the Jews were the opposite pole from the German people, and sooner or later there would have to be a showdown between National Socialism and World Jewry—that was even in peacetime. On the basis of these doctrines, I assumed that other people would sooner or later be convinced of the Jewish danger, and would likewise take a stand against it. All these books and writings and speeches said that the Jewish people were a minority in all countries, but, because their material power was so great, they influenced and controlled people to such an extent that they could maintain their power. It was shown how their control of press, film, radio, and education controlled German life. We assumed it was likewise the case in other countries, and that in time other countries would break their power as we did. And if anti-Semitism did not succeed in wiping out this Jewish influence, the Jews would succeed in bringing about a war to wipe out Germany.—But *everybody* was convinced of this; that was all you could bear or read. That was even before the war.

"Then, after the war started, Hitler explained that World Jewry had started a showdown with National Socialism—that was in a Reichstag speech at the time of the French campaign—and the Jews must be exterminated. Of course, nobody at that time thought that it was meant so literally. But Goebbels expressed himself more and more sharply against the Jews. He did not attack England or Holland or France, so much as the Jews, as our enemy. And he quoted Roosevelt and Morgenthau and others as people who actually intended to reduce Germany to a primitive state, and it was always stressed that if Germany was to survive then World Jewry must be exterminated and we all accepted it as truth.

"That was the picture I had in my head, so, when Himmler called me to him, I just accepted it as the realization of something I had already accepted—not only I, but everybody. I took it so much for granted that even though this order, which would move the strongest and coldest nature—and at that moment this crass order to exterminate thousands of people (I did not know then how many)—even though it did frighten me momentarily—it fitted in with all that had been preached to me for years. The problem itself, the extermination of Jewry, was not new—but only that I was to be the one to carry it out, frightened me at first. But after getting the clear direct order and even an explanation with it —there was nothing left but to carry it out."

"So, that was the background for accepting a mass murder order?"

"Yes, when I think back on it all, it is hard to figure out—but at that time I didn't think of it at all as propaganda, but something one just had to believe."

"You said you accepted this propaganda like church dogma. Was your early training strongly religious?"

"Yes, I was brought up in a very strict Catholic tradition. My father was really a bigot. He was very strict and fanatical. I learned that my father took a religious oath at the time of the birth of my youngest sister, dedicating me to God and the priesthood, and after that leading a Joseph married life [celibacy].—He directed my entire youthful education toward the goal of making me a priest. I had to pray and go to church endlessly; do penance over the slightest misdeed—praying as punishment for any little unkindness to my sister, or something like that."

"Did your father ever beat you?"

"No, I was only punished by prayer—if I teased my sister, or tried to lie, or any little thing like that. The thing that made me so stubborn and probably made me later on cut off from people was his way of making me feel that I had wronged him personally, and that, since I was spiritually a minor, he was responsible to God for my sins, and I could only pray to expiate my sins. My father was a kind of higher being that I could never approach, and so I crawled back into myself—and I could not express myself to others.—I feel that this bigoted upbringing is responsible for my becoming so withdrawn. My mother also lived in the shadow of this fanatic piety."

Hoess described how he became more and more alienated from religion, until he broke with the Church completely in 1922. Once having done so, he seems to have substituted Nazi propaganda for religion.

---

LUNCH HOUR: Fritzsche started the discussion on propaganda, quoting somebody who called propaganda "the first step to hell." He insisted against Schirach's protest that Rosenberg was the father of Nazi ideology. He traced the new German anti-Semitism to the *Handbook of the Jewish Question*, by Fritsch, a little known author.

"Yes, that was until *The International Jew* was published by the same publisher, and gave the whole movement a boost," Schirach observed.

"Yes, and then Rosenberg became the high priest of the Nazi ideology," Fritzsche added. He went on to say that one can carry on propaganda with all kinds of means; one can even lie with the truth, merely by stating facts out of context and robbing people of the proper concept of the whole truth.

Fritzsche continued his analysis of anti-Semitism. "Aside from the century-old anti-Semitism, the Nazi propaganda was first based on a few one-sided facts like the anti-nationalism of the Jews and the cases of Jewish Communists." (He implied that his own propaganda was of this mild nationalistic variety, taking his stand only against the internationalism of the Jews.) "But then the fanatics like Goebbels, Streicher, and Rosenberg whipped it up to a fever pitch and came out with the most extreme Jew baiting in every direction."

"—Like Rosenberg digging up the old forged *Protocols of Zion*," I remarked.

"Yes, that is lying with lies. I never gave the *Protocols* a moment's serious thought."

In the Elders' lunchroom von Papen turned the discussion to the anti-Semitism of the Nazi leadership, and focused his criticism on Rosenberg for his pagan philosophy. Doenitz did not think that Rosenberg had much influence on the Nazi ideology because less than 1 per cent of his own naval officers had ever read the *Mythus*.

"Oh, yes, he did!" von Papen objected. "You cannot become the Minister of Ideological Education, or whatever it was, and say that you had no influence on the Nazi ideology. I know, as a matter of fact, that Rosenberg did influence Hitler to let him spread his pagan philosophy. He came to him several times until Hitler finally gave him a grant to publish the *Mythus*. Even so, nobody read that tripe until Cardinal Faulhaber came out and denounced it, and then the Nazis grabbed it up and made it a best seller, as a symbol of their pagan protest against the Church."

I suggested that the Nuremberg Laws were an early manifestation of this perverted Nazi philosophy. Von Neurath agreed and replied that he had warned Hitler against the injustice and dangerous consequences of such laws.

"But I told Hitler," von Neurath explained, "entirely apart from the legal aspects, what dangerous repercussions it was going to have and *did* have in foreign countries—apart from the issue of justice, which didn't interest him."

"And then the Nazis felt hurt," I added, "when Jews all over the world protested against this crass discrimination, as if they expected a minority to be satisfied if it was being persecuted." Von Neurath and von Papen agreed that the Nazis had asked for trouble and then used this hostility in foreign countries and among their own persecuted minorities to justify more and more harsh measures. As it became obvious that they should have realized this at the time, von Papen remarked defensively:

"The one thing I am sorry about is that I did not flatly break with the administration in 1938 and refuse to have anything more to do with it."

---

AFTERNOON SESSION: *In the afternoon session, Rosenberg defended his activities as Commissioner for the Eastern Territories, by showing that he had disapproved atrocities but could not do much about it. As far as concentration camps were concerned, he had not seen one; in fact, he had refused to see any. He admitted having used "very strong words" about the Jews and having said something about extermination, but all of that propaganda was not to be taken literally. He also did not intend the Führerprinzip to*

abolish personal liberty. Things just turned out differently from
the way they were intended.

───────────── April 17 ─────────────

## MASTER RACE THEORY AND PRACTICE

MORNING SESSION: Mr. Dodd cross-examined Rosenberg, exposing
a good deal of the hypocrisy behind Rosenberg's mask of innocence, particularly in his responsibility for the deportation of slave
laborers and the reign of terror in the East. Mr. Dodd presented
several documents showing that Rosenberg was not content to
philosophize, but ruthlessly put the Nazi ideology into practice as
Governor of the Eastern Occupied Territories.

[When a document was read to Rosenberg showing that the
fighting in Russia was to be conducted outside of humanitarian
principles, Goering whispered to Raeder, "I wish the Americans
would fight Russia and see how they would do it." But as Rosenberg was tied up with the responsibility for atrocities in the East,
Goering said to Doenitz, "That Dodd is smarter than he looks."]

Correspondence presented by Mr. Dodd, between Rosenberg
and Bormann, showed substantial agreement on the execution of
the Nazi ideology with respect to the Slav races: "The Slavs are to
work for us. Insofar as we don't need them, they may die . . .
The fertility of the Slavs is undesirable. They may use contracep-
tives or practice abortion, the more the better. Education is dangerous. It is enough if they can count up to 100 . . . Every educated person is a future enemy. Religion we leave to them as a
means of diversion. As for food, they don't get any more than is
necessary. We are the masters; we come first." Rosenberg said he
was only trying to appease Bormann. As for his advocating the extermination of the Jews, Rosenberg could only quibble over the
meaning of the word "extermination."

─────────────────

LUNCH HOUR: At lunch von Papen commented, "Dodd asked
him if he knew that Hoess, the Commandant of Auschwitz, had
read his works. That was, of course, the crux of the whole thing.
Rosenberg just gave an evasive answer."

"Yes," said Schacht, "Rosenberg wrote too much."

In the Youth lunchroom that question also was commented upon and a lively argument was started on the psychological aspects of the trial. Fritzsche was most emphatic in criticizing the failure of the trial to recognize that the German people should also be represented among those sitting in judgment of their leaders, and assured me again that the judgment would be even more harsh than that of the foreigners who are interested only in the crimes against their own nations. There was general agreement among the four that Hitler had betrayed Germany, but there was some disagreement as to whether this would have been realized and would have created a revolution in case of victory. Fritzsche was of the opinion that millions of betrayed Germans would have revolted at the end of the war, but von Schirach commented that a victorious country never revolts against its victorious leaders.

Frank was overheard preparing his audience for his defense, "No matter what you admit or deny on the stand, if they have got a document with your signature on it, it goes down as evidence against you. All we can do when we get up there is our best, and let things work out as they may. We can knock our heads against the wall but it doesn't change the facts. Our lawyers have to do the talking for us but there is no use of our trying to deny what all of the world knows . . . Ja, it was a great Reich while it lasted."

Keitel also reminisced a little. "Yes, Hitler had charge of the whole Reich and he didn't like lots of things; he didn't like the Jews, he didn't like democracy and he didn't like diplomacy. As far as politics are concerned, seeing how England and America were grabbing things, I don't blame him for trying to see what he could get away with."

Frank then read a note he had gotten from one of the other defendants saying, "Well, we did our duty and it doesn't matter if we do get hung."

As soon as Goering came down to the dock, he called Rosenberg over and told him he was right to argue about the word Ausrottung (extermination) and told him he should have explained that it has different meanings in different dialects too. He then continued giving advice on evasive tactics in handling the prosecution, "Now that the Americans are finished, the worst is over; you don't have to be afraid of Rudenko. If you get a tough question, just stall and say the translation was incorrect, or anything like that.—You saw how I handled Jackson. Now all you have to do is wait until they ask the right question then give it to them!"

Doenitz laughed at Goering's expert coaching and said, "That is right—you handle it, papa."

Goering turned around and said laughingly, "Quiet, children. You stick to your U-boats."

Hess contributed a witty observation: "Yes, they cannot say you killed Jews with your U-boats." He thought that was very funny and gave one of his buck-toothed laughs.

---

AFTERNOON SESSION: [True to the instructions Goering had given him, Rosenberg continued to obstruct General Rudenko's cross-examination by complaining about the translations and using other obstructive techniques when asked questions that were too uncomfortable for him.] *It was Rosenberg's unruly subordinates who were responsible for atrocities in the East; Rosenberg tried to modify things. Having executed the Nazi ideology so well in the East, he had asked to become Foreign Minister, but he really had no influence on Hitler. M. Monneray, of the French prosecution, then accused Rosenberg of using the deportation and shooting of French Jews for the looting of their valuables.*

---

——— EVENING IN JAIL ———

*Doenitz' Cell:* I visited Doenitz in his cell in the evening. "That Rosenberg—he is a man who has his head in the clouds. I have no doubt that he is a man who would not hurt a fly but there is also no doubt that these propagandists were really responsible for paving the way for these terrible anti-Semitic acts . . . It is too bad Hitler isn't here. He did so much of all that is discussed here." He then drew a rectangle and shaded 90 per cent of the area. "As to Kaltenbrunner, well, even if everything he says. is true —let us assume so for the sake of argument—how can he hide behind the excuse that somebody forged his signature? Why, if any man court-martialed for falsification of documents—and I am responsible for what goes in my organization."

"Do you believe it is true that he knew nothing and his subordinate forged his signature?"

"Well, that hardly seems likely." Doenitz then continued to expound his thesis of the Russian danger to Germany, trying to point out that it is not to America's interest to let Russia control Europe, and he would like to talk with some sensible American official about it after the trial.

---

*Frank's Cell:* Frank was sitting calmly smoking a pipe. "We are glad it went so smoothly with Rosenberg.—It is just as well that they cut off the philosophical arguments. I asked him at the end if he wasn't glad of it himself. He said he was . . . Of course, his quibbling over the translation of the word *Ausrottung* [extermination], that was weak.—Yes, he was mixed up with it all right as we all were. I told the others that we were tied up in this whole Nazi movement for 25 years, more or less, and what's the use of denying it now. There is no getting around the facts.—I am going to come right out and say something the others will be shocked at; so will my attorney. But what is there to do? . . . The horrible testimony of Hoess is still ringing in my ears—2,000 murders a day!—Hitler has disgraced Germany for all time!—He betrayed and disgraced the people that trusted and loved him!—How the people loved him!—I will be the first one to get up and say that I simply did not believe the SS when they denied the atrocities—I will be the first to admit my guilt."

"Well, just in what way do you feel guilty?" I asked him.

The answer was quick and pat. "Because I was an ardent Nazi and did not kill him!—One of us should have killed him."

# 12. Frank's Defense

## FRANK'S "CONFESSION"

MORNING SESSION: *Frank told how he passed the bar exams in 1926, became legal advisor to Hitler and the Nazi Party, a member of the Reichstag in 1930, President of the German Academy of Law in 1933, Governor-General of Poland in 1939. Then came the decisive question: "Did you ever participate in the destruction of Jews?" Frank took a deep breath and answered: "I say yes . . . We have fought against Jewry; we have fought against them for years; and we have allowed ourselves to make utterances, and my own diary has become a witness against me in this connection —utterances which are terrible . . . A thousand years will pass and this guilt of Germany will not be erased."*

[Goering shook his head in disgust as another defendant dared to tell the truth. He whispered to his neighbors and passed notes around the dock. Then as Frank artfully stated that he had never found time to collect art treasures during wartime, Goering and those around him remained studiously dead-pan, while those at the other end of the dock grinned and glanced at each other.]

*Frank went on to admit his setting up of ghettos in Poland, the stigmatization of Jews, the exportation of slave labor, etc.*

———————————

In the morning recess Frank returned to the dock for a few minutes, very nervous and self-conscious, looking around for some sign of approval from the other defendants. Von Papen and Seyss-Inquart gave him some words of encouragement.

His attorney, Dr. Seidl, asked him: "Shall I ask you what part of the intellectual responsibility—?"

"No, let it go as it is," Frank interrupted. Then, turning to me after Seidl left, he said, "Ha! Little Seidl is priceless! Goering calls him Mickey Mouse.—He wants to narrow down my admission of guilt.—I am glad I got it out, and I'll let it go at that."

At the other end of the dock, Fritzsche was displeased that Frank had identified his guilt with the German people. Schacht, however, said that Frank had clearly admitted his guilt, and was right in saying that Hitler had degraded the German people.

Sauckel whispered to Goering, "Did you hear him say that Germany is disgraced for a thousand years?"

Goering retorted contemptuously, "Yes, I heard it . . . I suppose Speer will say the same thing. The weak-kneed cowards!"

———————

*Frank continued his testimony on the stand, sharing knowledge of the atrocities with the SS, but (with a dig at Goering, Ribbentrop, Keitel and Kaltenbrunner) "in contrast to those around the Führer who did not know anything about these things, I must say I was more independent, I heard about these things and read about them in the foreign press." [Goering shook his head painfully.]*

———————

LUNCH HOUR: Several expressed open satisfaction at these digs at Goering. Goering walked around the hall unhappily watching me talk to the others who were laughing about it. In the Youth lunchroom and in the Elders' lunchroom the expressions of satisfaction and amusement indicated that the resistance against Goering was still going strong.

Frank was waiting for my visit. "I kept my promise, didn't I? I said that, in contrast to the other people around the Führer who seemed to know nothing, I did know what was going on. I think the judges are really impressed when one of us speaks from his heart and doesn't try to dodge the responsibility. Don't you think so? I was really gratified at the way they were impressed by my sincerity."

There was a general agreement that one could not fool the judges.

In the Youth lunchroom Speer and Fritzsche had some reservations about their willingness to credit Frank with too much natural honesty. "I wonder what he would have said if he hadn't turned in his diary," Speer speculated. "Naturally, there is nothing left for him to do now but to admit what his diary has already proven."

Fritzsche was still bothered that Frank was "trying to identify his guilt and betrayal with the German people—but, as a matter of fact, he is more guilty than any of us. He really knows about those things."

―――――――― EVENING IN JAIL ――――――――

*Goering's Cell:* Sweating in his cell in the evening, Goering was defensive and deflated and not very happy over the turn the trial was taking. He said that he had no control over the actions or the defense of the others, and that he had never been anti-Semitic himself, had not believed these atrocities, and that several Jews had offered to testify in his behalf. If Frank had known about atrocities in 1943, he should have come to him and he would have tried to do something about it. He might not have had enough power to change things in 1943, but if somebody had come to him in 1941 or 1942 he could have forced a show-down. (I still did not have the desire at this point to tell him what Ohlendorf had said to this: that Goering had been written off as an effective "moderating" influence, because of his drug addiction and corruption.) I pointed out that with his "temperamental utterances," such as preferring the killing of 200 Jews to the destruction of property, he had hardly set himself up as champion of minority rights. Goering protested that too much weight was being put on these temperamental utterances. Furthermore, he made it clear that he was not defending or glorifying Hitler.

We got around to the subject of war again and I said that, contrary to his attitude, I did not think that the common people are very thankful for leaders who bring them war and destruction.

"Why, of course, the *people* don't want war," Goering shrugged. "Why would some poor slob on a farm want to risk his life in a war when the best that he can get out of it is to come back to his farm in one piece. Naturally, the common people don't want war; neither in Russia nor in England nor in America, nor for that matter in Germany. That is understood. But, after all, it is the *leaders* of the country who determine the policy and it is always a simple matter to drag the people along, whether it is a democracy or a fascist dictatorship or a Parliament or a Communist dictatorship."

"There is one difference," I pointed out. "In a democracy the people have some say in the matter through their elected representatives, and in the United States only Congress can declare war."

"Oh, that is all well and good, but, voice or no voice, the people can always be brought to the bidding of the leaders. That is. easy. All you have to do is tell them they are being attacked and denounce the pacifists for lack of patriotism and exposing the country to danger. It works the same way in any country."

────────── April 19–22 ──────────

## EASTER RECESS IN JAIL

*Frank's Cell:* Frank was sitting in the cell calmly smoking a pipe, and he proceeded immediately to soliloquize on his reaction to his own defense, soon working up a passion with arm-waving histrionics.

"Well, today is Good Friday, and I am at peace because I kept my oath. Yesterday I stood before the black gates, and now I have passed through to the other side.—I stood before the black gates in bare feet and sackcloth with a candle in my hand like a penitent sinner—or a Vestal Virgin—and spoke once more before God and the world.—Now I have paid my bill and passed through the black gates and do not belong to this world any more . . . God is a most generous Host. He allows you to run up as big a bill as you please.—He lets you order anything you want—a room —a castle—wine—women—power—anything you want—but He demands payment in full at the end! He doesn't allow any default of payment! Haha! He is a most generous Host, but he demands payment in full!" Frank paused for a minute, having exhausted the possibilities of his metaphors, than went on with a review of his defense.

"I was the first one to say how guilty we were. But Goering should have said it right at the beginning instead of striking such a pose. The world was crying to hear one of us say, as we stand before death, that our system was evil and we have sinned! But Goering did not say it—and Ribbentrop—well, he was a weak character—and Kaltenbrunner just lied. Why didn't Goering come out and tell the truth? Can you understand it, *Herr Doktor?*"

"Obviously because he wanted to maintain a pose to the bitter end," I answered.

"But he could have said that we had certain ideals in the beginning, and that Hitler betrayed us and disgraced us, and we are guilty because of our ambition and the evil that was in us."

"Well, he is too conceited a man to admit any wrong. It would spoil his pose. Anyway, I see you got in a few good digs at him."

Frank laughed. "Yes, his attorney raised hell with my attorney because I did so.—But let him stew! He glared at me but didn't say anything. I really had good reason to be mad at him. He should have done something to stop these horrible crimes; he was closest to the Führer. I am glad Mr. Dodd gave me the chance to bring out even more clearly that Goering was enriching himself while Europe was in agony . . . But these people do not understand these things. They think it is just a legalistic match of wits, instead of a decisive point in a fateful historical development. Rosenberg told me I am lost. Huh! What does he think? That he is saved? He wanted me to say how the Jews had threatened our State, so as to justify our anti-Semitism. But I had to confess my sin, so that I may be at peace with God, and perhaps raise my eyes to him a little bit . . .

"Do you know what was the last straw in making me decide that I had to expiate my guilt? A few days ago I read a notice in the newspaper that Dr. Jacoby, a Jewish lawyer in Munich, who was one of my father's best friends, had been exterminated in Auschwitz. Then, when Hoess testified how he exterminated 2½ million Jews, I realized that he was the man who had coldly exterminated my father's best friend—a fine, upright, kindly, old man—and millions of innocent people like him, and I had done nothing to stop it! True, I didn't kill him myself, but the things I said and the things Rosenberg said made those things possible!

"That testimony by Hoess—an order to murder a whole race!—I can never get that out of my mind. That is the final damnation of the whole system, and we can't get around it! Hitler spoke about the extermination of the Jewish race, and we all knew it—and Rosenberg had the nerve to quarrel about the translation of the word *extermination!*"

"You all had your share in saying such things."

He shook his head solemnly. "Yes—God knows we did. We

cannot deny it. But Hitler cold-bloodedly gave the order; Hoess told us how he got the order and carried it out.—*Herr Doktor,* will history ever get over this degradation of human civilization that Hitler brought us to? There is no doubt that that demon Hitler brought us to this. If Himmler had tried to do it on his own hook, and then Hitler had found out about it and had hung him for it, it would have been different. But no, Hitler gave the order himself—he indicates it even in his 'Last Testament'*—And that man wore the mask of a human being!—the head of a State! . . . I am going to write you that essay on Hitler that I promised you, but do you know that he is actually repulsive to me now? Now that he is unmasked and I see what a horrible repulsive man I have been following, I am nauseated." He leaned on the table with his elbow, his face in his hands, with eyes squinting as if in a trance. "—It is as if Death put on the mask of a charming human being, and lured workers, lawyers, scientists, women and children—everything—to destruction!—And now we see his face unmasked as it really was—a death's-head skeleton! *Herr Doktor,* it is terrifying!—it is repulsive!"

---

*Rosenberg's Cell:* Rosenberg was not unduly impressed by Frank's confessional stand. " . . . Yes, Frank is an impressive speaker, just as I told you. He shoots his mouth off and five minutes later he calms down. This time he let loose at the prisoners' dock instead of at the judges' bench or the prosecution.—But he is sensitive and musical, and those musical people are all whacky! You can never predict what he is going to say. '*Germany is disgraced for a thousand years!*'—That is going pretty far!"

"But don't you think it's about time that somebody did admit his guilt and call a spade a spade?" I asked. "These mass murders are the most horrible things that have ever taken place in the history of mankind!"

Rosenberg stopped his pacing up and down his cell and considered the question, then resorted to his usual historical defensive rationalization. "Well, yes—I suppose so.—But how about the

---

*Blaming "International Jewry" for the second World War, the so-called Political Testament of Hitler stated: "I left no one in doubt that this time—the real culprits would have to pay for their guilt, even though by more humane means than war."

murder of 3,000 Chinese in the Opium War and the degradation of perhaps 3 million Chinese by the British, through their opium traffic? And how about the 300,000 exterminated by an atomic bomb in Japan? And how about all the air attacks on our cities? That is all mass murder too, isn't it?"

"The whole war was unnecessary mass murder, and you can thank your Führer for deliberately starting it when the people of no country in the world wanted it—not even your own. Even Goering admits that. You might take a share of the blame yourself for your *Führerprinzip* and your own propaganda that constantly stirred up hatred instead of seeking some conciliation."

Rosenberg squirmed and protested, rationalized and counteratttacked. It was certainly not his fault, he said, that the war started and that things have gone to such extremes. It was the Versailles Treaty and the vicious, vengeful French and the imperialistic British and the threat of Communist world revolution, etc., etc.

---

*Von Papen's Cell:* Von Papen agreed that all the defendants who had spoken so far had shown their guilt and were lost, with the possible exception of Hess, whose mental responsibility was in question.

" . . . I found Ribbentrop the most lamentable of all of them," he said. "—What an excuse for a Foreign Minister! You could see how unscrupulously and irresponsibly he made pacts and broke them with no regard for national honor or world peace or anything."

"What do you think about Kaltenbrunner?" I said. "The others think *he* made the worst showing."

"Oh, Kaltenbrunner!—a stupid policeman!—I don't even count him. I always said there were two kinds of service for shady characters like that: one is Counter-Intelligence and the other is Security Police."

He asked for the latest news on the international front, and I quoted the headline that England had suggested that Franco resign now. Von Papen diplomatically refrained from showing approval or disapproval of this move, although he had already expressed his approval of Franco as a religious man in contrast to Hitler. He agreed, however, with my opinion that it was necessary to get rid of statesmen who had been in league with Hitler. Von Papen was sure that some other upright Spanish leader could be found who would be neither fascist nor Communist.

---

*Ribbentrop's Cell:* Ribbentrop was reading the transcript of his cross-examination. He made some feeble remarks about the prosecution questions being very mean. He seemed to have suffered a relapse into an aphasia-like condition with depression.

"I either can't find—the words—or I can't make the sentences . . . I have—thoughts—but I can't—control—. Do you understand? It takes a lot of effort—it's funny. I can either talk slowly —or the words come out quickly and uncontrolled—it's funny. I have trouble writing, too, and can hardly push the pencil across the page . . . I had the same—trouble in court—."

As for Frank: "He should not have said that Germany was disgraced for a thousand years." I asked him whether he didn't think that was true. "Well, a German should not say that anyway . . . Tell me—I wasn't in court on Monday.—Did Hoess actually say—that Hitler had ordered the mass murders?"

"He said that Himmler gave him a direct *Führerbefehl* for extermination of the Jews in 1941."

"In 1941?—did he say that?—in '41?—in '41?—did he really say that?

"Of course he did. You might have known; the whole Party leadership was talking about solving the Jewish problem—a problem that they themselves had made acute."

"But Hitler only spoke of transporting them to the East or to Madagascar."

"Even at that—how can you justify such colossal mistreatment of a mass of innocent people?"

"Did Hitler really order the extermination?—in '41?—in '41?"

"I've already told you Hoess said it started in Auschwitz in '41 and had already been in progress since '40 in other camps."

Ribbentrop held his head in his hand and repeated in a descending whisper, "—'41—'41—'41—My God!—Did Hoess say in '41?"

"Yes, transports started arriving right after he got the *Führerbefehl.* From all over occupied Europe—men, women, and children who had been living a perfectly peaceful family life. They were undressed, led into gas chambers and murdered by the thousands. Then the gold rings and teeth were removed from the corpses, the hair was cut off the women's heads, and the bodies were burned in the crematory—"

"Stop! Stop! *Herr Doktor*—I cannot bear it!—All those years—a man to whom children came so trustingly and lovingly. It must have been a fanatic madness—there is no doubt now that Hitler ordered it? I thought even up to now that perhaps Himmler, late in the war, under some pretext—. But '41, he said? My God! My God!"

"What did you expect? You were all making reckless statements about solving the Jewish problem. There is no reasonable limit to human hatred when you have whipped it up to such a fury as you Nazi leaders did."

"But we never dreamed it would end like this. We only thought they had too much influence—that we could solve the problem with a quota system or that we would transport them to the East or Madagascar.—You know, I didn't know anything about the exterminations—until the Maidanek affair came out in '44—My God! . . . "

---

*Frick's Cell:* Frick was a little less cold and unconcerned than usual, as he prepared the last-minute notes for his defense. He said he would not take the stand himself but would have one witness, Gisevius, one-time Gestapo official, who would also testify for Schacht. He didn't think he had much to say except that he had not even seen the Führer after '37 and he never approved of the atrocities. I asked him whether he didn't realize that the Nuremberg Laws were the beginning of a State-sponsored racial discrimination and hatred whose outcome was not all too obvious.

To this he shrugged his shoulders and said, "Well—every race has the right to protect itself, just as the Jewish race has done for thousands of years."

"Don't you think it was madness to try to revive this racial-clan rivalry concept from the Dark Ages, when people cannot avoid living together in modern society? Can you justify that as a lawyer?"

"Well, you will have the same problem in America. The whites don't want to intermarry with Negroes. The mass murders were certainly not thought of as a consequence of the Nuremberg

Laws . . . It may have turned out that way, but it certainly wasn't thought of that way."

---

*Streicher's Cell:* Streicher has become slowly subdued by the months of cool contempt by all of the other defendants and the accumulating disgrace of anti-Semitism. He did not launch into his usual anti-Semitic tirade when I visited him in his cell to see how he was anticipating his defense. He said he would probably require only one day, and did not sound as if he would have very much to say. He thought that Rosenberg was a very profound philosopher, and had handled his defense well. He himself was still convinced that World Jewry and Bolshevism were identical and would one day rule the world—but he sounded as if he really didn't expect anybody else to believe it any more. What Hitler had done, he said, was very embarrassing to his own Zionistic leanings—but his wife and former secretary would testify that he was completely out of touch with things after 1940—except for continuing the publication of his *Stürmer.*

---

*Von Schirach's Cell:* The effect of separation from Goering's influence is beginning to tell in the form of a return to his previously repentant attitude, and Frank's confession seems to have turned the tide.

He said that Frank's confession had brought the trial to a new and critical phase. He was going to take a more forthright stand himself in admitting his guilt on the anti-Semitism issue. He discussed the questions that he was going to have his attorney put to him to bring out how he became anti-Semitic, how he was deceived by Julius Streicher, and Hitler and the whole Nazi leadership on this issue; and he would admit that the racial policy was Germany's tragic mistake.

An element of exhibitionism entered into all of this, as if he saw the chance of making good the heroic expiation that had been denied him at the end of the war at Buchenwald. "You see, the exposé of the atrocities will not in itself put an end to anti-Semitism and racial prejudice. Neither punishment nor vengeance will do it, either, for it may even rebound in later years. The only one who can put an end to anti-Semitism is an anti-Semite. Perhaps that is the one historical mission that I can still fulfill. If I

get up as the Leader of German Youth and proclaim before all
the world that our racial policy was a mistake—that will put an
end to it once and for all."

---

*Seyss-Inquart's Cell:* We got into a discussion on anti-Semitism, as
a result of the recent testimony. There was no discussion of
Streicher, because his lurid bigotry was just beyond the pale of
discussion for intellectual Seyss-Inquart. As for his own anti-
Semitism, it was now an academic question, but he still thought
that his "quantitative concept of the Jewish problem" had had
some basis in fact. He had thought that there were too many Jews
in Germany and that some kind of a readjustment was necessary.

"How about the American concept of tolerance and peaceful
living together as a means of handling the minority problem?" I
asked him.

Well, that of course was quite logical for America, he thought,
because the various peoples had not arisen as national entities
through the centuries, but as streams of immigrants who were
being amalgamated into a new kind of cosmopolitan society. This
new *social* rather than genetic concept was a natural development
for America, and perhaps for the future in general; but that was
not the way things had developed in Germany. There had always
been too many nationalistic differences.

Speaking of nationalistic and sub-nationalistic differences, I remarked that Doenitz and Goering had said that Hoess was a southern German, and a Prussian could never do the thing that he had
done. Seyss-Inquart did not take issue with this, although I had
mentioned the popular notion that Bavarians and Austrians were
somewhat akin. Seyss analyzed German fanaticism as follows:

"Yes, as I told you, the southern German has the imagination
and emotionality to subscribe to a fanatic ideology, but he is ordinarily inhibited from excesses by his natural humaneness. The
Prussian, on the other hand, does not have the imagination to
conceive in terms of the abstract racial and political theories, but
if he is told to do something, he does it. When he has an order,
he doesn't have to think.—That is the categorical imperative; orders are orders. In Hoess you have an example of how Nazism
combined the two. Hitler would never have gotten anywhere if
he had remained in Bavaria, because while the people would have

followed him fanatically they never would have gone to such excesses. But the system took over the Prussian tradition as well and amalgamated the southern emotional anti-Semitism with the Prussian thoughtless obedience.—Besides, the Catholic authoritarianism achieves the same effect as Prussian militarism—you need only look to the Jesuits for an example of that. When fanatic ideology is combined with authoritarianism, there is no limit to the excesses it can go to—just as in the Inquisition."

As for Frank, Seyss-Inquart remarked that he naturally had no choice but to take some stand that could be reconciled with his diary. Aside from that, Seyss-Inquart was very cagey about making any remarks about any of the defendants.

---

*Schacht's Cell:* Schacht was very pleased that the criminality of the other defendants was coming out more and more clearly and did not conceal his pleasure at the digs that Frank had made at Goering.

"I told Frank that confessing was the best thing for him to do. After all, it was all in his diary. What else could he say but to admit that he was guilty? Kaltenbrunner was disgraceful in the way he lied. Ribbentrop—well, he is such a pitiful spectacle. Keitel showed he was honest and obedient but he had no character at all. Goering, at least, struck a good pose."

"But his united front of loyalty and defiance seems to have collapsed, and probably will even get worse.—I imagine you will stand up pretty well yourself."

"Well, I hope so. I lose my temper so easily if people ask me stupid questions." He gave a thinly-veiled explanation that few people were intelligent enough to talk on his level and flattered me by telling me that he could talk intelligently to me . . . The trouble with the German Government, he went on, was that they were a bunch of ignorant upstarts, including Hitler. "By the way, this will interest you psychologically. Goering told me himself even in 1933—mind you, 1933—he referred to Hitler as 'that vagabond from a Viennese café!' Of course, he then had to keep swearing loyalty to him and has to do so even now, because Hitler kept covering and tolerating his corruptions—that is quite clear. . . . And what kind of people do you think are running the German Civilian Government now?—a bunch of characterless turncoat racketeers and radicals with no education, no background, and no standing in German society . . .

"I wonder who's going to cross-examine me. Those youngsters they have working up my case—what do they know? Who are they anyway?—law students, I suppose." I told him that I had heard that, in recognition of his intelligence, the big chief himself would probably take him on. Schacht was half-flattered, half-apprehensive. "So? Well, I am sure he will see that I am ready to give an honest answer to a fair question—let the chips fall where they may . . . I am coming right out against the whole system—not as it originally was—but as it was perverted by Goering and Hitler and those generals. I cannot spare them, especially if I am asked questions under oath and the court requires me to answer. There are four people whom I consider especially guilty: Goering, Ribbentrop, Keitel and Raeder.—It may be unpleasant but I cannot help it: I cannot spare them. My people must be shown how the Nazi leaders plunged them into an unnecessary war."

He suddenly became indignant. "How *dare* they plunge a country into a war without even asking the people! After that Hoszbach speech of Hitler's in 1937, the leaders had the solemn duty to tell Hitler to his face that he was leading the country to war! And they could have protested the necessity of the march into Poland! —But those damn military men know nothing but how to click their heels and say '*Jawohl*, we'll arrange a war for you any time!' . . . I can't spare them now . . . Next to Streicher, Goering is the most repulsive character in the dock—a vulgar, corrupt thief! Ugh!"

---

*Jodl's Cell:* Jodl smiled at Frank's confession. "I wonder how *genuine* it was.—In the old days he was like a little king building up his own particular empire in Poland. I had a lot of trouble with him. He wanted railroads and everything under his control."

When I mentioned Frank's dig at Goering's looting, Jodl showed his satisfaction with a broad grin.

He then asked me whether it was in 1941 that Hoess had gotten the *Führerbefehl* to start the extermination of the Jews in Auschwitz—i.e., before the military situation had become serious. I confirmed that, also reminding him that extermination had already started in Treblinka in 1940, but that Hoess had improved the methods. Jodl hung his head and I ventured to read his thoughts: "—And that man sat in GHQ with you and spoke of protecting the Fatherland and preserving German honor—" I suggested.

Jodl nodded his head solemnly. "Yes—that is right. But he had no conception of honor and no feeling for human beings except as masses and pawns in his ambitious schemes. That much was clear to me even then. He judged people only by their usefulness to him. He was not in the least interested in any human considerations.—I realize that more and more.—Now I even doubt—in fact, I don't believe that the Russian campaign was necessary as he insisted it was, or that all the diplomatic possibilities had been exhausted. I am rather inclined to believe that he just decided he wanted to beat Russia and he thought that was the right time to try it.—We took it for granted then that it was only a desperate necessity as a last resort and that otherwise he would never have insisted on it.—But we were certainly kept in the dark on all the political developments."

"How about the attack on Poland?" I asked.

"The same thing applies there. It is obvious now, that the war was not at all necessary. We assumed that all the diplomatic possibilities had been exhausted, but obviously they weren't."

He discussed the blame of Hitler's and the propagandists' responsibility for keeping the people and the Wehrmacht in the dark about Hitler's true aims, and again expressed the opinion that Hitler had betrayed the faith and patriotism of German Youth. Identifying himself in this betrayal, he added, "—Especially in the clever way he appealed to the intelligent people. It wasn't just the desperate unemployed and the emotions of women. He appealed to the understanding of intelligent men too. The movement would never have gained such impetus if men of repute had not been swept along with it and given the movement some prestige before the German people. That is where propaganda did a terrific job."

I asked him what would have happened if the soldiers and generals had been clearly shown even in 1942 that they were fighting a war that nobody wanted and for a government that had already instituted cold-blooded mass murders as an instrument of international policy. Jodl thought for a moment, "There would have been a terrible reaction throughout the whole Wehrmacht. I don't know what would have happened. German soldiers are no beasts. They believed in the honor of the cause and the officers rigidly refrained from allowing any kind of religious intolerances.—The realization of what they were fighting for would have been terrible."

"Would it have brought revolution?"

"Well, that is hard to say. In war the moral pressure of obedience and the stigma of high treason are pretty hard to get around."

---

*Doenitz' Cell:* "Well, it was all right for Frank to talk that way, but he should have spoken for himself. He was one of the wildest and he should not give the impression that the whole German people were wild. But, anyway, my position as a soldier was entirely different."

Then, anticipating Schacht's defense: "These politicians needn't get on such a high horse. After all, it was not the soldiers and sailors but the voters and politicians who put Hitler into power, and, if he turned out bad, it is not our fault. We didn't have a thing to say about declaring war; we only had to fight it."

# 13. Frick's Defense

LUNCH HOUR: At lunch several defendants expressed disappointment that Frick was not going to take the stand himself. Fritzsche pointed out that, as chief of the government officials, he could clear up a lot of things. Funk said he wanted to ask him some questions. I commented that I had the impression that if Frick couldn't save his own neck he was not interested in the trial altogether. Speer nodded agreement.

Frick himself was quite cool about the whole thing and said that his witness would merely straighten out his relationships to the police system, but outside of that there wasn't much to say.

Down in the dock, Goering, who was feeling very ill at ease because of the developments in the trial and the coolness shown by many of the defendants, started to make conversation, but nobody was paying much attention. Finally, nervous little Sauckel went over to him and asked him if he thought it was really true that 2½ million Jews had been exterminated at Auschwitz.

"No, no—of course not," Goering said offhandedly. "I've thought it over—it's technically impossible."

"You heard Hoess's testimony," I reminded him, "and you know that Hoess described the whole procedure to me in detail. It was a regular mass production system."

"Were you there?" Goering asked.

"Where were you?" I retorted. "Now you claim that it isn't true, but it would have been better if you had prevented it from being true!"

Goering fidgeted and tried to change the subject. I proceeded to tell Sauckel what Hoess had told me: the gassing was easy; it was the burning that took all the labor and required 24-hour shifts to man the ovens. He had about 3,000 Germans working there, all loyal to the Führer and to Himmler. The whole Goering clique could not help hearing this exposé. Goering slumped into the corner of the dock and contented himself with some whispered remark after my back was turned.

# April 24

## GISEVIUS EXPOSES GOERING

Before court, Streicher (overheard) asked Frick whether that witness, Gisevius, was really going to appear. Frick assured him he was. Streicher asked whether he would really say all those nasty things about Goering that people were saying he had written in his book. Frick said he supposed he would. To Streicher's question whether that would be bad for Goering, Frick answered coolly, "I should worry. I only care about staying alive myself."

LUNCH HOUR: In the Elders' lunchroom, von Papen and von Neurath were condemning "that fat one" for precipitating a forceful Anschluss of Austria instead of letting the Austrians vote for Anschluss. Von Papen became heated and pointed a finger out to the hallway where Goering was walking up and down by himself. "That's the man who was guilty!—that fat one out there. He is the one who refused to let the election take place! He even persuaded Hitler to march."

As the defendants came back to the dock, great excitement began to reign in anticipation of the testimony of Gisevius, whose book, Kampf Bis Zum Letzten (Fight to the Finish) had recently come to their attention. Rosenberg was overheard scolding Frick for calling him as a witness when he knew perfectly well that the book contained damaging testimony against the Nazi leadership.

"Will you please leave my defense to me!" Frick retorted. "I didn't stick my nose into yours; just let me handle my own.—If I hadn't called him, Schacht would have called him anyway."

Goering told Doenitz he needn't pay any attention to Gisevius' testimony because he admits right at the beginning of the book that he committed high treason. Doenitz asked Goering what he thought of Frick's defense. Goering replied, "Frick was a hard man to understand. I don't know if you can trust him."

AFTERNOON SESSION: *Witness Gisevius started his testimony.*
*[Goering noticed that Judge Parker, who was watching him,*
*slipped Biddle a note and then both judges started to watch him.*
*Goering then went into his act, started shaking his head at the*
*witness' testimony, whispering and making gestures of denial to*
*Doenitz and Hess. Then, as Gisevius denounced Goering for his*
*part in building up the Gestapo and participating in Nazi scan-*
*dals, expressions of attention, hostility and amusement swept the*
*dock, according to their attitudes toward Goering.] The witness*
*exposed the Roehm putsch as being really a Goering-Himmler*
*putsch to keep control of the government. That ended the inter-*
*rogation by Frick's attorney. Then all hell seemed to break loose*
*in the courtroom as Schacht's attorney brought to light that Goer-*
*ing had attempted to intimidate the witness through Dr. Stahmer.*
*Goering had used the scandal of von Blomberg's marriage as an*
*excuse to get Dr. Stahmer to request Schacht's attorney not to ask*
*any questions about General von Blomberg. He had threatened to*
*"get even" with Schacht if he did. The witness explained that*
*Goering was hiding under the cloak of chivalry to conceal his own*
*role in the dirty scandal.*

---

During the afternoon recess, the pent-up emotions of the defendants exploded into an uproar. Jodl jumped up, purple with
fury, and shouted in the midst of the discussion over the Roehm
blood purge: "—then one pigsty was worse than the other! It is a
disgrace for the decent people who followed in good faith into
this dirty *Schweinerei!!"* Jodl was wrought up to the point of tears
and could not control himself.

Frick coolly commented, "It may be so, but I am convinced
that there was no putsch planned and that one gang was just liquidating the other."

Jodl continued, in heated rage, "What do you mean—no
putsch!—We had to sit in headquarters with our pistols on the
goddam table!—They were a bunch of dirty swine!—on both
sides!"

Fritzsche, Schacht and Speer could hardly conceal their satisfaction despite their discomfiture over the sensational revelations.
"Well," said Schacht to me, beaming, "what did I tell you? Now
all the rotten business is coming to light.—It was so stupid of the
prosecution to indict me!—My witness is their best witness . . .

What do you think of that dirty business with the intimidation of the witness? That shows you what kind of an underhanded character he was."

From the other end of the dock Goering saw us talking and glared. He then tried to break the tension around him by denouncing the witness as a traitor and saying that he had never seen him before. He kept repeating, "I never heard of that witness in my life—he's lying a blue streak. Frick is trying to blame me for things he has done—." (Overheard.)

---

*The testimony continued with further denunciation of Goering and the dirty politics behind the scenes, while Schacht was supposed to be trying to bring together some opposition against Hitler.*

---

At the end of the session, Goering tried to harangue the defendants and defense attorneys and to resist going back to the jail first, as ordered. He virtually had to be pushed into the elevator.

Then Schirach commented, "Well, Frick's witness isn't helping him much, but he's doing Goering a lot of harm . . . but Schacht was as good a party member as anybody else."

──────── EVENING IN JAIL ────────

*Schacht's Cell:* Schacht was tense and elated when I came into his cell. "Well, what did I tell you? Does that finish the Goering legend or doesn't it?—I must say that I am really happy—after all these years, to have that *criminal*, who ruled and terrorized *decent* Germans, shown up for the gangster he is!—Now at last—thank God!—he is unmasked! It was really stupid of the Tribunal to indict me.—I could have been their best witness myself.—It is excellent that that scandal with his attorney came to light. That was the most disgraceful thing that has happened in the trial.—Now the people will see what kind of a man he is."

---

*Speer's Cell:* Speer was overjoyed for the same reasons. "There, you see how the rottenness of these men comes out if you just give them enough rope? I guess there is no danger now that the people will fall for Goering's pose of being an honest, patriotic German."

---

*Von Schirach's Cell:* Von Schirach could not conceal his concern over the unmasking of his hero. I took this occasion to point out the hypocrisy of Goering's heroic pose and how it looked to the outside world, now that these additional facts are coming to light. I reminded him of his own conclusion that Hitler and Himmler had "had something" on each other over the Roehm purge, and were therefore bound in criminal confidence to each other. Now that Goering's implication in this affair had become clear, I was also of the opinion that all three men were bound to each other in a criminal alliance. Von Schirach was very defensive and explained that he was only a young boy when Goering was a big war hero from the first World War.—But that had nothing to do with his own defense and his own political convictions. He had never wavered in his conviction, since the collapse, that Germany's racial ideology had been its misfortune.

*Frick's Cell:* Frick knew perfectly well that his witness was cooking Goering's goose and he didn't seem to mind it a bit. He simply said that the witness was just telling the truth as he knew it, and that the background of Himmler's rise to power was now coming out into the open. "I could have broken Himmler's neck myself," he said, "but Hitler always supported him. Besides, Hitler didn't want to do things my way. I wanted things done legally. After all, I am a lawyer." Frick's attitude clearly betrayed a malicious satisfaction in getting back at Goering for helping Himmler to get power at Frick's expense, just as Goering had supposed.

However, it was ironic to see the promoter of the Nuremberg Laws hiding behind the virtuous cloak of legality while backbiting against the gangsters who beat him at his own opportunistic game.

# April 25

## NAZI PLOTS AND SCANDALS

As the defendants filed into court this morning they immediately started discussing the Goering intimidation-of-witness scandal. Schacht, Speer, and others around them made cynical remarks about the shameful behavior of "German patriot" Goering before an international tribunal. Doenitz said to Raeder and von Schirach that it was stupid of Goering to tell his attorney to do a thing like that. Keitel turned around and said, "Goering should have known that they would blow the lid off if he tried to pull something like that." Just then Goering came in and they all became poker-faced. Doenitz asked him if he had seen Dr. Stahmer last night. Goering lamely started to explain that it was not really the way it looked, and his conversation had just been a private conversation between him and his lawyer.

Still trying to save face with the admirals, Goering turned to them as soon as witness Gisevius came in to take the stand again, and said, "Look at the traitor! Why, he was just a small-fry official. Where does he get off talking as if he knows something?—Look at him sitting there like a traitor.—Don't worry, in 10 or 12 years history will take an entirely different view of these traitors."

---

MORNING SESSION: *Gisevius testified to Goering's complicity in the von Blomberg marriage scandal, and it became clear why he had wanted to intimidate the witness against giving testimony on the von Blomberg affair. With Goering's knowledge and help, Field Marshal von Blomberg had married a "woman of ill repute." Then Goering had used the scandal to make Hitler remove von Blomberg as Commander in Chief of the Wehrmacht. Goering's complicity in the von Fritsch scandal was also revealed, showing how von Fritsch had been railroaded into a charge of homosexuality and removed as Commander in Chief of the Army. Schacht, Canaris, and others had then started to plot a putsch against Hitler.*

---

Goering tried to laugh it all off with "Ach! He is just a sensationalist reviewing all of the rumors that have been circulated for the past 10 years."

Doenitz told me, "Let him keep talking. It shows how the politicians got themselves into a hole and then expected the generals to pull them out."

Keitel was upset over the revelation of the von Blomberg marriage scandal. "It is an unheard of disgrace to dig this scandal out into the open like this! Even that is not spared me!"

Goering caught it up, "It is no use complaining, Field Marshal —those people do not have our breeding. They don't understand these things. It is just as I have always told you."

"Yes, it was a dirty trick to make political capital out of it at the time," I told Keitel. "Now it is inevitable that it comes out in public to expose the rottenness of the Nazi leadership."

"I don't care, it was an indecent thing to bring it out," Keitel protested. "I have been an honorable soldier for 44 years and now they are trying to make a monkey of me and my whole tradition."*

---

LUNCH HOUR: As they went to lunch, von Schirach wore a hang-dog look over the unmasking of his hero, and most of the defendants filed out in embarrassed or angry silence.

Even Schacht was a little nervous as he spoke to me because he had gotten dirty looks from members of the military clique and some of the others. "You see, even many decent Germans are upset by their idea of patriotism. It would have been better if Gisevius hadn't tried to bring up the issue of treason [Landesverrat] but simply stated the facts. However, the truth is the truth and there is no way of preventing it from coming out." Doenitz was strutting up and down the lunchroom deliberately avoiding our conversation for the first time. "You see that [militarist] mentality which goes beyond all understanding and human feeling. There it was, the threat of war; it meant the lives of millions of Germans, the destruction and desperation—all that has happened. But, when it came to a showdown to prevent it, some people simply could not get over their narrow feeling of duty."

I tried to engage Doenitz in conversation but he deliberately started talking about the flowers outside in the garden. It was obvious, now that it had come to a showdown, that Doenitz' sympathies were strictly with the military men whom the witness had blamed for starting the war together with Hitler.

Von Papen finally joined the conversation. "It is too bad I didn't have closer contact with you in those days myself. There

---

*Keitel's son had married von Blomberg's daughter by a previous marriage, so that the marriage scandal reflected on Keitel's family tradition as well.

was not enough united co-operation among those who opposed Hitler. Even the generals had no support."

"No, the generals simply fell down on the job!" Schacht insisted. "If just a dozen energetic men had stuck together and didn't get cold feet when it came to a showdown. That is all that it would have taken to stop Hitler.—And millions of lives would have been saved! But, when it came to a showdown, the generals clicked their heels; von Neurath here merely resigned—I don't mean to get personal, understand, but there were very few people who were willing to see it through to a final showdown."

———

AFTERNOON SESSION: *In the afternoon session the witness revealed the details of the Hitler assassination plot which misfired on the 20th of July, 1944, and other intrigues and scandals in which Goering and the generals were involved. Even General Rommel came in for his share of intrigue when he saw the jig was up and he still wanted to be one of the men on top after the collapse.*

———

During the afternoon intermission, Schacht told me that this meant the end of the Hitler legend, now that the rottenness of the whole system was being exposed. Fritzsche again on the verge of tears had put on his dark glasses to hide his eyes. He said, "On the contrary, my friends, this means the beginning of the Hitler legend."

"Do you mean that the corruption, intrigue and scandal of the Hitler regime make Hitler even more admirable in German eyes?" I asked him.

Seyss-Inquart interrupted at this point, "No—but the picture is too gross—too much intrigue, too many assassination plots. I think the German people will be repulsed by it all."

———

*Under cross-examination by Justice Jackson, Gisevius revealed Goering's complicity in the Reichstag fire plot. Hitler had ordered "a large-scale propaganda campaign." Goebbels therefore arranged with Goering and the SA leader, Carl Ernst, to have the Reichstag building set on fire and the Communists blamed for it. Goering later had most of the SA men who had participated in the plot murdered during the Roehm purge, along with a prepared list of enemies.*

──────── EVENING IN JAIL ────────

*Schacht's Cell:* Schacht explained the Hitler legend argument. "What they were trying to say is that all of these plots against Hitler may help to give birth to another stab-in-the-back legend like the one after the first World War.—But the things that have come out in the testimony are really very damaging for Hitler's reputation. Just imagine this scene: Field Marshal von Fritsch comes to Hitler and declares on his word of honor that the homosexual accusation against him is untrue. Hitler, the leader of the State, then *personally* opens the door for this little jailbird and confronts him with his accuser. Now, just get this—the head of the German State takes the word of the homosexual jailbird against the word of honor of the Commander in Chief of the German Army.—No, Germans will never forgive a thing like that!"

He repeated what he had said about a dozen courageous men at lunch. "—And now von Papen wants to know why I didn't enlist his support.—Why, how could I when he let the Nazis assassinate his own subordinates one after another and he *still* played along?—After the Anschluss I thought he was through, but then he *again* accepted an ambassadorship.—Now I ask you, does that sound like a man you could plot with against Hitler? Now he wants to say he was against Hitler too.—No, there isn't one who was against him *then!*"

──────── **April 26** ────────

MORNING SESSION: *Witness Gisevius further testified under cross-examination by Justice Jackson that it was the brutality of the SA men from the very beginning which set the pace for the cruelty that reached its culmination in the murders in the concentration camps. The details of Goering's intimidation of the witness were once more made clear.* [*Goering tried to study the effect on the judges and the other defendants out of the corner of his eye while covering his annoyance with an affected air of indifference.*]

During the morning intermission, Dr. Stahmer, upset by the intimidation exposé which discredited his own honor as a lawyer,

came over to Goering and was overheard reading an explanation
he was going to make to the court. He wanted to discredit the witness and request that a statement be gotten from Goering on the
intimidation of the witness and the various intrigues Goering was
supposed to have participated in. Goering was reluctant to have
the matter pursued any further, obviously anxious to let it blow
over without attracting any further attention. Dr. Stahmer said
that he had to take some stand on it to clear himself. Goering told
him to let it go for the time being until he had thought it over.

Then Goering turned to his clique and changed the subject by
falling back on one of his favorite pep talks. "Don't worry, England couldn't lick us; England and Russia couldn't lick us; and it
took England, Russia and America a hell of a long time to lick us
—and if we had another crack at it they would never lick us even
so!" Goering's audience of military men, plus Ribbentrop and
absent-minded Hess, agreed heartily and enjoyed the heroic boast.
Thus, their attention was diverted, at least for the time being, from
Goering's own disgrace.

———————————

LUNCH HOUR: At lunch, however, it was obvious that Goering
knew he wasn't kidding anybody. He sulked in a corner of his
room, not even coming out to take his walk and face the averted
glances of the other defendants. When he came down from lunch,
he told Dr. Stahmer that he had been thinking it over and had
decided that it would be best not to make any more of the issue
just now.

# 14. Streicher's Defense

## STREICHER TAKES THE STAND

AFTERNOON SESSION: *Streicher started off his defense by denouncing his own defense counsel for not conducting his case along the lines he wanted. This forced the defense counsel to defend himself before the court for not wishing to defend Streicher's anti-Semitism, and to request the court's decision as to whether he should continue to defend his client under the circumstances. He was told to continue. Streicher then started with a bombastic oration, describing himself as the fate-ordained apostle of anti-Semitism. He described with dramatic fervor how he met and was inspired by Hitler and the halo around his head.* [The judges listened quizzically. Signs of embarrassment were obvious throughout the dock. Goering ostentatiously buried his head in his hand as though sick. Doenitz shook his head very sadly and closed his eyes.] *In the course of the examination Streicher had to be reprimanded for calling the previous witness, Gisevius, a traitor.*

-----

As they filed down out to the elevator after the court recessed, all except Frick showed signs of disgust by word or gesture. Frick thought that Streicher had spoken well.

──────── April 27-28 ────────

## WEEK END IN JAIL

*Jodl's Cell:* Jodl was depressed. I told him I understood how he felt, with obvious reference to his outburst in court three days ago. He spoke with quiet earnestness. "Yes—it is bitter—and it is no pleasure to be torn between the bitter revulsion against this dirty politics and the natural patriotic feeling that I have even now."

We discussed the week's events, and Jodl did not conceal his malicious amusement over the unmasking of Goering's tactics. He had known that Goering had gotten rid of von Blomberg's love rival, and considered it entirely probable that Goering had deliberately let von Blomberg get into the trap because he couldn't stand having him or anybody else as his superior officer. "Yes, he was certainly a contemptible, conceited, ambitious and arrogant cur in those days. The way he took advantage of von Blomberg's embarrassment just made our blood boil. We despised him anyway for his uncouth vanity. I know for a fact that he was anxious to get rid of von Blomberg. But that von Fritsch affair was even worse. It may be, as Gisevius says, that Goering had his finger in that disgraceful affair too, because he could stand von Fritsch even less than von Blomberg as Commander in Chief of the Wehrmacht. Von Fritsch was a hidebound Prussian who stood for no monkey business. It is quite possible that Goering dug up that homosexual frame-up to get him out of the way."

Jodl had to laugh at Streicher for starting off his case by denouncing his own counsel. I mentioned that the editor of the Stürmer, Hiemer, would also appear as a witness. Jodl pointed out that both Streicher and Hiemer had been schoolteachers. "These schoolteachers were always looking for a chance to get some power and respectability." I asked him what particular significance there was behind that. "Well, you may not realize it, but a grammar school teacher was the most looked-down-upon profession in the country—especially in Bavaria. The schoolteachers in Catholic towns were merely looked upon as the priest's lackey—they used to be obliged to play the organ in church on Sunday and more or less teach what the priest allowed them to."

---

*Von Schirach's Cell:* Von Schirach was unwilling to talk about Goering, now that he had been unmasked and disgraced. However, he had a lot to say about Frick. "That's really a good one— Frick would have it appear now that he was always against the Nazi system. Why, when I was a school kid, Frick was the big leader of the Nazi faction in the Reichstag. He was the one who helped to bring Hitler to power. He was the chief government official as Minister of the Interior after the Party came to power —and now he tries to ride Schacht's coat-tails as somebody who also said something against Himmler. That is why he called Gisevius as a witness. He knew that Schacht would make a good showing and probably be acquitted. He didn't even take the stand to testify for the others, because he is afraid he will hurt himself, and all he cares about is his own neck.—I must say, that is something awful.—When I think of what an important leader of the Party he was, when I was only a kid—and now he doesn't want to know anything about it. I am at least still doing something to relieve German Youth from the burden of this anti-Semitic madness that I felt partly responsible for, and doing something to ease things for the future. But I think that all that Frick cares about is himself. I think he was afraid to take the stand. He knew he had a lot to answer for in this dirty anti-Semitism business, and he just didn't feel like answering for it. By the way, what did you think of Streicher?"

"He certainly showed what a fanatic fool he was in court," I answered.

"Well, do you know, I think he is going to follow it through and still try to maintain his anti-Semitism regardless of the disgrace it has fallen into." We discussed the issue further. Von Schirach made it subtly clear to me that if Streicher had his way there would be no peace over this issue. I followed his cue by assuring him that it would take a more respectable individual, who had been deluded into anti-Semitism and had already awakened to the madness of racial prejudice, to expose the falsity of this doctrine. This was just what von Schirach wanted me to say.

Von Schirach is by now convinced that the future of anti-Semitism in Germany lies in his hands and that German Youth is listening for a word from their former leader. If he remains silent on that issue, they will accept it as a tacit confirmation of his former convictions; but if he tells them how they were deceived, they will end anti-Semitism once and for all as far as German Youth is concerned. I then told him that the only way he could make up in a small measure for what he had done was to come right out, speaking to and for German Youth, and declare flatly that Hitler had betrayed them. I pointed out that, furthermore, history and the German people would not regard as honest patriots the dirty politicians like Goering but a man like Speer who turned against Hitler when he realized he had deceived the people. All of this seemed to make a profound impression on von Schirach.

---

*Ribbentrop's Cell:* Ribbentrop said he was still having speech difficulty but talked a blue streak, repeating many of his previous arguments and rationalizations: they had made the mistake of losing the war; they had not broken the Munich Pact; Hitler was a fascinating personality—he wished that Colonel Amen had tried to cross-examine Hitler and he'd see where he would get off; he was not an anti-Semite—some of his best friends were Jews; he was only the member of an anti-Semitic government and naturally couldn't follow a pro-Semitic policy; the prosecution had produced a few documents to prove that he was guilty of anti-Semitism and aggressive war, but he was sure the prosecution could have also produced documents to prove just the opposite. A new line was added—his assertion that America had used its army to suppress opposition by force 150 times in the past 150 years. He did not say where he had gotten this information. He then asked what people are saying about him since his case was finished. I could not give him much encouragement . . .

He thought that it was not nice of Gisevius to say all those nasty things about other Germans, and wanted to know what I would say if an American said such things about other Americans. I told him that if such things were true about Americans, I would naturally be quite ashamed of it, but would not think that keeping quiet could change the truth. I asked him what *he* thought of the intimidation of the witness and all the scandal that had been uncovered. He repeated that it wasn't nice for Germans to talk that way about other Germans.

---

*Schacht's Cell:* Schacht said that everybody was cutting him except Speer, but he didn't give a hang because they were a bunch of criminals anyway, as he had always said. "You just have to look at that worm Streicher on the stand and see the kind of man that Hitler protected to the very end!—Ugh! That man Hitler had no conception of decency and honor and dignity. He kept the criminal scum in power and forced the decent men to resign, or he liquidated them one after another."

———————— April 29 ————————

## "DER STÜRMER"

MORNING SESSION: *Streicher tried to prove that he destroyed Jewish synagogues only because of architectural taste. He admitted that the anti-Jewish demonstrations of November 10, 1938, was not a spontaneous affair but a pogrom precipitated by Goebbels, of which he had previous knowledge. Himmler and von Schirach, among others, gave him written support when the "Stürmer" was under threat of suppression. As an anti-Semite, he was naturally not interested in describing the positive characteristics and accomplishments of the Jewish people.*

During intermission he went back to the dock and looked around for signs of encouragement and approval, but all had their backs turned to him. Finally Ribbentrop told him that he could say if he wished that Ribbentrop was not a fanatic anti-Semite.

Rosenberg then urged him to tell how Jewish writers were attacking the Nazi regime so that Nazi writers were justified in retaliating. (This is something that Rosenberg has been trying to sell all the defendants who have gotten up so far, without success, but Streicher agreed to bring that in.)

Back on the stand, *Streicher admitted responsibility for all issues of the "Stürmer," including the special numbers such as that devoted to alleged Hebraic ritual murders. He also took occasion to embarrass and insult his own attorney, and the court had to warn him that any further insolence to the attorney or to the court would require a termination of his examination.*

LUNCH HOUR: During lunch there was a general reluctance even to discuss Streicher as someone beneath contempt.

AFTERNOON SESSION: *Streicher continued to deny any connection with or knowledge of the extermination of the Jews. The cross-examination by Mr. Griffith-Jones slowly but surely tied up*

Streicher with knowledge of the atrocities and persistence in advocating extermination even after it was reported in the foreign press, which he admitted reading. Streicher kept saying that even if he had read those things he would not have believed it. He had spoken about exterminating the Jews but hadn't meant it literally.

[This produced a contemptuous reaction from Frank, who glared at him during the intermission and hissed: "The swine did not know anything about the murders!—*I* am the only one who knew anything about it!—How can he lie under oath like that?—When I swear an oath by Holy God Almighty—how can I tell a lie!! I seem to be the only one who knew anything about it!"]

Streicher kept excusing himself for his incitement to extermination on the grounds of literary license, retaliation for incitement in the foreign press, etc.

Finally, Mrs. Streicher testified that her husband was a nice man. The prosecution did not bother to cross-examine her.

———— EVENING IN JAIL ————

*Fritzsche's Cell:* His comment on Streicher was brief and to the point. "Well, they've put a rope around his neck after all; at least our end of the dock thinks so."

He then started to fight back his tears again as he told me of his desperation over the whole business. He was not very coherent, but said that he was disillusioned over Schacht's case. If so many people had known all along what Hitler was doing, why didn't someone have the guts to risk his own life and go right up to him and shoot him, instead of always planting bombs that didn't work because they didn't want to be at the scene of action? He explained the danger of another stab-in-the-back legend. But he was sick and tired of everything.

*Doenitz' Cell:* Doenitz' attitude was that he didn't want to know or say anything about this dirty politics and dirty propaganda. None of his naval officers would ever have touched Streicher's filthy sheet even with a pair of tongs. He said it was bad enough to have to sit through it all in court, but he was glad that his case was coming up soon and he was being represented by an upright example of a clean-cut young German naval officer who would present his case simply and honestly. Then he hoped some day to get as far away from this mess of politics and propaganda as he possibly could.

# 15 Schacht's Defense

## SCHACHT TAKES THE STAND

MORNING SESSION: *Schacht began his defense with a self-portrayal as a patriotic nationalist, idealist, and democrat. He had made common cause with Hitler because Hitler had been the leader of the largest party and his program had not sounded so radical at the time. He spoke scornfully of Hitler as a demagogue politician, describing Mein Kampf as a political tract written in bad German by a poorly-educated fanatic. Schacht maintained that he was justified in objecting to the Versailles Treaty, since even America refused to ratify the treaty as a betrayal of Wilson's 14 Points.*

During the morning intermission Goering came out of his corner and started whipping up sentiment in the middle of the dock against Schacht. He got Sauckel, von Schirach, Frank, Rosenberg, and Ribbentrop into a huddle and described how Schacht had greeted Hitler with both hands in the Reichstag and couldn't get in fast enough to shake hands with him. He denounced Schacht as a turncoat and hypocrite whom the German people would renounce—an obvious warning to those who have yet to testify.

LUNCH HOUR: During lunch a lively discussion was held in the Youth lunchroom with Speer trying to keep wavering von Schirach to the anti-Hitler line of resistance. Von Schirach voiced the opinion that if Hitler was such a fanatic half-educated man who had no conception of industrial problems, he wondered why Schacht had supported him in the beginning. Speer answered that it was obvious that Hitler had fooled him, "just as he fooled the rest of us." Von Schirach still did not think that Hitler was as ignorant as Schacht was making him out to be. He may not have had much education, but he read a great deal and showed considerable knowledge in many fields.

"That's just the trouble," said Speer. "Like many people who have a smattering of reading in many fields, he thought he was an expert in all fields. Speaking for architecture and armaments, the two things that I know something about, he thought that he was an expert in these fields because he accepted everything he read as authoritative. Such self-taught people have an unholy awe for what they see in print. Unlike scientists, they don't understand that authorities become revised in time and science progresses and the printed word is far from absolute. But he considered his opinion absolutely authoritative on all subjects because he too had once read a book."

I contributed something about the dangerous combination of a smattering of knowledge and an obsessive personality.

This got von Schirach back on the anti-Hitler track. "Yes, he persisted in his anti-Semitic obsession to the very death, and even in his Testament he tried to blame the Jews for the war and justify the extermination." Turning to Speer, he added, "We'll have to say something about that in our defenses."

Speer seized the opportunity to drive home his point. "Yes, we must. As I once mentioned to you, Hitler clearly said that he didn't care if the German people lost their last possibility of existence, because only the inferior population remained. Now, do you consider the German Youth inferior population who do not deserve to exist?"

Von Schirach raised his eyebrows. "So? You must show me that statement." Speer said he would, and would also show how Hitler actually gave the orders to destroy all further means of livelihood for the German people.

---

AFTERNOON SESSION: [Goering kept grumbling to his neighbors hostile remarks about Schacht, and said he hoped that Jackson would get the goods on Schacht too. The admirals and von Schirach, however, paid no further attention to him, and he was forced to pour his grumblings into the unretentive ear of Hess.] Schacht continued to denounce Hitler as the betrayer of German idealists like himself, telling how Hitler had taken an oath to uphold the Weimar Constitution, but broke all its laws; had promised minority rights for the Jews, but actually rendered them stateless and unprotected; promised to protect positive Christianity, but hurt and insulted the Church; promised peaceful trade, but instead destroyed it. When he realized that Hitler was bent on war and getting rid of all who stood in his way, Schacht turned *against him and plotted to overthrow him, as Gisevius had testified.*

———————— EVENING IN JAIL ————————

*Schacht's Cell:* Schacht was playing solitaire again, calm and self-confident. "Did you hear me this afternoon? I told them a thing or two. I told them what Hitler had promised and what he had accomplished. Of course, those Nazis didn't like it a bit. They were grumbling all over the dock, except for the couple who agree with me—Speer, Funk, and von Papen. That little runt, Streicher, said it was terrible to talk that way about our dead Führer. Those swine talk about respect for the dead after they have murdered 5 million innocent people and millions of decent Germans who have fallen in a useless war! . . . I've only just begun! Wait until I get to the outbreak of the war. The military men will have a fit. They're mad already, although Jodl at least spoke to me and tried to explain the difference between pacifism and love of peace. I know there is a difference. I explained it in court. If the military profession is honorable, it is the most self-effacing profession in the world because its duty is to prevent its use." We discussed militarism a little further and agreed that experience had shown that, when German militarism was faced with a showdown between peace and war, the training, obedience, and ambition of the generals swung the decision in favor of war.

——————————— **May 1** ———————————

MORNING SESSION: *Schacht explained how little he had to do with the Nazis and how much contempt he had for the crowd for social reasons.* [Although Goering no longer had a very interested audience around him, he kept making remarks loud enough for them to hear. "Now he has the nerve to say that!—Just listen to how he lies!"] *Then came a long discussion on disarmament and rearmament and his intentions only to keep on a par with Germany's neighbors while they refused to disarm.* [When Schacht said that, if he had known that Hitler was going to use the money for rearmament, he would never have given it, Goering laughed out loud and Raeder said, "Who's going to believe that!"]

————————

During the morning intermission, Goering was overheard telling the attorneys sitting in front of him, "He's lying! He's lying! He's lying! I was there myself when Hitler said we needed some more money for armaments and Schacht said, 'Yes, we need a big army, navy and air force.' "

Ribbentrop chimed in with, "Yes—I heard that too.—It was in 1940." Goering confirmed the time of the incident.

Hess turned around and asked von Schirach if he had heard that, but von Schirach ignored the whole conversation, and Goering showed his annoyance at von Schirach's recalcitrant attitude.

---

*Schacht quoted Davies' "Mission to Moscow" in describing how enthusiastically Schacht greeted Roosevelt's proposal to limit rearmament to arms that a man could carry on his back. He admitted that, as President of the Reichsbank, he used the so-called "Mefo Bills" to finance rearmament, but it was not his fault that it was kept secret; that was the responsibility of the Finance Minister.*

---

LUNCH HOUR: In the Youth lunchroom, Speer was working on von Schirach and Fritzsche. He showed them the correspondence between himself and Hitler, documenting Hitler's determination to destroy the "inferior remains" of the German people rather than surrender. Von Schirach was reading it with intense interest when I came in, and he gasped, "Horrible! Horrible!"

"And here are the orders that show he not only said so but was starting to carry it out!" Speer pointed out.

Fritzsche was pacing up and down excitedly. "That's the thing that will destroy the Hitler myth once and for all! That will wipe out the danger of a stab-in-the-back legend on account of the plots against Hitler."

"Exactly! That's why I asked you to confirm that, before the Yalta Conference, Hitler ordered a propaganda campaign with the slogan 'WE WILL NEVER SURRENDER!!' He didn't want a peace offer!"

Von Schirach kept repeating, "Terrible! Terrible!"

Down in the dock several of the defendants made snickering remarks to me to the effect that Schacht was not the Hitler-hater that he now pretends to be, back in the earlier years when he was riding the bandwagon. Frank, annoyed at anyone who tried to pretend innocence, after he had admitted his guilt, remarked, "If Hitler had won the war, Schacht would be running around with the loudest 'Heil Hitler!'" Jodl and Doenitz remarked to me as they came down into the dock that it was all very interesting and very amusing—hinting the same thing.

---

AFTERNOON SESSION: *Schacht continued to show his opposition to illegal, rowdy, and anti-Semitic measures, and claimed to be the "No-man" that Goering said did not exist, as far as obedience to Hitler was concerned. Finally, on the question of the oath of loyalty to Hitler, he claimed that he gave it not to Hitler the man, but Hitler the head of the State. "I never hold the oath of loyalty to a perjurer, and Hitler proved himself to be a perjurer hundredfold."* [Goering, smarting under the dig at his pose of loyalty, leaned his chin doggedly on his fist, and stared at Schacht.]

---

## ———————— May 2 ————————

## SCHACHT IS CROSS-EXAMINED

Before court started in the morning, there were many snickering comments among the defendants about Schacht's alleged antipathy to Hitler in the early days. The military men were particularly scornful of Schacht's attempt to disclaim intentions to rearm for war. Even security-conscious Raeder gave me his direct opinion of one of the defendants for the first time, as if he didn't mind being quoted on this one. "He is a terrible man—that Schacht—what he says is just not true." In the context of the conversation there was no doubt that he was referring to the rearmament issue.

When Goering came into the dock, he was glad to see that some hostile sentiment was being expressed toward his enemy, Schacht. Ribbentrop started to complain that Schacht was talking too much about German foreign policy. Goering comforted him with the remark: "That's all right—if you wanted to condemn Germany as much as that, you could have talked much longer too—so could I." After I left the courtroom, Goering told his attorney that he was going to smuggle two letters out through him today. The guard reported this to me and I took necessary precautions to watch the passing of papers between the two.

MORNING SESSION: *Schacht concluded his defense by portraying himself as a paragon of virtue and emphasizing his leading role in the plots to remove Hitler. He said he could get no support from German intellectuals and the military men always left him in the lurch at the last minute.*

LUNCH HOUR: There was little discussion of Schacht's case at lunch, since the theme of his too-exaggerated virtue had been pretty well exhausted. The comments overheard in the dock as well as at lunch disclosed a malicious anticipation of the unmasking of the anti-Nazi Schacht in cross-examination. For the first time they all seemed to wish the prosecution Godspeed.

AFTERNOON SESSION: [When the cross-examination started in the afternoon, the Goering clique showed extreme pleasure as Prosecutor Jackson began to show that Schacht was much more enthusiastically tied up with the Party accession to power than he had been willing to admit.] *Then Jackson quoted to Schacht some excerpts of his speech of November, 1938, on the "Wonders of Finance."* [Goering, Sauckel, von Schirach and the admirals looked at each other, nodded and winked. Goering nudged Hess and said, "Put on your earphones; this is going to be good." The military men and propagandists enjoyed Schacht's embarrassment over the evidence that he had contributed a thousand RM yearly to the Party after getting the golden Party badge. Goering laughed until he shook.] *Then the prosecutor turned to the subject of Schacht's knowledge of the growing Wehrmacht, which was hardly reconcilable with his peaceful aims.* [Goering was tickled, and told the others, "Now it comes out."]

*With reference to the Koenigsberg speech, Jackson pointed out, "You stopped the quotation just at the point where I get interested." Schacht laughed in good-humored embarrassment, saying that he naturally left the other parts for the prosecution to quote.* [This brought a snicker from Goering. "He giggles just like an innocent girl who's getting it for the first time!" He thought that was pretty good and repeated it to the boys in the back row.] *Mr.*

*Jackson* quoted the part in which Schacht supported Hitler and the Nazi line.

A revealing character trait was brought out when Jackson asked him how he could reconcile his glowing tributes to Hitler with his alleged hostility to him. Schacht explained innocently that he naturally had to maintain a false face in order to have his way.

────────── EVENING IN JAIL ──────────

*Doenitz' Cell:* Doenitz had plenty to say as soon as I came into his cell. "What did I tell you—that's politics for you! Now, I can respect anybody who sticks to his guns.—I always despised Goering, but I must say I was impressed by his consistency.—I never even invited him to my house; that shows you how little I thought of him. As Chiefs of the Luftwaffe and Navy we were always at odds, but at least he got up and stuck to his guns and I have changed my mind about him. I am also diametrically opposed to Rosenberg, but if he defends his viewpoint, that is his affair. Speer is one of my best friends and he feels justified in having tried to assassinate Hitler in January, 1945. That is also his affair and his honest conviction. But that does not change our friendship even though I may feel differently about it . . . But I smelled a rat when Schacht tried to make himself out an enemy of the regime from the very beginning. So did Biddle and Parker. I could see it on their faces. In fact, so did Jackson. Jackson asked him why he made so many pretenses, and Schacht says that if you want to influence somebody you have to put up a false front. All Jackson said was, 'Thanks for the advice.'—If a man goes around strutting like a peacock with the golden Party badge, it is hypocrisy to say that he wore it just to enjoy certain pleasantries on the train or in ordering a car.—Did you notice Biddle's and Parker's faces? They nearly burst out laughing at that . . . No, I believe in being upright and consistent. You can get along with anybody if they are upright, regardless of what their viewpoint may be . . . Thank God, I never had anything to do with politics until the end of the war. Today it is just one year since I undertook my first political mission, and I never had anything to do with politics before that. That is why I have had a very rich life and a clean one."

*Speer's Cell:* Speer felt it was obvious that Schacht had been a little insincere about his hostility to the Nazi Party in the early years. He should have admitted his co-operation with Hitler in the be-ginning and then his disillusionment and renunciation would have been more convincing. "That convinces me all the more that I am right in the line that I am taking.—I am going to admit my own share of guilt right off, and then explain why I decided to try to as-sassinate Hitler." He stressed once more that he was doing it not to save his own neck but to let the German people know what a traitor Hitler was to his own people.

The conversation then turned to Goering again. "He is up to a new trick. He is spreading it around that he is getting permis-sion to have his say once more at the conclusion of the defense in order to retaliate against Schacht and Gisevius, and he'll make Schacht sorry he ever started to attack him. Of course, his purpose in saying that is to scare anybody else who might have something to say against him. There isn't a Nazi in the dock who doesn't have something he'd rather not have mentioned, and Goering knows perfectly well that they are all afraid he might have some-thing on them. These little tricks work like a kind of moral black-mail.

"Anyway, as far as Goering's marble casket is concerned, I am afraid neither I nor any other architect will ever get the order to design one for him. The testimony of Gisevius just about finished him."

## May 3

## SCHACHT'S FINANCE AND GOERING'S LIPSTICK

MORNING SESSION: *Schacht's characterization of Goering as "an immoral criminal type," his pompous showmanship and egocen-tricity, was brought out in cross-examination by Jackson. Goering's reception of officials dressed in a toga and sandals like Nero, with painted face, lipstick and red fingernails, was read, to the amuse-ment of everyone in the court, except Goering. [Goering squirmed in his seat and grumbled, "This is no place to bring up a thing like* that—even if it is true. It can't help him any—I don't know why he brought that up." Hess laughed his buck-toothed laugh, but the others at that end of the dock had sufficient presence of mind to control their amusement. Goering continued with dark references to his threat to get even with Schacht. "You can be sure of one thing—just wait; you can be sure of that."]

*The cross-examination brought out that Schacht had, in fact, financed the rearmament; that even though he disapproved of the Anschluss of Austria and the rape of Czechoslovakia, he gladly took over their banks after these countries were invaded, and made grand speeches glorifying Hitler. Nevertheless, Schacht admitted that the invasion of Poland, Norway, Holland, Belgium, France, etc. was absolute aggression.*

---

During the morning intermission, several of the defendants commented on the fact that the cross-examination was now taking on a new phase in going into the moral issues above and beyond the factual ones. Von Papen said that for his part he was glad of it, although he knew he would be asked why he continued to support Hitler even though he knew Hitler was guilty of aggressive war. He did not indicate how he would answer for it but implied that it would be a rather unfair question. Turning to von Schirach he said, "For instance, they will probably ask you, 'Did you approve of the invasion of Poland, Holland and Belgium? No!—Then why did you educate the Youth to invade Poland, Holland, Belgium?' "

Von Schirach condemned Schacht for requiring loyalty from the financial employees at a time when he himself says he was in opposition to Hitler. Rosenberg popped in at this point, "He swore them to loyalty—*swore* them . . . If he opposed Hitler, all well and good. Then he should have gone to Hitler and shot him and taken the consequences. This business of inciting others to do it while straddling the fence himself—that doesn't go. As a matter of fact, I don't think he did oppose Hitler at the time of the Anschluss. He had a flare of decent feeling in supporting the Führer at that time, but now he is trying to backtrack on it."

---

*The cross-examination continued with Schacht quibbling that Czechoslovakia had been presented to Germany on a silver platter and that one could therefore not speak of the "rape of Czechoslovakia." He also claimed that if he had had the opportunity he*

*would have killed Hitler himself.* [At that point Goering ostentatiously sat up in his seat, glared at Schacht, shaking his head; then
buried his face in his hands, shaking his head as if in great pain
over this admission of treason.]

---

LUNCH HOUR: In the Youth lunchroom all were agreed that
Schacht had gone too far in maintaining his innocence and opposition to Hitler. Von Schirach said he simply could not believe
him and had no respect for him any more. As for his pretending
that he was a democrat and not an anti-Semite—the less said about
that the better. Fritzsche characterized Schacht's defense as
"propagandistic suicide."

Funk quoted Stresemann as saying, "The only thing clean about
Schacht is his white collar."

"He held those inspiring speeches and greeted Hitler enthusiastically even after the aggression had started," von Schirach
pointed out. "All that means to me is that he was sitting on the
fence and playing safe."

Speer agreed to all this, but defended Schacht as at least a man
who tried to put an end to the catastrophe, in contrast to Goering who made a feeble gesture to delay the war, but then submitted very willingly to the declaration of war.

In the next lunchroom Keitel was overheard telling the others
with a sigh, "I guess they're finishing off Schacht too.—It's a misfortune to be a German altogether these days." To this Sauckel
replied that it had started that way in 1920 and poor Germany
has had no rest ever since. Frank looked up from his paper and
declared that it was terrible the way Russia was robbing everything Germany had. The conversation turned to the beginning of
World War II, and Keitel commented that the men who fought
in Spain were forced to go; they weren't volunteers.

Several of the defendants commented that Jackson was doing a
particularly good job on Schacht.

--------- EVENING IN JAIL ---------

*Schacht's Cell*: Still convinced of his innocence, Schacht wanted
to know whether the prosecution wasn't going to release him. I
reminded him that there wasn't anything in the Charter that pro-

vided for such a move. In an attempt to see whether he didn't have any regrets at all about his early support of Hitler, I reminded him that the prosecution had shown that he did have a big share in the rise to power and rearmament.

"But so did all the other powers," Schacht protested. "That is no crime, and anyway that is not what I am indicted for. They can attack my character, my duplicity, or anything they please—but I am indicted for planning aggressive war. That charge has not been proved . . . Now will they keep me sitting here for another three months and listening to all that stuff that doesn't concern me?"

He giggled at the discomfiture he had caused Goering and the other criminals, but remained unshaken in his own self-righteousness.

---

*Goering's Cell:* Goering had a headache and asked me to tell the German doctor to give him some pills. He looked haggard and depressed, and it was obvious that it was Schacht who had given him the headache. "That fool! Bah! He probably thought he could save his own neck by attacking me—but you see how far he got.— The way I behave in my own house is my own business. But I thought that a man of his intelligence would not be so stupid as to stoop to such things.—Anyway, I didn't use lipstick.—And he can compare me to Nero or anybody he likes, but what has that got to do with his defense? He had an easy case. He did not have to stoop to such things." Goering wore a very hurt, sick look as he lay on his cot, mumbling as though to himself, and seemed to be on the verge of whimpering like a slapped child.

"Well, it is obvious that you two were not friends," I commented, to draw him out further.

"Sure, but did you know that it was through him that I got into the industrial field altogether? He recommended me for Minister of Raw Material and Foreign Exchange; then that gradually led to my talking over the Four Year Plan. Naturally, I had to tell him that he would have to take orders from me, because industry was involved in the Four Year Plan.—Anyway, the cause of his dismissal was not the differences he had with me, but with the Minister of Agriculture, Darré."

He paused and blinked his eyes, apparently quite hurt, and continued to mumble in a low voice: "The fool—when people begin to get scared of their necks, they become stupid.—He had an easy case; he didn't have to do that."

Upon further reflection, he decided that the testimony by Schacht and Gisevius offered an excellent means of tying up both the war and the defeat with a new stab-in-the-back betrayal legend.

"Now I know why the Poles were so insolent in answer to our demands in 1939. Those traitors told them to put up a stiff front, and there would be a revolution in Germany. If they hadn't been encouraged to be so insolent, we probably could have dealt with them peacefully ourselves and there wouldn't have been any war." He scowled with dilated nostrils and fairly snorted his contempt for Schacht's plans to attack Hitler and sabotage the war. " . . . Do you think I would ever put myself in the position of letting a foreign prosecutor ask me if I claimed credit for my country's defeat in the war?—I'd sooner die!"

We continued talking a little while longer, but Goering carefully avoided any reference to his part in the von Blomberg and von Fritsch scandals, or his attempted intimidation of the witness in court.

---

*Von Schirach's Cell:* Von Schirach's mind is all made up about Schacht. "Schacht is all washed up as far as I am concerned—I know too much about him.—When he tells what an enemy he was of National Socialism, I can only smile and call to mind certain scenes, and I know that there is something that just doesn't check. For instance, I remember a reception in the Reich Chancellery which my wife and Schacht's wife and many others attended. Do you know what his wife was wearing?—a big *diamond-studded swastika*, which Schacht had given her to wear.—It was so out of place—nobody else thought of such a thing at a formal reception. Even the regular Nazis would not use their wives with such bad taste. We all smiled and thought it amusing that Schacht wanted to be the super-Nazi in the crowd.—And then his wife went and asked Hitler for his autograph.—Now obviously there was just one reason why Schacht sent her to Hitler for his autograph at such a reception. He wanted her to attract Hitler's attention to the super-Nazi Schachts . . . And then these speeches praising the Führer. I know how those speeches were held. He couldn't tell me he was just doing it for bluff. When I think of these scenes and see the film on how he greeted the Führer at the *Anhalter Bahnhof*, and then he says in court that he was never a great supporter of Hitler, I just know that something doesn't smell right."

I wondered how Schacht would have defended himself if Hitler had won the war and Schacht was put on trial for treason. Von Schirach described Schacht's hypothetical defense in that case with great gusto.

"Why, then he would have said: 'How can you say I plotted against Hitler when I was always one of his most enthusiastic supporters? Just because Gisevius said so? Why, he was a traitor himself in contact with the enemy during the war. Didn't you see in the *Wochenschau* [newsreel] how wholeheartedly I greeted Hitler at the *Anhalter Bahnhof*? And then don't forget it was *I* who arranged the big businessmen's fund for the election in 1933.—And how about the Mefo Exchange which financed our rearmament? Do you think we would have won the war without me?—As for those contacts with foreign countries before the Polish campaign —why, that was the pretext by which I helped rope them in.— And you know my speeches after the Anschluss and in Prague. Can you doubt my loyalty to the Führer? . . . ' That's the way he would speak.

"No, I think he played safe all along. I think he had just one ambition: to become Reich President. He didn't make it in the Weimar Government; so he saw his chance with Hitler; and then it didn't work with Hitler, either, so he thought he could plot with Goerdeler and get it that way. I see him now in his true character; a really sly and unscrupulous character, though you cannot pin specific criminal acts on him. It is just like his business dealings. His Mefo Exchange is probably something that other financiers could do too, but they don't consider it quite cricket. I have less respect for him now than I ever did, and I don't even think he is as smart as I used to think."

Von Schirach then went to the theme of his own defense, pointing out that no one yet had the guts to admit that anti-Semitism and the racial policies of the Nazi regime were a tragic mistake. He still felt that German Youth was waiting for a Nazi leader to tell them this, and no amount of Allied propaganda would ever convince them unless a German anti-Semite did so. This, he felt, was his mission. He was finally and irrevocably convinced that Hitler was a destructive demon who had deceived German Youth, after having read the documents that Speer was going to use in his defense. He thought that Hitler's orders to destroy the inferior remains of the German people was something that would have a terrible effect on the most ardent Nazis.

He still wondered whether he wouldn't have a chance to address the German Youth leaders once more before his execution and tell them what a terrible mistake he had made, and that he was taking the blame to exonerate them. I told him that the best thing he could do for his people was to come out with his opinions courageously whether it pleased Goering or not, because continued fanaticism on the part of the Nazis would only hurt Germany and world peace in the long run. He agreed to this heartily. "As far as Goering is concerned," he said, "he is a big man, but he belongs to an outworn, medieval tradition, and that is a matter for itself. But I am thinking of the future of German Youth."

## May 4-5

### WEEK END IN JAIL

*Funk's Cell:* As far as Schacht's defense was concerned, Funk commented, "I used to have a very great respect for Schacht, but I think he has become morally discredited. He is responsible for rearmament. There isn't the slightest doubt about that. Don't forget he was War Armaments Minister.—No, he just goes after his goal without scruple.—He was always that way and he is that way now."

*Frank's Cell:* "I think Schacht exaggerated too much . . . But what he said about Goering was very true.—That's the kind of man he really was—a brutal, corrupt character . . . That Streicher is such an inferior person.—He didn't even have the guts to admit that he advocated the persecution of the Jews.—He tried to justify

his anti-Semitism and handed out that stupid nonsense about finding a Jewish homeland.—Ugh! He is such a repulsive character!—
You see, I am still the only guilty one."

He laughed at the fact that Streicher had attributed the title
of one of his anti-Semitic books to Luther. Frank thought it was
amusing that some people consider Luther the first Nazi. He himself thought there was something to it, "although one must, of
course, take that with a grain of salt." But, to show that he was
impartial in his disparagement of Church history, he drew some
analogies between the Catholic Church and the fascist hierarchy.
He said that they both had *Führerprinzip* and authoritarian hierarchy. He thought that that, too, helped predispose the Germans to authoritarianism. (It seems that he must have discussed
this with Seyss-Inquart, who gave me this opinion several weeks
ago.) He wanted me to understand that Germans have, after all,
been brought up as an obedient nation for many centuries. That is
why he did not think that Schacht's attack on Hitler and his plots
against him would be appreciated by the German people. He, too,
thought that Schacht was finished as far as the German people
were concerned.

---

*Von Papen's Cell:* Von Papen diplomatically asked me for my
opinion of Schacht's defense before giving his own. I said I
thought that Schacht had exaggerated somewhat. Von Papen then
felt free to give his own opinion. He recalled that Schacht, who
was, of course, a businessman looking for the place to do business, came to him in 1932 and told von Papen that he would have
to step down as Reich Chancellor to make room for Hitler. Without saying so directly, von Papen gave me to understand that
Schacht was an opportunist who had bet on the wrong horse. He
had been all out for Hitler in the beginning, but he did not doubt
that Schacht was sincerely opposed to Hitler after 1938. Von
Papen thought that it did, in fact, look as if Hitler really intended
to solve the industrial and political crisis peacefully in the beginning. It wasn't because of the industrial program that Nazism
failed, but because of Hitler's ignorance of foreign relations, his
unwillingness even to listen to his own ambassadors.

I asked him about the racial persecution and his disregard for
human rights. Von Papen agreed that naturally that was part of

it. I suggested that all of the members of the government were guilty of tolerating a breach of human rights in the Nuremberg Laws as long as it didn't disturb business, and asked him how a religious man like him had put up with it. Von Papen said that he was in Austria at the time and really did not pay too much attention to these things. It was not until the pogrom of 1938 that the people really began to realize what was going on—but then it was too late to do anything about it. The Gestapo was already in control of the country. Von Papen did not explain why he continued to accept ambassadorships in such a government.

---

*Jodl's Cell:* Jodl naturally reacted to the reflections made on the generals by the politician Schacht. "What kind of a way is that? —to go and tell the generals they ought to assassinate the Commander in Chief and commit treason, so that I can sit on the sidelines and become Chief of State if the plot works.—That's a hell of a business, and it's asking for an awful lot . . . Yes, there is a lot to be said about that.—My conception of loyalty is not something to be bought and sold out like a banker's stock. I wouldn't greet a man [referring to film] with both hands when he is victorious and start looking for a dagger as soon as his stock looks as if it is going down. Bankers can do that, but not officers."

"But isn't there a moral issue involved?" I asked.

"That, of course. I may withdraw my loyalty because of moral grounds, but not because of the stock market trend.—Naturally I recognize certain moral limits to obedience and loyalty."

We discussed the issue further and he made the point that a Bavarian was much more independent in that regard than a Prussian like Keitel. He repeated how violent his quarrels had been with Hitler because he had not submitted to the Führer's will so readily. As a matter of fact, he went on, Hitler turned on the screws even more when he saw he had a soft subject like Keitel, and made him do things which he knew Jodl would fight about.

The subject of Streicher's wife started a discussion on the position of women in Germany. Jodl thought that Streicher's wife was surprisingly charming for a skunk like Streicher—"which shows you how strange are the ways of love." Speaking of German women in general, Jodl said that Bavarian and Austrian women were not very independent, especially in Austria where the Catholic influence on the law restricted their rights to a great extent. They were not even allowed to have bank accounts without their husbands' signature, and the various laws of marriage, inheritance, etc. were prejudicial to them. Prussian wives, on the other hand, were more domineering. They sometimes even dictated the conduct of other officers' wives (according to rank), checked on church attendance, and influenced the husbands' decisions on matters of promotion, etc.

---

*Ribbentrop's Cell:* Ribbentrop is getting into an increasingly agitated state. He paced the cell, sat down, got up, paced the cell again, sat down, snapped his fingers rapidly out of sheer nervous tension, his face twitching as he spoke rapidly with wild gestures, as if in a panic over the denunciation of the Nazi leadership by Schacht and Gisevius.

"I have been thinking over and over again the incredible things that have happened.—The future looks so black—for Europe.— If I only didn't have children.—Stalin is a tremendous power—a mighty man greater than Peter the Great—I know, I dealt with him—I even saw an airplane factory with an output greater than all of German aircraft production.—I think that is why Hitler decided to attack him. He was a terrible threat—I wanted a policy of conciliation, but I think history will show the Führer was right. The Russians are a terrible power—you will see.—But the Jewish murders—that is terrible. That is where my loyalty stops— that is the most horrible thing imaginable, there is no doubt about it. But the political questions—there is so much to be said about it; if I could only talk to a few reasonable Americans.— You know, I have never been an anti-Semite. I have been in absolute opposition to Hitler on that issue, but you have no idea how terrible he was on that subject.—That is what my terrible argument was about in 1941—didn't I tell you?—the time he got that attack. I told him it was a mistake to incite World Jewry against us. It was like having a fourth world power against us: England, France, Russia, and World Jewry. But he had a fit over it. I fought with him over it. God knows how I fought. It takes less courage to go into ten battles against—against atomic bombs or what not, than to argue with the Führer on the Jewish issue. But I was against this anti-Semitic policy. What he says about World

Jewry starting the war is nonsense—sheer nonsense.—I fought him tooth and nail on it.—"

"Why couldn't you say that at the trial?"

"Oh, I couldn't stand there and attack the Führer—it just couldn't be done. I am not like certain Germans—now I don't want to say anything against any other defendant, but I can't say I was against him.—Oh, I might still say I don't believe the Jews started the war, but I can't bring out how I opposed the Führer on that issue."

"Did you really?"

"Oh, I may have made certain remarks agreeing with the policy —after all, I was working for an anti-Semitic government.—But I have never myself been anti-Semitic . . . "

# 16. Doenitz' Defense

## DOENITZ TAKES THE STAND

LUNCH HOUR: By coincidence Admiral Doenitz, who negotiated the surrender as Hitler's successor, takes the stand on the anniversary of V-E Day. I reminded him of this at lunch, and he merely commented dryly, "That's why I'm sitting here. . . . But if I had it to do over again, I don't know that I could have done it any differently."

"Even if you knew then what you know now?"

"Oh, since then I have become 100,000 years wiser. I mean, just knowing and thinking what I did *then* I couldn't have acted any differently."

Von Papen noticed in the paper that DeGaulle had declined to attend the victory celebration of the government in Paris, and had said that he was visiting the grave of Clemenceau instead. I asked him what significance he saw in this. "Well, he is showing that he doesn't want to have anything to do with the present Socialist Government, but is showing his respect for Clemenceau, a symbol of French nationalism."

"French chauvenism!" von Neurath corrected.

This led to a discussion in which von Papen and von Neurath pointed out that America had a great share of the guilt for bringing about conditions that produced Hitler and the second World War, because they did not join the League of Nations. "If you had, the League would not have degenerated to a police club for preserving the Versailles Treaty—Hitler would not have been possible—the whole post-war history would have been different." They explained that America's voice would have been sufficient to revise the peace treaty as Wilson had expected. Neither the Munich Pact nor the breaking of it would have been possible, and that upstart, Hitler, would never have come to power in the first place.

AFTERNOON SESSION: *In the afternoon session, Doenitz took the stand and started his defense by declaring that as an officer he had no concern with deciding whether a war was aggressive or not, but had to obey orders. The orders for U-boat warfare came from Admiral Raeder. He explained how the arming of merchant vessels forced them to issue attack-without-warning orders. Orders from the British Admiralty were also read to justify the German procedure. The British, he alleged, had violated the rules of naval warfare just as much as he had.*

---------- EVENING IN JAIL ----------

*Jodl's Cell:* This evening Jodl told me how he signed the actual surrender with the Western powers in Reims on May 7, 1945. He said he had told Eisenhower's Chief of Staff, General Bedell Smith that he (Jodl) could order anything he pleased but the soldiers on the Russian front would not stand fast if there was any possibility of their moving back into the British or American zones. He therefore asked for a 4-day lapse between the signing of the Armistice and the date of its taking effect, so that he could order the troops on the Eastern front back in an orderly fashion. He said Eisenhower turned this down, but he managed to wangle 48 hours for this purpose. He then transmitted the arrangements to Doenitz by a censored, coded message. A colonel of the German General Staff was then taken in an American tank through the fighting area in Czechoslovakia so that orders could be issued for units on the Eastern front to retire. "In that way I saved 700,000 men from capture by the Russians; if we had had the 4 days, I could have saved more." He laughed and said that he did not think the Russians knew to this day how it happened, because when they came looking for the airplanes and troops that had been fighting against them, they were all gone.

---

*Keitel's Cell:* Keitel said he knew only too well what day this was, and remembered the signing of the surrender, but not with a great deal of pleasure. The greatest cause of his displeasure, however, seemed to be the fact that Hitler was not there to sign it and take the responsibility for all that had happened. "As I told Jodl, if Hitler wanted to be Commander in Chief, then he should have remained it to the bitter end.—He gave us the orders. He said, 'I

take the responsibility!'—And then when the time comes to face
the responsibility, we are left to answer for it . . . It is not fair.
He should have shouldered his responsibility as a soldier to the
very end." Keitel suddenly became heated and waved his arms for
emphasis. "He deceived us! He did not tell us the truth! That is
my absolute conviction, and nobody can tell me differently! If he
did not deceive us by deliberate lies, then he did it by deliberately
keeping us in the dark and letting us fight under a false impression!"

I raised the issue of loyalty again, but Keitel still felt he had no
choice as an officer but to obey his Commander in Chief. He
could not be like certain politicians (meaning Schacht) who expressed loyalty while plotting behind his back. "I have been a
soldier for forty years and that is the only code I know."

––––––––––––––– **May 9** –––––––––––––––

## MORE ORDERS

MORNING SESSION: *Doenitz described Germany as surrounded by
enemies and any attempted putsch in war time as a threat to the
state and (with a dig at Schacht) anybody who plans it, as a traitor.
[Goering shook his head in violent affirmation, leaned forward
and looked down the dock at Schacht.] Doenitz repeatedly sought
to justify his orders to sink ships without notice and not to rescue
the survivors. It is necessary to understand conditions of military
expediency. He completed his direct examination by explaining
why he did not think it would have been wise to surrender earlier,
implying that millions would have perished in the East if they had
surrendered sooner.*

Doenitz' testimony brought the opposition lineup into sharp
focus. During the intermission Goering jumped up, rubbed his
hands, and declared to those around him, "Ah, now I feel great
for the first time in three weeks!—Now we finally hear a decent
German soldier speak for once. That gives me new strength; now
I am ready to listen to some more treason again."

Frick and Streicher thought that he had spoken very well. Even

Frank said he was speaking like a fine officer, because after all, orders are orders.

Speer, smarting under the reference to treason and the impossibility of ending the war earlier, snapped back at Frank, Frick and Streicher: "Of course—orders for the destruction of the German nation are immaterial!—Just follow orders, that's all!"

Frank turned to me. "I am speaking as a soldier. I must say that Doenitz makes a marvelous impression. I told you that the German people would never approve of treason."

"I should think that betrayal of the people is a worse crime than your so-called treason," I said.

"Oh, but the soldier cannot help that. It is the politicians who have misused the soldiers' honor. The soldiers can only obey orders."

Frick took up the argument. "Well, what do you expect a man to do when he has orders to carry out?"

"If it is a question of one man's will against the lives of millions of people, I would say that one is morally obligated to kill the dictator rather than carry out such orders, if that is the only way out."

"A moral obligation to murder?—That is a very peculiar obligation. That is a crime against social convention, you know."

"I see. Killing a murderous dictator is a crime against social convention, but war and extermination were quite legal in Nazi Germany."

Frick shrugged his shoulders. "Oh, that is another matter."

---

*Upon cross-examination by Sir David Maxwell-Fyfe, Doenitz declared that he had not been interested in whether naval arms production was done by foreign slave labor or not, but was interested only in the production itself. Sir David had great difficulty making him give a direct answer to the question whether he approved of the order for shooting captured enemy commandos. Doenitz said he didn't approve of it now, but was vague about what he thought of it at the time.*

——————— EVENING IN JAIL ———————

*Speer's Cell:* Speer was rather hurt that his friend, Doenitz, had branded the putsch-planners as traitors, since he knew that Speer had planned to assassinate Hitler at the end. I said that I had noticed lately that when it came to a showdown, Doenitz' militaristic training and mentality came to the fore.

"Of course, that's it," Speer commented grimly. "No matter how decent they are, all they can understand is that orders are orders. The people can die, but they must stand there like loyal heroes . . . To hell with it! I am all the more resolved now to carry my line through.—It is not so easy. Those military men have it much easier. All they have to say is, 'We can only obey orders,' and they don't have to answer any questions about conscience or morality or the welfare of the people. They know that many people, maybe even most people, will respect them for saying that they were just loyally following orders and could not think of treason. That's the only line they can follow, and it makes it easy for them.—I only hope that I am in the right mood when the time comes.—Don't worry, I'm not wavering like Frank or von Schirach. I'll go through with it all right, but I hope that I don't choke up and fail to make myself clear. I had to fight with my attorney to make him accept my line, and he has warned me that a confession will justify any kind of a sentence; but to hell with it! This is the way I've felt since January, 1945, and I am not going to back down for the sake of getting off with life imprisonment and hate myself for the rest of my life.—I saw the whole country thrown into despair and millions of people killed because of that maniac and nothing can make me change my mind!"

---

*Doenitz' Cell:* Doenitz said he was glad that he could finally get that murder business straightened out. He felt that the Allied naval officers who were present in the courtroom understood perfectly that he had conducted naval warfare the same as anybody else.

I asked him whether he meant Speer when he referred to the traitors who tried to assassinate Hitler. He said that he had specifically stated that anyone who planned it had to be sure that it was necessary for the good of the German people, and that way he left an opening for Speer. He asked me what I thought of his defense and I said it is noticeable that the military men still refuse to say anything against Hitler even if they know he was a murderer.

"But the court did not give me a chance to say anything about the black side of Hitler," Doenitz protested. "I was just saying something about him when they interrupted, and I didn't have a chance to say that there was a black side to him that I didn't see."

## May 10

MORNING SESSION: *Sir David made him admit several things he had neatly glossed over or concealed in his direct examination: He had requisitioned 12,000 concentration camp workers for naval production, but was not concerned about where these workers came from or how they were treated. He had ordered the sinking of unarmed neutral ships in war zones, but that was a matter of military expediency. He had objected to withdrawing from the Geneva Convention while saying that the navy could always take whatever measures it considered expedient anyway.*

LUNCH HOUR: At lunch Doenitz explained to me that he considered the sinking of ships in war zones was perfectly proper, because they had been warned to keep out. Even Roosevelt, he said, recognized that merchant ships who sailed into war zones for the sake of making profit, had no right to risk the lives of their crews, and for that reason, he forbade ships from going into the war zones. Other merchant ships that did take the risk for the sake of profit, had to take the consequences. I tried to argue the matter of moral indifference of military procedure, but we could not get very far. He was quite sure that every naval man throughout the world appreciated his position. The responsibility for starting the war is a political responsibility.

AFTERNOON SESSION: *Sir David concluded the cross-examination by bringing out that Doenitz had advocated the occupation of Spain for seaports, and had supported Hitler on various other issues to prosecute the war with ruthless energy.*

---------- **May 11** ----------

## DOENITZ PUTS OUT A FEELER

---------- EVENING IN JAIL ----------

*Doenitz' Cell:* "Well, what do you think now?—I showed that I was on your side. I moved our whole fleet to Western waters before the Armistice.—That is why the Russians are so mad at me. —I have shown that I am a friend of the West.—That is also why I said in court, Germany belongs to the Christian West."

Doenitz then told me that an American admiral in the audience had sent his aide to his defense counsel to say that he considered Doenitz' naval warfare beyond reproach. "I told Kranzbühler to tell him that the Russians have been trying to get hold of the technicians who have been working on our new submarine—the one that can cruise around the world without surfacing." I told him that such a move would probably look as if he was trying to play the West against the East and get some personal advantage for himself, while on trial by the International Military Tribunal. Doenitz said he knew that, and had changed his mind about letting his attorney tell that to the admiral's aide.

"—But you ought to tell him that," Doenitz urged me. "It is your duty. Ever since the Armistice the Russians have been trying by all possible means to get those technicians and experts on the X U-boat. And do you know why? Because it has a cruising range all around the world without surfacing for recharging of the batteries, and it is foolproof against any weapon—even the atomic bomb!" He drew a sketch of the U-boat, showing how it could recharge its batteries by merely rising to 20 M. below the surface, sending up a tube to the surface to get oxygen for the diesels which recharged the batteries. Its fishlike shape gave it a speed of X m.p.h., faster than any U-boat speed even at the surface. "—And if Stalin is generous, as I believe he is in these matters, it will be a simple matter for him to build a few thousand of these U-boats, and then he will control the seas of the world. And what will you be able to do against a submarine that never has to surface? Even your atomic bomb won't help you.—Now I have imparted this information to you, and it is your duty to inform that admiral, because six months from now I will say that I told you about it, and you don't want to carry it around in your heart."

For an honest soldier who condemned dirty politics, it was a pretty clever move. I told him I might transmit the information as a matter of security, but he needn't think we were at all interested in going to war against Russia.

# 17. Raeder's Defense

<hr>
## May 15
<hr>

## GOLD TEETH IN THE REICHSBANK

MORNING SESSION: Before Admiral Raeder's case got fully under way, a little backfire on Funk's case had to be disposed of.* The witness, Puhl, who had testified to the arrangements for depositing SS confiscated gold in the Reichsbank, was examined by Funk's attorney to establish Funk's ignorance of the details i.e., that gold teeth, wedding rings, eyeglass rims, etc. from concentration camp victims had been deposited in the Reichsbank.

Then the witness, Toms, further testified how the deliveries of confiscated gold and valuables were actually made. He was just a little bank official who told sweetly how the gold teeth were melted down for the gold, how he had seen tags from Auschwitz and Lublin concentration camps, had told the previous witness, Puhl, about the kind of material the SS was storing in the bank, but did not think that the Reichsbank could do any wrong. He merely thought that the gold, currency, and other valuables were confiscated in places where the SS had been active, such as Warsaw, and confiscated gold was nothing unusual to the Reichsbank. Anyway, his superior, Vice-President Puhl, knew about it, and therefore he had no further responsibility in the matter.

Finally Raeder started his defense by explaining how Germany had to build up her navy against the threat of aggression from Poland, in spite of the Versailles Treaty. New warships had to be built, merchantmen armed, etc.

<hr>
## EVENING IN JAIL
<hr>

Jodl's Cell: Jodl dismissed the beginning of Raeder's defense as trivial, saying that he did not think the court really cared whether this or that merchantman had a gun on it. However, he felt that the military men showed how superior they were to the

<hr>

*Funk's defense (following Schacht's) has been omitted, in the interest of economy of space. Other defenses omitted are: Sauckel, Seyss-Inquart, von Neurath, Fritzsche, as well as the indicted Nazi organizations.

dirty politicians who dealt in bloody gold. Perhaps Funk did not know the details of the gold teeth in the Reichsbank, but it was a sample of civilian dirty work. The Wehrmacht had, of course, turned confiscated gold over to the Reichsbank, but it was clean gold confiscated according to military law. This concentration camp gold, however, was a dirty *Schweinerei*, and of course reflected the most abject disgrace on the Hitler Government. "I could understand it if somebody hates certain people so much that he kills them. He might be in a rage, and then he is glad to get rid of them. But to cold-bloodedly extract the gold from their corpses—that is something that I cannot understand. I wonder to whom the thought occurred anyway. Somebody—Hitler or Himmler—must have gotten the idea that it would be a good idea to salvage the gold from the corpses." Jodl shook his head and gazed grimly at the cell floor.

When I again raised the question of how anybody could still be loyal to a man like that, obviously referring to Goering, Jodl again emphasized that Goering was tied up so deep in the dirty business, that he had no choice but to hide his guilt behind the pose of loyalty.

---

*Fritzsche's Cell:* Fritzsche was again in desperation, and said he would not be able to last through the trial. Every day brought a new moral torture for him. "What good is it if Funk is partly exonerated from the knowledge of these gold deposits? Germany is not exonerated.—It is a chain of partial responsibility that extended into every sphere of German government.—I just cannot stand it any longer." He mentioned that not one of the defendants had had the courage to come out and put the blame where it properly belongs—on Hitler. Schacht had done so, but his defense sounded too exaggerated to be sincere.

We discussed racial politics. He said that it had been made clear for all time that advocating racial bigotry was intellectual conspiracy in murder; anybody who still advocated it was a spiritual father of a new wave of mass murder. I pointed out to him that this was not so clearly understood by the general public as he thought it was. He expressed surprise that there was anybody who would still have any doubts on that score. He then said that

he would have to put something on that into his defense—if he
lasted that long.

───────────────── **May 16** ─────────────────

## RAEDER'S TESTIMONY

MORNING SESSION: *Raeder testified that Hitler did not want to
compete with England in naval rearmament, and therefore made
the Naval Pact of 1935 which preserved a 3-to-1 ratio of the British and the German naval tonnage. That was a breach of the Versailles Treaty on both sides, of course. Raeder did not deny even
breaking the breach by exceeding the limits agreed upon.*

*He disputed the aggressive implications of Hitler's Hoszbach
speech, but admitted that he was at that meeting and heard it.*

───────────────── **May 17** ─────────────────

MORNING SESSION: *Raeder described the plans for attack on
Czechoslovakia and Poland as simply security measures. Then he
admitted the sinking of the "Athenia" "by oversight," as well as
the official denial ordered by Hitler even though it had been
reported to him. He had been annoyed at reading the accusation
in the "Völkischer Beobachter" that Churchill had supposedly
sunk one of his own ships for propaganda purposes. Raeder
quoted Fritzsche as having told him that Hitler himself had ordered the editorial, and must, therefore, conclude that Hitler
deliberately lied about it.*

LUNCH HOUR: As they went up to lunch, Goering whispered
something to Fritzsche. In the lunchroom Fritzsche was incensed.
"Did you hear what Goering said to me? He said, 'How could
you tell a thing like that to Raeder about the Führer!' I am sorry
you were standing there, Doctor, because I would have given him
a short answer—'You arse-licker!!'—Of course Hitler deliberately
lied about it!—I swear to that! And I myself screamed about the

*Athenia* propaganda stunt on the radio for a month, because they lied to me about it too!"

There was another heated discussion on Goering's tactics in trying to keep the truth about Hitler's guilt from coming out, because it exposed Goering as a co-criminal. In this instance it was clear that Goering preferred to let Raeder and Fritzsche appear as deliberate liars rather than let anything be said against the Führer, to whom Goering still maintained his pose of loyalty. Speer and Fritzsche agreed that they would put an end to this rotten deceit for the sake of setting the German people straight.

---

AFTERNOON SESSION: *Raeder continued his defense with his justification of the attack on Norway as a preventive measure in which they merely beat England to the punch. Hitler, however, had deceived Raeder on his peaceful intentions. Nevertheless, he participated in deliberate circumvention and breach of the Versailles Treaty through deliberate pretexts and forms of deceit.*

At the end of the session, Schacht summarized his reaction: "He disapproved of aggressive war and was deceived by Hitler, but he planned and began the aggressive war just the same.—That's a militarist for you."

---

## May 18

MORNING SESSION: *Raeder testified that he and Hitler had advised Japan to attack Singapore to frighten America out of the war but that Pearl Harbor was a complete surprise to them. He concluded his direct examination by citing what a hard time he had getting along with Hitler and how he finally had to insist on handing in his resignation. He gave the impression that although he managed to have his way in a few little things, he considered Hitler unreasonable and impossible to get along with.* [To all this Doenitz listened impassively in the dock and then unwittingly gave his judgment in one word: "Crap!"]

---

### EVENING IN JAIL

*Doenitz' Cell:* I asked Doenitz what he meant by that last remark. "As I told you, I cannot stand it when people turn their coats because the wind is blowing the other way. Why the devil can't people be honest!—I know how Raeder talked when he was the big chief and I was just a little man in the navy. It was altogether different then, I can tell you that. It gives me a pain to hear them change their tune now and say they *always* opposed Hitler.—Same thing with Schacht.—Of course, we all know better now, but we cannot deny that we followed him then.—Do you see what I mean? That is why I did not want to attack Hitler."

---

*Frank's Cell:* Frank thought that the trial was dragging out too long and that the high moral purpose was somehow getting lost sight of in the maze of evidence. "Of course, that gives the others courage, because they are still trying to save their necks, and the longer it drags out, the better for them."

He discussed this in a manner which indicated that the "high moral purpose" had also been lost on *him* again, and that he was taking a grim kind of satisfaction out of the mess that the whole world was in. He, too, harped on the Russian menace and chuckled at America's task in solving the problems of Europe.

This led to a discussion of the Polish DP's. "I know my Poles. —They are stinking-lazy!—Hahahahaha!" (His laughter is becoming more and more hysterical.) "There are 400,000 of them living off UNRRA in Germany. They don't want to go back to Poland. Why should they? They get something to eat and don't have to work. They say they have been thrown out of their homeland by the bad Nazis. Then why aren't they dying to go home?—Because it is easier to live off the soft-hearted Americans!—America is rich; so why not?—Hahahahaha! You will have to support all of Europe!—Hahahahahahahaha! You're *stuck!!*—Hahahahahahaha!—" He was by now red-faced in his hysterical laughter and I left him.

—————————— **May 20** ——————————

## RAEDER'S MILITARY CODE

MORNING SESSION: *Sir David Maxwell-Fyfe brought out in cross-examination that the German-British Naval Pact of 1935 was intended to curb German submarine production, but that the Nazis were most flagrant in their violation of this aspect of the pact.*

Raeder was somewhat embarrassed by having the statement which he made to the Russians about Goering read to him for confirmation. He had stated that Goering used the marriage scandal of von Blomberg and the homosexual frame-up against von Fritsch to get rid of his rivals for Commander in Chief of the Wehrmacht. This was a confirmation of Gisevius' testimony from an unexpected source. Raeder hemmed and hawed but had to admit that that was what he thought at the time. Sir David pointed out the more ominous aspect of the frame-ups; namely that the two Commanders in Chief who might have protested against aggressive war were thus eliminated.

Sir David then reminded him of the various occasions at which Raeder must have recognized Hitler's aggressive intentions. Hitler's Hoszbach speech of November 5, 1937, had already been dismissed by Raeder as something not to be taken seriously. Hitler's expressed intention of smashing Czechoslovakia merely brought forth Raeder's comment, "Well, he wanted to smash lots of things." Hitler's speech of May 23, 1939 (Schmundt speech) was only an "academic" discussion full of "exaggeration." And how about the order to march against Poland on the 27th of August, 1939, the prosecutor wanted to know. Raeder shifted uneasily in his seat, looked at the clock as though hoping to be "saved by the bell," and stammered something about Hitler's skill in avoiding war, and how he still did not believe that there was going to be war when Hitler gave the order to attack Poland.

[Raeder came back to the dock a little unnerved. Keitel and Ribbentrop made perfunctory comments of encouragement. Doenitz sat immobile. "Well, that's just the way it was," Raeder said nervously. "—I am sorry I had to show up Goering, but that's true too."]

——————————

LUNCH HOUR: Schacht laughed at Raeder's unwillingness to confirm what he had said about Goering's instigation of the General von Fritsch frame-up. "Why are people so afraid to stick to what they know is true? I came right out and told them what I thought about Goering. He is a crooked character!"

Von Neurath was most interested in Raeder's version of the Hoszbach speech. "I had an entirely different view of that Hoszbach speech," he said. "It was not so 'academic' as Raeder pretends."

Von Papen showed what bothered him most about the question of aggression. "That Russian Non-Aggression Pact was the real betrayal! They called it a Non-Aggression Pact and at the same time had that secret clause partitioning Poland in advance!"

Down in the dock Sauckel was overheard trying to defend Raeder for being blamed for his presence at Hitler's Hoszbach speech. He mentioned to Keitel, Ribbentrop, and von Schirach that they all had been present at a Gauleiter meeting, (Keitel remembered that it was on May 31), at which Hitler discussed the extermination of the Jews. Ribbentrop remembered it and said, "Yes, if we had objected to it we would have been treated worse than the Jews."

---

AFTERNOON SESSION: *Sir David forced Raeder into admitting that he had considered an attack on neutral ships, while he was flying false flags, as permissible in war, though it was considered piracy in maritime law. Raeder had also suggested an attack against Soviet submarines even six days before the attack on Russia. He had also advocated unrestricted submarine warfare against British shipping, and all neutral shipping, and following international law only as long as it was expedient. Raeder sought to justify all this as perfectly understandable measures in conducting a war.*

*The Russian prosecutor, Colonel Pokrovsky, then took Raeder's petty differences with Hitler as a point of departure. Raeder had testified that he had offered his resignation rather than consent to the marriage of one of his officers to a woman below his station. The Russian prosecutor wanted to know whether the planned war against Russia, which Raeder claimed to have disapproved of, was not more serious cause for threatening to resign. Raeder apparently did not think so, because the former issue was a matter of principle. The question of aggression against Russia, however, was not for him to decide.*

A statement made by Raeder while in captivity in Moscow was read in part, denouncing Goering in scathing terms and pointing accusing fingers at various other people, including Doenitz and Keitel. Raeder's counsel objected to the reading of the statement, the court took the objection under advisement.

────────── EVENING IN JAIL ──────────

*Doenitz' Cell:* Doenitz was annoyed at the day's testimony and worried about what Raeder had said about him in his Moscow statement. Anyway, all he cared about was the statement that was forthcoming from Admiral Nimitz. His attitude seemed to be that the others will hang anyway, so why should he worry what they say about him.

─────────

*Raeder's Cell:* Raeder was somewhat overstimulated by the cross-examination, but relieved to have it over. He therefore opened up to me for the first time in six months. He explained that when he had signed that statement in Moscow, he was under the impression that he would not be tried as a war criminal. He thought that the Russians were very fine people, but they could lie like hell for political reasons. He made the statements freely enough, he said, but before signing it asked whether he would have to confront the others as a war criminal and was assured that he would not. However, what was said was true and it is just too bad if it embarrasses some people.

In any case, it really was madness to attack Russia, and he felt there was not the slightest doubt that they could have kept the peace with Russia. The Russians are actually very friendly people. Naturally, they now want hegemony in Europe after sacrificing so much, but that means that they will have to control the Mediterranean, and they do not know enough about seamanship for that. (It occurred to me why Goering had mentioned to me slyly that the Russians would not let Raeder be executed, and hinted that the Russians had better use for Raeder. Doenitz had apparently decided that his trump card was to show the Americans that they had better use for him. Thus, the game of playing the East against the West continues behind the scenes, with the admirals already choosing up sides for the next war, before the peace treaty has even been signed for this one.)

Raeder was already reconciled to the death sentence, however. "I have no illusions about this trial.—Naturally, I will be hanged or shot.—I flatter myself to think that I will be shot; at least I will request it. I have no desire to serve a prison sentence at my age."

---

## May 21

## RAEDER'S MOSCOW STATEMENT

I obtained a copy of Raeder's Moscow statement, which is creating so much consternation among the military men in the dock, because of its psychological value. Apparently this explains why Raeder has been so unwilling to commit himself about the other Nazis during the trial.

"The person Goering had a disastrous effect on the fate of the German Reich. His main peculiarities were unimaginable vanity and immeasurable ambition running after popularity and showing off, untruthfulness, impracticality and selfishness, which were not restrained for the sale of State or people. He was outstanding in his greed, wastefulness, and soft unsoldierly manner.

"According to my conviction, Hitler realized his character very soon, but took advantage of him if it served his purposes and he burdened him with ever new tasks in order to avoid his becoming dangerous to the Führer. Goering placed the utmost importance on outwardly appearing particularly loyal to the Führer, but, despite that, was very often unbelievably tactless and mannerless in his behavior toward Hitler, which was deliberately overlooked by the Führer.

"In the beginning he posed as outwardly full of comradeship and friendship for the navy, but soon began to show an intense jealousy and an ambition to imitate the best the navy could offer or to take it away in order to apply it to his Luftwaffe, belittling and degrading the navy behind their backs.

"The Führer considered it important that his relationship to me should seem outwardly normal and good. He knew that I was well thought of in all the really important circles of the German people, and that they generally had great faith in me—this in contrast to Goering, von Ribbentrop, Goebbels, Himmler, Ley. . . .

(With respect to Doenitz) "Our manner was very cool, since his somewhat conceited and not always tactful nature did not appeal to me. The mistakes resulting from his personal viewpoint, which were known to the Officers' Corps, soon became apparent, to the detriment of the navy.

"But Speer flattered Doenitz' vanity—and vice versa. So all the tried and proven naval procedures were pushed aside in order to make room for new methods and new men at a crucial moment. Doenitz's strong political inclinations brought him into difficulties as head of the navy. His last speech to the Hitler Youth, which was ridiculed in all circles, earned him the title of 'Hitler-Boy Doenitz,' which of course did not help his prestige any. On the other hand, his manner won for him the confidence of the Führer, for otherwise there is no explanation for his appointment as Administrative Chief for Northern Germany. His acceptance of this post, while Commander in Chief of the Navy, shows how little he was interested in the command of the navy, for which he was hardly qualified. By calling for continued resistance, he made a fool of himself and harmed the navy.

"A personality of quite a different kind must be mentioned at this time, who, holding a most influential position, has affected the destiny of the Wehrmacht adversely—the Chief of the OKW, General of the Army Keitel, a man of unimaginable weakness, who owes his long stay in his position to this characteristic. The Führer could treat him as badly as he wished—he stood for it . . . "

As the defendants came into the dock in the morning, it was very obvious that Raeder's Moscow statement, which they had seen in the meantime, had greatly strained relations among the military clique. Doenitz was very glum and annoyed and spoke to no one. (Goering was unfortunately still staying out of court because of his slight ailment.) Keitel sat erect in silence and slipped his attorney a note telling him not to ask Raeder any questions in view of his damaging statements. Von Schirach was overheard telling Raeder that he did not blame him for making that statement about Goering. "The Reichsmarschall knew more about the things that were happening in Germany than any other man in the dock. Yet, although he had admitted great responsibility, he actually admitted less guilt than any other man in the dock." For a former hero-worshipper of Goering's, this spontaneous statement is certainly a revelation of his changed attitude, even though it was made in Goering's absence.

MORNING SESSION: *An argument took place on the question of reading Raeder's complete Moscow statement into the record.*

*Raeder's counsel objected to the reading, and Colonel Pokrovsky insisted on it.* [During the argument Jodl and Keitel excitedly called to their attorneys; Jodl saying, "Let him!" and Keitel saying, "Stop him!" Doenitz sat back in stern silence. Hess laughed in half-witted amusement at the consternation among the military men. Ribbentrop leaned over the dock and talked excitedly to Dr. Horn. The defense counsels got into a huddle and debated it heatedly.] *Finally the court ruled that it was unnecessary to read the document. Dr. Siehmers immediately terminated the reexamination of Raeder and beat a hasty retreat.*

---

LUNCH HOUR: At lunch, Keitel expressed his annoyance over the document and said it was very nasty of Raeder to say those things about him, but it was very decent of the judges to have denied permission to read it in court.

Doenitz tried to conceal his annoyance and merely said he was getting wiser every day. Now feeling the need of defending himself, he got into a conversation with the "politicians," Schacht, von Neurath, and von Papen, for the first time in two weeks, and explained how Raeder had probably been under a false impression in Moscow. Raeder had probably not understood that he had delayed the surrender only to allow the Germans to escape to the West, and not to prolong the war.

Jodl revealed why he had no objection to having the document read. He had copied the part of Raeder's Moscow statement that concerned him and read it to me, emphasizing that even Raeder recognized that Jodl, in contrast to Keitel, was independent in his attitude toward Hitler, and often succeeded in having his way.

I showed Jodl the article in *Stars and Stripes* on the Dachau trial over the shooting of 500 American PW's in the Bulge at Malmedy and elsewhere. The article quoted Sepp Dietrich as saying that Hitler had ordered the Sixth SS Panzer Army to fight "without any human inhibitions." Jodl said it was entirely out of the question that Sepp Dietrich had received or given any orders to shoot PW's, because then he and von Rundstedt would have known about it and they would not have tolerated it for a moment. As a matter of fact, they had taken some 74,000 (?) Anglo-American prisoners in the Bulge and that proved that no such order had been given. He considered Sepp Dietrich an honorable soldier, and one who had, as a matter of fact, ridiculed Himmler's

"Nordic superiority." Kaltenbrunner came over to defend the SS. Jodl and Kaltenbrunner decided that the thing started with one of Hitler's usual hot speeches in GHQ to fight without mercy and so on, and this was handed down the line until the local commanders, outdoing each other for the Führer's favor, took it upon themselves not to take any prisoners. Kaltenbrunner gave the speech as he imagined Hitler had given it: Fight with fanatic zeal, stop at nothing, sacrifice for the Fatherland, and show your bloody courage and hardness.

So that is why the GI's were murdered at Malmedy.

──────── EVENING IN JAIL ────────

*Doenitz' Cell*: Doenitz was still quite unhappy about Raeder's Moscow statement. While changing to his prison clothes, he complained, "I still tell you the same thing.—I cannot understand why a man who followed Hitler with flying banners tries to change his whole story now.—As for what he said about me, it is clear that he was under Russian influence at the time. I told him this morning he should never have put such a thing in writing. I have refrained from writing or saying a single thing that could hurt anybody on our side . . . He said that I had made a laughing stock out of the navy by taking over the administration of the northern area.—But obviously I had to do that for the sake of the northern ports, which were of vital interest to the navy . . . Then he complained about the way I held up the Armistice negotiations. But that was all written from the Russian point of view. He probably was trying to make a good impression on the Russians at the time."

I tried to get some reaction on the personal relationship between him and Raeder, but he warily evaded committing himself; merely saying they weren't exactly friends because Raeder was 16 years older.

## May 22

## THE ADMIRALS

LUNCH HOUR: At lunch Doenitz was tickled over the statement he had just gotten from Admiral Nimitz in answer to his questionnaire. "Do you know what he said? He conducted unrestricted warfare in the whole Pacific Ocean from the first day after Pearl Harbor!—It is a wonderful document!"

In the next room Ribbentrop and Raeder were also taking great comfort from the document, which Doenitz had shown them. "You see," said Raeder, "unrestricted warfare!—anything is permitted as long as you win! The only thing you mustn't do is lose!"

Ribbentrop sought to use this even to justify the breaking of the Munich Pact. "There you are—unrestricted warfare in the whole Pacific Ocean, where America really doesn't belong! And when we make a Protectorate of Bohemia and Moravia, which belonged to Germany for a thousand years, it is considered aggression!"

"But there is still a difference between the two situations," I pointed out. "You had signed a pact in Munich not to take more than the Sudetenland, while we were attacked without warning in the Pacific in the midst of negotiations. There is a clear difference there between aggression and defense."

Ribbentrop refused to concede the point.

In the Youth lunchroom, Speer was giving von Schirach his last-minute advice on telling the truth in defiance of Goering's hypocritical stand. I caught only the tail-end of it, where von Schirach was agreeing to tie in his explanation with Speer's.

## EVENING IN JAIL

Doenitz' Cell: I came into Doenitz' cell with a copy of Raeder's Moscow statement. "Look here, Admiral, I don't know if I ought to associate with you any more! Your own superior officer doesn't seem to think much of your character."

Doenitz was taken aback and dropped his guard, excitedly attacking each sentence in the document. "—But look, Captain, everything here is absolutely wrong!—Don't forget, he wrote that as a disillusioned old man in Moscow who had just attempted suicide. This business about Speer and me—. Do you know why he wrote that?—Because he was jealous over our increased U-boat production over his old-fashioned methods!—That's why! I said to him this morning, 'Which is a higher number, 44 or 21?' —Well, by improving on the old-fashioned methods, Speer and I produced 44 U-boats a month instead of the measly 21 that he was able to squeeze out . . . This 'Hitler-Boy' business is a damn lie!—I was never called that. Raeder is just a jealous old man who is sore because I not only succeeded him, but actually accomplished more than he did, and finally I became Chief of State, although I was once his subordinate.—That part about my ordering the troops to fight on at the end—I've already explained to you.—It was only to save two million Germans from falling into Russian hands, and for that I had the support of General Eisenhower and General Montgomery.—No, I told my lawyer, Kranzbuhler, not to say a word about this gripe of a pissed-off jealous old man . . . and Raeder is ashamed to death of it himself. He's been trying for weeks to get that document withdrawn, but he didn't say anything about it because he thought he could get away with it. He couldn't get up on the stand and say that he wrote the statement under pressure, because his family is still in Russian hands.

"Well, I have to put up with him in the dock anyway; I don't want the prosecution to see me hitting him over the head. I've got to stand all kinds of people in that dock, like Schacht and Goering, just to mention two opposites.—But you should see the comments written on the margin of the copy of that document which was passed around among us: 'Jealousy'—'Conceit'—'Jealous griping.'—What do you expect me to do with a jealous old fogey like that?"

I said I was satisfied and we laughed it off. He reminded me again how well he was thought of by the American admiral who had sent his aide to tell him through his lawyer that he had the highest regard for him.

# 18. Von Schirach's Defense

## VON SCHIRACH TAKES THE STAND

AFTERNOON SESSION: Von Schirach started his defense by assuming full responsibility for the education of German Youth. Unable to restrain himself from a bit of cultural narcissism, he explained expansively that he was a propagandist not only for National Socialism but for Goethe and German Kultur. He had to be interrupted several times to get on with his story. He described German Youth as more or less a Boy Scout organization that was interested in sports and was not given military training. He had also refrained from letting the Hitler Jugend participate in the pogrom of 1938. Von Schirach then came to the point and started to tell how he became an anti-Semite, mentioning the great influence of the American book "The International Jew."

During the day, Dr. Thoma, Rosenberg's attorney, told me that he was getting sick of Rosenberg's hateful attitude. Rosenberg has been constantly badgering him to present evidence that the persecution of the Jews was justified. He keeps insisting, for instance, on presenting the Pototsky document. "So I told him, 'For God's sake, Rosenberg, you want me to make them think that you disapproved of the extermination, and didn't know anything about it, and yet you want me to present the document to show that the extermination was justified!' —He makes me sick!"

I asked him what the Pototsky document was supposed to show. He said it was a statement by the former Polish Ambassador to the USA, stating that the Jews around Roosevelt were hostile to Nazi Germany. "—But if you ask me," Dr. Thoma said, "it is a credit to the Jews that they recognized this vicious evil of Hitlerism that has ruined Europe, and wanted it stamped out. I can tell you that many decent Christians were glad of the war for only one reason: it meant the end of Hitlerism." He told what a difficult time he was having with Rosenberg, whom he described as an arrogant heathen. Rosenberg keeps insisting on searching

347

for historical justification for the war and persecution of the Jews, and blaming him for not defending his viewpoint. He is struggling by all possible means to justify his position and save his neck. "—But he ought to be glad I have *not* presented so many documents to show what a vicious anti-Semite he is.—I have found the most damaging documents against him, myself, and he ought to be glad that I have *not* presented them!"

—————————————— May 24 ——————————————

## VON SCHIRACH DENOUNCES HITLER

MORNING SESSION: Von Schirach explained his anti-Semitic attitude; he and the German Youth had expected a peaceful solution to the "Jewish problem." He had nothing to do with the Nuremberg Laws but had thought that the problem had already been solved and the Nuremberg Laws were superfluous. However, German Youth had to accept it as official State policy. [At this Frick scowled from the dock.] As for Streicher's "Stürmer," the Youth had rejected it. [An ugly snicker from Streicher.] He had called the pogrom of 1938 a cultural disgrace and crime. After that he thought the Jews would be better off if settled in the East. He admitted having approved of the transportation of the Jews from Vienna while he was Gauleiter there and having backed up the action with a speech on September 15, 1942, in Vienna.

To this von Schirach could only add, "I made that statement, which I regret sincerely now, and out of false loyalty to the Führer, I identified myself morally with that action. That I have done and I cannot undo it now." He described his break with Hitler in 1943 over cultural and anti-Semitic issues.

Then came the denunciation of Hitler and anti-Semitism. In reference to Hoess's testimony about Auschwitz, he stated: "That is the greatest and most devilish mass murder of history. But that murder was not committed by Hoess: Hoess was only the executioner. The murder was ordered by Adolf Hitler. That can be seen from his *Last Testament.—That Last Testament* is genuine. I have seen the photostatic copy of that Testament. He and Himmler together committed that crime which for all times is the darkest *blot on our history. It is a crime which is shameful to every German . . . "* [There was tension throughout the dock. Frank, Funk, and Raeder wiped their eyes at various points in this testimony. Streicher's ugly snicker grew uglier.]

*" . . . It was my guilt, which I will have to carry before God and the German nation, that I educated the Youth of that people; that I raised that Youth for a man whom for many years I considered impeccable as a leader and as a head of State; that I formed a Youth for him who saw him just as I did. It is my guilt that I educated the German Youth for a man who committed murders millionfold . . . But if on the basis of racial politics and anti-Semitism an Auschwitz was possible, then Auschwitz must become the end of racial politics and anti-Semitism . . . "*

---

During the intermission Rosenberg told his attorney not to ask him any questions. The attorney argued that he simply could not keep pretending that the extermination of the Jews was in the slightest way justified, and von Schirach was decent in saying what he said, denouncing anti-Semitism and putting the blame squarely on Hitler.

Fritzsche and Speer were quite moved and rather pleased that von Schirach had had the nerve to come out as emphatically as he did in spite of Goering's pressure. I mentioned that it was too bad that Goering was still out of court. Schacht said, "Oh, it wouldn't make any impression on that thick-skinned pig anyway!" Fritzsche and Speer nodded emphatic affirmation.

Frank, disturbed at being outdone in his repentant attitude argued that von Schirach had no business passing such judgment on Hitler. I told Frank that I was surprised to hear him say that, since he had so often denounced Hitler so violently himself, and I wondered why he didn't have the nerve to say so on the stand too. Frank argued that it was entirely a legal matter; when taking the stand as a witness, one does not assume the role of judge.

---

LUNCH HOUR: At the close of the morning session, a question by Rosenberg's attorney revealed that von Schirach had never been able to read the *Myth of the 20th Century*. This made Rosenberg furious and he scolded his attorney for having asked such a stupid question. As they filed out of the courtroom to go to lunch, I asked each one if he had ever read Rosenberg's *Myth*. None of them had. Most of them laughed at it, and only Streicher claimed that it was a very profound study which was a little "too deep" for him. I told Rosenberg that he could console himself that none of the defendants had read the *Myth*. "But I don't write books for nobody to read them! Who asked that stupid attorney to ask that question?" Rosenberg fumed.

In the Youth lunchroom, von Schirach's confession was greeted as a victory over Goering's cynicism and a service to the German people. Fritzsche, Funk and Speer complimented him most highly.

Von Schirach himself was quite pleased to have created such a sensation. "Well, I guess that ends the Hitler myth. I told them that Hitler's Testament was genuine, that he himself admitted this horrible crime; that he really hated the people of Vienna and that his anti-Semitic policy was a crime, and anybody who was still anti-Semitic is a criminal.—This will no longer leave any doubts in the minds of German Youth."

Von Schirach was perfectly well aware that he was showing up Goering's heroic cynicism. Speer said he could now follow up by showing how Hitler had wanted the destruction of the entire German nation when he could not realize his ambitions, and Fritzsche said he would summarize the whole betrayal theme when he defended his propaganda at the end.

In the Elders' lunchroom von Papen, von Neurath and Schacht agreed heartily that von Schirach was absolutely right about Hitler.

"Yes, he was the biggest murderer of all times!" von Papen exclaimed heatedly. "—And he even said at the end that the rest of the inferior German people did not deserve to exist!"

I asked Doenitz if he did not agree to these sentiments. He answered abruptly, "Of course," and would not say anything further.

Streicher had "no comment." Ribbentrop buried his face in a newspaper.

---

AFTERNOON SESSION: *In the cross-examination, Prosecutor Dodd showed that von Schirach had good reason to be repentant, and brought up a few things that von Schirach neglected to mention: During the early part of the war he had not been averse to taking credit for having helped educate German Youth to be patriotic warriors. He had inspired them by composing provocative songs* for the Hitler Jugend of a bellicose and anti-Semitic nature. Large numbers had been trained in small caliber shooting and glider piloting. An anti-religious tendency had been fostered in various ways, drawing Youth away from the churches. Finally, it was shown that he had even had an agreement with Himmler to recruit members for the "Totenkopf" units (which were used in concentration camps) and his office had gotten weekly reports on the SS extermination activities.

---

At the end of the session, Frank, who had criticized him this morning for denouncing Hitler, now criticized him for evading much of the guilt on specific issues.

Frick remarked with his characteristically opportunist outlook, "There—his denunciation didn't help him anyway.—The prosecution kicked him around just the same."

---

## May 25-26

## WEEK END IN JAIL

*Von Schirach's Cell:* Von Schirach was satisfied with the impression he had made in confessing the guilt of anti-Semitism and denouncing Hitler as a murderer. Reviewing his break with Hitler, he emphasized the Führer's ingratitude and betrayal. "Just imagine! Just because I raised the issue of the atrocities—I, who built up the whole Youth organization, was cut off in such a way that I had to fear for my life and my whole family.—And then he even discussed with Himmler whether I shouldn't be stood up before a People's Court. And at the same time he was praising the accomplishments of the *Hitler Jugend*, while calmly thinking he would liquidate me as soon as I did not suit his purpose."

He spoke of Hitler's peculiar unnaturalness with women. He had always noticed that Hitler was really never at ease with them, but covered this with an inordinate politeness and show of gallantry. For instance, he adopted the gesture of kissing a lady's hand, as had been customary in court circles and still used to

some extent by the officer-nobility class. "In our circle there was
an understood limit to the appropriateness of this gesture. I
might kiss the hand of a minister's or officer's wife, for instance,
but never an unmarried girl.—You can imagine I sometimes felt
embarrassed to see our Chief of State kiss the hand of just a common young girl who happened to be presented to him. He had no
sense of the appropriateness of things in such situations—a man
who put on an artificial polish."

His wife, von Schirach told me, had said that she was sure that
the relationship between Hitler and Eva Braun was not normal,
and he had noticed something wrong about it himself. He did not
think that there was a normal healthy sex relationship between
the two. He thought that perhaps Eva Braun was more of a pup-
pet he needed to make things look normal.

We discussed the effect that von Schirach's denunciation
might have on German Youth. He was particularly anxious that
his statement be spread around among German Youth so that he
would at least have the satisfaction of knowing that he had to
some extent mitigated the harm he had done. He gave me the
original notes that he had written for his denunciation and asked
me to show them to the Youth leaders, Hoepken and Wieshofer,
who were in the witness wing. He felt that if these Youth leaders
saw the statement in his own handwriting, they would be convinced that that was the word of the leader, and would spread it
around among the German Youth. I agreed to do this.

---

*Witness Wing:* I took the statement denouncing Hitler and anti-
Semitism and the betrayal of German Youth to the two Youth
leaders in the witness wing. They read it and were both apparently impressed. They said that that expressed their sentiments
exactly. They were sure that it would have a wholesome influence
on the hundreds of thousands of Youths who still thought of von
Schirach as the only leader they had ever known. It was particularly effective because he admitted being an anti-Semite and
follower of Hitler for a long time, as they all were, but renounced
this belief out of sincere conviction that Hitler's policies had led
to murder. They asked permission to copy the statement to take
it along with them and spread the word around among the former
Hitler Youth.

Later I had a longer talk with Fritz Wieshofer, 31, one of the chief Austrian Youth leaders. He said he was inspired by reading von Schirach's statement and could see something worth living for to spread the word of denunciation of Nazism and anti-Semitism. German Youth, he said, was in such despair, not knowing what to think, that this word from their former leader would have a great effect.

"But how about your country?" he asked. "I am amazed to hear American officers express anti-Semitic sentiments even now! Hasn't the world learned anything from Germany's horrible example? How can there still be anti-Semites after what has happened in Germany? Of course, there are some who may say they never realized before what racial prejudice can lead to. But now?—After Auschwitz, as von Schirach says? German Youth certainly learned its lesson. It is quite right as he puts it here, '—What Hitler has done to both the *Jewish and German* people.' We have learned in bitterness and misery what racial prejudice leads to. But hasn't the rest of the world learned yet?"

---

*Von Schirach's Cell:* I then went back to von Schirach's cell and told him how thoroughly sympathetically his statement was received by the two Youth leaders. He was extremely pleased and declared, "There! I knew they would see it my way!—Do you know what one of the defendants told me after I came back to the dock? He said that German Youth would not believe me because they believed in Hitler and would regard me as a traitor. So I told him that I know my German Youth better than he did, and all the rest of them who made the big speeches.—So I told Rosenberg: 'If you think that the Youth still believed in Hitler to the very end, you are very much mistaken. Don't forget that my generation was the generation that had to go out and fight at the front while you were making fine ideological speeches. The kids who thought Hitler was a great man began thinking differently after they had fought at the front—2-3-4-5-6 years, had seen their comrades die, had gotten wounded and come home just long enough for their wounds to heal and then gone back to the front again. They were obedient to the end, of course, but it was an embittered Youth, I can tell you!' "

He felt that his statement had broken the last moral tie to Hit-

ler and if the Americans were smart, they would capitalize on
that to the utmost. "It may seem strange to an American that a
whole generation can be so influenced by a leader, but the fact is
that German Youth has been brought up to follow a leader, and
this can be exploited to a positive end, rather than just jumping
in and talking about democracy while they are still too confused
to know what to think . . . "

He became expansive. "Well, now I have made my statement
and ended my life. I hope the world will realize that I only
meant well."

To this I replied that in view of his confession, I was surprised
that he disputed so much of the evidence that Mr. Dodd had
presented on cross-examination. I hinted that I was not completely unaware of the fact that his stand had its ego value,
though it was taken with a good deal of sincerity and in any event,
was more decent than Goering's hypocritical pose of loyalty. Von
Schirach did not dispute this. "Of course, I realize perfectly well
that this stand will find sympathetic response among the Youth,
and especially among the mothers of the nation who will say, 'He
at least did something to point the way for my boy out of his confusion.'—Naturally, I am enough of a politician to realize that. But
at least I am bowing out gracefully."

He even thought that German Youth might some day want to
erect a monument to the Jewish sacrifices to Hitler's madness.
"Of course, that's only a symbol, but German Youth has been
brought up to think in terms of symbols."

---

*Rosenberg's Cell:* Rosenberg was annoyed at von Schirach's belittling his influence. He said he never forced anybody to read the
*Myth,* but had been surprised to see how many people read it in
all walks of life. I raised the question of von Schirach's condemnation of anti-Semitism. He argued heatedly that it was all well and
good to say that now in view of the exterminations, but sought
to rationalize racial ideology as something that has been going
on for centuries in many countries. "Now it has suddenly become a crime, just because Germans have done it!"

I asked him once more, regardless of the reasons for his previous attitude, whether he did not realize now that racial prejudice
was a dangerous thing to play with, and whether von Schirach was

not right in saying that anybody who still maintained it after the mass murders at Auschwitz, was a criminal. Rosenberg refused to recognize that, but persisted in harking back to further historical rationalizations. The Catholic Church had a fanatic ideology too and had directed Polish politics toward the persecution of Germany for 150 years. Martin Luther preached an anti-Catholic ideology, which was justified at the time, but brought about the great bloodshed of the 30 Years' War, etc. etc. One cannot blame the originators of ideology for the consequences.

Finally I asked him whether he would not agree that *all* fanatic ideologies were dangerous, and that mankind must realize now that reason and tolerance were necessary for survival. He thought that that was a very nice sentiment in theory, but that it was an impractical idea because there are different races and nationalities in the world and struggle is inherent in human nature. Now the Anglo-American, or better expressed, American-Anglo people have the leadership of the world and must maintain it or Russia would dominate the world. He considered UNO only a vehicle for one or the other to force its domination on the world. There was no escaping the *Führerprinzip*. Anyway, America would soon come to grips with its own racial problem, Rosenberg repeated hopefully.

---

*Goering's Cell:* Goering is still sulking in his cell, complaining of sciatica and treachery. Major Goldensohn, who examined him, felt that in addition to the plausible symptoms, his failure to go to court this week was partly explained by his desire to dodge the unpleasantness of Raeder's and von Schirach's statements. When the chaplain, psychiatrist, and I made the rounds, he indicated to each that he had already known in advance about Raeder's Moscow statement and von Schirach's intention to "sell out." Even in the confines of his cell he still could not overcome the ingrained tendency to play up sympathies and prejudices to his own advantage. He made snide remarks about the psychologist to the psychiatrist, about the Catholic chaplain to the Protestant chaplain, and vice-versa, to the psychologist about the chaplains, and to the chaplains about the psychologist. Major Goldensohn and I are of the opinion that although he has been deprived of drugs, his drug addiction is far from cured and he is still a basically

weak character resorting to other means of frustration-evasion and
ego-protection.

Chaplain Gerecke has just about given up the vain struggle to
bring a little of the fear of God to this arrogant heathen.

---

## May 27

MORNING SESSION: *Prosecutor Dodd forced von Schirach to admit
that among his cultural interests was the proposal to Bormann to
bomb a cultural English town in reprisal for the killing of Heydrich; another suggestion being to remove all Czechs en masse
from Vienna. He also admitted discussing the forceful evacuation
of the remaining 50,000 Jews from Vienna to Poland with Himmler and Frank, whereupon Minister Frank had protested that
there was no room for them in Poland. He was also in charge of
war commitments for German Youth, but quibbled about his responsibility on other issues such as the importation of 10–14 year-
olds from foreign countries for war exploitation. Von Schirach denied having read the reports submitted to him on the extermination of Jews and partisans in eastern territories.*

---

In the intermission Frank said to me, " 'Minister Frank protested.' Did you hear that? You see what I mean? He doesn't
sound as innocent and betrayed as he did on Friday, does he?
Don't forget that such grandiloquent confessions don't have any
meaning legally and don't change the guilt."

I made a remark about the fantastic way the Nazis had of proposing the shifting of populations hither, thither, and yon as
though they were dealing with carloads of cattle instead of human
beings. This called forth a heated rebuttal from Frank and Seyss-
Inquart, who started cursing about the way Russia was doing exactly the same thing now, and the Americans were blinding themselves to that fact.

---

In the course of the cross-examination by the Russian prosecu-
tor, General Alexandrov, von Schirach stated that his Hitler
Jugend was far behind the Russian Youth in military training.
[Frank laughed until he was red in the face.]

──────── EVENING IN JAIL ────────

*Frank's Cell:* In the evening Frank explained his attitude toward von Schirach's defense. "You were wondering why I criticized von Schirach on Friday. You were thinking, Frank thinks one thing about Hitler one day and another thing the next day. It isn't as simple as all that. I know the situation, and I knew that von Schirach was trying to simplify things too much with his grand confession. Did you notice how all the dirt came out in cross-examination? That is just what I expected. He wanted everybody to think he was just a misguided innocent boy. Why, he even tried to make it appear as if Henry Ford was responsible for Auschwitz.—That isn't it at all . . . I know what his relationship was to Hitler and what the fear of losing influence with him meant. Why do you think he sent that teletype to Bormann proposing the bombing of an English cultural city?—Because he was afraid he was losing his influence with Hitler and was being scorned as a weakling by Bormann, who was always at Hitler's ear. —So he makes this brave suggestion to bomb an English cultural city.—That's the sort of thing that burns me up. I had at least thought that one moral accusation we could make against the Allies was their unnecessary bombing of our cultural cities like Rothenburg.—But then this comes out and we don't even have that left.—I could sense that there was something a little too theatrical about that confession of his. Of course, it makes wonderful propaganda, and it is a good thing and all that, but don't forget that he was part of the whole system, and if he really wanted to make a confession, he should have made it all the way and not evade moral guilt here and formal responsibility there."

────────

*Ribbentrop's Cell:* Ribbentrop thought it was terrible the way von Schirach spoke about the Führer. I asked him whether it was not the truth. "Well, I don't know, but it was the way he brought it out . . . It is not such an easy matter to fix the guilt." He wanted to explain that one cannot say that Hitler or Ribbentrop was guilty of planning and executing an aggressive war; it was much more complicated than that. Neville Henderson had accused him of being a Talleyrand, and of advising Hitler that the decadent British would not fight. Suddenly Ribbentrop decided he had fought hard to warn Hitler that the British would fight in case of any further encroachment after the breaking of the Munich Pact —in fact, he fought like the devil over it. (This after telling me repeatedly that the Munich Pact had not been broken, and that there was no reason why the British should fight over a little thing like their reasonable demands on Poland.)

---

*Doenitz' Cell:* I showed Doenitz the headline in the German paper saying that von Schirach had denounced Hitler as a murderer. He agreed that that was true enough; but he thought that von Schirach was trying to cover up a little too much, especially the anti-Christian influence on the German Youth. "It is the same old story with these Nazi leaders. They started this whole turmoil and we military men who did nothing but our duty are the sufferers. Now take this issue of Christianity and German Youth. I brought up my children as good Christians. I had them confirmed and baptized. The two sons I lost in battle were good Christians and good soldiers. So was I; so are your admirals—we are the same type.—Anyway I had my children baptized even though they belonged to the *Hitler Jugend,* and the *Hitler Jugend* was definitely anti-Christian.—I know it was anti-Christian! That is what makes me mad. It is these politicians—.

"Now I don't want to blame von Schirach especially—but take a man like Frick. He is the oldest Nazi in the dock. He helped bring the Party to power and put it in the saddle, as you say in English.—We soldiers did nothing but our duty to the head of the State.—Now he looks for some little rat-hole to crawl into!" Doenitz could hardly control his anger and made contemptuous gestures as if he were looking around the cell for a rat-hole. "He didn't even have the guts to get up and defend himself, and to take his share of the responsibility, but tried to give the false smell of an anti-Nazi with that witness Gisevius.—But it was these politicians who brought the Nazis to power and started the war! They are the ones who brought about these disgusting crimes, and now we have to sit there in the dock with them and share the blame! There are two classes of people in that dock: soldiers and politicians. The soldiers only did their duty, and I for my part didn't get a pfennig besides my regular salary and allowances, but these politicians, like von Schirach, and Frick, etc. got estates, big gifts, and whatnot." I asked him whether he considered Goering a soldier or a politician. Doenitz indicated scornfully enough that Goering belonged to the grafting politician class.

*Fritzsche's Cell:* Fritzsche was in the depths of another wave of despair because even von Schirach was tied up much more with the criminal policies than he had suspected. Von Schirach's failure to go any further into the matter of the SS reports on the killing of Jews and partisans in the East and his weak denial of the Hitler Youth anti-religious trend only added to his conviction that there was simply nothing in the Nazi movement that was not based on deceit. Again he did not know if he would last until his case came up. I pointed out that von Schirach's confession and denunciation did have some constructive propagandistic value and Speer's revelations would have more, and that he might take advantage of this in exposing the betrayal through propaganda. Fritzsche replied in despair that he didn't think it mattered a damn what he said.

*Speer's Cell:* Speer was still elated over von Schirach's denunciation of Hitler and the complete break in Goering's "united front." He said that von Schirach was now his *Dutzfreund*, (i.e. they now address each other as intimate friends with the familiar *Du*). "It's a far cry from the time that Goering sent him to warn me about saying anything against Hitler. I reminded him about that at lunch today, and how I had told him that Goering should go to hell with his heroics, and should have been more heroic during the war to face his responsibility instead of doping himself up and letting Germany get destroyed and disgraced. Von Schirach finally admitted that I was entirely right about that—and now we are *Dutzfreunde*.—Hah! Wait till Goering hears that—he'll have a fit!"

# 19. Jodl's Defense

## JODL TAKES THE STAND

MORNING SESSION: [As Jodl took the stand, Goering whispered to Hess, "Well, this is my last hope."]

Jodl started his defense with a brief description of himself as one who had the profession of soldier in his blood, was not interested in party politics. He had been very skeptical of Hitler at the time of the Munich putsch and Hitler's accession to power. As far as he was concerned, he associated with Jews who recognized their fatherland. His misgivings about Hitler's accession to power were quieted by the presence of such men as von Papen, von Neurath, Schwerin-Krosigk in the government.

---

AFTERNOON SESSION: In the afternoon session Jodl characterized Hitler's attitude as "a masterpiece of secrecy and a masterpiece of deception through Himmler." [Goering did not like that. When Jodl told how he had had a break with Hitler in 1942 and could hardly get along with him since, Goering mumbled in the dock, "Huh! It wasn't as bad as that!" Later, impatiently waiting for Jodl to say something in confirmation of his own assertions, Goering mumbled, "I wish he would talk faster and get on with it. He makes me nervous."]

Jodl angrily denied the assertions by the witness, Gisevius, that he had withheld information from Hitler. In fact, he had reported anything by way of war atrocities immediately, as in the case of the Malmedy shootings. On the contrary, he regretted his inability to withhold certain kinds of information from Hitler, because Hitler would get his information from nosey-bodies like photographers and accept it in preference to his own professionally evaluated military information. Then he, too, sharply denounced those who planned putsches while the soldiers were fighting. [Doenitz, Goering and Ribbentrop shook their heads in a violent affirmative. Doenitz looked over to my corner from the dock with the same cocking of the head which indicated, "You see?"]

Jodl described himself as one of the few who dared oppose Hitler, even violently at times.

---

The attack on the putsch-planners again brought out the sharp differences between the officers and politicians in the dock. Goering and Doenitz were elated at this crack against Schacht. Frank, still identifying himself as an officer declared with dramatic respect, pointing to Jodl, "There speaks a German officer!—The Germans are a soldierly people, *Herr Doktor*. You can never get around that. They would never have been able to maintain themselves for a thousand years if they weren't."

Schacht and Speer were of an entirely different opinion. They thought that such statements merely condemned the German people. Political revolution may have been out of the question, but it was the responsibility of the leaders to do something about that madman Hitler.

---

*Jodl was interrupted when he started to give a characterization of Hitler. However, he mentioned that after the murdering of the 50 British fliers who escaped from PW camp, he knew that Hitler had no concern for human rights. Jodl himself felt responsible for observing international law after July, 1944. (The Canaris office had been put under his jurisdiction after the assassination attempt.) The prosecution's charge that the officers had enriched themselves was a slander against all honest German officers. [All the officers in the dock except Goering showed satisfaction with that remark.]*

--------- EVENING IN JAIL ---------

*Jodl's Cell:* I asked him what he was going to say about Hitler when he was interrupted. He was going to say that his feelings toward Hitler fluctuated between admiration and hatred: "The things that made me hate Hitler were: his contempt for the middle class [Bürgertum], with which I identified myself; his suspicion and contempt for the nobility, to which I was married; and his distrust and hatred of the General Staff, of which I was a member."

I asked Jodl why Hitler hated these groups. Jodl explained that Hitler hated the *Bürgertum* because he considered them cowardly and not in sympathy with his revolutionary ideas; the nobility filled him with distrust because they smacked of internationalism and an aristocratic code of behavior that he could not understand; and the General Staff was always to blame when anything went wrong, even though he always thought he knew better than they did when it came to taking advice.

I drew him out on his attitude toward the putsch-planners. "I am surprised that you attacked the putsch-planners so violently. Knowing what you do about Hitler, do you still blame them for trying to do something to get rid of him?"

That seemed to stop Jodl in mid-air in the act of blowing his nose. He thought about the question for about half a minute. Finally he said, "Well, if they knew then what we know now, that is different. But I rejected the idea, as an officer who disapproved of National Socialism from the very beginning and then obeyed the head of the State whom the politicians chose. Then they say it was all a mistake and the Wehrmacht ought to get rid of him.—It is the idea of double-dealing that disgusts me. I don't think they ought to shake his hand and tell the officers to assassinate him. I detest this business of following somebody in good weather and rejecting him because he failed." He was obviously talking about Schacht again.

"You mean you think that once having chosen a leader, he should be followed to the bitter end? Couldn't the politicians realize that they were mistaken and then try to correct the error?"

"That is another matter, but then the politicians should take the consequences."

He said that he hated to think what he would have done about it himself if he had known then what he knows now, but in any case he would have acted according to principle, and not opportunism. He felt that as far as he was concerned, he had acted in accordance with principle by drawing the line at clearly criminal acts that Hitler had wanted to enforce, like the order to kill all captured commandos. He is going to go into detail tomorrow.

——————— June 4 ———————

## IMPROVISED AGGRESSION AND BLUFF

MORNING SESSION: *Jodl described how Hitler wanted him to give out an order that all commandos were to be shot when captured. Jodl told Hitler's adjutant, General Schmundt, that he would refuse to do so. Hitler then gave the order himself. Jodl later put out a directive without Hitler's or Keitel's knowledge, that commandos were to be regarded as prisoners of war.*

*Jodl swore that he had not the slightest notion of death and terror in the concentration camps, or of Hitler's and Himmler's program for the extermination of the Jews of Europe. He knew about the transportation of Jews from Denmark, for example, but he merely informed his generals that it was no concern of theirs. The only time he became suspicious about Himmler's activities, he said, was when Himmler reported the "uprising" in the Warsaw Ghetto, which he had had to quell with violence.*

———————————

LUNCH HOUR: A picture showing the hanging of Karl Hermann Frank, the butcher of Lidice, appeared in today's *Stars and Stripes*. At lunch von Neurath commented that it served him right. He was the one who had lied to him and exercised the reign of terror in Czechoslovakia. Von Neurath said there was nothing he could do about it, but resigned as Protector, because Frank was answerable only to Himmler. The SS is apparently the only point on which the militarists agree with the politicians. Doenitz agreed to this explanation.

"The SS Police was a state within a state," Doenitz explained. "It was a question who was more powerful at the end, Hitler or Himmler. At the end you didn't know who was going to arrest whom. When I came to GHQ meetings, they said I was crazy to go around without a bodyguard." Doenitz gave the impression of being an innocent boy in a den of gangsters and politicians.

———————————

AFTERNOON SESSION: *In the afternoon session Jodl described Germany as entirely unequipped for a world war. It could meet Po-*

*land but not any combination of powers. It was a mystery to him why France and England remained stationary at the Maginot Line with 110 divisions against Germany's 23, while Germany was busy finishing off Poland.*

---

During the intermission Keitel told me this was absolutely true. He had told Hitler in 1939 just before the Polish campaign that they had ammunition for only 6 weeks and that he hoped there wouldn't be any outbreak of hostilities, because they would simply have to stop at the end of 6 weeks. He said that if the foreign powers had not given in at Munich, Hitler could not have done anything about it. They were not in a position to wage a world war over the issue.

Doenitz could not understand how the politicians could have started a war under those conditions.

Von Schirach told Sauckel, "Our foreign policy was madness! Madness!" (Ribbentrop was busily discussing some irrelevant subject with his attorney and was "not available for comment.")

Keitel continued: "You see, that was why we really didn't believe Hitler meant war—especially after he had arrived at an understanding with Russia. We were sure it was all a bluff."

Frank declared that starting the war was madness. I said it was clearly madness on Hitler's part because nobody wanted war except him. Frank agreed. But Rosenberg refused to concede any such thing. "It was none of America's business whether or not Germany wanted to settle the Danzig problem," he sneered.

At the far end of the dock Schacht was telling his attorney again what criminal madness it was to go to war without asking the cabinet or even being prepared for it.

---

*Jodl admitted that the German generals were "frightened like a gambler staking his entire fortune" on the reckless gamble of occupying the Rhineland with 3 battalions in 1936. "There couldn't be any mention of aggressive intentions because the French Army alone could have blown us off the earth, considering the situation we were in."*

*Jodl described the march into Austria as completely improvised within a few hours. Nevertheless, it was a triumphal entry in which the population greeted them with rejoicing and flowers. The Sudetenland was a gift of the Munich Pact, and nobody was* surprised when they marched in. However, he expected no further action and the taking over of Czechoslovakia was a surprise to him. He did not have any idea of the impending attack on Poland either.

---

## June 5

## "STRATEGIC NECESSITY" AND WAR GUILT

MORNING SESSION: Jodl explained how the occupation of Norway was undertaken to beat England to the draw. Holland and Belgium were also overwhelmed to prevent France from doing so. He cynically stated that morality had nothing to do with those things. He assumed that the head of the State would not have thus increased the number of their enemies unless it was a strategic necessity. He defended the principle of military obedience to the head of the State, saying that the prosecution could thank its own obedient soldiers for being in a position to prosecute.

---

During the intermission Keitel assured me again that Hitler had never told them about the English and French guarantee of Poland. I asked Ribbentrop how come the General Staff had no knowledge of the political situation that made it clear that they were starting another world war. Ribbentrop turned to Keitel and said wearily, "Well, it was announced on September 1st.—Maybe you didn't see it." There was something incredibly phony about the way the former Foreign Minister and the former Chief of Staff of the OKW did not seem to know what they were doing at the time.

"I suppose you didn't consider the political aspect any concern of yours," I said to Keitel.

Keitel replied that Hitler was the one who decided on the campaign and later took over the actual command of the Army. (After December, 1941, when von Brauchitsch resigned.) "Hitler had the authority over us and pushed his authority all the way down past us, and did not even tell us what he was doing."

"But how did he dare attempt such a reckless political and military strategy when your own army, as Jodl says, was not ready for a European war?"

"We never thought the French would fight," Keitel answered. "Why should we? They didn't even make a move against our couple of divisions on the Maginot Line. It just looked as if the French simply did not want to fight. Well, neither did we. I was sure it was only a bluff on both sides and Hitler could get what he wanted."

---

*Jodl continued to testify how Hitler had started talking to him about the possible hostilities with Russia in July, 1940, and had asked if they should not get ready to forestall an attack by Russia in the fall. Hitler ordered him to improve campaign conditions in the East. Two divisions were sent to Poland for readiness "to protect the Rumanian oil fields." Hitler was convinced that Russia would squeeze or attack them in the near future, and England would encourage it. Incidents at the demarcation line in Poland increased. There were reports of increasing strength of Russian troops near the border. Jodl said that it never occurred to him that Hitler would have attacked Russia except through necessity, and Hitler insisted on it in spite of all advice to the contrary. They began their troop movements in February and Hitler set the plan for the attack around April 1st. It was, of course, "a defensive war."*

---

LUNCH HOUR: Doenitz and Goering expressed their complete satisfaction with Jodl's defense. Doenitz was particularly pleased with Jodl's support of the principle that the politicians started the war and the soldiers could only obey.

But the politicians were of an entirely different opinion. Schacht turned to me indignantly at lunch and declared, "He could hardly have given a more terrible indictment of German foreign policy and leadership! *Improvising* a war!—Did you hear that?—Taking a reckless chance in the Rhineland, going to war with a few divisions on another reckless bluff with Poland!—I tell you, *Doktor*, it is a crime without parallel!—not against you but against the German people! We ought to hang them; not you!"

Von Papen was more diplomatic in his expression of opinion because of the presence of Doenitz. He shook his head and said that it certainly was a lot of bluff and that he was amazed that

the Allies had allowed Hitler to bluff them all the time. I began
to raise the issue of why the German diplomats allowed Hitler to
bluff them all the time, but von Papen saw that coming and ran
to cover by turning to a discussion of the day's news.

---

AFTERNOON SESSION: *In the afternoon session Jodl renounced the
conspiracy, saying that there was nothing but the plan of war
against Poland in 1939. They had never thought of attacking
Norway or Holland in the beginning, but that developed presum-
ably as a matter of military necessity. He further testified that
Generals von Rundstedt and Rommel had advised Hitler as
early as 1944 that the war was lost and that he should sue for
peace. Most high-ranking generals shared the opinion, but Hitler
refused to be budged from his decision to fight to the bitter end.*

--------------- EVENING IN JAIL ---------------

*Jodl's Cell:* Jodl discussed the defense with me in the cell in the
evening. He said he was sorry that he had not been given the opportunity to express his opinion of Hitler as a "military genius."
He was of an entirely different opinion than Keitel about that, although he was surprised how Hitler had guessed right on the success of the campaign in the West.

He repeated that he had been quite sure that Hitler would not
dare to make war after the English guarantee of Poland. "You can
be damn sure that we generals didn't want the war.—God knows
we veterans of the first World War had our belly full of it.—
When I heard about the English guarantee, I took it for granted
that that settled the matter and Hitler would not dare to fight in
the face of another world war.—I assure you that the day we heard
that war had actually been declared, we were a pretty long-faced
bunch of generals in the War Ministry."

"Do you mean to say that Hitler and Hitler alone wanted war,
and was able to force it in spite of the general reluctance to fight?"

Jodl stopped in the middle of his supper and answered with
conviction and emphasis, "There is absolutely no doubt about it!
In this case it was Hitler's will alone that forced the issue! I can
only assume that he had his mind dead set on it and all the negotiations were bluff.—I don't know, but it certainly looks that way.
Nobody really knows what went on in his mind." Jodl gave the

impression that he had been led to believe that the military preparations were bluffed at the time, but he had since come to the
conclusion that the political negotiations were the real bluff, and
the generals were fooled by him. "I thought he was clever enough
to make all the appearances of meaning business in order to get
what he wanted, but that he would never really go to war. When
England made it clear that they would fight, I took it for granted
that he would back down and negotiate.—But instead he just gave
the order to march, knowing perfectly well that it meant at least
a European war, if not a world war, and once he gave the order
there was nothing left for us to do but to obey. Wars are decided
by politicians and not soldiers.—Maybe in deciding future wars
the General Staffs should be consulted.—But in this war the absolute guilt rests with one man, one man only—Adolf Hitler!"

---

## June 6

## POLITICS, MILITARISM, AND HONOR

MORNING SESSION: Mr. Roberts began the cross-examination of
General Jodl by questioning his honor. Jodl blushed, glanced at
the ceiling, at the prisoners' dock, and at the judges, clutched the
railing, trying to control his temper. He admitted that he had discussed the question of creating an incident to justify the attack on
Czechoslovakia, but could not explain why that was necessary
when he considered the attack justified by the mistreatment of the
Sudeten Germans. Mr. Roberts put to him the honesty of the
guarantees of neutrality of Holland, Luxembourg and Belgium
while at the same time calling the invasion of these countries the
only means of attack against France. Jodl evaded the issue, since it
was a political question.

---

LUNCH HOUR: The Stars and Stripes carried a big spread to com-
memorate the second anniversary of D-Day. I showed it to Jodl
at lunch. "Yes, we were expecting the landing around that time,"
he said. "I never found out how many losses you had."

"I don't know either," I said.

Jodl then added with a malicious gleam, "Your troops had pretty rough going in some places."

Ribbentrop joined the discussion as we stood at the open doorway between the two lunchrooms and inquired blandly, "Why did you join the war anyway?"

"Why did you *start* the war? Has the Foreign Minister forgotten that Germany declared war on the United States?"

"Oh, that was a formality. We were already practically at war. Roosevelt was openly hostile toward us." Rosenberg also chimed in with some remarks that the declaration of war was a formality, but everybody was being hostile toward poor Germany.

"Is it any wonder?" I retorted. "After Hitler broke his word by violating the Munich Pact, it was clear to all the world that there was no appeasing him, and that he was absolutely bent on war. You signed the Munich Pact for Hitler and then you broke it."

"Oh, no we didn't! There was nothing in the pact about a guarantee. Formally it was not a breach of the treaty when we established a Protectorate of Bohemia and Moravia—," and so it went.

Rosenberg and Frick laughed maliciously as if Ribbentrop had gotten the best of the argument with his legalistic explanation. Jodl, however, reserved his opinion about this "dirty politics" until I saw him in the evening.

The politicians all took comfort from Ernest Bevin's statement in Parliament supporting Secretary Byrnes's warning on "Russia's Satellite System," as reported in today's newspaper. Ribbentrop waved the Communist Bogey in my face again. "Doesn't America care if Russia gobbles up all Europe?"

---

AFTERNOON SESSION: *The cross-examination of Jodl became more and more acrimonious. With respect to the bombing of defenseless Rotterdam, Jodl retorted that the losses were not as heavy as from the bombing of the Leipzig after the Allies knew that they had won the war. The attack on Russia was based on the opinion of the "politicians" that the Non-Aggression Pact was not being observed by Russia. Mr. Roberts asked him whether this record of broken pledges did not disgrace Germany for centuries to come.*

"If it is proven that Russia had no intention of attacking us, then yes; if not, no."

He approved of the ruthless suppression of partisan fighters, but he admitted that the order to kill sabateurs upon capture was against his conviction. The killing of the escaped British fliers, he had to admit, was outright murder.

Finally Mr. Roberts asked him whether he considered the breaking of promises consistent with an officer's honor. Jodl replied acidly that it was not consistent with an officer's honor, but in politics it is another story.

─────── EVENING IN JAIL ───────

*Goering's Cell:* Whatever Goering's "last hope" was, he could take little comfort from Jodl's defense, with its slams at dirty politics, broken words of honor, the incorruptible honesty of the real Wehrmacht officer, etc. etc. When he came down to the cell block after Jodl's cross-examination had been finished, he was wearing a deep scowl. When he saw me, however, he said he was delighted at the way Jodl had shown up Prosecutor Roberts with his sharp answers. But he could not conceal his displeasure at the barbed references to the morality of "certain people." This continued our argument over moral issues from where we left off. He is more frank than ever in his cynicism.

"What the devil do you mean, morality?—word of honor?" Goering snorted. "Sure, you can talk about word of honor when you promise to deliver goods in business.—But when it is the question of the *interests of the nation!?*—Phooey! Then morality stops! That is what England has done for centuries; America has done it; and Russia is still doing it! Why do you suppose Russia won't give up an inch of her territory in the Balkans? because of morality?—" He thrashed around the cell as he changed his uniform. "Herrgott! When a state has a chance to improve its position because of the weakness of a neighbor, do you think it will stop at any squeamish consideration of keeping a promise? It is a statesman's *duty* to take advantage of such a situation for the good of his country!"

"That is just it," I broke in. "That is why these struggles of selfish national interests go on endlessly, leading to wars. That is why decent statesmen of the world hope that UNO— . . . "

"Ach, we piss on your UNO! Do you think that any one of us takes that seriously for a minute? Why, you see already that Russia won't budge, and why should they? It is only your atomic bomb that keeps them in check at all.—Just wait 5 years when they have it too! England doesn't want to give in on the Balkan issue, because then Russia threatens the Mediterranean, and what the hell good is England without the Mediterranean? Morality doesn't have a damn thing to do with these things . . .

"You Americans are making a stupid mistake with your talk of democracy and morality. You think all you have to do is arrest all the Nazis and start setting up a democracy overnight. Do you think that Germans have gotten one bit less nationalistic because the so-called Christian parties are securing a majority of the votes now? Hell no! The Nazi Party is banned, so what can they do? They can't go Communist or Social Democratic, so they hide behind the skirts of the priests for a while. But don't think that Germans have become more Christian and less nationalistic all of a sudden . . .

"All this trial is achieving is breaking down the willingness to follow orders. No wonder you can't find any people with real leadership to take the responsibility of administration in Germany. Do you know why? Because the best nationalist leaders are in jail and the rest figure if they carry out the de-Nazification laws now, who knows but that in 10 years—after America leaves, or a fight between the East and West changes the situation—they will be stood up before a German national court and tried for treason.— And then they won't even be able to hide behind the excuses that they were following orders. So they figure why the hell should they stick their necks out.—And what do the German people think? I've already told you: 'Whenever things are lousy, we have democracy!'—Make no mistake about it, the people know that they were better off when Hitler was in power before the war.—What he did was right from the nationalistic point of view—except for the mass murders, which really made no sense even from a nationalistic point of view.—"

"Well, you didn't even concede that Hitler was wrong on that issue, but maintained your loyalty even though you knew he was a murderer."

"But, *Gott im Himmel, Donnerwetter nochamal!* I can't stand there like a louse and call the Führer a millionfold murderer, as that fool, von Schirach, did!—I denounced the deed but not the doer!—Don't forget that Hitler was more than just a person to us—"

"If the deed was murder, then the doer was a murderer, wasn't he?"

"That is something else again.—That is not for us to say.—Don't forget that even little von Schirach lived off his good graces to the very end too! You just can't turn around and denounce somebody who gave you so much for 23 years!"

"Anyway, I think it was good that he made that clear denunciation for the sake of German Youth who might also be bound by these false concepts of loyalty."

This obviously stung Goering's concept of his nationalistic heroism. "Do you think that German Youth gives a damn what a run-down Youth leader says from his cell? And do you think they give a damn about the atrocities when they are having plenty of trouble of their own? No, the next generation is being led by its own leaders and they will see that their own national interests are being threatened, and you can take your morality and your repentance and your democracy and stick it up!"

---

*Jodl's Cell:* Jodl was sitting in his shirt sleeves, resting from his strenuous cross-examination. He said he was really sweating, but thought that he had acquitted himself well and that the judges had been impressed by what he said. He also thought that he had done a good job of controlling his own temper except once or twice. He found the situation very much like the arguments with Hitler in GHQ, where he had to learn to control his temper, and often was cut off in the middle of an argument.

There was no doubt that his slam at the politicians was well-calculated. "I told them what I thought of this double-dealing politics.—But of course, it was easier for me because I wasn't tied up with the Nazi Party from the beginning the way Goering was.—And I want to tell you this: I am not like those politicians at lunch today who tried to say that there was no breaking of the Munich Pact.—Never mind what it said in so many words; it was absolutely a broken pledge! The whole world knows what the Munich Pact meant, and never mind these legalistic twists.—It even astounded me at the time when Hitler ordered the march into the rest of Czechoslovakia.—Even Goering told me that he advised Hitler against it, because it would have a terrible effect on world opinion, and he could achieve his aim by peaceful means anyway, because the rest of Czechoslovakia could not exist without us."

Jodl repeated that there was no doubt whatever that Hitler had wilfully started the war. He was surprised that the prosecution had not worked on that question in the cross-examination instead of wasting a lot of time attacking his own honor as a soldier and getting nowhere.

Referring back to the July 20th assassination plot, which had been brought up in cross-examination, he repeated that he certainly did not have any love for the assassins after he was almost killed in it himself. He thought that Count Stauffenberg and General Beck probably acted out of idealistic motives, but there were a lot of people who merely climbed the assassins' band wagon because the wind was blowing the other way, and that's what makes him mad. Some of the generals (he did not specify which) were just getting ready to be on the right side when the collapse came.

## June 7

## FIGHT TO THE FINISH

### AFTERNOON IN JAIL

*General von Rundstedt's Cell:* While Jodl underwent a rather unproductive cross-examination by Colonel Pokrovsky, I went down to the witness wing and had a talk with General von Rundstedt. General von Rundstedt confirmed that he and Rommel had told Hitler in July, 1944, that it was time to quit. His own adjutant, General Blumentritt, had said that if it had been any other general who had given that advice, he would have been stood up against the wall and shot for "defeatism." Hitler was a man who refused to hear the truth. He really should have seen that he was licked after Stalingrad in 1943, but certainly at the very last after the successful landing in 1944. He repeated that the so-called von Rundstedt counteroffensive was really a Hitler counteroffensive and was strategic madness. Von Rundstedt's soldierly pride rebelled against taking credit for the counteroffensive at a time when defeat was certain. "If old von Moltke thought that I had planned that offensive he would turn over in his grave." As far as the Allied landing in southern France was concerned, it was not entirely a surprise, although their propaganda had led them to expect a landing more likely on the northern coast. Their propaganda machine made them think that the V-bombs were so devastating, that he thought the British would stop at nothing to knock out the launching sites on the northern coast first, in spite of the greater cost. Anyway, just as at Stalingrad, Hitler insisted on giving the order to hold their ground.

" 'Hold your ground!'—It is easily said. They held until they were killed or captured. It was the same thing with that so-called Rundstedt offensive. A counterattack is all well and good, but you've got to have the wherewithal.—With our Luftwaffe knocked out, we had to move only at night, while Patton could wind up his tanks and move day or night right into our positions. Our manpower was all shot too. All we had was the run-down old men who couldn't fight and the foreigners who kept deserting.—And Hitler kept hollering, 'Hold your ground.'—Like at Bastogne, just to mention one name.—It was absolute madness!—And that was the man who wanted to be considered a great field general!—He didn't know the first thing about strategy!—All he knew was bluff."

Von Rundstedt spoke with the depression of a man who had reached the end of the road and did not even summon up enough inspiration to express his anger with sufficient vehemence. I asked him whether he considered the war necessary or inevitable.

"Over the lousy Corridor?" he asked, with barely a snicker. "Not for a minute.—They could have settled that with a deal any time. The Poles were not fit to govern themselves. They could have told Russia to let us have the Corridor, and they could do what they liked with Poland. Poland would have collapsed sooner or later anyway; they have never been able to govern themselves. But to go to war over a little thing like that? It was madness! The whole war was madness."

He was perfectly willing to admit that the responsibility for starting the war lay with Hitler, but pointed out that he was only suddenly called to lead the Western armies when the campaign was about to start. It was Hitler's failure to quit when he had lost, however, that was the most inexcusable part of his behavior.

---

*Jodl's Cell:* I had another talk with Jodl after he came down from court and again broached the subject of the needless prolongation of the war.

Jodl smiled foxily. "Well, naturally after what Hitler and Goebbels had on their conscience, it is no wonder that they insisted on fighting on. Now I can see it all clearly. They knew that they would be hung in any case, and made up their minds that they would commit suicide if they lost. Under those conditions it is very easy to keep insisting on fighting on and on to total destruction. I see that all clearly now."

"But thousands of human lives had to be sacrificed to keep them living a little while longer."

Jodl admitted that that was so, and said he didn't know what he would have done if he had known then what he knows now. He agreed with General von Rundstedt in saying that the time to quit was really after the successful landing in France at the latest, and that the war was obviously lost after the failure to take Stalingrad.

---

## June 8–9

## WEEK END IN JAIL

*Von Papen's Cell:* Von Papen said that Goering had attacked him at the end of the court session on Saturday. I asked him why.

"One of my documents showed that I had some connection with the plotters of July 20th. I was supposed to make negotiations.—Well, anyway, Goering asked me if I was going to dare to attack the Führer and justify the assassination plot. Well, do you know what I told him? I said, 'Goering, I had great faith in you as an old officer and a man of good family, and I thought that if

Hitler ever went too far, you would just grab him by the scuff of the neck and throw him out. I thought you were a man of energy and principle, and so did thousands of others.' That is what I told him.

"Do you know what he answered? He says, 'Well, I would have done something, but I needed three psychiatrists to certify that he was not in his right mind.' So I said, 'My dear Goering, did you need three doctors to see that Hitler was leading Germany to destruction?' Such nonsense! We really did put a lot of stock in him, you know. But after the way he covered himself with jewels, started taking big bribes left and right, paying no attention to his duties, while Germany was bleeding—." Von Papen threw up his hands in a gesture of contemptuous despair.

Concerning the unnecessary prolongation of the war, he told how he had made the proposal in January, 1945, that he negotiate with the Western powers. He proposed to Ribbentrop's assistant that he (von Papen) be sent to deal with the Western powers, to let them make a quick advance against German forces from the West, so that the Allies would occupy Germany and Russia would be held off.

---

*Ribbentrop's Cell:* Ribbentrop was scribbling feverishly some notes on the Jewish question. Apparently completely demoralized, he handed out the same old jumble of contradictory rationalizations, lies, quibbles, defensive and retaliatory arguments. Forgetting the versions of incidents that he had related to me before, he was inventing some new ones. The proposals he had made to Hitler for a conciliatory policy were now supposed to have been made in 1943, and he had not made them directly, but through a third party, and it showed that he was not an anti-Semite, wanted to put an end to the war, etc. etc. He is not an anti-Semite, he assured me, but World Jewry is making a terrible mistake, and the Allies are making a terrible mistake in the way they are treating Germany, because Germany was the key to peace in Europe, etc. etc.

I asked him why he complained about the present deplorable state that Germany and Europe were in, after his own and Hitler's reckless diplomacy had brought the catastrophe about. He smiled obsequiously and assured me that I didn't understand those things, that Hitler really meant well, etc. I pointed out that he was about the only one left in the courtroom who still did not admit Hitler's guilt in starting the war. No, Ribbentrop insisted it was Britain's fault for not telling the Poles to give in. And the mass murders? Well, he must have been talked into it somehow, though he takes the responsibility in his Last Testament, but Hitler was really a man of such good intentions, it is difficult to see how these things came about, and it is all very sad and complicated, and the Allies are making a terrible mistake, etc. etc. . . .

——————————————— June 13 ———————————————

## THE HITLER LEGEND FALTERS

Morning Session: *In the morning session there was considerable argument over the court's proposal to limit the time for argumentation after all the evidence was in.*

————————

During the intermission, while some of the attorneys protested that they needed more time for argumentation, Goering kept shouting, "That's all right, that's good!—Then the people will see that this trial is a political farce and has no meaning!—Let them set a time limit; that's all right with me." Goering repeated it several times.

"That is a pretty cheap argument for the Nazi leadership to get away with its responsibility for war and mass murder!" I remarked.

"Atrocities! Atrocities!—That's all you ever talk about! What do you know about politics? This is a political trial by the victors and it will be a good thing for Germany when they realize that!"

"No excuses in the world will wipe away the cold-blooded murder of millions of people—I do not even choose to believe that the German people wanted it, or are thankful to the Nazi leadership for leading them to a war of destruction!"

"Ach, phooey! Nobody approves of the mass murders, but you are trying to confuse the political issues with those things!"

"Do you mean to deny that Hitler ordered the mass murders when he himself admits it in his own Last Testament?"

"That is no proof. I think he only covered it at the end. He was roped into it somehow by Himmler, and since he was going to kill himself, at the end, he took the responsibility." The argument was so ridiculous on the face of it that Goering felt a little abashed at offering it, but he had apparently already discussed it with Ribbentrop as a way of protecting. the good name of the Führer.

"You see?" Ribbentrop put in excitedly. "That is just what I told you the other day! That is just what I think."

"Yes, I see.—It is very interesting that you two have decided between yourselves to promote a Hitler legend. Do you mean to say that in your Führer State where your Führer had such absolute power that it becomes the main argument of your defense, that he knew nothing about a little thing like the extermination of a race?"

"Oh, he probably knew about it—but not to that extent," Goering answered uncomfortably, seeing that some of the others were looking at him accusingly.

———————

LUNCH HOUR: The argument continued during the lunch hour. Guido Schmidt, former Austrian Foreign Minister, one of Seyss-Inquart's witnesses, had stated under examination by von Papen's attorney, that Schuschnigg had proposed sending a psychiatrist instead of a diplomat to negotiate with Hitler on the Austrian issue. Goering took this as another excuse to try to browbeat von Papen just before the beginning of his defense. Before they went to lunch, Goering flew at von Papen fiercely, "How dare you let anybody talk that way about Hitler! Don't forget that he was our Chief of State!"

"The Nazi Chief of State!" von Papen retorted angrily. "A Chief of State who murdered 6 million innocent people!"

"No, you can't say that Hitler ordered it," Goering scowled.

"Well then, who did order those mass murders?" von Papen challenged, flushing and throwing out his hands in indignation. "Did you order them?"

Goering was rather taken aback by this and mumbled, "No, no —Himmler." He looked bewildered as the other defendants filed past him out of the courtroom without even looking at him.

At lunch von Papen grumbled about the nerve of the fat one trying to dictate to him what he could say and could not say to conceal the Nazis' guilt.

Speer, Fritzsche, and von Schirach began to laugh at how Goering's hypocrisy and attempts to browbeat the defendants were being rebuffed even by timid diplomatic von Papen. Von Schirach mentioned that the big shot was not doing so well in the arguments in the dock any· more. Fritzsche repeated with bitter mockery what he had said downstairs. "No, of course Hitler didn't order the mass murders. Some sergeant must have done it."

In the next lunchroom Keitel and Frank began to discuss how Hitler had betrayed the honorable tradition of the Wehrmacht. "Excuse me if I say this, Seyss-Inquart, but Hitler was an Austrian and did not comprehend the honorable Prussian tradition."

"I'll say he didn't!" Keitel agreed vehemently. "He double-crossed us right and left. For us it was a matter of absolute certainty that one could depend on his Commander in Chief and not be lied to! He disrupted the whole Wehrmacht by putting Himmler and his SS in competition with us and letting them expand way beyond what he had promised. It is all clear to me now why he did it too! The SS carried out his atrocities and now we're tied up with them."

Later Sauckel was overheard telling Keitel that it was disgraceful to get into such long discussions because it reflected discredit on the Vaterland. Goering was overheard announcing from his corner that they'd better not talk to that Gilbert any more; Americans do not have the breeding to understand the German point of view.

# 20. Von Papen's Defense

## A GENTLEMAN OF THE OLD SCHOOL

MORNING SESSION: Von Papen began his defense by describing himself as a man of a conservative, religious background, brought up on a family estate that had been in the family for 900 years. He was in Mexico at the outbreak of World War I and went to the United States to negotiate for war materials. He has been greatly maligned by false propaganda ever since. Von Papen heatedly rejected such propaganda epithets as "master spy."

LUNCH HOUR: As they went to lunch, Ribbentrop remarked wearily, "Yes, they have slandered me too."

Von Papen vehemently denounced the Black Tom scandal in our lunchroom discussion. Stresemann had been willing to pay the 50 million dollars that had been demanded by the United States, just to patch up good relations with the United States. "So I told Stresemann, 'If you pay one cent of that claim, I will denounce you before the Reichstag!' " He claimed that the counsel for the firm that was making the claim had gotten 2 million dollars in fees to exploit the case. A Senate investigating committee, however, had found that there was no substance to the charges.

AFTERNOON SESSION: In the afternoon session von Papen continued to denounce the slander and libel of his character, as in the book, "Devil in Top Hat." He then described how he had joined the Catholic Center Party, working for a conservative collaboration to avoid the extreme Party differences after the war. He stated that Goering had spoken for the Nazi Party but von Papen was speaking for the "other Germany." He defended the Weimar Republic and paid homage to von Hindenburg, "the last great German statesman." He described how he tried to wrestle with the problem of unemployment and inflation which had proletarianized the middle class. At the Lausanne Conference in 1932 they tried to improve Germany's position and to correct some of the injustices of the Versailles Treaty, but achieved no results. He attributed Hitler's success to the failure of foreign powers to give Germany any hope. In the Reichstag, Goering actually prevented him from taking the floor in a crisis. Von Papen was finally unable to stop the rising tide of Nazism and Hindenburg was forced to appoint Hitler as Chancellor. Von Papen remained in the Cabinet on the earnest plea of von Hindenburg.

─────────────── June 15 ───────────────

## STATESMAN RIBBENTROP

*Ribbentrop's Cell:* Stimulated by von Papen's self-portrayal as a statesman and man of culture, Ribbentrop started to impress me this morning with his qualities as a statesman and a man of culture too. He launched into a long, confused and abstruse speech on "political dynamics": The dynamic of Russian one-party politics led inevitably to the spreading of Communism all over Europe, just as the National Socialist dynamic naturally had to lead to the spreading of National Socialism in the conquered territories, but America, with its two-party system, had a better-balanced dynamic, whereas the dynamic of the British Empire naturally led dynamically to Empire politics, etc., etc. Finally he asked me if I understood what he was talking about. To avoid argument I said Yes. Ribbentrop was so tickled he started to hiccough. He obviously did not understand it himself.

Then he asked me if I had read Otto Spengler, (of course, he meant Oswald). He said when he thought of Otto Spengler he just hated to think of it, because he hated to think of the future of the West, which America, of course, was part of, and we ought to think about that too.

Then it occurred to him that France has him to thank for the fact that Paris was not bombed. I asked him whether the French had not declared Paris an open city. Well yes, but Hitler had decided to bomb it and he used his influence to make him change his decision, even before it was declared an open city. I don't think he believed that I would believe him, but hearing himself talk like this is the only pleasure he has left in life. . . .

His next thought was that if America had only listened to him, the whole catastrophe would have been avoided. He had sent somebody to America in 1940 to tell the Standard Oil people and the Jewish bankers not to let America get into the war. If they only had not been so hostile toward Germany . . .

He complained again about the pain in his head and said that you could write the word "Jew" on that spot in his head, because it came from his nerve-wracking efforts to steer Hitler off his course of anti-Semitism in 1941. "I knew that Hitler was of the opinion that the Jews had started the war, but that was absolutely untrue, and I always told him that that was not right." He has just finished writing a long dissertation for his attorney on the Jewish issue. He said he would give me this dissertation, because even if it did not have any bearing on the trial, he wanted the world to know that he really was not an anti-Semite and had nothing to do with the atrocities.

--------------------------------- June 17 ---------------------------------

## NAZISM AND RELIGIOUS BIGOTRY

MORNING SESSION: *Von Papen continued his defense, explaining that the law putting Hitler into power was forced by the seriousness of the political situation, but it was supposed to be based on a Christian solution of social problems. He concluded a Concordat with the Vatican, but Hitler proceeded to consider it merely a scrap of paper. His attitude toward the Jewish problem is that which the Catholic Church expects from every good Catholic. He denied participation in the Jewish boycott in 1934 and implied that Hitler and Goebbels double-crossed him on a peaceful solution to the Jewish problem.*

During the intermission the Catholics in the dock as well as anti-Catholic Rosenberg began to discuss the attitude of the Catholic Church on anti-Semitism.

Rosenberg said that von Papen merely meant that in a Christian country there should not be too much Jewish influence.

Seyss-Inquart remarked that 85 per cent of the lawyers in Vienna were Jews. He then went on to explain the tie-up between the priesthood and anti-Semitism.

He said that as a matter of fact, most of the priests were basically anti-Semitic, especially in Poland. That is where the pogroms have been going on for centuries even up to the present day, and it was the immigration of Polish Jews that carried a wave of anti-Semitism with it into Germany.

Frank agreed to this, giving a little more of the historical background. "Yes, the priesthood has been essentially anti-Semitic ever since the Inquisition. Hahaha! They tortured people all over Europe out of religious intolerance, and later they started burning witches."

Here Rosenberg added, glad of a chance to see Frank admitting that the Inquisition was a disgraceful chapter in Catholic Church history, "Yes, and that went on for four or five centuries—not just a momentary outburst of emotion!"

Frank sobered up and added, "The predecessors of Auschwitz were the torture chambers of the Inquisition.—It was a horrible period in our history really!" Frick and Rosenberg remarked that compared to the Inquisitors, Hitler was a white lamb. Frank disputed this, but with the same unfeeling perverted humor. "No, he wasn't a white lamb but it really was a hell of a period in history.—Hahaha! You see, my dear professor, mankind has always been in a terrible state. The beast in man keeps coming out again and again."

Rosenberg and Kaltenbrunner added further details of the tortures of the Inquisition, the adventures of Torquemada, etc. To keep the record straight, Frank pointed out that the Protestant rulers of northern Germany, not to be outdone in religious fanaticism took up the trying and torturing of "witches." These trials had apparently interested Frank as a lawyer. "I read some of the protocols of those trials out of the 15th and 16th centuries. They actually asked old women how many times they had sexual intercourse with the devil! It is recorded right in the protocols, and they tortured them until they got the answer.—Hahaha! Really it is grotesque!"

LUNCH HOUR: At lunch the discussion on the attitude of the Catholic Church toward anti-Semitism contained in the Elders' lunchroom, but von Papen had a more Christian conception of it. "Why, everybody knows what the Catholic Church's attitude is," he said to Schacht and me. "It is the principle that all men are equal before God and that racial differences are no indication of inequality." Von Papen said that he assumed that Hitler recognized that in recognizing Germany as a Christian state, but it turned out that Hitler was just a liar—a pathological liar at that.

Schacht said that he is now convinced that Hitler was a liar from the very beginning, but being a pathological liar, he was not so easily detected, and he fooled everybody. "Why, I was standing there·when he made his speech of acceptance upon becoming Reich Chancellor. I tell you, his expressions of constructive idealism sounded so sincere and convincing that it was impossible to imagine that it did not come from the depths of his soul. I tell you, we were moved to the depths of our souls and felt that a new era had dawned for Germany."

---

AFTERNOON SESSION: Von Papen said that when the Nazi Party Government turned out to be a dictatorship instead of a coalition, he decided to go before the people in his Marburg address of 1934. He denounced the restriction of human rights, freedom of speech and religion, Godless materialism, rejection of intellectualism, restriction of justice, Byzantinism, materialistic education, regimentation, and the many excesses covered by the pretext of revolutionary necessity. [In the dock Doenitz and Goering agreed that von Papen was turning traitor.] The publication of the speech was forbidden by Goebbels. Von Papen went to Hitler and offered his resignation. Hitler said it was a mistake and held him off. But von Papen realizes now that Hitler lied to him, because Funk got instead an order from Hitler to tell Hindenburg that von Papen had gotten out of hand and would have to be dismissed. [Then, as von Papen described the details of his arrest during the Roehm blood purge, Goering's ears got red and he sat in the dock with the studied indifference which he always brings to bear on such occasions.] During the purge one of von Papen's assistants was shot, two were sent to a concentration camp. After three days of arrest Goering pretended it was a misunderstanding. Von Papen went to Hitler and demanded that his resignation be accepted.

---

During the intermission Schacht remarked that up to this point von Papen's story is entirely in order, but he could bet the prosecution would ask him why he went back into the Hitler Government after this atrocious treatment.

Funk confirmed that he had that order from Hitler and brought it to President von Hindenburg. Old von Hindenburg had merely answered, "Anybody who can't keep discipline, must go."

Von Schirach was talking to his attorney and said that it was still a mystery why von Papen went back into the government. He thought that he had probably done so at the bidding of the Catholic Church to protect their interests.

---

*Von Papen continued with his story. He was offered the ambassadorship to the Vatican soon after his resignation, but refused. The day of the Dollfuss murder he was urged to take the ambassadorship to Vienna. He insisted on the condition of recalling Habicht, the Nazi instigator of the Dollfuss murder.* [Goering got excited at this and said to Hess, "That's a dirty lie, because Habicht was removed before that."] *Von Papen continued to explain that he accepted the post only as a matter of conscience and to do his duty to obtain order.* [Goering was still annoyed. "I won't stand for this nonsense; it is not true!" He kept cursing von Papen and was overheard calling him names like "coward . . . scared rabbit . . . liar."]

---

When von Papen came back to the dock at the end of the session, Frank and several of the others congratulated him for his statesmanlike performance. As soon as von Papen left the dock to go back to the prison, Frank said to the others while waiting their turn: "Now we can talk . . . Now he gets up there and tries to make himself a good and famous man. Why the devil didn't he go to the United States after January 30 [1933]? He could have come back now and still be a famous man and sit out there in the audience and laugh at us." Frick and Frank kept grumbling that von Papen is trying to get out of the fact that he played along with the Party and was an ardent Hitler supporter all along.

--------- EVENING IN JAIL ---------

*Frank's Cell:* In the evening Frank had another version of his attitude toward von Papen when he spoke to me in his cell: "Ah, that good old von Papen. He is like a trapped fox.—Hahaha! He tried to do his best as a good nationalist but naturally people will say, 'Why did you stay after the way Hitler kicked you around?' Hahahaha!—He really should have been with Gisevius plotting against Hitler in Switzerland.—Up to 1934 he was perfectly in order, after he resigned, but then he came back thinking he could do some good. He wrote the drama wrong. Hahahaha!—He should have written a different last act. Now it ends as a tragedy instead of a comedy! Hahahahaha!!!" Frank laughed himself into red-faced hysterics again, telling how von Papen should have rewritten the last act of his life.

Then he turned to his denunciation of Hitler again. "He must have known that he was in danger of losing the war in 1941, and said, 'These Jews are to blame for everything and I will extermi-nate them!!' " Frank clenched his teeth and hissed through them, pounding his fist on the frail writing table until it rattled. "*I will exterminate them!!*—Don't you think it was like that? It is a stu-pendous psychological problem.—In centuries to come people will tear their hair and say, 'My God, how did such an action come about?' . . . It is—. You cannot call it just a crime—crime is too mild a word for it. Stealing is a crime; killing one man is a crime —but this—this is just beyond human imagination!—Reducing murder to mass production! Two thousand a day—gold teeth and rings to the Reichsbank; hair packed for mattresses!—God Al-mighty!—And all ordered by one devil who appeared in human form! . . . But you should have heard his speeches to women. You would have thought he was goodness itself.—And yet he did this horrible thing in cold fury—. —He really should not have done such a thing to the German people who believed in him so—."

Frank soon calmed down into a mystic mood. "Did God ordain all this? Did God nod his head 6 million times and say Yes as the Jews were led into the gas chambers?" Frank shook his head and reflected softly and solemnly. "It is enough to make one despair of divine justice. No, an American or English author—I forget his name—expressed it rightly: 'No, be assured, this time God him-self is just as outraged as is all of humanity.'—That is well put.— It was really the work of the devil."

--------------------------------- June 18 ---------------------------------

## VON PAPEN IS EMBARRASSED

MORNING SESSION: Von Papen described how he was recalled from Vienna before Hitler ordered the march into Austria at Goering's instigation. His assistant, Keppler, was murdered and he turned to Goering, head of the Gestapo, for satisfaction, but got no results. [Goering kept mumbling and shaking his head throughout the whole recital, and was overheard telling Ribbentrop, "That whole Keppler story is an absolute lie!—The old boy should have kept his mouth shut about that.—Anyway, I was not head of the Gestapo at that time and I can prove it. I'll bring that up one way or another."]

Von Papen explained that Hitler gave him the golden Party badge to camouflage their differences. Perhaps he should have declined it, but he was afraid of getting into another fight with Hitler. [In the dock Goering kept mumbling, "coward . . . liar . . . " He also cursed von Papen's attorney for asking such questions and sent him a note.] Von Papen continued to explain how he had made proposals to von Ribbentrop to stave off war, but Ribbentrop told him that he was conducting Germany's foreign policy, not von Papen. [Ribbentrop was overheard whispering to Goering, "He should have been shot long ago."] Von Papen declared that he had warned Ribbentrop of the danger of a world war. [This time, for the benefit of the audience, Goering looked askance at Ribbentrop. Ribbentrop pouted and nodded that it was true.]

Von Papen said he accepted the ambassadorship to Turkey only to prevent a hostile encirclement of Germany, not to start a war. In fact, he was astounded when he heard of the outbreak of war in 1939. "Provoking this war was the greatest crime and the greatest madness Hitler has committed . . . Germany cannot win this war and will lie in ruins at the end of it," was the reaction he claimed to have given to diplomatic friends. However, he remained in Turkey because there was nothing else left to do. He said he repeatedly approached the question of peace feelers to end the war, but Ribbentrop told him that Hitler wanted to hear nothing about peace and he should not make any moves in that direc-

*tion.* [Again Goering very ostentatiously looked askance at Ribbentrop, then sat back wth a disgusted expression, to show that he himself blamed Ribbentrop.]

*Von Papen also considered the waging of war against Russia a crime. He described a plan in which he was supposedly involved to surround GHQ and capture Hitler to bring him to trial. His attorney then submitted an affidavit by Bismarck's grandson showing that von Papen was thought of as Foreign Minister by the July 20 plotters.* [Goering laughed and shook his head. Jodl turned red and looked as if he was seeing red.]

---

LUNCH HOUR: At lunch Ribbentrop was nervous and discontented. "Tsk! Tsk!—Washing that dirty linen in court.—It is not right. —It really is not right. Do you think so?—There are certain things that should not be mentioned . . . Oh, of course, he was never really a National Socialist; that is true.—But washing that dirty linen—." He did not mention what was really bothering him: the exposure of his stubborn and blind adherence to Hitler's catastrophic foreign policy.

Von Papen told me that he had given them a good piece of his mind. "The fat one did not like that. He just bawled me out and said he was going to testify again and get even." This was obviously the "moral blackmail" Speer had referred to. I assured von Papen that Goering was not being given any special privileges by the court, and would have nothing more to say except in his final plea, the same as everybody else. Schacht said that there was no doubt that Goering was tied up with the Gestapo all along, even though he was the head of it only a short time. Doenitz kept to his corner, decisively detaching himself from the politicians.

In the next room Streicher had caught Jodl's ear across the threshold between the two lunchrooms, and was haranguing him on the impropriety of attacking such gigantic characters as Hitler, who are brought about by supernatural forces. "There are metaphysical forces which bring about such great figures in history; one cannot say if he was right or wrong . . . Anyway, World Jewry controls this trial. It is a diabolical thing how World Jewry has concentrated its power to bring about this trial." He turned to me. "Do you remember what I wrote on your copy of the indictment in the beginning?—*'This trial is a triumph of World*

Jewry!' That is right. Practically the whole prosecution consists of Jews."

Later Jodl turned his back on Streicher and started to discuss von Papen's defense. "Concerning today's evidence, there is one thing you can be damn sure about: they wouldn't have killed three of my adjutants and found me still working with the regime— you can bet your life on that!"

---

AFTERNOON SESSION: *Upon cross-examination, Sir David Maxwell-Fyfe embarrassed von Papen by quoting back to him his own speeches in which he called Hitler as heaven-sent to the German people to lead them out of their misery.* [Goering laughed and all but thumbed his nose at von Papen. Doenitz slid his colored glasses down his nose and looked at me with the same "You see?" expression with which he always signals to me his contempt of the politician-hypocrites.] *Von Papen stammered that he was under the impression at the time that Hitler would keep the coalition. Sir David further confronted him with documentary evidence that he had actually prepared the coalition beforehand.*

*Sir David relentlessly pursued the theme of von Papen's collaboration with a gang of criminals. Didn't he know that thousands of political opponents were thrown into concentration camps as soon as the Nazis came to power? Von Papen equivocated over the number; there were some, perhaps hundreds.* [In the dock Goering insisted on his due. "No, thousands!" he grumbled.] *Why had he appealed to the Catholics to support Hitler? Von Papen explained that he had concluded the Concordat and had assumed that Hitler would support religion.*

---

During the intermission, Jodl described, grinning, how von Papen's embassy in Ankara had been used by the Abwehr for espionage work. "—They did a good job too. Once they swiped the records of a British agent, showing how Britain was trying to get Turkey to put some airfields at her disposal."

Rosenberg and Frank declared that many of those thrown into concentration camps deserved it for besmirching the national symbols, like that swine Carl von Ossietzky (Pacifist, Nobel Peace Prize winner 1935). Piscator was one of the leaders of this nationalist-defamation movement on the stage, and there were a lot of Jews that participated in that movement. "No, there is no doubt that Germany was faced with one choice," Frank assured me. "—Either Communism or National Socialism. Even von Papen and Schacht agree to that."

---

Sir David proceeded to tear apart von Papen's motives for resigning after the Roehm purge and accepting another post three weeks later. He read him his own letter reaffirming his support of Hitler and hailing his masterful consolidation of power after the "heroic suppression" of the Roehm purge. "You were prepared to serve these murderers as long as your dignity was put right!" Sir David shot at him. Von Papen rejected the insinuation, [but Goering snickered, "That's right!" and Ribbentrop agreed.] "You knew that his prestige especially among Catholics was valuable to Hitler at a time when world opinion turned against him, and you might have helped ruin him by opposing him," Sir David continued. Von Papen answered hesitatingly that that was right, but if he had done so he would have disappeared like his colleagues. Sir David kept hammering to a climax: in spite of the Roehm purge, in spite of the murder of his own assistants, in spite of the murder of Dollfuss, in spite of a warlike foreign policy, von Papen still remained in the government—why? why? Von Papen could only keep replying lamely and finally indignantly that it was his sense of duty.

--- EVENING IN JAIL ---

*Von Papen's Cell:* Von Papen was really bothered by those letters of his with which Sir David had confronted him. He laughed in embarrassment as I came into the cell. "—You know, I had completely forgotten those letters. As a matter of fact, so did my secretary.—Of course, one sees things differently now from the way one saw them at that time after 3 days arrest.—Those questions about why did I stay in the government.—Now I ask you again, what could I do when war broke out? Come back home and go to the front as a soldier?—Emigrate and write a book?— What could I really do?" He threw out his arms at each question to show how useless the alternatives were.

"I was surprised that the court did not want to go into my Turkish affairs. That must mean that they have given up the idea of a conspiracy, because if they were still considering it, they would have to know more about my activities at the time . . . Of course, it is the task of diplomacy to get support from other countries. That is what diplomats are for." He then told me how he had saved 10,000 Jews from transportation to concentration camps from France. They were former Turkish nationals, and he had said that the Turkish Government would consider it an offense to their national interests.

But he wanted to talk about more interesting things: the current meeting of the Big Four Foreign Ministers in Paris, for instance. He said that the peace of Europe depended on whether Russia showed a willingness to compromise. Bevin and Byrnes showed a reasonable attitude, but what about Molotov?

--------------------------- June 19 ---------------------------

MORNING SESSION: *Sir David continued to show that von Papen had given aid and comfort to Austrian Nazis during his stay as Ambassador in Austria; that he had, in effect, offered himself as a Catholic Trojan Horse to further Nazi interests in Austria. Von Papen replied that as a diplomat he naturally had to accept any support offered. He said he never denied that pressure had been exerted on Schuschnigg to affect the Anschluss (though Sir David pointed out that Ribbentrop had denied it).*

During the intermission Frank and the group around him put their heads together and defended the Anschluss. "What do they mean, Catholic Trojan Horse!" Frank demanded. "You can't go against a law of nature. The Austrian and German people simply could not be kept apart. It was like trying to keep apart an irresistible force in nature."

Frick volunteered, "I don't think that Sir David really understands the Austrian situation."

"Oh, yes, he does," Rosenberg sneered. "Leave it to that Englishman; he understands it well enough—as much as he wants to understand it.—It is the height of gall for that Englishman to make it a crime even to associate with National Socialists. What do they expect? It was the most natural thing in the world for the German Ambassador to get co-operation from Austrian National Socialists."

Seyss-Inquart repeated what he had said the other day about Dollfuss being really a dictator backed up by only a small clerical minority, and not really representing the will of the people.

Frank fell back on the old reliable Russian line. "I'd just like to see them examine the Anschluss of Azerbaijan by the Russians with the same kind of arguments and documents.—Hahaha!" He waved his finger at the judges' bench. "Let them just examine those things and we'll see whose face won't turn red." He then went on with some more historical arguments, exclaiming how "we Bavarians created Austria—," how the tyrant kings of the Middle Ages and Renaissance slaughtered each other's populations, etc., etc.

---

*Sir David wanted to know how, two years after the Concordat, von Papen could have written to Hitler, in July, 1935, a statement calling his diplomacy "the clever hand which eliminates political Catholicism without touching the Christian foundations of Germany." [Goering snickered, "Now he's trying to figure out a good answer to that one."] Von Papen did not actually answer that. Sir David then quoted the Pope in describing the persecution of the Church by the Nazis. Von Papen agreed that that was so, but tried to explain that political Catholicism and the Christian basis of the State were two entirely different things. He further confirmed the statement that Hitler treated the Concordat as a scrap of paper and persecuted both Catholics and Jews. He knew about the sacrilegious invasion and looting of Cardinal Innitzer's church by rowdy Nazis, but was not in a position to do anything about it because he was a private citizen.*

*As a parting shot, Sir David threw up to him once more why he had remained after repeated murders of his own assistants, political opponents, leading statesmen, etc., by the Nazis. Von Papen repeated heatedly that he did it out of patriotism, and that was something he could answer for to his own conscience.*

---

LUNCH HOUR: At lunch von Papen, visibly upset, said, "Sir David has no facts, and so he has to try to besmirch my character. I told him I had to stay as a good German patriot, hard as it was to do so."

Schacht consoled him. "Yes, how well I know those struggles with one's conscience—weighing patriotism against those other things.—How well I know.—I had the same problem."

Von Papen accepted this consolation eagerly. "Naturally, I had the most terrible struggles with conscience," he exclaimed, waving his arms and twisting his Mephistophelean eyebrows. "My God, after they shot my own assistant!—And yet I had to say to myself: 'You still have your duty to the Fatherland!'—Do you think it was easy? It was a *terrible* conflict!"

In the other lunchrooms many of the defendants were shaking their heads over various parts of the cross-examination, some making snickering references to "political Catholicism"; the militarists stressing the point that they would not have let anybody get away with killing *their* adjutants.

---

AFTERNOON SESSION: *In the afternoon session, Chief Justice Lawrence asked the rather pointed question: How could von Papen claim credit for saving 10,000 Jews from extermination unless he had known about extermination at the time. Von Papen could not explain that very well.*

[When the witness, Hans Kroll, took the stand, Goering whispered to Hess, "There goes von Papen's arse-licker!" Doenitz yawned and said he was getting bored, and thought he ought to be home in three months. Then he and Goering started to size up the blonde translator, saying she was pretty nifty. Goering said he wouldn't mind having her, but having been without it for so long, he didn't know if he had what it takes.]

# 21. Speer's Defense

## SPEER DENOUNCES HITLER

MORNING SESSION: Speer described how he took over the supervision of the German war production, increasing his power from 1942 to 1944, until he had 14 million workers working under him. He admitted using some PW labor, though not all of it was in violation of the Geneva Convention. He also admitted using foreign workers, although he was frequently at odds with Sauckel over their use and procurement. He did not think that the German labor supply had been completely exhausted, and for another thing he was not in favor of bringing the workers to Germany, but thought that they could work just as well in occupied territories. He also admitted using concentration camp labor, but these represented only 1 per cent of the total labor in the armaments industry.

LUNCH HOUR: During lunch Keitel was overheard telling Sauckel, Frank and Seyss-Inquart that if somebody had guts enough in 1943 to tell Hitler that the war was lost, they could have saved a great deal. The only man who could have done it was Speer, because he was the one who knew that they could not turn out enough tanks, planes, and ammunition to win the war.

Sauckel was very angry at Speer for having put him in a bad light with respect to slave labor. He complained angrily that Hitler and Speer were always putting through orders to squeeze all the labor they could out of both the Wehrmacht and foreign countries for the war industries. Both Keitel and Sauckel seemed to think that Speer was to blame for everything.

AFTERNOON SESSION: In the afternoon session Speer made his statement of common responsibility, "all the more so since Hitler shirked that responsibility before the world by committing suicide." [Rosenberg looked down the dock at Goering. They exchanged looks as if to say, "Here it comes."] Speer declared that the war was strategically lost in 1943, but he realized that it was actually utterly lost from a production viewpoint in January, 1945, at the latest. Nevertheless, Hitler gave orders to continue fighting and to destroy industrial installations in the occupied territories upon retreat. Speer was able to have these orders circumvented to a large extent. The situation was hopeless, "but Hitler betrayed us all." Rumors of "wonder-weapons" were spread to keep up an unrealistic optimism among the public. Phony diplomatic discussions were mentioned to deceive everybody. General Guderian told Ribbentrop the war was lost, but Ribbentrop came back with orders from Hitler that such defeatist expressions would be treated as treason.

Hitler ordered a press campaign with the slogan "We will never surrender" so that no real peace negotiations could take place. Even in his speech before the Gauleiters in 1944, Hitler had indicated that the German people were not fit to survive if they could not win the war. He blamed the German people for the catastrophe, not himself. He insisted on fighting to victory or total destruction at a time when it was absolutely obvious to everyone that only destruction remained. But this "scorched earth" policy continued to apply even to German territory as the armies retreated. It became clear that if the war was lost, Hitler really wanted the German people to be destroyed with him. In his despair, Speer decided the only way out was to assassinate the Führer. Speer was reluctant to tell the details, but the court asked to hear it after the recess.

---

During the recess there was great tension and excitement throughout the dock. Frank expressed his typical violent ambivalence toward the Führer. First he declared to the others that it was obviously necessary to bring out the truth; then he denounced the attempt to assassinate the Führer. Rosenberg said that as long as Speer's attempt didn't succeed, he ought to keep his mouth shut.

Goering exercised a good deal of self-control not to express himself openly.

---

Speer described his plan to kill Hitler with poison gas to be thrown into the air-intake of his bunker. He said that at this time it was easy to get sensible men who were eager to co-operate with anybody who was willing to take responsibility for trying to stop the war and the insane orders of destruction. But Hitler only insisted on giving wilder orders for destruction. Speer then quoted from his own letter confirming his conversation with Hitler. Hitler had said: "If the war is to be lost the nation will also perish. This fate is inevitable. There is no necessity to take into consideration the basis which the people would need to continue a most primitive existence. On the contrary, it would be wiser to destroy even these things ourselves, because then our people have proved to be the weaker and the future belongs solely to the stronger eastern nation. Besides, those who remain after the battle are only the inferior ones; for the good ones have fallen."

Hitler gave orders to continue the war without consideration of the German population. Speer took measures for protecting German industry into his own hands, even passing out machine guns to protect installations from destruction by Nazi Gauleiters. "The sacrifices which were made on both sides after January, 1945, were without sense. The dead of this period will be the accusers of the man responsible for the continuation of that fight, Adolf Hitler, just as much as the cities destroyed in that last phase, who had lost tremendous cultural values and a tremendous number of dwellings. Many of the difficulties under which the German nation is suffering today are due to the ruthless destruction of bridges, traffic installations, trucks, locomotives and ships. The German people remained faithful to Adolf Hitler until the end. He has betrayed them knowingly. He has tried to throw them into the abyss."

Speer defended his actions on the basis of loyalty to the people. It was clearly the duty of the leaders to act when Hitler betrayed the people and gambled with their fate.

---

At the end of the court session there were evidences of a profound reaction both for and against Speer. Schacht declared, with feeling, "That was a masterful defense! That was the position decent Germans were in!"

Funk, half blubbering, added, "Really—one must hang his head in shame."

Goering left the dock without a word. As the others waited their turn to go down to the prison, Rosenberg cursed at this denunciation of the Nazi leadership. "Well, he didn't have the courage to go to Hitler and shoot him, so what is he talking about? It is easy enough to beat your chest about something you tried to do."

———————— EVENING IN JAIL ————————

*Speer's Cell:* Down in his cell, Speer lay on his cot all fagged out, complaining of a stomach pain. "Well, that was quite a strain, but I got it off my chest.—It was the truth and that is all there is to it. I wouldn't have been so mad at Goering if he had not tried to falsify history by making a heroic legend out of this rotten business. He, especially, has no right to make himself a hero, because he failed so miserably and was such a coward in our hour of crisis."

———————————— June 21 ————————————

## SPEER IS CROSS-EXAMINED

MORNING SESSION: *Upon cross-examination by Prosecutor Jackson, Speer admitted using concentration camp labor and threatening slackers with being thrown into concentration camps. He had also made a deal with Himmler to let him have 5 per cent of the arms production produced by concentration camp labor. He further admitted that the war effort was definitely hindered by the anti-Semitic policy. He also admitted using PW labor and foreign slave labor without bothering about the legality of it. It was then revealed that Hitler had been planning to resort to gas warfare, although the Wehrmacht leaders were against it, knowing that Germany would get the worst of it. He confirmed that only a small group of fanatics around Hitler kept Germany fighting after the generals knew that the war was lost. Goering squirmed as Speer revealed Hitler's opinion of him; someone who had always been a corrupt dope addict. He also revealed how Goering forbade General Galland to tell the truth about enemy fighter power.*

During the intermission Frank said, "Well, I'd rather be sitting here than before a German court on account of treason. —Don't forget that Speer himself helped spread the confidence in victory with his own big speeches about how he would sweep the skies clean of enemy aircraft with his new planes. What else do you think kept us alive in Cracow?—The confidence in the victory of German arms."

Jodl said that he knew after the Russian campaign bogged down, that is was no use, but somehow he thought it was indecent of Speer to plot against Hitler after Hitler had shown such favoritism for him and concern for his children. Jodl implied that he himself had not shown the bad taste to assassinate Hitler even though he knew the war was lost, but Speer showed bad taste in trying to do so when he had been one of Hitler's best friends.

Frank told von Papen that he would have been better treated in the cross-examination if he had made an assassination attempt on Hitler too. He then lectured me on the sense of loyalty of the German people, and how they would never approve of assassinating the Commander in Chief. He warned me not to see things too one-sidedly.

Goering began to mumble dark threats and curses about traitors. Doenitz tried feebly to explain that Speer had to tell the truth as he saw it. To this Goering retorted angrily, "But he didn't have to say those things about me! I think he was just trying to get even."

LUNCH HOUR: At lunch von Papen declared with some satisfaction, "That finishes that fat one! Just imagine giving an officer a direct order not to tell the truth!" Schacht and von Neurath agreed that Goering was finished with the German people.

In the Youth lunchroom von Schirach, Fritzsche and Speer hailed the end of the Goering-Hitler legend, although von Schirach seemed to have an uneasy feeling as if he was sitting on a keg of dynamite.

Goering sat brooding in his room and said nothing. As soon as they came down to the dock after lunch, however, Goering said to Doenitz and Hess, "We never should have trusted him." Then he went to the middle of the dock and told Rosenberg and Jodl that Speer was lying about not having any chance to attack Hitler himself, because their briefcases were never searched. If he really had any nerve he would have gone to shoot Hitler himself. Then he went back to his own corner, mumbling, "You just wait and see —this isn't over yet."

AFTERNOON SESSION: After the cross-examination by the Russian prosecutor in the afternoon session, Judge Biddle asked Speer *what he meant by common responsibility and asked him to give specific examples. Speer said that the members of a government were responsible for the broad general policy and for such decisive actions as beginning and ending a war.*

## ———— EVENING IN JAIL ————

*Speer's Cell:* In the evening Speer said that the thing that was creating the greatest consternation in the prisoners' dock was his admission of a share in the common responsibility. They were all angry about that, except for Seyss-Inquart, who had always supported him on that issue against the misgivings of his own defense counsel. "Now they are all mad because their own necks are at stake. But you should see how they would be hollering to claim a share in the common responsibility for victory if we had won the war."

He said he had been caught a little unprepared to answer Judge Biddle's question, and wondered whether he couldn't send him a letter giving further details. He felt that the leaders of the government were responsible not only for the beginning and end of the war, but for the anti-Semitic policy and for lawlessness. By accepting the post of minister he knowingly accepted a share in the responsibility for a government which clearly adopted anti-Semitism and lawlessness and concentration camps as instruments of governmental policy. His guilt lay in accepting those things as a matter of course, though he came to his senses rather late in the game. He decided that he would elaborate on that in his final speech. He was all the more anxious to do so since Goering was already attacking him for being insincere in his admission of common responsibility. Goering was telling the others that it is easy enough for Speer to say that the leaders of a government share the responsibility for actions such as beginning and ending a war, because Speer had nothing to do with beginning it and at the end he performed one act of treason after another.

As far as his attack on Goering was concerned, he had actually spared Goering some of the extra details, such as the fact that it was Goering who really introduced corruption into the Wehrmacht.

## June 22-23

## WEEK END IN JAIL

*Goering's Cell:* Goering tried to be moderate in giving his reaction to Speer's denunciations. "What a tragicomedy!—Don't you think it's funny?—*I* was hated and ordered shot by the Führer at the end! If there is to be any denunciation of the Führer, *I* was the one who had the first right to do so—not these others like Speer and von Schirach who were favored by the Führer to the very end!—Where do *they* get off denouncing him like that? I didn't do it, and *I* am the one who had the best right. But I didn't do it because of the *principle* of the thing, that was all! . . . Do you think I have any personal love for him?—Not in the least!—I assure you, it's the principle of the thing!" (Psych. note: Substitute *pose* for *principle*.) "I swore my loyalty to him and I cannot go back on that. That has nothing to do with him as an individual. It is *my principle* that is in question. You must separate those two things. The same applies to von Schirach. He had no business calling Hitler a murderer.—All right, I know what you are going to say; it is true. But I mean he could have at least said it differently.

"But when I give my oath of loyalty, I cannot break it.—And I had a hell of a time keeping it too, I can tell you!—Just try being crown prince for 12 years some time—always loyal to the king, disapproving of many of his policies, and yet not being able to do anything about it, knowing at any moment that you might become king and have to make the best of the situation. But I couldn't plot behind his back with poison gas or sticking briefcases with bombs under his arse and cowardly tricks like that.—The only thing I could have honorably done was to make an open break; to declare openly that I renounce my loyalty, and fight it out—."

"You mean slap him in the face with your glove and challenge him to a duel?" I broke in.

"—Cast my gauntlet at his feet!" Goering corrected quickly,

showing that I had read his chivalrous thoughts correctly, but had misplaced the century of his fantasies.

"Then it would have come to an open showdown.—But I couldn't do that when we were in the middle of a four-front war —divide our forces by internal struggle. Suppose I'd tried after the Russian campaign went bad. Thousands would have joined me. But it would have meant chaos for Germany, and anyway he would have had Himmler and the SS behind him—it would have been no good. And of course, after the victorious French campaign, I would have been lucky to get a few hundred to join me, if I had been crazy enough to break with him then.—And as for trying it before the war—why, they simply would have thought I was sick in the head. They would have sent me to an asylum. No, I assure you, there was nothing I could do."

"But don't you know that history and your people would have thought better of you if you had said on the witness stand that you had kept your oath to Hitler, but Hitler betrayed you and the German people, just as von Schirach says?"

"Oh, no, there I understand German tradition better than you, believe me. It has not always been easy for German heroes, as I've told you, but they kept their loyalty just the same."

"Don't you think that all these medieval concepts of loyalty and nationalism are out-dated and that people will think differently in the future?"

"Well, then, let those who belong to the future think differently. I am what I have always been—'the last Renaissance figure,' if you please." He smiled as he quoted his witness Koerner's characterization of him, and I could have sworn that he had told Koerner to say that on the witness stand. "—You can't expect me at the age of 52 to change my entire concept all of a sudden."

It is evident that Goering is greatly bothered by the fact that as things stand now, he has confirmed his loyalty to a murderer, and is trying to figure out a new angle for his last stand.

He mentioned that he was going to bring up the case of the Katyn massacre at the end of the individual defenses, as an uncompleted part of his case. I asked him whether that had anything to do with his case. Again the sly smile. "No, but I am doing it out of my special love for the Russians." Then he added with another foxy grin, "—You don't think I'd be in a position to do this if I wasn't getting help from a non-German source, do you?" I asked him what he meant. "Oh, I can't say, but don't forget there is still a Polish Government-in-Exile in England."

Goering then resumed his campaign to convince me that he was really a man of culture. He must have been reading Dale Carnegie's *How to Win Friends and Influence People*. He now has a great interest in American culture, and asked his attorney to get a German copy of that American classic *Gone with the Wind*. Then too, he had always been a man of culture, and not a rabid anti-Semite like Rosenberg or Streicher. To be sure, he had fallen for a lot of the anti-Semitic propaganda himself. The whole Party was drenched with it. "It was Goebbels and Ley and a certain other philosopher among the defendants whom I will not name. He was the one who kept harping on how all the Communists were Jews, and even the Russian commissars were Jews—which we found out later was not so. But since he came from Russia himself, we thought he was an authority on the subject."

Finally, he professed a great interest in the field of psychology. He wanted to discuss that ink-blot test I had given him at the beginning of the trial, and learn more about the progress of American psychology.

---

*Speer's Cell:* While Goering was portraying himself as a reasonable man of culture, Speer revealed the latest evidence of Goering's gangsterism in the prisoners' dock. "He announced to the others in a way that I would be sure to hear, that even if I come out of this trial alive, the *Feme* [Kangaroo] Court would assassinate me for treason." Speer laughed a little nervously. He knew better than I that the *Feme* Kangaroo Courts had struck terror into the hearts of German revolutionaries for centuries. He implied that Goering was using this hint at assassination as a method of intimidating the others, if not himself. "You will see; as the trial nears its climax and their nerves begin to feel the strain, their polite masks will fall away, and you will see them for what they are." He asked me if I had noticed how Goering could turn on the good-humored charm and forthright bravado in the presence of the American officers and the press. I said I had. Speer assured me that this assassination threat was really more in keeping with Goering's true character.

Speer said that he hoped that Goering would really get nasty with his threats and his final statement on the stand, so that he himself will be in the mood to cut loose and tell the world what a coward and corrupt phony that Goering really was. He repeated that he never would have attacked him so much in the first place, if Goering had at least had the decency to admit his guilt instead of falsifying history and covering up the disgusting, selfish callousness and corruption of the whole regime. "He thought he had us all bulldozed so that he could get up and make a big grandstand play, and we would all immediately fall in line, concealing the truth about this dirty business, and just clapping 'Bravo, Goering!' "

Speer said the German prison doctor had told him that Goering had said Friday was the blackest day of his life. Goering had also told his attorney and some of the others that he was going to have to alter his whole line of defense in the summation and the final speech.

# 22. The Summations

―――――――――― July 3 ――――――――――

### RACIAL SCIENCE

Frick, in discussing the draft of his attorney's summation, told him that he never had been an anti-Semite, never had hated the Jews. He had formulated the Nuremberg Laws for scientific reasons to protect German blood. He refused to let his attorney apologize in any way for the Nuremberg Laws, and told him to make it clear that he formulated them out of scientific principles, not out of hatred.

At lunch another discussion of the Nuremberg Laws started. Frick and Rosenberg insisted that the Nuremberg Laws were based on fundamental laws of nature. German blood had to be kept pure. If these laws work with animals, why shouldn't they work with human beings? They did not seem bothered by the idea of treating human beings like animals nor by my arguments that their pseudo-science had no basis in fact. When I pointed out that the Jews could no longer be considered a race, they switched to the word *Volk* (people) and continued to talk about breeding livestock. I referred to Fritzsche's recent explanation of how the Nuremberg Laws were really forced down the people's throats. Rosenberg and Frick did not think that that was a fair criticism since according to the *Führerpinzip*, the Führer and the Party leaders decided what was good for the people.

―――――――――― July 5 ――――――――――

Dr. Stahmer made his plea for Goering this morning.

Speer explained at lunch that Goering was denying all moral and legal responsibility for any of the Nazi crimes. This is interesting from two points of view, he thought: First of all, it shows Goering's complete lack of moral sense, and it also shows that when it comes to a showdown, he is just as anxious to save his neck as anybody, and that the heroic pose of standing up to take the blame was just a farce.

Dr. Stahmer asked me to be sure to listen to the conclusion of his summation in the afternoon, because it gave a characterization of Goering which ought to be interesting to a psychologist. Goering must have put him up to that, because Stahmer doesn't do anything without a direct order from his client.

The "psychologically interesting" characterization of Goering amounted to a tribute to his medieval sense of loyalty and his national pride. After Dr. Stahmer was finished, he asked me what I thought of it. I told him that there was another side to Goering's character that he had neglected to mention. Dr. Stahmer laughed and said, "Of course, but that is for the prosecution to expose."

## July 8

Dr. Horn finished his summation in behalf of Ribbentrop.

Ribbentrop was assured by everybody that his attorney had made a good plea. At lunch he said that he was satisfied that Dr. Horn had explained that the foreign policy was really determined by Hitler and not by him, and that the question of aggression was really highly debatable. However, he was dissatisfied that his attorney had not used any of the material in his big essay on the anti-Semitic issue, showing that Ribbentrop was really not an anti-Semite; however, he would give me that essay, or maybe rewrite it in better style, because he wanted people to know that he was not really an anti-Semite although naturally, he was a member of an anti-Semitic government. At this point Streicher came over and assured Ribbentrop that he really did not rate as an anti-Semite. Ribbentrop was very pleased and said to me, "There, you see, there you have it from an authority."

The headline in today's Stars and Stripes, "GOERING HAD PLOT TO HIDE 50 MILLIONS," created some stir among the defendants. Von Schirach said that that was the most damaging thing revealed about Goering in a long time. The German people would be incensed over the idea that Goering had tried to salt away a little nest egg in America to come out on top after Germany was destroyed.

Speer laughingly remarked, "I see that I have a colleague in Goering in the matter of treason. The only difference is that our motives were entirely different."

Goering was embarrassed when I told him about the newspaper article resulting from a recent interrogation with John Rogge. Goering fumed that it was a dirty trick to let such things get into the papers, and said he would never answer any more questions by any interrogators.

─────────── EVENING IN JAIL ───────────

*Funk's Cell:* The summation speeches for Goering, Ribbentrop and Keitel are moving Funk to a sense of shame over the moral irresponsibility on the part of the political and military leaders of the Third Reich. He had asked me to come to visit him because there was something preying on his mind. When I dropped into his cell this evening, he told me dolefully that I was the only one who made him feel like a human being. "—But what I wanted to tell you was that there is really none of us—not a single one —who escapes a moral guilt in this matter. I have already told you how my conscience bothered me when I signed those laws for the aryanization of Jewish property. Whether that makes me legally guilty or not, is another matter.—But it makes me morally guilty, there is no doubt about that. I should have listened to my wife at that time. She said we would be better off dropping the whole minister business and moving to a small three-room flat, than to be involved in such a disgraceful business. I mentioned in court that I had misgivings about that, but, of course, I didn't tell them that the voice of conscience was my wife. But they are all guilty in the same way. Of course, von Papen is not as guilty as Goering, and Fritzsche was only a small man—but don't forget, even he knew more about the atrocities than I did. He got definite reports and then let himself be lied to.—That is just the trouble; we were all blinded.—Even Schacht does not escape this moral guilt. He was still President of the Reichsbank and Minister without Portfolio when this disgraceful thing came about. But he did not resign from his posts either. Maybe if we had all gotten together and refused to go any further, we might have prevented this final disgrace.—Every one of us has this moral guilt. I don't see how the court can acquit a single one of us."

---

## July 9

## CULTURAL ANTHROPOLOGY

MORNING SESSION: *Dr. Nelte finished his plea for Keitel and Dr. Kauffmann made his plea for Kaltenbrunner. Dr. Nelte's plea was based mostly on the Führerprinzip. Keitel had a terrible time with the Führer, but, as any fool can see, a soldier has to obey orders, not his conscience. Anyway, it was the SS and not the Wehrmacht that was responsible for the atrocities. Dr. Kauffmann held a sermon on virtue, not pretending that Kaltenbrunner was a model of virtue, but one who had good intentions, and although millions of people, alas, were killed in the concentration camps, that was really all Himmler's doing.*

---

LUNCH HOUR: As they went to lunch, Kaltenbrunner said to me, "I saw Colonel Amen holding his sides for laughter. You can tell him that I congratulate him on his victory over me in getting me such a stupid attorney."

At lunch I read to Frank the news article about the Kielce pogrom in Poland and the editorial in the Paris *Herald-Tribune* denouncing this new flare-up of Jewish persecution after the terrible catastrophe that had taken place under Nazi influence. Frank rejected the idea that this was the result of Nazi policies, and pointed out that pogroms have been going on in Poland for several centuries. He attributed it to the passionate prejudices of the Polish people. Seyss-Inquart was inclined to blame it on the leftover religious superstition of the Middle Ages, using the old slogan, "Save the faith and kill the Jews." Frank did not like this interpretation, but accepted Seyss-Inquart's alternative version that it was linked up with their anti-Communistic prejudices. However, Frank's preferred explanation was the innate characteristics of the Polish people. Seyss-Inquart agreed to that too, adding an anthropological explanation: the Poles are too much of a mixed race.

"Yes," agreed Frank, "they are a bastard mixture of Tartar, Slav, Ruthenian, and Germanic blood.—The Poles are a very polemic people.—They fight about everything. There are only three things they are agreed on; they are unified in their Church, and in their hatred of the Jews, the Germans and the Russians." I asked him how religion and hatred could be reconciled. "Religion has nothing to do with it," Frank replied. "People get out of religion only what they bring to it. Catholic teachings will mean one thing to a German and another thing to a Chinese convert, that is obvious.—Most of the Poles are simply a passionate and prejudiced people. Don't forget, they killed a bishop and all his priests last year. The Church certainly had nothing to do with that."

Frank began to dramatize his story with wild gesticulation, as Keitel left the room and Seyss-Inquart and Sauckel watched with quizzical expressions. "Somebody starts a rumor about a Jewish ritual murder, and WHEE! the whole population is up in arms screaming for Jewish blood! And I'll bet they are in church right now, crying in their confessions, 'Oh, my wretched soul, what an evil thing I have partaken of!'—And they will confess and beg forgiveness and will swear to lay off, and in 3 months they will be at it again." Frank described this with the same gestures and intonation he used to describe his own hysterical remorse, so that the projection was clear.

We got on to the Nuremberg Laws, and Frank expressed the opinion that the Nuremberg Laws were really not necessary, now that one looks back on it. The abuse of Christian girls could have been taken care of by normal, legal processes. It was really an unwarranted slap in the face to the Jews, many of whom were very fine industrious people, and when you get right down to it, they were just too industrious and successful for their own good. They evoked the jealousy of other Germans in business and in the professions who were not as industrious.

Frank thought the solution was for the Jews to go to France. France has expressed its need for more manpower. France could use such industrious people as the Jews, because the French are stinking lazy like the Poles. I asked Frank what good that would do, if the French would also show jealous hostility toward the industrious Jews. Frank, still making the comparison to Poland rather than Germany, said that that probably would not create any difficulty, because the French, in contrast to the Poles, are a *Kulturvolk* of sorts.

---

## July 12

MORNING SESSION: *Dr. Marx made his plea for Streicher. Much to Streicher's annoyance he characterized his client as somebody who was obsessed by anti-Semitism, but was really never taken very seriously by the German people. In fact, he was not even taken very seriously by Hitler, although Hitler supported his Stürmer to the end. Naturally, he also had nothing to do with the extermination of the Jews, and didn't even know about it, although it appeared that way.*

---

LUNCH HOUR: The innocence of the "white lambs" was beginning to become a sort of joke in the Youth lunchroom. It was apparent that nobody had anything to do with anything. The Foreign Minister was only an office boy; the Chief of Staff of the High Command of the Wehrmacht was only an office manager; the rabid anti-Semites were all in favor of chivalrous solutions to the Jewish problem and knew nothing about the atrocities, including Gestapo Chief Kaltenbrunner; and Goering, of course, was the most chivalrous of them all.

Today's news, as a matter of fact, stirred up a great deal more interest than the defense pleas which were being held. Molotov's objection to the partitioning of Germany for France's benefit, created something of a minor sensation. Von Papen actually popped his eyes at the headline and said it was incredible. But after a moment's reflection he added, laughing, that it was undoubtedly Russia's plan not to let France get too strong, now that the elections had turned out in favor of the Christian-Democratic MRP rather than the Communists and Socialists. In the next lunchroom Ribbentrop was surprised for a moment; then looked worried. He said that no doubt the Russians were figuring that sooner or later they would get all of Germany, so that they didn't want it to be partitioned in the meantime. Most of the defendants were of similar opinions, crediting the move to Russia's aims for hegemony in Central Europe, rather than any ulterior motives on Germany's behalf. However, they were inclined to accept the move as an ironic defense of Germany's territorial integrity.

## ———————————— July 13 ————————————

## MORE RACIAL SCIENCE

*Streicher's Cell:* I had another short talk with Streicher as an aftermath of his defense summation. He repeated some of his previously expressed attitudes. There was no doubt that Hitler had ordered the extermination of the Jews, and had, as a matter of fact, expressed that intention even before the war. Early in the war he must have realized that he would have to die, and decided to take the Jews with him. But that was no solution, because you would have to exterminate *all* the Jews, and there are still many Jews in all countries who can still keep breeding. So Hitler's idea of exterminating the whole race was obviously impractical. Anyway, Hitler made a mistake in killing so many Jews, because he made a martyr race out of them and that will delay a real solution of the Jewish problem for another 100 years. The solution must be a State solution, because people with the same blood belong together. It is one of the laws of nature that people with the same blood are drawn together and you cannot go against the laws of nature.

I asked him just what he meant by racial blood and laws of nature. Streicher mumbled something about 24 chromosomes. I told him I knew all about that, but I wondered whether there were any particularly Jewish characteristics, because modern research had failed to discover any. Streicher insisted that there were Jewish physical characteristics, although there were many exceptions, and it often took a real expert like himself to detect them. I asked him what some of these Jewish physical characteristics were. He said that for one thing one could frequently tell by the eyes. The Jewish eyes were different. I asked him in what way, but he said they were just different.

More significant than Jewish eyes, however, was the Jewish behind, he had discovered. I asked him what was characteristic about the Jewish behind. "Oh, the Jewish behind is not like a Gentile behind," he smirked wisely, apparently rather serious and superior about this. "The Jewish behind is so feminine—so soft and feminine," he said, glowering and virtually drooling as he shaped the Jewish behind in the air with lascivious hands, indicating its softness and femininity. "—And you can tell from the way it wobbles when they walk.—When I was at Mondorf, I was interrogated by four Jews—I could always tell by their behinds when they left the room, even though the others could not recognize it. And another thing is the way they talk with their hands. Of course, lots of them don't do that. But even if you cannot tell by these physical features, their behavior always gives them away. A German is so open in his manner—like a child—but a Jew is always two-faced. . . . I have made quite a study of this for 25 years, and nobody understands this problem as well as I do. I have studied the people in the courtroom, for instance, and I can recognize a Jew in a few minutes while the others have to study a man for days before they realize I am right. The prosecution is made up almost entirely of Jews." I asked him whether he considered Prosecutor Jackson a Jew. Streicher scoffed and said that of course Jackson's real name was Jacobson and he was a Jew like all the rest. (Same argument he gave Goldensohn the other day.)

———————————— July 18 ————————————

MORNING SESSION: *Dr. Sauter completed his defense plea for von Schirach, emphasizing von Schirach's renunciation of Nazism and anti-Semitism.*

During the intermission and before lunch, Goering agitated against von Schirach, seeking agreement among some of the defendants in rejecting von Schirach's renunciation of Nazism. Since relations at his end of the dock are somewhat cool now, he often shifts operations to the middle of the dock where he often gets a sympathetic ear from Sauckel, Rosenberg, and Frank. This time, after some urging, Frank agreed, "Yes, I disapprove of this servility before the court. It is like making a plea about a married man on the basis of the fact that he was once single."

LUNCH HOUR: Keitel and Jodl were nervous over the news that all 73 of the Waffen-SS murderers of American PW's at Malmedy were found guilty, 43 sentenced to death, and 30 to various terms of imprisonment. Keitel said that Colonel Peiper, who was sentenced to death, was a good leader. I commented that he must have been a very loyal officer who also was good at carrying out orders with inspiring faithfulness. Keitel said that regardless of this murdering of prisoners, which of course he never condoned, Peiper was a good leader just the same. In the next lunchroom, Jodl took some comfort from the fact that General Sepp Dietrich, Peiper's Division Commander, was sentenced only to life imprisonment. This showed that a higher officer might be considered less guilty than the subordinates who are directly responsible for the execution of the crimes. He was also interested in the fact that General Student was mildly sentenced and then pardoned in connection with another action, "—because some American officers testified to his character," he added suggestively.

In the dock after lunch, irrepressible Goering was at it again with his tactic of stirring up sympathy through common hostility. He was overheard telling Doenitz and the other Protestants around him that the court was getting full of Jews, and that the Catholic Church is teaching pure Bolshevism, but it is hard for those two to get together. Later he returned to the middle of the dock to spin the same yarn with Frank, but carefully omitted any reference to the Catholic Church this time, attacking only the Jews and Communists.

───────────── July 23 ─────────────

## AMERICA AND RUSSIA

LUNCH HOUR: Yesterday's Paris edition of the *Herald Tribune* carried the headline "McNARNEY INVITES ALLIES TO MAKE REICH AN ECONOMIC UNIT," as well as a review by Lewis Gannett of Ambassador Bullitt's book *The Great Globe Itself.* Schacht read both articles to Doenitz, von Papen, and von Neurath at lunch. They all took some half-amused satisfaction in this accumulating evidence of growing tension between Russia and America. The review of Bullitt's book created more interest than the statement by McNarney, which was already well-known. Schacht read as the others listened attentively:

### "Forgets a Few Million Lives."

"President Roosevelt should, Mr. Bullitt now holds, have set a bargaining price on lend-lease. 'Few errors more disastrous have ever been made by a President of the United States,' says Mr. Bullitt, adding, irresponsibly, that 'those citizens of the United States who bamboozled the President into acting as if Stalin were a cross between Abraham Lincoln and Woodrow Wilson deserve a high place on an American roll of dishonor.' In return for lend-lease, Mr. Bullitt actually dares to say, we asked and got 'nothing.' Nothing but five or six million Russian lives, whose death spared several million Americans—'nothing.' "

At this point Schacht explained, "That is, of course, the irony of the reviewer." The others groaned. Schacht continued to read the review.

"In his interpretation of the springs of Soviet policy, Mr. Bullitt utterly omits the possibly insensate but indubitably genuine Russian fear that the Western world desires to destroy the Soviet Union. That fear, as Mr. Bullitt was once well aware, had considerable historical justification in 1919; the events of 1938 revived it; and this naïvely hysterical little book will probably make a new contribution to it."

### "A Program That Spells War."

"For this is Mr. Bullitt's proposed 'constructive' policy: stop all aid to Soviet-controlled lands, move to create an anti-Soviet 'Demo-

cratic Federation of European States, including as many countries as
it may be possible to free from Soviet Control'; merge this in a large
'Defense League of Democratic States,' equally frankly directed
against the Soviet Union."

"Humph! A new Anti-Comintern Pact," von Neurath remarked
with a grin. There was a suggestion of "here we go again" in his
attitude.

Von Papen said something about the need for enlisting Russia's
co-operation rather than threatening her with war, which had been
Germany's big mistake.

Schacht continued his reading:

> "Of course, this really spells war. Mr. Bullitt's denial is oddly
> ambiguous. 'Let us first reject with absolute finality the idea that
> we should attack the Soviet Union,' he begins. 'Thanks to the pos-
> session of the atomic bomb and an air force of overwhelming
> strength, we are today stronger than the Soviet Union and could de-
> stroy it,' he continues. . . . Mr. Bullitt seems more than a bit con-
> fused and rather dangerously irresponsible."

Doenitz just grinned and didn't say much. He gave me one of
those knowing looks and then walked over to the window, shaking his head to himself as if deep in reflection. It was not hard
for me to figure out at this point what he was thinking about:
The Americans would need his X U-Boat after all; they have better use for him than to sentence him for war crimes.

Down in the dock Goering and Ribbentrop got wind of the
news and started to discuss it with me. Goering said that he knew
that Bullitt had always been anti-Russian, but had been anti-
Nazi also, which was a contradiction in terms, since Nazism was
the champion of anti-Bolshevism. This thought struck a responsive chord even in Hess's empty mind, "That's right, that is a contradiction in terms."

Ribbentrop had his first good laugh in several weeks at the reviewer's comment that Bullitt is in favor of using the atomic
bomb "to scare the pants off Russia." As Ribbentrop translated
the comment that Russia was only waiting to develop its own
atomic bomb to attack us, Goering replied expansively, "Why, of
course, every child in the street knows that—anybody who has the
slightest political knowledge . . . I give them about 5 years'
time."

They did not talk about it very much in my presence, but from their smug grins, it was easy to see that they received no small delight from this sign of tension between America and Russia.

───────────────── July 26 ─────────────────

## THE PROSECUTION SUMMATION

MORNING SESSION: *Justice Jackson made the summation speech for the American prosecution delegation.*

"Of one thing we may be sure. The future will never have to ask, with misgiving: What could the Nazis have said in their favor? History will know that whatever could be said, they were allowed to say. They have been given the kind of a trial which they, in the days of their pomp and power, never gave to any man . . .

"But in summation we now have before us the tested evidences of criminality and have heard the flimsy excuses and paltry evasions of the defendants. The suspended judgment with which we opened this case is no longer appropriate. The time has come for final judgment and if the case I present seems hard and uncompromising, it is because the evidence makes it so . . .

"The large and varied role of Goering was half militarist and half gangster. He stuck a pudgy finger in every pie . . . He was equally adept at massacring opponents and at framing scandals to get rid of stubborn generals. He built up the Luftwaffe and hurled it at his defenseless neighbors. He was among the foremost in harrying the Jews out of the land . . .

"The zealot Hess, before succumbing to wanderlust, was the engineer tending the Party machinery, passing orders and propaganda down to the Leadership Corps, supervising every aspect of Party activities, and maintaining the organization as a loyal and ready instrument of power. When apprehensions abroad threatened the success of the Nazi scheme for conquest, it was the duplicitous Ribbentrop, the salesman of deception, who was detailed to pour wine on the troubled waters of suspicion by preaching the gospel of limited and peaceful intentions. Keitel, weak and willing tool, delivered the armed forces, the instrument of aggression, over to the Party and directed them in executing its felonous designs.

"Kaltenbrunner, the grand inquisitor, took up the bloody mantle of Heydrich to stifle opposition and terrorize compliance, and buttressed the power of National Socialism on a foundation of guiltless corpses. It was Rosenberg, the intellectual high priest of the 'master race,' who provided the doctrine of hatred which gave the impetus for the annihilation of Jewry, and put his infidel theories into practice against the Eastern Occupied Territories. His woolly philosophy also added boredom to the long list of Nazi atrocities. The fanatical Frank, who solidified Nazi control by establishing the new order of authority without law, so that the will of the Party was the only test of legality, proceeded to export his lawlessness to Poland, which he governed with the lash of Caesar, and whose population he reduced to sorrowing remnants. Frick, the ruthless organizer, helped the Party to seize power, supervised the police agencies to insure that it stayed in power, and chained the economy of Bohemia and Moravia to the German war machine.

"Streicher, the venomous vulgarian, manufactured and distributed obscene racial libels which incited the populace to accept and assist the progressively savage operation of 'race purification.' As Minister of Economics Funk accelerated the pace of rearmament, and as Reichsbank President banked for the SS the gold teeth fillings of concentration camp victims—probably the most ghoulish collateral in banking history. It was Schacht, the façade of starched respectability, who in the early days provided the window dressing, the bait for the hesitant, and whose wizardy later made it possible for Hitler to finance the colossal rearmament program and to do it secretly.

"Doenitz, Hitler's legatee of defeat, promoted the success of the Nazi aggressions by instructing his pack of submarine killers to conduct warfare at sea with the illegal ferocity of the jungle. Raeder, the political admiral, stealthily built up the German Navy in defiance of the Versailles Treaty, and then put it to use in a series of aggressions which he had taken a large part in planning. Von Schirach, poisoner of a generation, initiated the German Youth in Nazi doctrine, trained them in legions for service in the SS and Wehrmacht, and delivered them up to the Party as fanatic, unquestioning executors of its will.

"Sauckel, the greatest and cruelest slaver since the Pharaohs of Egypt, produced desperately needed manpower by driving foreign peoples into the land of bondage on a scale unknown even in the ancient days of tyranny in the kingdom of the Nile. Jodl, betrayer of the traditions of his profession, led the Wehrmacht in violating its own code of military honor in order to carry out the barbarous aims of Nazi policy. Von Papen, pious agent of an infidel regime, held the stirrup while Hitler vaulted into the saddle, lubricated the Austrian annexation, and devoted his diplomatic cunning to the service of Nazi objectives abroad . . .

" . . . If we combine only the stories from the front bench, this is the ridiculous composite picture of Hitler's government that emerges. It was composed of: A No. 2 man who knew nothing of the excesses of the Gestapo which he created, and never suspected the Jewish extermination program although he was the signer of over a score of decrees which instituted the persecutions of that race; a No. 3 man who was merely an innocent middleman transmitting Hitler's orders without even reading them, like a postman or delivery boy; a Foreign Minister who knew little of foreign affairs and nothing of foreign policy; a Field Marshal who issued orders to the armed forces but had no idea of the results they would have in practice; a Security Chief who was of the impression that the policing functions of the Gestapo and SS were somewhat on the order of directing traffic; a Party philosopher who was interested in historical research, but had no idea of the violence which his philosophy was inciting in the 20th century; a Governor-General of Poland who reigned but did not rule; a Gauleiter of Franconia whose occupation was to pour forth filthy writings about the Jews, but who had no idea that anybody would read them; a Minister of the Interior who knew not even what went on in the interior of his own office, much less the interior of his own department, and nothing at all about the interior of Germany; a Reichsbank President who was totally ignorant of what went in and out of the vaults of his bank; and a Plenipotentiary for the War Economy who secretly marshalled the entire economy for armament, but had no idea it had anything to do with war . . .

"If you were to say of these men that they are not guilty, it would be as true to say there has been no war, there have been no slain, there has been no crime."

---

LUNCH HOUR: The reaction of most of the defendants was one of hurt surprise that the prosecution still considered them criminals. Von Papen dropped his mask of polite friendliness in my presence, and denounced the speech. "That was more the speech of a demagogue than of a leading representative of American jurisprudence! . . . What have we been sitting here for eight months for? The prosecution isn't paying the *slightest* attention to our defense. They still insist on calling us liars and murderers!"

Doenitz dropped his contempt of the hypocritical politicians long enough to agree heartily with von Papen on this issue, since he had also been attacked. He and von Papen supported each other in indignation over Jackson's denunciation.

Schacht joined the discussion, adding his own grievances, and agreeing heartily with the other two. "I suppose I am expected to tell a man to his face that I am planning to assassinate him!— That was a miserable speech. It had a very low *niveau!* [level]." They all agreed that the speech had a very low *niveau.*

Goering reacted with the typical shrug of the shoulders toward evidence that wounded his pride yet left him unable to do anything about it. "Oh, that was just about what I expected.—Let him call me names as much as he pleases—I didn't expect anything different from him." He expressed the attitude that sticks and stones will break my bones, but names will never hurt me, without saying so in so many words. However, he found a malicious satisfaction in the fact that his enemies had also gotten it in the neck. "Anyway, those who kow-towed to the prosecution and denounced the Nazi regime got it in the neck just the same. It serves them right.—They probably thought they would get off cheap that way."

Goering insinuated that Speer, von Schirach, and Schacht had made a deal with the prosecution to get off easy in exchange for denouncing the Nazi regime. I told him he must surely know that that was out of the question. "Well, if there wasn't a deal, then they must have at least expected to get off easy." I told him that I was convinced that Speer and von Schirach, at least, had made the denunciation out of bitter disillusionment, and had attempted to set the German people straight on the guilt of their leaders.

Goering didn't like that, and defended his own position by contrast to Schacht. "That's all right—at least I'd rather be called a murderer than a hypocrite and opportunist like Schacht. I certainly got off better than he did.—Now the people will say of him, 'On the one hand you were a traitor, and on the other hand you stand exposed as a hypocrite just the same.'—I'd rather do it my way." He kept mumbling about Jackson's undignified name-calling, and said that the British prosecution would probably be more dignified.—But of course, the whole trial is a farce, because the prosecution isn't paying the slightest attention to their defense. I reminded him that the defense will have lasted 6 months including the organizations, and that they would still have the last word. Goering laughed. "Unfortunately not—the judges will have the last word." Then to forestall the impression that he knew he was guilty, he added hastily, "—And the victors, as I've always told you, are always right."

Streicher was also elated that those who had "helped the prosecution" had gotten it in the neck anyway. Jackson's characterization of the "filthy Streicher," etc. had not penetrated his thick skin, and he started a harangue with a new twist: the current riots in Palestine had convinced him that the Jews have plenty of fighting spirit and spunk, and he was filled with admiration for them now; in fact, by God, he was now ready to fight for them in their ranks. "Anybody who can fight, and resist, [waving his arms, counting the Jewish virtues on his fingers] and stick together, and stick to their guns—for such people I can have only the greatest respect! Yes, even if Hitler was living now, he would also admit that they are a spunky race.—I would be ready to join them now and help them in their fight!—No, I am not joking!"

Jodl and Rosenberg pricked up their ears and looked at him in amusement.

"Absolutely! I am not joking!—And do you know why?—Because the democratic world is too weak and isn't fit to exist! I warned them for 25 years, but now I see that the Jews have determination and spunk.—They will still dominate the world, mark my word!—And I would be glad to help lead them to victory because they are strong and tenacious, and I know Jewry. I have spunk too! And I can stick to my guns!—And if the Jews would be willing to accept me as one of them, I would fight for them, because when I believe in a thing, I know how to fight!" By this time Jodl and Rosenberg were laughing themselves sick.

"I have studied them so long, that I suppose I have adapted myself to their characteristics—at least I could lead a group in Palestine.—I am not joking.—I'll give it to you in writing.—I'll make a proposition. Let me address a gathering at Madison Square Garden in New York.—It will be a sensation!"

I asked him how he thought the Jews could dominate the world when the Nazi regime had exterminated most of the Jews in Europe. Rosenberg and Jodl stopped laughing. Frick, Kaltenbrunner, and Ribbentrop, who had been cocking an ear to the fantastic conversation, were suddenly paying no attention.

"Oh, I don't think we have exterminated as many as they say," Streicher answered. "I don't think it was 6 million. I figure it was maybe 4 million.—And according to my figures there were 16 million Jews in the world—of course, including those of mixed blood—but they are spread in important positions all over the world, and they are destined to rule the world, and since I know their plans so well I could help.—Of course I will have to be given a furlough after the sentence."

---

AFTERNOON SESSION: *Sir Hartley Shawcross began his summation speech for the British delegation.*

"*That these defendants participated in and are morally guilty of crimes so frightful that the imagination staggers and reels back at their very contemplation is not in doubt . . . Great cities, from Coventry to Stalingrad, reduced to rubble, the countryside laid waste, and now the inevitable aftermath of war so fought—hunger and disease stalking through the world—millions of people homeless, maimed, bereaved. And in their graves, crying out, not for vengeance but that this shall not happen again, 10 million who might be living in peace and happiness at this hour, soldiers, sailors, airmen and civilians killed in battles that ought never to have been . . . Two-thirds of the Jews in Europe exterminated . . . And is the world to overlook the revival of slavery on a scale which involved 7 million men, women, and children taken from their homes, treated as beasts, starved, beaten, and murdered? . . .*"

Sir Hartley reviewed the consolidation of power by the Nazis, the aggression, the war crimes, the crimes against humanity, and denounced the defendants as "common murderers."

---

At the end of the session Goering said to Ribbentrop, "There, it's just as if we hadn't made any defense at all."

"Yes, it was a waste of time," Ribbentrop agreed.

Keitel, frozen-faced, went right over to the elevator door to be the first one to go down and get out of sight as quickly as possible.

———— EVENING IN JAIL ————

*Ribbentrop's Cell:* The cell was messier than usual. His laundry was strewn on the cot; his table covered with papers among which he was again scribbling notes; books, laundry, and papers were piled in the corner of his cell; he himself was more dishevelled than usual.

"Tsk! tsk! tsk!—Did you hear Sir Hartley Shawcross?" he asked me after a moment's delay, as if he was having difficulty getting his bearings. "Compared to him, even Jackson was a charming fellow this morning.—They say such nasty things about us—it really is not very dignified. Do you think it is dignified? Here, I've jotted down a couple of things—." He fished among his papers and read me some notes he had jotted down on Jackson's speech. "Here, in one place he says that I made an anti-Semitic remark to Minister Bonnet. Why, I never did such a thing, because I always thought Bonnet was a Jew himself, so obviously that was out of the question . . . And here he says I intimidated Schuschnigg. —Why, I only spoke to him two hours that time. How can any one say I exercised pressure on him?"

"Well, von Papen said it was so, right on the witness stand. when Sir David cross-examined him, if you remember."

"Oh, did he?—Well, maybe Hitler did.—I suppose he spoke very directly to him—but I didn't.—I mean I only assume that Hitler did. I don't know."

He went on with the usual hash of confused rationalizations to explain away the guilt of war and aggression, explaining how the Poles had been so insolent about the Polish Corridor question, etc. etc. I reminded him that it had been proven in court that Hitler had planned the war in advance, and framed up the Gleiwitz Radio Station incident to provoke the war that he had already planned against Poland. Ribbentrop assured me that he didn't know about that at the time, and had even cited the Gleiwitz incident in his White Book because he had believed it was the Poles' provocation of the war at the time.

As for the persecution of the Jews: "Nobody used up so much nervous energy trying to dissuade Hitler from such a course.—I had 4 or 5 very severe clashes with Hitler on that subject—as I told you, didn't I?—But there was simply nothing you could do

—in the beginning one could, but toward the end you couldn't even talk about it."

Ribbentrop's big clash with Hitler over some triviality in 1940 has developed in the course of time into a big clash in defense of the Jews, and finally into 4 or 5 big clashes. Ribbentrop is gradually becoming, in his own fantasy, the leading champion of the Jews in the Third Reich, while having to work with a regime that was admittedly anti-Semitic to the point of mass murder.

---

*Goering's Cell:* Goering called me in as I passed his cell. "I take back everything I said at lunch today. Compared to Shawcross, Jackson was downright chivalrous." (That explains where Ribbentrop got the idea) "They sure don't flatter us. Did you notice that one place where I really got mad? Well, that time I really had to show it.—That story about the 50 British fliers.—I proved that I wasn't even there.—But in the other places where I was not on such sure ground, I didn't respond.—Did you know some of the others were keeping a tabulation on how often we were mentioned in Jackson's speech? I was way out in front with 42 mentions, and Schacht was a poor second. But I certainly think that I got off better than he did, as I told you at lunch.—I've already read the rest of Sir Hartley's speech, and he's sure going to give the rest of them hell tomorrow morning. Compared to them, I'm getting off easy there too. Just listen to it tomorrow morning.

"You know when Jackson asks what would have happened if Hitler got up to defend himself, I could have told them all right. First of all, Hitler would have taken all the responsibility because that's the way he was. Secondly, I can assure you that a few of the defendants would not have been so cocky if he was there. They couldn't get away with that stuff of always being against him. But with Himmler, it would have been a different matter. He would have known that he was sunk, and he would be glad to hang a few Wehrmacht generals with him. He would have said this one knew about it, and that one participated in that atrocity, and so on."

"I suppose he would have made a few damaging statements about you too," I suggested.

Goering sensed the danger in that question and neatly dodged it. "Oh, I don't know.—He never had anything against me personally.—It was just political rivalry." Goering laughed. "—But here in the prisoners' dock he would have been glad to concede first place to me. I've always said, for instance, that the first 48 hours after Hitler's death would have been the most dangerous for me, because he would have tried to get me out of the way—an 'auto accident' or a 'heart attack over the death of the dear Führer,' or some such thing.—He was good at those things. But once the Wehrmacht had sworn allegiance to me, I would have been safe—and Himmler would have been on the way out."

---

*Schacht's Cell:* Schacht thought that both Jackson and Shawcross had made miserable speeches, so biased and so unfair. They had paid no attention to his defense, when he had proved conclusively that he was innocent. I asked him whether the prosecution wasn't justified in holding the secret financing of rearmament against him.

"But I *told* those people, it was none of my doing. I was only Reichsbank President. If the Finance Minister didn't announce it, then that was his fault.—And if he failed to pay the bills when due, that was an absolute crime!—But I have never done anything that could be in any way be considered immoral!" He waved his hand and placed it innocently over his heart. "That is the difference between me and von Papen and von Neurath. One can ask them why they still stayed in Hitler's regime after they saw what kind of a man he was.—But not me!—I did not accept a single post after 1939. Oh, I tell you, it would be an eternal disgrace to this Tribunal and to international justice if I am not acquitted!"

"Well, you played along with Hitler with enthusiasm in the beginning."

"With *enthusiasm?* Not in the least! I told you I had only hoped to restrain him . . . They may accuse me of lots of things. —They may even say that the brilliant Mr. Schacht was foolish enough to let Hitler deceive him.—But they cannot say I wanted war!—It is slander to say that I joined the Party as it rose to success, and abandoned it when it was starting to go down. Why, I left at the very height of its success and power—."

"—Because you knew they were headed for war," I said.

"No, at that time, in January, 1939, I had no reason to expect war, but left for *moral* reasons."

"What moral reasons, if not war?"

"Because Hitler wanted to keep financing rearmament with inflationary measures. He wanted to keep appropriating money and making me just print it. That is absolutely immoral, and I refused!"

---

*Speer's Cell:* Speer said he was delighted with the speech, after listening to all the stupid nonsense of the defense attorneys, each one trying to make his client look like a helpless, innocent little man, and helping them shirk their responsibility before the German people. He knows that Goering is angry and is saying that if it wasn't for Speer the prosecution would not still be trying to maintain its conspiracy charge. "His reasoning is clear.—He's already got his scapegoat for the death sentence that he knows most of them deserve. He will say, 'There, we can blame Speer for that.'—Anything to cover up his own guilt." He was glad that Jackson had set the record straight on Goering's hypocrisy. He thought the speech was brilliantly formulated and put the blame right where it belongs—on all of them. "Naturally, they all put up a good fight to save their necks, but even those fool defense counsels did not seem to realize that they also had a responsibility for the German people.—Imagine Sauckel's defense counsel trying to justify slave labor just to save Sauckel's neck. If the court was to agree with him, then the Allies would be justified in taking millions of Germans into slave labor. If they denounce it as a crime, then they morally obligate themselves to observe that principle."

--- July 27 ---

MORNING SESSION: *Sir Hartley Shawcross continued, coming to the horrors of the extermination of the Jews, quoting Streicher, Frank, von Schirach, and Hoess. "Mass murder was becoming a State industry with by-products—" Sir Hartley observed. [Unrest and hostility mounted in the prisoners' dock as Sir Hartley's cool but scathing attacks struck home. Von Papen covered his face as Sir Hartley reviewed the packing of murdered women's hair, the sending of gold rings and gold tooth fillings to the Reichsbank.*

Frank, Goering, Streicher, and Rosenberg busied themselves reading the transcript.] *Sir Hartley continued to read an eyewitness description of a mass execution by one of Himmler's 'Action Commandos.'*

"Without screaming or weeping these people undressed, stood around in family groups, kissed each other, said farewells, and waited for a sign from another SS man, who stood near the pit, also with a whip in his hand. During the 15 minutes that I stood near I heard no complaint or plea for mercy. I watched a family of about 8 persons, a man and a woman both about 50 with their children of about 1, 8 and 10, and 2 grown-up daughters of about 20–24. An old woman with snow-white hair was holding the 1-year-old child in her arms and singing to it and tickling it. The child was cooing with delight. The couple were looking on with tears in their eyes. The father was holding the hand of a boy about 10 years old and speaking to him softly; the boy was fighting his tears. The father pointed to the sky, stroked his head and seemed to explain something to him. At that moment the SS man at the pit shouted something to his comrade. The latter counted off about 20 persons and instructed them to go behind the earth mound. Among them was the family which I have mentioned. I well remember a girl, slim and with black hair who, as she passed close to me, pointed to herself and said, '23.' I walked around the mound and found myself confronted by a tremendous grave. People were closely wedged together and lying on top of each other so that only their heads were visible. Nearly all had blood running over their shoulders from their heads. Some of the people shot were still moving. Some were lifting their arms and turning their heads to show that they were still alive. The pit was already two-thirds full. I estimated that it already contained about 1,000 people. I looked for the man who did the shooting. He was an SS man, who sat on the edge of the narrow end of the pit, his feet dangling into the pit. He had a tommy gun on his knees and was smoking a cigarette. The people, completely naked, went down some steps which were cut in the clay wall of the pit and clambered over the heads of the people lying there, to the place to which the SS man directed them. They lay down in front of the dead or injured people; some caressed those who were still alive and spoke to them in a low voice. Then I heard a series of shots. I looked into the pit and saw that the bodies were twitching or the heads lying motionless on top of the bodies which lay before them. Blood was running away from their necks."

[Kaltenbrunner remained expressionless. Sauckel mopped his brow; Fritzsche, pale, bit his lips. Goering supported his head on his hand and looked tired, then stirred uneasily in the dock and changed position. Von Schirach knitted his brows, did not move. Frank and Rosenberg kept reading the transcript. Frick sat pouting until his name was mentioned in connection with the euthanasia murder of the ill, aged, and insane; he reddened a little, and lowered his head.] "What special dispensation of Providence kept these men ignorant of these things?" Sir Hartley demanded.

He quoted Goethe as saying that some day Fate would strike the German people because "they ingenuously submit to any mad scoundrel who appeals to their lowest instincts, who confirms them in their vices and teaches them to conceive nationalism as isolation and brutality." "With what a voice of prophecy he spoke," Sir Hartley added, "for these are the mad scoundrels who did these very things."

[Frank was cursing out loud against "that damn Englishman." Rosenberg was grumbling, and Frick was also cursing under his breath.]

"What matters it if some forfeited their lives only a thousand times whilst others deserved a million deaths? . . . Mankind itself—struggling now to re-establish in all the countries of the world the common simple things—liberty, love, understanding—comes to this court and cries 'These are our laws, let them prevail!' . . . You will remember when you come to give your decision the story [of the mass execution], but not in vengeance—in a determination that these things shall not occur again. The father—you remember—pointed to the sky, and seemed to say something to his boy."

END OF TRIAL DIARY

# Epilogue
## APPENDICES

# Epilogue—The Condemned

THE TRIAL WENT ON for another month while representatives of the indicted Nazi organizations* blamed each other for the atrocities and war crimes. Then, on August 31, 1946, the last day of the trial, the 21 defendants made their final speeches.

Goering deserted Hitler and made a grandiose protestation of his own innocence, calling upon God and the German people as witnesses to the fact that he had acted out of pure patriotism. This hypocrisy infuriated von Papen so much that he came over and attacked Goering at lunch, demanding furiously, "Who in the world *is* responsible for all this destruction if not *you!* You were the second man in the State! Is *nobody* responsible for any of this?" He waved his arms at the ruins of Nuremberg visible through the lunchroom windows.

Goering folded his arms cockily and smirked into von Papen's face: "Well, why don't *you* take the responsibility then? You were Vice-Chancellor!"

"I *am* taking my share of the responsibility!" von Papen retorted, red-faced. "But what about you? You haven't taken the least responsibility for anything! All you do is make bombastic speeches! It is disgraceful!" Goering laughed at the old man's fury.

Most of the other defendants acknowledged that there had been horrible crimes committed, but claimed that they had individually acted in good faith according to the standards of their respective positions and professions. The generals had only followed orders; the admirals had done no more than other admirals; the politicians had only worked for the Fatherland; the financiers had only attended to business.

Rosenberg acknowledged that genocide (racial and cultural extermination) was a crime, but protested that he had never dreamed of the consequences of his philosophy of forceful segregation. Frank admitted that the Nazis had never realized the deathly consequences of turning from God.

---

*A declaratory judgment had been asked to declare 7 Nazi organizations as criminal in nature: Gestapo, SD, SS, Reich Cabinet, Corps of Political Leaders, General Staff and OKW, and Storm Troops. Of these the first 3 were declared criminal, though no members can be punished without further trial.

Speer turned from his defense to warn the world of the destruction we might expect in a future war: radio-controlled rockets, aircraft flying at supersonic speed, and atomic bombs, destroying everything within reach; chemical and bacteriological warfare snuffing out all life that remained.

Hess suddenly recovered his memory through a haze of paranoid rambling during his final speech (the third recovery) and then retreated to an embarrassed silence in his cell.

As the defendants awaited the verdict, there was tense depression in the jail, in spite of the relaxation of prison rules to allow visits from their wives and among themselves.

Goering acknowledged defeat on the psychological front: "You don't have to worry about the Hitler legend any more," he said despondently. "When the German people learn all that has been revealed at this trial, it won't be necessary to condemn him; he has condemned himself." As the day of sentencing approached, he grew more and more nervous and found it harder and harder to laugh.

Keitel was depressed and keenly aware of his disgrace. He declined to see his wife, "because I just couldn't face her."

Sauckel, Rosenberg, Fritzsche, Funk paced their cells or lay on their cots staring at the ceiling. Raeder repeated that he had no illusions about getting off with less than the death sentence and would prefer that to life imprisonment.

Schacht, the only confident one, was being interrogated for information on the German industrialists to be indicted in the next trial. He laughed about it in his cell. "If you want to indict industrialists who helped to rearm Germany, you will have to indict your own too. The Opel Werke, for instance, who did nothing but war production, were owned by your General Motors.—No, that is no way to go about it. You cannot indict industrialists."

Ribbentrop was almost pathetic in his confused repetition of the old rationalizations and lies, and in the pale fear of death that crept into his haggard face. The day before the sentence he hinted that he could write a whole book, maybe even a series of volumes on the mistakes of the Nazi regime, if we only gave him enough time. He even went so far as to suggest to me that I could make a great historical gesture by interceding on behalf of the defendants for clemency, and he could write those memoirs . . .

Finally, on September 30–October 1, the Tribunal rendered its verdict, and read its judgment on each of the 21 defendants: Schacht, von Papen, and Fritzsche were found not guilty. All the rest were found guilty on one or more counts of the indictment. (See judgment.) The last Diary note follows:

OCTOBER 1, 1946. (*Afternoon in Jail*)

While the convicted defendants were getting ready to be called to hear their individual sentences, I talked to the acquitted defendants, Schacht, von Papen, and Fritzsche, as they packed their belongings and moved to cells on the third tier.

Fritzsche was so unnerved and overcome, he seemed to lose his balance and almost fell over as though he were dizzy: "I am entirely overwhelmed," he whispered "—to be set free right here, and not even be sent back to Russia.—That was more than I had hoped for." He was glad that the Tribunal had realized that unlike Streicher he had not incited hatred.

Von Papen was elated and quite obviously surprised. "I had hoped for it, but did not really expect it." Then, with a gesture of compassion for von Neurath, he took out of his pocket an orange he had saved from lunch, and asked me to give it to von Neurath. Fritzsche asked me to give his to von Schirach. Schacht ate his own orange.

Then the convicted defendants came down one by one after hearing their sentences. It was my duty to meet them as they returned to their cells. I asked each one what the sentence was.

Goering came down first and strode into his cell, his face pale and frozen, his eyes popping. "Death!" he said as he dropped on the cot and reached for a book. His hands were trembling in spite of his attempt to be nonchalant. His eyes were moist and he was panting, fighting back an emotional breakdown. He asked me in an unsteady voice to leave him alone for a while.

Hess strutted in, laughing nervously, and said that he had not even been listening, so he did not know what the sentence was—and what was more, he didn't care. As the guard unlocked his handcuffs, he asked why he had been handcuffed and Goering had not. I said it was probably an oversight with the first prisoner.

Hess laughed again and said mysteriously that he knew why. (A guard told me that Hess had been given a life sentence.)

*Ribbentrop* wandered in, aghast, and started to walk around the cell in a daze, whispering, "Death!—Death! Now I won't be able to write my beautiful memoirs. Tsk! tsk! So much hatred! Tsk! tsk!" Then he sat down, a completely broken man, and stared into space . . .

*Keitel* was already in his cell, his back to the door, when I entered. He wheeled around and snapped to attention at the far end of the cell, his fists clenched and arms rigid, horror in his eyes. "Death—by *hanging!*" he announced, his voice hoarse with intense shame. "*That,* at least, I thought I would be spared.—I don't blame you for standing at a distance from a man sentenced to death by hanging.—I understand that perfectly.—But I am still the same as before.—If you will please only—visit me sometimes in these last days—." I said I would.

*Kaltenbrunner's* clasped hands expressed the fear that did not show in his insensitive face. "Death!" he whispered, and could say no more.

*Frank* smiled politely, but could not look at me. "Death by hanging," he said softly, nodding his head in acquiescence. "I deserved it and I expected it, as I've always told you. I am glad that I have had the chance to defend myself and to think things over in the last few months."

*Rosenberg* sneered agitatedly as he changed into his prison overalls. "The rope! The rope! That's what you wanted, wasn't it?"

*Streicher* smiled a crooked smile. "Death, of course.—Just what I expected. You all must have known it all along."

*Funk* watched the guard unlock his handcuffs in simpering bewilderment. Then he walked around the cell with bowed head, mumbling, as if he couldn't quite grasp it, "Life imprisonment! —What does that mean? They won't keep me in prison all my life, will they? They don't mean that, do they?" Then he grumbled that he was not surprised at Fritzsche's acquittal, but was surprised that they let Schacht and von Papen off—very surprised.

*Doenitz* didn't know quite how to take it. "Ten years!—Well— anyway, I cleared U-boat warfare.—Your own Admiral Nimitz said—you heard it." He said he was sure his colleague Admiral Nimitz understood him perfectly.

As *Raeder* came into the cell block, he asked the guard at the gate in a high-pitched voice, in a desperate attempt to be casual, whether they were going walking this afternoon. He limped to his cell, and, as I approached, signified that he did not want to talk. I did not enter his cell, but asked him through the portal what his sentence was. "I don't know. I forget," he said, waving me away. (A guard told me he had been given life imprisonment.)

*Von Schirach's* face was grave and tense as he marched to his cell, head high. "Twenty," he said, as the guard unlocked the handcuffs. I told him his wife would be relieved to know that he had not gotten the death penalty, which she had feared. "Better a quick death than a slow one," he answered. He asked what the other sentences were so far and seemed to agree that each one was about what he had expected.

*Sauckel* was perspiring and trembling all over when I entered his cell. "I have been sentenced to death!" he sputtered. "I don't consider the sentence fair.—I have never been cruel myself.—I always wanted the best for the workers.—But I am a man—and I can take it—." Then he started to cry.

*Jodl* marched to his cell, rigid and upright, avoiding my glance. After he had been unhandcuffed and faced me in his cell, he hesitated a few seconds, as if he could not get the words out. His face was spotted red with vascular tension. "Death—by *hanging!*— That, at least, I did not deserve. The death part—all right, somebody has to stand for the responsibility.—But that—." His mouth quivered and his voice choked for the first time. "—That I did not deserve."

*Seyss-Inquart* smiled, but the crack in his voice belied the casualness of his words. "Death by hanging." He smiled again and shrugged his shoulders. "Well, in view of the whole situation, I never expected anything different. It's all right." He asked if they would still get tobacco, then apologized for being so trivial at a time like this.

*Speer* laughed nervously. "Twenty years.—Well, that's fair enough. They couldn't have given me a lighter sentence, considering the facts, and I can't complain. I said the sentences must be severe, and I admitted my share of the guilt, so it would be ridiculous if I complained about the punishment. But I am glad that Fritzsche got off."

*Von Neurath* stammered, "Fifteen years." He could hardly talk, but was touched by von Papen's orange.

*Frick* shrugged, callous to the end. "Hanging.—I didn't expect anything different." He asked about the others and I told him there were eleven death sentences, including his own. "So. Eleven death sentences. I figured fourteen. Well, I hope they get it over with fast."

When Goering collected himself enough to talk, he said that he had naturally expected the death penalty, and was glad that he had not gotten a life sentence, because those who are sentenced to life imprisonment never become martyrs. But there wasn't any of the old confident bravado in his voice. Goering seems to realize, at last, that there is nothing funny about death, when you're the one who is going to die.

---

The three acquitted defendants found it difficult to enjoy their freedom. No sooner had their acquittal been announced, than the German civil administration declared its intention to arrest them and try them for betrayal of the German people. A cordon of Nuremberg police was thrown around the Palace of Justice to catch them as they came out. For three days and nights they remained in the jail at their own request, fearing to face their own people. Von Papen declared, "I am a hunted animal and they will never leave me in peace!" In desperation, Fritzsche asked me for a pistol, saying that he could not stand this torture any longer. Finally, Fritzsche and Schacht ventured out of the jail in the dead of night. They were arrested, released, and arrested again. Von Papen continued to bide his time.

As Frank heard of all this in his death cell, he paused in his penitent meditations long enough to laugh himself into hysterics over it. "Hahaha!—They thought they were free!—Don't they know, there is no freedom from Hitlerism! Only we are free of it! We got the best deal after all! Hahahaha . . . "

But Goering could no longer laugh. He lay on his cot completely worn out and deflated. In our conversations he still toyed feebly with the heroic legend idea, like a child holding the torn remnants of a balloon that had burst in its hand. A few days after the verdict he asked me again what those psychological tests had shown about his personality—especially that ink-blot test—as if it had been bothering him all the time. This time I told him. "Frankly, they showed that while you have an active, aggressive mind, you lack the guts to really face responsibility. You betrayed yourself with a little gesture on the ink-blot test." Goering glared apprehensively. "Do you remember the card with the red spot? Well, morbid neurotics often hesitate over that card and then say there's blood on it. You hesitated, but you didn't call it blood. You tried to flick it off with your finger, as though you thought you could wipe away the blood with a little gesture. You've been doing the same thing all through the trial—taking off your earphones in the courtroom, whenever the evidence of your guilt became too unbearable. And you did the same thing during the war too, drugging the atrocities out of your mind. You didn't have the courage to face it. That is your guilt. I agree with Speer. You are a moral coward."

Goering glared at me and was silent for a while. Then he said those psychological tests were meaningless, and he didn't give a damn what that double-crosser, Speer, said. A few days later he told me that he had given his lawyer, Dr. Stahmer, a statement that anything the psychologist or anybody else in the jail had to say at this time was meaningless and prejudiced . . . It had struck home.

The night before the executions Goering asked the chaplain for the rites of the Last Supper and the blessing of the Lutheran Church. Chaplain Gerecke, sensing another theatrical gesture, declined to administer the rites, telling Goering that since he had never shown the slightest sign of repentance, he would not put on a show for someone who did not really mean it. The next night, when Goering showed that he had intended to make a mockery of the Last Supper by committing suicide right after it, the chaplain realized how right he was about Goering.

So did I.—For Goering died as he had lived, a psychopath trying to make a mockery of all human values and to distract attention from his guilt by a dramatic gesture.

During the night of October 14–15, Goering joined Hitler, Himmler, Goebbels, and Ley in choosing suicide. The 10 other condemned men were executed as prescribed by the Tribunal.

The day after the death of the last top Nazi leaders, I asked

one of the German lawyers what the German people were thinking about this end of the Third Reich. He thought a while, then
said, "To tell you the truth, they think whatever you want them
to think. If they know you are still pro-Nazi, they say, 'Isn't it a
shame the way our conquerors are taking revenge on our leaders!
—Just wait!' If they know you are disgusted with Nazism, the misery and destruction it brought to Germany, they say, 'It serves
those dirty pigs right! Death is too good for them!' You see, Herr
Doktor, I am afraid that 12 years of Hitlerism has destroyed the
moral fiber of our people."

# Appendix I—The Judgment

The four counts of the indictment were: 1—Conspiracy to commit crimes alleged in other counts; 2—Crimes against peace; 3—War crimes; 4—Crimes against humanity.

(NB. *Not all defendants were indicted on all counts.*)

GOERING: "From the moment he joined the Party in 1922 and took command of the street fighting organization, the SA, Goering was the adviser, the active agent of Hitler and one of the prime leaders of the Nazi movement. As Hitler's political deputy he was largely instrumental in bringing the National Socialists to power in 1933, and was charged with consolidating this power and expanding German armed might. He developed the Gestapo and created the first concentration camps, relinquishing them to Himmler in 1934; conducted the Roehm purge in that year and engineered the sordid proceedings which resulted in the removal of von Blomberg and von Fritsch from the army . . . In the Austrian Anschluss he was, indeed, the central figure, the ringleader . . . The night before the invasion of Czechoslovakia and the absorption of Bohemia and Moravia, at a conference with Hitler and President Hacha he threatened to bomb Prague if Hacha did not submit . . . He commanded the Luftwaffe in the attack on Poland and throughout the aggressive wars which followed . . . The record is filled with Goering's admissions of his complicity in the use of slave labor . . . He made plans for the spoliation of Soviet territory long before the war on the Soviet Union . . .

"Goering persecuted the Jews, particularly after the November, 1938 riots, and not only in Germany, where he raised the billion-mark fine as stated elsewhere, but in the conquered territories as well. His own utterances, then and in his testimony, show his interest was primarily economic—how to get their property and how to force them out of the economic life of Europe. . . . Although their extermination was in Himmler's hands, Goering was far from disinterested or inactive despite his protestations from the witness box . . .There is nothing to be said in mitigation . . . His guilt is unique in its enormity. The record discloses no excuses for this man."

*Verdict:* GUILTY on all 4 counts.
*Sentence:* Death by hanging.

HESS: " . . . As deputy to the Führer, Hess was the top man in
the Nazi Party with responsibility for handling all Party matters
and authority to make decisions in Hitler's name on all questions
of Party leadership . . . Hess was an informed and willing participant in German aggression against Austria, Czechoslovakia,
and Poland . . . On September 27, 1938, at the time of the
Munich crisis, he arranged with Keitel to carry out the instructions of Hitler to make the machinery of the Nazi Party available
for a secret mobilization . . . With him on his flight to England,
Hess carried certain peace proposals which he alleged Hitler was
prepared to accept. It is significant to note that this flight took
place only 10 days after the date on which Hitler fixed the time
for attacking the Soviet Union . . .

"As previously indicated, the Tribunal found, after a full medical examination of and report on the condition of this defendant,
that he should be tried, without any postponement of his case.
Since that time further motions have been made that he should
again be examined. These the Tribunal denied, after having had
a report from the prison psychologist. That Hess acts in an abnormal manner, suffers from loss of memory, and has mentally
deteriorated during this trial, may be true. But there is nothing to
show that he does not realize the nature of the charges against
him, or is incapable of defending himself. He was ably represented
at the trial by counsel, appointed for that purpose by the Tribunal.
There is no suggestion that Hess was not completely sane when
the acts charged against him were committed."

*Verdict:* GUILTY on counts 1 and 2.
*Sentence:* Life imprisonment.

RIBBENTROP: "Ribbentrop was not present at the Hoszbach
Conference held on November 5, 1937, but on January 2, 1938,
while Ambassador to England, he sent a memorandum to Hitler
indicating his opinion that a change in the *status quo* in the East
in the German sense could only be carried out by force and suggesting methods to prevent England and France from intervening
in a European war fought to bring about such a change . . . Ribbentrop participated in the aggressive plans against Czechoslovakia. Beginning in March 1938, he was in close touch with the
Sudeten German Party and gave them instructions which had the

effect of keeping the Sudeten German question a live issue which might serve as an excuse for the attack which Germany was planning against Czechosolvakia . . . After the Munich Pact he continued to bring diplomatic pressure with the object of occupying the remainder of Czechoslovakia . . .

"Ribbentrop played a particularly significant role in the diplomatic activity which led up to the attack on Poland. He participated in a conference held on August 12, 1939, for the purpose of obtaining Italian support if the attack should lead to a general European war. Ribbentrop discussed the German demands with respect to Danzig and the Polish Corridor with the British Ambassador in the period from August 25 to August 30, 1939, when he knew that the German plans to attack Poland had merely been temporarily postponed in an attempt to induce the British to abandon their guarantee to the Poles . . .

"He played an important part in Hitler's 'final solution' of the Jewish question. In September, 1942, he ordered the German diplomatic representatives accredited to various satellites to hasten the deportation of the Jews to the East . . . Ribbentrop participated in all the Nazi aggressions from the occupation of Austria to the invasion of the Soviet Union . . . It was because Hitler's policy and plans coincided with his own ideas that Ribbentrop served him so willingly to the end."

Verdict: GUILTY on all 4 counts.
Sentence: Death by hanging.

KEITEL: " . . . Keitel was present on May 23, 1939, when Hitler announced his decision 'to attack Poland at the first suitable opportunity.' Already he had signed the directive requiring the Wehrmacht to submit its 'Fall Weiss' timetable (for the attack on Poland) to OKW on May 1 . . . Hitler had said, on May 23, 1939, that he would ignore the neutrality of Belgium and the Netherlands, and Keitel signed orders for the attacks on October 15, November 20, and November 28, 1939 . . . Keitel testified that he opposed the invasion of the Soviet Union for military reasons, and also because it would constitute a violation of the Non-Aggression Pact. Nevertheless, he initialed 'Case Barbarossa' (for the attack on Russia) signed by Hitler on December 18, 1940, and attended the OKW discussion with Hitler on February 3, 1941 . . .

"On Aug. 4, 1942, Keitel issued a directive that paratroopers were to be turned over to the SD. On September 16, 1941, Keitel ordered that attacks on soldiers in the East should be met by putting to death 50 to 100 Communists for 1 German soldier, with the comment that human life was less than nothing in the East . . . There is nothing in mitigation. Superior orders, even to a soldier, cannot be considered in mitigation where crimes as shocking and extensive have been committed consciously, ruthlessly."

*Verdict:* GUILTY on all 4 counts.
*Sentence:* Death by hanging.

KALTENBRUNNER: " . . . When he became Chief of the Security Police and SD and head of the RSHA on January 30, 1943, Kaltenbrunner took charge of an organization which included the main offices of the Gestapo, the SD and the Criminal Police . . . During the period in which Kaltenbrunner was head of the RSHA, it was engaged in a widespread program of War Crimes and Crimes Against Humanity. These crimes included the mistreatment and murder of prisoners of war. Jews, commissars, and others who were thought to be ideologically hostile to the Nazi regime were reported to the RSHA, which had them transferred to a concentration camp and murdered . . . The order for the execution of commando troops was extended by the Gestapo to include parachutists while Kaltenbrunner was Chief of the RSHA. An order signed by Kaltenbrunner instructed the police not to interfere with attacks on bailed out Allied fliers . . .

"The RSHA played a leading part in the 'final solution' of the Jewish question by the extermination of the Jews. A special section under the Amt IV of the RSHA was established to supervise this program. Under its direction approximately 6 million Jews were murdered, of which 2 million were killed by the Einsatzgruppen and other units of the Security Police. Kaltenbrunner had been informed of the activities of these Einsatzgruppen when he was a Higher SS and Police leader, and they continued to function after he had become Chief of the RSHA. The murder of approximately 4 million Jews in concentration camps . . . was also under the supervision of the RSHA when Kaltenbrunner was head of that organization . . . "

*Verdict:* GUILTY on counts 3 and 4.
*Sentence:* Death by hanging.

ROSENBERG: " . . . Recognized as the Party's ideologist, he developed and spread Nazi doctrines in the newspapers *Völkischer*

*Beobachter* and *NS Monatshefte*, which he edited, and in the numerous books he wrote . . . As head of the APA, Rosenberg was in charge of an organization whose agents were active in Nazi intrigue in all parts of the world. His own reports, for example, claim that the APA was largely responsible for Rumania's joining the Axis. As head of the APA, he played an important part in the preparation and planning of the attack on Norway.

"Rosenberg bears a major responsibility for the formulation and execution of occupation policies in the Occupied Eastern Territories. He was informed by Hitler on April 2, 1941, of the coming attack against the Soviet Union, and he agreed to help in the capacity of 'Political Adviser' . . . On July 17, 1941, Hitler appointed Rosenberg Reich Minister for the Eastern Occupied Territories, and publicly charged him with responsibility for civil administration . . . He helped to formulate the policies of Germanization, exploitation, forced labor, extermination of Jews and opponents of Nazi rule, and he set up an administration which carried them out . . . Rosenberg had knowledge of the brutal treatment and terror to which the Eastern people were subjected. He directed that the Hague Rules of Land Warfare were not applicable in the Occupied Eastern Territories. He had knowledge of and took an active part in stripping the Eastern Territories of raw materials and foodstuffs, which were all sent to Germany. He stated that feeding the German people was first on the list of claims on the East, and the Soviet people would suffer thereby. His directives provided for the segregation of Jews, ultimately in Ghettos. His subordinates engaged in mass killings of Jews, and his civil administrators considered that cleansing the Eastern Occupied Territories of Jews was necessary . . . He gave his civil administrators quotas of laborers to be sent to the Reich, which had to be met by whatever means necessary. His signature of approval appears on the order of June 14, 1941, for the *Heu Aktion*, the apprehension of 40,000 to 50,000 youths, aged 10–14, for shipment to the Reich . . . "

*Verdict:* GUILTY on all 4 counts.
*Sentence:* Death by hanging.

FRANK: " . . . Frank was appointed Chief Civil Administration Officer for occupied Polish territory and, on October 12, 1939, was made Governor-General of the occupied Polish territory. On October 3, 1939, he described the policy which he intended to put into effect by stating: 'Poland shall be treated like a colony; the

Poles will become the slaves of the Greater German World Empire.' The evidence establishes that this occupation policy was based on the complete destruction of Poland as a national entity, and a ruthless exploitation of its human and economic resources for the German war effort . . . Frank was a willing and knowing participant in the use of terrorism in Poland; in the economic exploitation of Poland in a way which led to the death by starvation of a large number of people; in the deportation to Germany as slave laborers of over a million Poles; and in a program involving the murder of at least 3 million Jews."

*Verdict:* GUILTY on counts 3 and 4.
*Sentence:* Death by hanging.

FRICK: " . . . An avid Nazi, Frick was largely responsible for bringing the German nation under the complete control of the NSDAP . . . The numerous laws he drafted, signed, and administered abolished all opposition parties and prepared the way for the Gestapo and their concentration camps to extinguish all individual opposition. He was largely responsible for the legislation which suppressed the Trade Unions, the Church, the Jews. He performed this task with ruthless efficiency . . . Always rabidly anti-Semitic, Frick drafted, signed, and administered many laws destined to eliminate Jews from German life and economy. His work formed the basis of the Nuremberg Decrees, and he was active in enforcing them . . . He had knowledge that insane, sick and aged people, 'useless eaters,' were being systematically put to death. Complaints of these murders reached him, but he did nothing to stop them . . . "

*Verdict:* GUILTY on counts 2, 3, and 4.
*Sentence:* Death by hanging.

STREICHER: " . . . For his 25 years of speaking, writing, and preaching hatred of the Jews, Streicher was widely known as 'Jew-Baiter Number 1.' In his speeches and articles, week after week, month after month, he infected the German mind with the virus of anti-Semitism, and incited the German people to active persecution . . . Streicher had charge of the Jewish boycott of April 1, 1933. He advocated the Nuremberg Decrees of 1935. He was responsible for the demolition on August 10, 1938, of the synagogue in Nuremberg. And on November 10, 1938, he spoke publicly in support of the Jewish pogroms which were taking place at that time. But it was not only in Germany that this defendant advocated his doctrines. As early as 1938 he began to call for the annihilation of the Jewish race . . . With knowledge of the extermination of the Jews in the Occupied Eastern Territories, this defendant continued to write and publish his propaganda of death . . . Streicher's incitement to murder and extermination at the time when Jews in the East were being killed under the most horrible conditions clearly constitutes persecution on political and racial grounds in connection with war crimes, as defined by the Charter, and constitutes a crime against humanity."

Verdict: GUILTY on count 4.
Sentence: Death by hanging.

FUNK: " . . . Funk became active in the economic field after the Nazi plans to wage aggressive war had been clearly defined . . . On October 14, 1939, after the war had begun, Funk made a speech in which he stated that the economic and financial departments of Germany working under the Four Year Plan had been engaged in the secret economic preparation for war for over a year . . . In 1942 Funk entered into an agreement with Himmler under which the Reichsbank was to receive certain gold and jewels and currency from the SS and instructed his subordinates, who were to work out the details, not to ask too many questions. As a result of this agreement the SS sent to the Reichsbank the personal belongings taken from the victims who had been exterminated in the concentration camps. The Reichsbank kept the coins and banknotes and sent the jewels, watches, and personal belongings to Berlin Municipal Pawn Shops. The gold from the eye-glasses and gold teeth and fillings was stored in the Reichsbank vaults. Funk has protested that he did not know that the Reichsbank was receiving articles of this kind. The Tribunal is of the opinion that Funk either knew what was being received or was deliberately closing his eyes to what was being done . . ."

Verdict: GUILTY on counts 2, 3, and 4.
Sentence: Life imprisonment.

SCHACHT: "Schacht was an active supporter of the Nazi Party before its accession to power on January 30, 1933, and supported the appointment of Hitler to the post of Chancellor. After that he played an important role in the vigorous rearmament program which was adopted, using the facilities of the Reichsbank to the

fullest extent in the German rearmament effort . . . As Minister
of Economics and as Plenipotentiary General for War Economy
he was active in organizing the German economy for war . . .
But rearmament of itself is not criminal under the Charter. To be
a crime against peace under Article 6 of the Charter it must be
shown that Schacht carried out this rearmament as part of the
Nazi plan to wage aggressive wars . . . The Tribunal has considered the whole of this evidence with great care, and comes to
the conclusion that this necessary inference has not been established beyond a reasonable doubt."

Verdict: NOT GUILTY.

DOENITZ: "Although Doenitz built and trained the German
U-boat arm, the evidence does not show he was privy to the conspiracy to wage aggressive wars or that he prepared and initiated
such wars . . . The Tribunal is of the opinion that the evidence
does not establish with the certainty required that Doenitz deliberately ordered the killing of shipwrecked survivors . . . The
evidence further shows that the rescue provisions were not carried out and that the defendant ordered that they should not be
carried out . . . Doenitz was also charged with responsibility for
Hitler's Commando order of October 18, 1942 . . . [by which]
the members of an Allied motor torpedo boat were . . . turned
over to the SD and shot . . . "

Verdict: GUILTY on counts 2 and 3.
Sentence: 10 years imprisonment.

RAEDER: "In the 15 years he commanded it, Raeder built and
directed the German Navy; he accepts full responsibility until re-
tirement in 1943. He admits the navy violated the Versailles
Treaty, insisting it was 'a matter of honor for every man' to do
so . . . He was one of the 5 leaders present at the Hoszbach
Conference of November 5, 1937 . . . The conception of the invasion of Norway first arose in the mind of Raeder and not that
of Hitler . . . Raeder endeavored to dissuade Hitler from em-
barking upon the invasion of the USSR . . . But once the decision had been made, he gave permission six days before the
invasion of the Soviet Union to attack Russian submarines in the
Baltic Sea . . . It is clear from this evidence that Raeder participated in the planning and waging of aggressive war . . . "

Verdict: GUILTY on counts 1, 2, and 3.
Sentence: Life imprisonment.

VON SCHIRACH: " . . . Von Schirach used the *Hitler Jugend* to educate German Youth 'in the spirit of National Socialism' and subjected them to an extensive program of Nazi propaganda . . . When von Schirach became Gauleiter of Vienna the deportation of the Jews had already begun . . . On September 15, 1942, von Schirach made a speech in which he defended his action in having driven 'tens of thousands upon tens of thousands of Jews into the Ghetto of the East' as 'contributing to European culture' . . . The Tribunal finds that von Schirach, while he did not originate the policy of deporting Jews from Vienna, participated in this deportation after he had become Gauleiter of Vienna. He knew that the best the Jews could hope for was a miserable existence in the Ghettos of the East. Bulletins describing the Jewish extermination were in his office . . . "

*Verdict:* GUILTY on count 4.
*Sentence:* 20 years imprisonment.

SAUCKEL: " . . . Shortly after Sauckel had taken office, he had the governing authorities in the various occupied territories issue decrees, establishing compulsory labor service in Germany . . . That real voluntary recruiting was the exception rather than the rule is shown by Sauckel's statement on March 1, 1944 that 'out of 5 million workers who arrived in Germany, not even 200,000 came voluntarily.' . . . His attitude was thus expressed in a regulation: 'All the men must be fed, sheltered, and treated in such a way as to exploit them to the highest possible extent at the lowest conceivable degree of expenditure.' The evidence shows that Sauckel was in charge of a program which involved deportation for slave labor of more than 5 million human beings, many of them under terrible conditions of cruelty and suffering."

*Verdict:* GUILTY on counts 3 and 4.
*Sentence:* Death by hanging.

JODL: " . . . Jodl discussed the Norway invasion with Hitler, Keitel, and Raeder on December 12, 1939; his diary is replete with late entries on his activities in preparing this attack . . . He was active in the planning against Greece and Yugoslavia . . . Jodl testified that Hitler feared an attack by Russia and so attacked first. This preparation began almost a year before the invasion. Jodl told Warlimont as early as July 29, 1940 to prepare the plans since Hitler had decided to attack . . . A plan to eliminate Soviet commissars was in the directive for 'Case Barbarossa.' The decision whether they should be killed without trial was to be made by an officer . . . His defense, in brief, is the doctrine of 'superior orders,' prohibited by Article 8 of the Charter as a defense. There is nothing in mitigation. Participation in such crimes as these has never been required of any soldier and he cannot now shield himself behind a mythical requirement of soldierly obedience at all costs as his excuse for commission of these crimes."

Verdict: GUILTY on all 4 counts.
Sentence: Death by hanging.

VON PAPEN: " . . . Von Papen was active in 1932 and 1933 in helping Hitler to form the Coalition Cabinet and aided in his appointment as Chancellor on January 30, 1933. As Vice-Chancellor in that Cabinet he participated in the Nazi consolidation of control in 1933 . . . Notwithstanding the murder of his associates, von Papen accepted the position of Minister to Austria on July 26, 1934, the day after Dollfuss had been assassinated . . . The evidence leaves no doubt that von Papen's primary purpose as Minister to Austria was to undermine the Schuschnigg regime and strengthen the Austrian Nazis for the purpose of bringing about the Anschluss. To carry through this plan he engaged in both intrigue and bullying. But the Charter does not make criminal such offenses against political morality, however bad these may be . . . Under the Charter von Papen can be held guilty only if he was party to the planning of aggressive war . . . but it is not established beyond a reasonable doubt that this was the purpose of his activity . . . "

Verdict: NOT GUILTY.

SEYSS-INQUART: " . . . Seyss-Inquart participated in the last stages of the Nazi intrigue which preceded the German occupation of Austria . . . As Reich Commissioner for Occupied Netherlands, Seyss-Inquart was ruthless in applying terrorism to suppress all opposition to the German occupation, a program which he described as 'annihilating' his opponents. In collaboration with the Higher SS and Police leaders he was involved in the shooting of hostages for offenses against the occupation authorities and sending to concentration camps all suspected opponents of occupation policies including priests and educators . . . Seyss-Inquart contends that he was not responsible for many

of the crimes committed in the occupation of the Netherlands
. . . But the fact remains that Seyss-Inquart was a knowing and
voluntary participant in War Crimes and Crimes against Humanity which were committed in the occupation of the Netherlands."

*Verdict:* GUILTY on counts 2, 3, and 4.
*Sentence:* Death by hanging.

SPEER: "The evidence introduced against Speer under counts
3 and 4 relates entirely to his participation in the slave labor
program . . . As Reich Minister for Armaments and Munitions and General Plenipotentiary for Armaments under the
Four Year Plan, Speer had extensive authority over production
. . . The practice was developed under which Speer transmitted
to Sauckel an estimate of the total number of workers needed,
Sauckel obtained the labor and allocated it to the various industries in accordance with instructions supplied by Speer. Speer
knew when he made his demands on Sauckel that they would be
supplied by foreign laborers serving under compulsion . . .
Sauckel continually informed Speer and his representative that
foreign laborers were being obtained by force . . . In mitigation
it must be recognized that . . . in the closing stages of the war
he was one of the few men who had the courage to tell Hitler
that the war was lost and to take steps to prevent the senseless destruction of production facilities . . . "

*Verdict:* GUILTY on counts 3 and 4.
*Sentence:* 20 years imprisonment.

VON NEURATH: " . . . As Minister of Foreign Affairs, von
Neurath advised Hitler in connection with the withdrawal from
the Disarmament Conference and the League of Nations on October 14, 1933; the institution of rearmament . . . Von Neurath
took part in the Hoszbach Conference of November 5, 1937. He
has testified that he was so shocked by Hitler's statements that
he had a heart attack. Shortly thereafter he offered to resign, and
his resignation was accepted on February 4, 1938, at the same
time that von Fritsch and von Blomberg were dismissed. Yet with
knowledge of Hitler's aggressive plans he retained a formal relationship with the Nazi regime as Reich Minister Without Portfolio . . . Von Neurath was appointed Reich Protector for Bohemia and Moravia on March 18, 1939 . . . The free press, polit-·
ical parties, and trade unions were abolished. All groups which

might serve as opposition were outlawed . . . He served as the chief German official in the Protectorate when the administration of this territory played an important role in the wars of aggression which Germany was waging in the East, knowing that War Crimes and Crimes Against Humanity were being committed under his authority . . . "

*Verdict:* GUILTY on all 4 counts.
*Sentence:* 15 years imprisonment.

FRITZSCHE: " . . . The Radio Division, of which Fritzsche became the head in November 1942, was one of the twelve divisions of the Propaganda Ministry . . . It appears that Fritzsche sometimes made strong statements of a propagandistic nature in his broadcasts. But the Tribunal is not prepared to hold that they were intended to incite the German people to commit atrocities on conquered peoples, and he cannot be said to have been a participant in the crimes charged . . . "

*Verdict:* NOT GUILTY.

# Appendix II—Chronology

## THE RISE AND FALL OF NAZI GERMANY

──────── 1919 ────────

January 5. Founding of the *Deutsche Arbeiterpartei* (German Workers' Party, original name of the Nazi Party).

──────── 1920 ────────

May 11. Party name changed to *Nationalsozialistische Deutsche Arbeiterpartei* or NSDAP (National Socialist German Workers' Party).

──────── 1921 ────────

July 29. Hitler becomes first Party chairman.

──────── 1923 ────────

November 8. "Beer-hall putsch" in Munich. Breaking up a nationalist meeting at the *Bürgerbräuhaus Keller*, Hitler announces, "The National Revolution has started!" The next day a march to the *Feldherrnhalle* is dispersed by Bavarian police. Goering, Hess, Streicher, Frank, and Rosenberg are among those who participate in the putsch. Goering is wounded and escapes; the other ringleaders are arrested.

──────── 1924 ────────

April 1. Hitler is sentenced to 5 years imprisonment in Landsberg fortress for treason.

April 28. Hess, Streicher, and several others are sentenced to prison terms. (Hitler starts to write *Mein Kampf* and keeps alive the fanatic spirit of the Party nucleus of "old fighters" in prison.)

December 20. Hitler is released.

──────── 1925 ────────

July 18. The first volume of *Mein Kampf* appears.

──────── 1926 ────────

December 1. Hitler appoints Goebbels District Leader of the Party for Berlin.

—————— 1928 ——————

May 20. The Nazis elect 12 Reichstag deputies, polling 2½ per cent of the total vote.

—————— 1930 ——————

January 23. Frick becomes Minister of the Interior and Popular Education of the State Government of Thuringia, paving the way for the spread of Nazism.

September 14. The Nazis elect 107 Reichstag deputies, polling 18 per cent of the vote.

September 18. Japan attacks Manchuria.

—————— 1932 ——————

February 25. Hitler becomes German citizen.

April 10. Von Hindenburg re-elected President of the Weimar Republic. Hitler gets 37 per cent of the vote.

June 1. Von Papen appointed Reich Chancellor.

June 15. Von Schirach named Leader of Hitler Youth.

November 6. The Nazis elect 196 Reichstag deputies, polling 33½ per cent of the vote.

December 2. General von Schleicher appointed Reich Chancellor, as one cabinet crisis succeeds another.

—————— 1933 ——————

January 4. Secret meeting of von Papen and Hitler at the home of the banker Kurt von Schroeder in Cologne. Hess and Himmler are present. Hitler's participation in a future German Government is discussed.

January 30. Adolf Hitler is appointed Reich Chancellor. His cabinet includes von Papen as Vice-Chancellor, von Neurath as Foreign Minister, Goering as Minister Without Portfolio, Frick as Minister of the Interior, and General von Blomberg as Reichswehr Minister.

February 27. The Reichstag fire. A reign of terror is started against the Communists, who are immediately blamed for the fire, and other opposition parties.

*February 28.* Basic civil rights of the Weimar Constitution are suspended as an "emergency measure."

*March 5.* The Nazis elect 288 Reichstag deputies, still not quite a majority.

*March 13.* Goebbels appointed Reich Minister for People's Enlightenment and Propaganda.

*March 16.* Schacht becomes Reichsbank President.

*March 21.* The new Reichstag meets. By excluding the Communists from their seats, Goering assures the Nazi Party an absolute majority.

*March 27.* Japan announces her withdrawal from the League of Nations.

*March 29.* The government enacts a new law imposing the death penalty for "crimes against the public security."

*April 1.* A nationwide boycott against Jewish doctors, lawyers, and business houses is ordered.

*April 27.* Hitler appoints Hess as deputy leader of the Party.

*May 2.* The Free Trade Unions are taken over by Robert Ley's "German Labor Front."

*May 10.* Book burning: books out of line with Nazi ideology or written by "Non-Aryans" are publicly burned all over Germany.

*June 22 to July 6.* The Social Democratic Party is banned and "voluntary" dissolution of all other parties is enforced.

*July 8.* A Concordat between Germany and the Vatican is signed by von Papen and Cardinal Pacelli.

*October 14.* Hitler announces Germany's withdrawal from the League of Nations.

*November 24.* Himmler is given sweeping police powers in various states to quell opposition by the terror methods sanctioned by the March 29 decree.

———————— 1934 ————————

*January 6.* Bishop Mueller is given dictatorial power to unite German Protestants in one Reich Church over the protests of the majority of German Protestants.

*January 26.* A 10-year Non-Aggression Pact with Poland is signed by von Neurath and Polish Ambassador Lipsky.

*April 24.* Von Ribbentrop is appointed Hitler's representative for disarmament questions.

*June 30.* The "Roehm purge." Ernest Roehm, homosexual Storm Troop chief who succeeded Goering, is killed along with numerous other Nazis in a sweeping Party purge led by Goering and Himmler. A number of prominent Catholics and Reichswehr officers are also assassinated, including Dr. Erich Klausner, head of the Catholic Action Society, General von Schleicher and his wife, and three secretaries of von Papen. Von Papen is temporarily placed under "protective arrest."

*July 25.* Nazi putsch in Austria. The Austrian Chancellor Dollfuss is assassinated.

*July 26.* Von Papen is appointed German envoy to Austria.

*August 2.* President von Hindenburg dies. Hitler declares himself head of the German State.

---------- 1935 ----------

*March 9.* Germany officially discloses the existence of a Luftwaffe (Air Force), in violation of the Treaty of Versailles.

*March 16.* The Reich Government introduces military conscription, also a violation of the Treaty of Versailles.

*June 18.* Germany concludes a naval agreement with Great Britain, giving Germany the right to construct a navy up to 35 per cent of British naval strength.

*September 15.* The Reichstag convening in Nuremberg passes the sweeping anti-Semitic "Nuremberg Laws," which virtually disenfranchise all those of "Jewish blood."

*October 3.* Italy invades Ethiopia.

*December 19.* Hans Frank, Hitler's lawyer, is appointed Minister Without Portfolio.

---------- 1936 ----------

*March 7.* Hitler denounces the Locarno Pact and marches troops into the demilitarized Rhineland.

July 11. Germany signs an agreement recognizing the complete sovereignty of Austria and promising to abstain from interference in Austrian affairs.

July 17. Spanish Civil War starts.

October 25–27. Count Ciano visits Berlin. The Italo-German Axis Pact is announced.

November 18. Germany and Italy recognize the Franco Junta as the legal government of Spain.

November 25. Von Ribbentrop signs the Anti-Comintern Pact with Japan.

———————— 1937 ————————

April 26. Luftwaffe "dress rehearsal" in Spain. German planes, fighting for Franco, destroy the undefended Spanish town of Guernica, killing thousands of civilians.

July 7. Japan reopens war on China. A skirmish at the Marco Polo Bridge at Peiping is used as the pretext.

September 7. Hitler declares the Versailles Treaty is dead.

October 13. In a formal exchange of notes, Germany pledges herself to respect the inviolability and territorial integrity of Belgium.

November 5. In a secret meeting attended by Goering, von Fritsch, Raeder, and von Neurath, Hitler announces his aggressive plans for the domination of Europe by force ("Hoszbach speech").

November 6. Italy joins the Anti-Comintern Pact.

November 26. Funk is named Economics Minister, replacing Schacht, who remains Reichsbank President and Minister Without Portfolio.

December 11. Italy gives notice of her withdrawal from the League of Nations.

———————— 1938 ————————

February 4. Shake-up of the German High Command. Reichswehr Minister von Blomberg and Commander in Chief von Fritsch are removed and 13 other generals forced to resign. Keitel is appointed Chief of Staff. Von Ribbentrop replaces von Neurath as Foreign Minister.

*February 12.* Austrian Chancellor Schuschnigg is summoned to Berchtesgaden and presented with an ultimatum by Hitler.

*February 15.* The main German demands are accepted by Austria. Seyss-Inquart is appointed Austrian Minister of the Interior.

*March 9.* Schuschnigg announces a plebiscite on Austrian independence, to be held on March 13.

*March 11.* Yielding to German threats,. Schuschnigg resigns. President Miklas appoints a Nazi Government under Seyss-Inquart.

*March 12.* The new Austrian Chancellor, Seyss-Inquart, announces the *Anschluss* (incorporation of Austria within the Reich). German troops march in the next day.

*March 17.* The Soviet Government suggests a conference to stop further Nazi aggression.

*April 24.* Konrad Henlein, Führer of the Sudeten German Nazis in Czechoslovakia, asks for autonomy for Sudeten Germans.

*August 17.* Henlein rejects a compromise proposal of the Czechoslovak Government and increases his demands.

*September 15.* Chamberlain flies to Berchtesgaden. Sudeten Nazi leader Henlein demands reunion of the Sudetenland with Germany.

*September 22.* Chamberlain flies to Godesberg for a second meeting with Hitler.

*September 25.* Czechoslovakia rejects Hitler's Godesberg demands for cession of the Sudetenland with all its installations.

*September 26.* President Roosevelt sends a personal appeal to Hitler and President Benes to settle the controversy by negotiation. Hitler makes a violent speech saying that the Sudetenland is the last territorial claim which he has to make in Europe.

*September 27.* President Roosevelt appeals to Hitler again, asking for a conference of all nations concerned in the Sudeten dispute.

*September 29–30.* The Munich Pact. Hitler, Mussolini, Chamberlain, and Daladier meet in Munich and decide to let Hitler take over the Sudetenland. Czechoslovakia yields to the Munich decision.

*October 1.* German troops enter the ceded Sudeten territory.

*November 7.* Ernst von Rath, a secretary in the German embassy in Paris, is shot by a 17-year-old Polish youth, Herschel Grynszpan, and dies two days later.

*November 9–10.* Pogroms are staged all over Germany as a "spontaneous" reaction to von Rath's slaying. Organized mobs burn synagogues, destroy Jewish property and beat up Jews, killing many.

*November 12.* The German Government enacts new anti-Jewish laws. A collective fine of one billion marks is imposed on the German Jews as penalty for the slaying of von Rath.

———————— 1939 ————————

*January 20.* Funk succeeds Schacht as Reichsbank President.

*March 15.* German troops enter Prague "by agreement," after threats by Hitler, Goering, and von Ribbentrop.

*March 16.* Hitler signs a decree establishing a Protectorate of Bohemia and Moravia; Slovakian Premier Tiso also places Slovakia under German protection.

*March 18.* France and Great Britain notify Germany that they do not recognize the annexation of Bohemia and Moravia by Germany.

*March 20.* The United States Government notifies Germany that it does not recognize the annexation of Bohemia and Moravia. Russia again suggests a conference to stop further Nazi aggressions.

*March 27.* Franco Spain joins the Anti-Comintern Pact.

*March 28.* Franco occupies Madrid.

*March 31.* Great Britain and France guarantee Polish independence.

*April 7.* Italy seizes Albania.

*April 14.* President Roosevelt, in a personal message to Hitler and Mussolini, asks for a promise that the independent nations of Europe and the Far East will not be invaded. The Reichstag laughs as Hitler reads them the letter.

*April 28.* In a Reichstag speech Hitler announces the abrogation of the Polish-German Non-Aggression Pact.

*May 22.* Von Ribbentrop and Ciano sign a military alliance between Germany and Italy.

*May 31.* Von Ribbentrop signs a Non-Aggression Pact with Denmark.

*August 5.* An Anglo-French military mission leaves for Moscow.

*August 8.* Hitler receives Albert Foerster, Nazi leader in Danzig. Two days later Foerster asks for the return of Danzig to the Reich.

*August 22.* France and Great Britain officially reaffirm their pledges to Poland. Chamberlain appeals to Hitler for a peaceful solution to the German-Polish dispute.

*August 23.* A Soviet-German Non-Aggression Pact is signed in Moscow by Molotov and von Ribbentrop. (A secret clause, not revealed until the Nuremberg Trial, fixes a demarcation line for the  mutual occupation of Poland in case of a German attack on Poland.)

*August 24.* President Roosevelt appeals to Hitler and Polish President Moscicki for a solution by arbitration. Pope Pius XII broadcasts an appeal for peace.

*August 25.* President Moscicki accepts the offer of mediation. President Roosevelt sends another plea to Hitler to arbitrate and avert war.

*August 26.* Premier Daladier of France appeals to Hitler to avert war.

*August 30.* Von Ribbentrop reads the latest German demands on Poland to British Ambassador Henderson, refusing to give him the text in writing.

*August 31.* Polish Ambassador Lipski informs Germany that Poland is ready to settle the dispute through negotiation. Pope Pius appeals to Germany and Poland to abstain from war.

*September 1.* Germany invades Poland.

*September 3.* England and France declare war on Germany.

*September 14.* Warsaw is virtually cut off by the Wehrmacht.

*September 17.* Russian troops cross the Polish border.

*September 28.* Warsaw falls.

*October 12.* Hans Frank is appointed Governor-General of the conquered Polish territory.

*November 30.* Russia invades Finland.

————— 1940 —————

*March 12.* Russia and Finland sign a peace treaty in Moscow.

*April 9.* Germany invades Norway and Denmark.

*May 10.* Germany invades the Netherlands, Belgium, and Luxembourg. Chamberlain resigns and Winston Churchill becomes Prime Minister of Great Britain.

*May 14.* The Dutch Army capitulates. Goering's Luftwaffe destroys the Rotterdam business center in spite of the surrender of the city.

*May 28.* King Leopold of Belgium surrenders the Belgian Army.

*June 10.* Italy declares war on Great Britain and France.

*June 14.* Paris falls.

*June 22.* Germany and France sign an Armistice at Compiègne.

*August 8.* The "Battle of Britain" starts with an intensified air offensive.

*September 17.* As a result of heavy air losses, Hitler decides to postpone the invasion of Britain.

*September 27.* A Tri-Partite Pact is signed by Germany, Italy, and Japan.

*October 6.* German troops enter Rumania.

*October 28.* Italy invades Greece.

————— 1941 —————

*March 11.* President Roosevelt signs the Lend-Lease Bill.

*April 6.* Germany invades Yugoslavia and Greece.

*May 10.* Rudolf Hess parachutes onto Scottish soil.

*May 14.* Martin Bormann is named successor to Rudolf Hess.

*June 22.* Germany invades Russia.

*July 12.* A Soviet-British mutual assistance pact is signed in Moscow.

*July 17.* Rosenberg is appointed Reich Minister for the Eastern Occupied Territories.

*August 14.* The Atlantic Charter is announced by President Roosevelt and Prime Minister Churchill after a secret meeting at sea. They declare their intention to defeat the Axis and preserve the "four freedoms," but renounce any "territorial aggrandizement."

*November 8.* Hitler promises the fall of Moscow.

*December 7.* "Pearl Harbor." Japanese planes attack the American fleet at Pearl Harbor, Hawaii, while Japanese envoy Kurusu is negotiating a peaceful settlement of Pacific problems in Washington. Japan then declares war on the United States and Great Britain.

*December 11.* Germany and Italy declare war on the United States.

*December 19.* As Moscow still refuses to fall, Hitler removes General von Brauchitsch as Commander in Chief of the Wehrmacht and assumes the post himself.

——————— 1942 ———————

*February 9.* Albert Speer, Hitler's architect, is named Armaments Minister to succeed Dr. Todt, who is killed in an airplane crash.

*March 28.* Fritz Sauckel, Gauleiter of Thuringia, is named chief of manpower mobilization to speed up slave labor recruitment.

*June 10.* Berlin announces that the Czech village of Lidice has been exterminated in reprisal for the murder of Gestapo chief Heydrich.

*August 23.* 35 German divisions start the attack on Stalingrad.

*October 23.* General Montgomery attacks El Alamein to destroy Rommel's North Africa Corps.

*November 5.* General Montgomery announces that Rommel's army is in full retreat.

*November 7–8.* Allied armies land in North Africa.

*November 11.* German troops invade unoccupied France.

*November 27.* German troops enter the French naval base of Toulon. The French fleet is scuttled by her own crew.

——————— 1943 ———————

*January 14–24.* Casablanca Conference. President Roosevelt and Prime Minister Churchill confer at Casablanca and demand unconditional surrender of the Axis powers.

*January 30.* Ernst Kaltenbrunner is appointed Chief of the RSHA (Gestapo, etc.) under Himmler to succeed Heydrich. Admiral Doenitz, Commander of the U-boat fleet, is appointed Commander in Chief of the German Navy to succeed Admiral Raeder.

*February 2.* Moscow announces the end of the Battle of Stalingrad. Field Marshal von Paulus surrenders his battered army.

*May 13.* The last German units surrender in North Africa.

*July 10.* Allied troops invade Sicily.

*July 25.* Mussolini is forced to resign.

*August 24.* SS and Gestapo Chief Himmler is appointed Reich Minister of the Interior to combat "defeatism," extending his reign of terror to every phase of German life.

*September 3.* Allied troops land on the Italian mainland. Italy signs a secret Armistice.

*October 31.* The Italian Government of Marshal Bodoglio declares war on Germany.

*October 30.* The Moscow Conference ends. Secretary Hull, Molotov, and Eden renew demand for unconditional surrender. Roosevelt, Churchill, and Stalin promise to pursue Axis war criminals "to the uttermost ends of the earth."

*November 28–December 1.* Teheran Conference of Roosevelt, Churchill, and Stalin.

*December 24.* President Roosevelt announces that General Eisenhower has been named Supreme Commander of the Allied invasion forces.

———————— 1944 ————————

*June 4.* Rome falls.

*June 6.* Allied landing on the Normandy coast.

*July 20.* Assassination attempt on Hitler by a group of German officers headed by Count von Stauffenberg.

*August 8.* After a summary trial before a "People's Court," 8 high-ranking German officers are hanged, among them Marshal von Witzleben, for complicity in the assassination plot. Many others are purged unofficially.

*August 15.* The Allies invade southern France.

*August 25.* Paris is liberated.

*December 16.* Rundstedt launches a counter-offensive through the Ardennes Forest.

*December 28.* The German counter-offensive is repulsed; "Battle of the Bulge" begins.

———————— 1945 ————————

*February 12.* Yalta Conference of Roosevelt, Churchill and Stalin is announced. They declare: "It is our inflexible purpose to destroy German militarism and Nazism and to . . . bring all war criminals to just and swift punishment."

*March 8.* The American First Army crosses the Rhine at Remagen.

*April 12.* President Roosevelt dies.

*April 21.* The Red Army enters Berlin.

*April 28.* Mussolini is executed by Italian partisans.

*April 30.* Suicide of Hitler, Eva Braun, and Goebbels with his entire family.

*May 1.* Admiral Doenitz takes over as head of the German Government.

*May 2.* Berlin falls to the Red Army.

*May 7.* General Jodl signs the surrender at Reims, effective May 8.

*May 9.* Field Marshal Keitel signs Germany's unconditional surrender in Berlin.

*June 26.* The United Nations Charter is signed in San Francisco.

*August 1.* The Potsdam Conference between Truman, Attlee and Stalin ends.

*August 5.* The first atomic bomb is dropped on the Japanese city of Hiroshima.

*August 8.* The Soviet Union declares war on Japan.

*August 14.* Japan accepts Allied surrender terms.

*September 2.* Formal Japanese surrender aboard the battleship "Missouri."

*November 20.* Opening of the Nuremberg Trials.

# Index

N.B. This is merely an Index to the present volume. It is not an exhaustive index to the trial.